# The Travels of Ibn Battuta

## In the Near East, Asia and Africa

**IBN BATTUTA**
**TRANSLATED BY SAMUEL LEE**

COSIMOCLASSICS

NEW YORK

**The Travels of Ibn Battuta: in the Near East, Asia and Africa**
Cover Copyright © 2009 by Cosimo, Inc.

*The Travels of Ibn Battuta: in the Near East, Asia and Africa* was
originally published in 1829.

For information, address:
P.O. Box 416, Old Chelsea Station
New York, NY 10011

or visit our website at:
www.cosimobooks.com

**Ordering Information:**
Cosimo publications are available at online bookstores. They may
also be purchased for educational, business or promotional use:
- *Bulk orders:* special discounts are available on bulk orders for reading groups,
organizations, businesses, and others. For details contact
Cosimo Special Sales at the address above or at info@cosimobooks.com.
- *Custom-label orders:* we can prepare selected books with your cover or logo of
choice. For more information, please contact Cosimo at
info@cosimobooks.com.

Cover Design by www.popshopstudio.com

ISBN: 978-1-61640-262-4

In this part, I also saw those women who burn themselves when their husbands die. The woman adorns herself, and is accompanied by a cavalcade of the infidel Hindoos and Brahmans, with drums, trumpets, and men, following her, both Moslems and Infidels for mere pastime. The fire had been already kindled, and into it they threw the dead husband. The wife then threw herself upon him, and both were entirely burnt. A woman's burning herself, however, with her husband is not considered as absolutely necessary among them, but it is encouraged; and when a woman burns herself with her husband, her family is considered as being ennobled, and supposed to be worthy of trust. But when she does not burn herself, she is ever after clothed coarsely, and remains in constraint among her relations, on account of her want of fidelity to her husband.

—from Chapter XIV

# LIEUTENANT-COLONEL FITZCLARENCE,

FELLOW OF THE ROYAL SOCIETY OF LONDON,

HONORARY MEMBER OF THE ASIATIC SOCIETY OF CALCUTTA,

MEMBER OF THE ASIATIC SOCIETY OF PARIS,

MEMBER OF THE ROYAL SOCIETY OF LITERATURE,

VICE-PRESIDENT OF THE ROYAL ASIATIC SOCIETY OF GREAT BRITAIN AND IRELAND

AND

TREASURER OF THE FUND APPROPRIATED TO THE TRANSLATION OF ORIENTAL
WORKS BY THE COMMITTEE OF TRANSLATION ATTACHED
TO THAT BODY.

---

DEAR SIR:

I think myself fortunate in having it in my power to dedicate to you the first-fruits of an Institution, which owes its origin and efficiency almost entirely to your exertions : and, as my author traversed and described many parts of the East, of which you, nearly five hundred years after his time, have given so many interesting and confirmatory accounts, this will constitute an additional reason for doing so.

The principal motive, however, which has induced me to inscribe this work to your name has been, the consideration of public utility. No one, perhaps, can better estimate than your-self the duty incumbent on this country to possess an accurate knowledge of the history, geography, commerce, manners, customs, and religious opinions of the East. Placed as we are in the proud situation of legislating to perhaps its richest and most important part, and hence looked up to by its almost countless inhabitants for protection, instruction, government,—nothing can be more obvious, than, that it is just as binding upon us to acquaint ourselves with their wants, in order to these being provided for and relieved, as it is that we should calculate upon the wealth of their commerce, or the rank and influence which our Governors, Judges, and Magistrates, should hold among them. Unhappily, however, prior to the times of Sir William Jones, knowledge of this kind was scarcely accessible to the bulk of Society; and, since that period, notwithstanding his glowing predictions to the contrary,* the study of Oriental literature has seldom been carried beyond its first elements. A few Scholars have, from time to time, appeared among the servants of the Honourable East-India Company: but, when we take into the account the vastness of the means which we possess, together with the duty laid on us as a nation, accurately to know the condition of so many of our fellow subjects in the East, it must appear, that all which has been done, so far from being matter of exultation, must rather tend to lower us in the opinion we would entertain of ourselves, and much more in that of the surrounding nations. It is not my intention to dwell here, with the admirable Sir William Jones, on the beauty of their poetry, the value of their sentiments as moralists or philosophers, or the almost boundless extent and variety of their languages: but on the paramount necessity of our possessing an accurate knowledge of their countries, histories, laws, commerce, connexions, tactics, antiquities, and the like for purely practical

---

* Preface to his Persian Grammar.

purposes. Other considerations, indeed, will, and ought to weigh with the Divine, the Gentleman, and the Scholar; and, here, perhaps, our knowledge of philology may be mentioned as likely to receive as much improvement, as any science cultivated in polite society possibly can.

It is customary, I know, to look to the Universities for the tone of learning in any country: but, in this respect, these bodies are with us very inadequately provided for. The majority of students is interested in other pursuits; while those which are intended for the East are expected to keep Terms at one or other of the seminaries provided by the Honourable Company. The utmost, therefore, that can be brought to bear here upon the ardour of youth, or to stimulate the enterprising to the toil of years, which is indeed necessary to a moderate acquaintance with the languages of the East, is, perhaps, a Professorship with an endowment of forty pounds a year, accompanied with duties and restraints of no ordinary nature. And, the natural consequence has been, that, whatever may have been known on these subjects, few have been found hardy enough to undertake laborious and expensive works, with no other prospect than of being eulogized by their biographers, as having " immortalized and ruined themselves."

Our Institution, therefore, will, I trust, even here be the means of creating a stimulus to the cultivation of learning, for which, indeed, some provision has been made, and which the greatest ornaments of our Church and Nation have deemed of the very highest importance: I mean, that which immediately bears on the study of the Christian Scriptures, an acquaintance with the Hebrew and its sister dialects. As things formerly were, a Whelock, Castell, or Pococke, may have delivered lectures; but, as it was then facetiously said, "the Lecture-room would exhibit an *Arabia deserta*, rather than an *Arabia felix :*" and for the most obvious of all reasons, namely, that where neither emolument nor consideration are to be had, there will never be any considerable public effort made. In this point of view, therefore, I believe, that under prudent government our Institution may be productive of the greatest public good, in filling up a chasm in our means of information which nothing else could effect. And, I think I may say, that whether we consider the amazing extent of its operations, the unprecedented support which in so short a time it has experienced, the aggregate quantity of literary power concentrated in its Committee, or the number of works of the first importance which it already has in the progress of publication, to have projected and brought into active operation such an institution, cannot but be gratifying to every one (and particularly to yourself), who took any part in its formation.

I have the honour to be,

DEAR SIR,

Your most obliged humble Servant,

THE TRANSLATOR AND EDITOR.

*Cambridge,*
*January 24th* 1829.

# PREFACE.

———◆———

SOME years having elapsed since I first made known my intention to translate and publish these travels,* and having at length succeeded as far as my abilities and opportunities would allow me, it now becomes a duty to say, why the work has been so long delayed, and to give some account of the manner in which it has been completed.

Soon after I undertook this translation I was informed by a gentleman, a native of Tripoli† then residing in this country, that he had in his own library at Tripoli a copy of the entire original work; and, that if I would wait till he should have returned, he would send me that copy. Upon this, I deemed it most prudent to wait. Hearing, however, two or three years afterwards, that the same promise had been made to several gentlemen in London, not one of whom ever heard again from Mr. Dugais on the subject, I naturally gave up all further expectation from that quarter. But, as I had then engaged in other undertakings, and besides, had not within my power the means of publication, I had no resource but to let the work lie dormant until opportunities for completing it should present themselves. Finding myself, at length, a little more at leisure, I determined to complete the translation; and accordingly, during the last summer-vacation, more than one half of it was made, and a few notes were written. Since that time the rest has been completed in the manner now presented to the Public: and I have now only to give some account of the manuscript copies used, and of the rules by which I have been guided in my proceedings.

---

* As afterwards published in the **Quarterly Review** for May 1820, p. 238.

† Mr. Dugais, son of a rich merchant in Tripoli (Mr. D'Ghies of Major Denham's Africa).

The Arabic manuscripts of this work are three in number, and are all copies of the same abridgment.  They were originally bequeathed to the library of the University of Cambridge by the late Mr. Burckhardt, where they may at any time be seen.  It is, indeed, much to be regretted that they are only abridgments ; but, as they contain much curious and valuable information, and that obtained at a time of very considerable interest ; namely, when the Tartars were making progress in Asia Minor,  and  the empire of Hindūstān was verging towards its final subjugation to the Mogul dynasty, I have thought it would be quite unpardonable to let the manuscript lie any longer untranslated, especially as its publication may possibly be the means of bringing the entire work to light, which Mr. Burckhardt has assured us is still in existence.*

About the time these MSS. were deposited in our public library, some parts of the abridgment were published in Germany, by Mr. Kosegarten, and Mr. Apetz, both of Jena.†

The work of Mr. Kosegarten contains in its first section a very learned dissertation on the itinerary of Mohammed Ibn Batūta,‡ which is followed by the preface to his copy § with some notes.  His second section contains the journey through Persia into

---

* Travels in Nubia, p. 534.

† I have lately been informed, that there is now also a copy in France.

‡ Mr. Kosegarten's work appeared in 1818, bearing the following title, " De Mohammede Ebn Batūta Arabe Tingitano ejusque Itineribus—Commentatio Academica, A.D. VII. Martii cıɔıɔcccxviii.   Auctor Joannes Gothofrehdus Ludovicus Kosegarten Lingua. Oriental.......In Universitate Litterar. Jenensi Professor Publicus Ordinarius."

§ The following is the text which forms the preface to our work ; it is here given in order to enable the Oriental scholar to form some estimate of the difference observable in our several texts :

بسم الله الرحمن الرحيم الحمد لله رب العالمين وصلى الله على سيدنا محمد وعلى اله وصحبه
اجمعين وبعد فيقول فقير عفو ربه الغنى محمد بن فتح الله البيلونى هذا ما انتقيته مما لخصه الامام
الكاتب محمد بن جزى الكلبى رحمه الله تعالى من رحلة الفقيه ابى عبد الله محمد بن عبد الله
اللواتى الطنجى المعروف بابن بطوطه وما انتقيت الا ما كان غريبا غير مشهور او مشهور النقل لكن
ربما لا يعتمد عليه لغرابته وتسامح المورخين فى النقل غالبا فاثبته لكون صاحب الرحلة ثقة وكتب
ما ثبت عنده من اخبار الامم والاقطار فنقل الصدوق اوقع فى الاعتبار والاستبصار وبعض ما نقله قد
يخالف ما ذكره غيره كما فى وصفه بعض ما شاهده من عقاقير الهند فان خرج الشيخ ابن بطوطه
صاحب الرحلة لقصد الحج والسياحة من بلدته طنجه عام خمس وعشرين وسبعماية وانما اذكر بعض
اسماء البلاد التى اجتازبها فى رحلته وان لم يكن فى ذلك كبير فائدة للتنبيه على كمال همته
وتوكله وعدم سآمته من المحل والترحال وقطع مشاق الفيافى والجبال فاول مدينة وصل اليها تلمسان
ثم الى مدينة مليانه &c. ; a translation of which will be found at the outset of the travels.

Tartary, which, although apparently a copy of the same abridgment with our's, contains scarcely half the quantity of matter which we have, as the reader will see by comparing the translations. Mr. Kosegarten's third section contains the account of the Maldive Islands, which differs less from ours than the preceding. The fourth section of Mr. Kosegarten's work contains the travels into Africa : and here also our difference is but little. These extracts are all accompanied with a Latin translation, and some very ingenious notes, with a few geographical extracts from some other works. The work of Mr. Apetz contains only the account of Malabar given by our traveller ; its title is " Descriptio Terræ Malabar ex Arabico Ebn Batutæ Itinerario edita, interpretatione et annotationibus instructa per Henricum Apetz. Jenæ MDCCCXIX." The copy here followed is that used by Mr. Kosegarten, as Mr. Apetz himself informs us in his preface. The varieties observable between this text and ours are not many, nor of much importance : some of these, however, I have marked, as the reader will find in the notes. A few notes accompany the translation of Mr. Apetz, some of which I have also noticed. In some instances Mr. Kosegarten's copy gives the orthography of the proper names of places : one of our copies also occasionally does this, while one or other of the others supplies the vowels. But this is neither constant, nor indeed always to be relied on when found : and, when this is the case, and such name is not to be found in any of the dictionaries, which often happens, I must now say, I cannot be at all answerable for my own orthography of such words. In some cases, indeed, we find the same word written differently in the same MS. and in the same line : and when this happens, and I have no means of rectifying the mistake, I must make the same apology.

In making my translation, I have followed those readings which appeared to me to be the most correct ; and, where the differences have been important, I have marked them in the notes. It has not been thought worth while to print the Arabic text, as it presents nothing remarkable, being in general very plain and entirely void of every attempt at what is called fine writing. Where I have had any doubt, however, as to the sense of the passage, I have given the original Arabic in a note. Still, should the original be called for, there will be no difficulty in putting it to press.

---

Who brought Mr. Kosegarten's text into Europe he does not inform us, only that it came from Cairo, and was first presented to him by a dear friend (pp. 8, 9). Mr. Seetzen's name he only mentions, to regret his having made the attempt to translate a part of the travels, whence one would suppose, that Mr. Kosegarten did not follow his copy.

In translating I have followed the original as closely as our idiom would generally allow; and in a style as nearly assimilated to that of my author as the nature of the case would permit. My attempt to put the poetical extracts into verse will, I hope, be excused, my only object being to give my translation throughout the spirit of the original, as nearly as I could.

The notes which have been added will, I trust, be found neither tedious nor entirely uninteresting. I thought it important both to examine and to explain many of the statements of my author; and for this end the notes were added. That they are either so extensive or so good as the subject requires, I do not so much as suppose: and my apology must be; it has not been in my power to command either the time, or the opportunities, which many others can. I have done then, if not the best, the best in my power; and as such, I hope it will be received. My principal object in making these inquiries, was to ascertain the accuracy and fidelity of my author; and, in this point of view I have succeeded to my own satisfaction at least, having no doubt that he is worthy of all credit. Superstitious, and addicted to the marvellous, indeed, he occasionally is; but for this allowance must be made, as it occasionally must in travellers of much later times. It is for his historical, geographical, and botanical notices, that he is principally valuable; and I concur with his Epitomator, Mr. Burckhardt and Mr. Kosegarten, in believing, that in these he is truly valuable. In botany, perhaps, his skill may be called in question; and, in this respect, I am sorry to say, it has not been in my power to correct him. In some of his geographical excursions, too, I have been unable to follow him; not because I have not endeavoured to do so, but because no geographer accessible to me has noticed such places. Those who have been in the East themselves, or those who may hereafter visit those parts will, perhaps, make all clear, and to them I leave such instances. As I have occasionally cited some Arabic and Persian works in the notes, I take the opportunity here of apprizing the reader what they are, and where the copies cited are to be found.

1. The ªRauzat El Safâ is a very celebrated and well known history of Persia, written by Mīr Khānd in seven volumes. The copy here cited, formerly belonged to the Right Honourable Lord Teignmouth, and is now in my own possession; copies, however, are to be found in most of the public libraries.

---

ª روضة الصفا .

2. The [b] Khulāsat El Akhbār, an abridgment of the Persian historians generally. This is also in my possession.

3. The [c] Gwālior Nāmah, a history of the fortress of Gwālior, by Herāman Ibn Kardhar Dās the Munshī, a small neatly written quarto, bearing the class-mark 324 of the library of Eton College. From this the notice of Gwālior has been taken.

4. The [d] Tārīkhi Badāyūnī, a valuable history of Hindūstān, by [e] Abd El Razzāk Malūk-shāh of Samarcand. A neatly written thick folio, bearing the class mark of the Eton library 439.

5. The first volume of the [f] Matlaa El Saadain by [g] Abd El Razzāk Ibn Is-hak of Samarkand, a general history of Persia. A moderate-sized folio, incorrectly written, bearing the Eton class mark 366. These three volumes were lent me for this work, by the kindness of the Reverend the Provost and Fellows of Eton College, for which, and the very ready access they afforded me to their valuable library, I take this opportunity of returning my warmest thanks.

6. The [h] Tabakāti Akbarī, a history of the Emperors of Hindūstān prior to the times of Akbar, compiled at that monarch's request, by [i] Nizām Oddīn Mohammed Mukīm of Herāt. The copy cited formerly belonged to my late valued and learned friend Jonathan Scott, Esq. of Shrewsbury: it is a thick quarto very neatly written, and is now in my possession.

7. The citations from Ferishta are taken from a copy also in my possession.

8. The [k] Kānūn El Tijārat is a well-written work in Persian on the nature and value of jewels, silks, &c. taken from the A-īni Akbarī and other works, written originally in the Hindūstānī language by [l] Iatimād El Daulat, and translated into the Persian, A.D. 1806. The copy is in my possession; it is a thin neatly written folio.

9. The [m] A-īni Akbarī, a most valuable work giving a statistical account of Hindūstān, with particulars as to its officers, customs, &c. compiled under the superintendence of Abul Fazl, prime minister to the Emperor Akbar; large folio, in the University library of Cambridge. This work has been translated into English by Mr. Gladwin, but the copies are very scarce: our library does not possess one.

---

[b] خلاصة الاخبار.   [c] كواليار نامه.   [d] تاريخ بدايوني.   [e] عبد الرزاق ملوكشاه.

[f] مطلع السعدين.   [g] عبد الرزاق بن اسحق السمرقندي.   [h] طبقات اكبري.

[i] نظام الدين محمد مقيم الهروي.   [k] قانون التجارة.   [l] اعتماد الدولت.   [m] آئين اكبري.

10. The Medical Dictionary of Ali Ibn El Husain, known by the [n] Hāji Zain El Attār. This work is entitled [o] Ikhtiārāti Badīaī, and contains a list of medicines simple and compound, arranged according to the Arabic alphabet; it is neatly written, and in the Persian language. The form is small folio, and contains about 300 closely written pages. The copy cited is in my possession.

11. The [p] Dabistān, a very valuable and interesting work on the religious opinions of the Orientals, usually ascribed to [q] Mohammed Mohsin Fānī of Kashmire: the real author, however, seems to be yet unknown. This work was first brought to notice by Sir William Jones; but has not yet been translated, if we except the first book on the religion of the ancient Persians, which was translated and published in India by Mr. Gladwin. The whole Persian work was printed in Calcutta in 1811. Two MS. copies of this work are in my possession, one of which is the very copy noticed by Sir William Jones. If I can ever command leisure sufficient, it is my intention to translate this work.

12. The [r] Heft Iklīm, a very valuable biographical and geographical work in Persian, by [s] Amīn Ahmed Rāzī, giving notices of some of the most eminent Persian writers of every clime. The copy here cited is in large folio, very thick, and neatly written; it was lately purchased by the public library of Cambridge.

The [t] Maathari Rahīmī, a valuable and elaborate history of some of the Emperors and other eminent men of Tartary, Hindūstān, &c., by [u] Mohammed Abd El Bākī El Rahīmī El Nahāwendī. The copy used by me formerly belonged to Mr. Hindley, but has lately been purchased by the Cambridge public library: it is fairly written in large folio, and contains perhaps 2,000 leaves.

13. The [x] Nafahāt El Ins, a History of the Mohammedan Saints by the celebrated Jāmī. This work contains all that was valuable in two writers who had preceded him, together with considerable additions made by himself from other works, as well as from information obtained by personal inquiry. It was dedicated to the Emīr [y] Nizām Oddīn Ali Shīr, A. H. 881. A. D. 1476; but according to a note at the end, in 1478. The work, which is in my possession, is a large octavo of about three hundred and fifty leaves, very neatly but not very accurately written in Pattan in Hindūstān, A. D. 1612.

---

[n] علي بن الحسين المشتهر بحاجي زين العطار. [o] اختيارات بديعي. [p] دبستان المذاهب.
[q] محمد محسن فاني. [r] هفت اقليم. [s] امين احمد رازي. [t] ماثر رحيمي.
[u] محمد عبد الباقي الرحيمي. [x] نفحات الانس. [y] امير نظام الدين علي شير.

14. The [z]Khulāsat El Ansāb, a short history of the Afghāns by [a]Ibn Shāh Aālam of the tribe *Kot-ha Khail*. A work in one small octavo volume, Persian. There are two copies of this work in the public library of Cambridge.

The Arabic works cited are the following :

15. The [b]Kitāb El Ishārāt by El Harawī. This is an account of the pilgrimages performed by the Sheikh Alī of Herāt early in the thirteenth century. The book is but short, and, according to the author, contains only an abstract of a larger work, which had been taken from him by the King of England, when engaged in the Crusades. This abstract was made from memory ; but of this the author does not fail to remind his reader when treating of particulars, which might have escaped him. I had the use of two copies, one in the collection of Mr. Burckhardt in our public library, the other was lent me by the kindness of Mr. Lewin. These copies are near the size of our duodecimos. Mr. Burckhardt's contains part of two copies, the latter of which was written 537 years ago, perhaps in the time of the author. I have generally cited him by the name of El Harawī.

16. [c]Abulfeda's Geography. The copy used by me is in the hand-writing of Erpenius, which is probably a transcript of that in the University Library of Leyden. It is in very large folio, and like its original presents many unintelligible readings; it is preserved in the public library at Cambridge, and has the class marks Dd. i. ii. This work is, I understand, either entirely or for the most part, given in a translation by Reiske in Buesching's Magazine ;* a work published some years ago in Germany, but which has never come to my hands.

17. The Geographical Work of Edrīsī is too well known to need any description. I used the Roman impression.

18. The [d]Marāsid El Itlāa. This is a sort of geographical dictionary not unlike our gazetteers. It is occasionally cited in M. De Sacy's Chrestomathie Arabe. Like all

---

[z]خلاصة الانساب .      [a]ابن شاه عالم كوته خيل .      [b]كتاب الاشارات في معرفة الزيارات

تأليف الشيخ الولي الشيخ علي الهروي .      [c]تقويم البلدان لابي اسمعيل ابي الفدا ·

[d]كتاب مراصد الاطلاع علي اسماء الامكنة والبقاع تاليف ... عبد المؤمن بن عبد الحق مدرس الحنابله

&c. بالبشيرية

---

* Buesching's Magazine, für Historie und Geographie, tom. iv.

other Arabic dictionaries it is very defective: otherwise many places unnoticed by me, would have been more exactly described.

19. The geographical work of Ibn El Wardī is too well known to need description. The copy I have cited belongs to the public library of Cambridge, and bears the class-marks Ll. 5. 30. There is also another copy in the collection of Mr. Burckhardt.

20. The ᵉYatīmat El Dahar, a remarkably elegant and interesting work on the principal Arabian poets, with some extracts from their writings, compiled A. H. 384, A. D. 994, by Abu Mansūr El Thaālabī. The work is occasionally cited by M. de Sacy in the second edition of his Chrestomathie Arabe. The copy used in this work is a large sized neatly written octavo containing about 250 leaves. It formerly belonged to Mr. Hindley; but is now in my possession.

21. The ᶠSukkardān, a work by Ibn Hajela on Egypt: it is occasionally noticed by M. De Sacy, in his Chrestomathie Arabe. The copy here used is a moderately sized octavo. tolerably well written; it is to be found in the collection of Mr. Burckhardt in the public library of Cambridge.

22. The ᵍKhulāsat Tahkīk El Zunūn, a biographical dictionary, apparently an abridgment of Hāji Khalfa; but of this I am not certain, as the copy of Hāji Khalfa with which I have compared it, contains scarcely half the number of works of which this gives some account. I suspect, however, that this copy of Hāji Khalfa is only an abridgment itself. The Epitomator's name is ʰKamāl Oddīn Abu Futūh Ibn Mustafa Ibn Kamāl Oddīn Ibn Ali El Sidīkī. The book is in Mr. Burckhardt's collection.

23. Another book from which some citations have been made is, Ibn Khaldūn's history of the Berbers: and, as this book is extremely scarce and valuable, I may be excused if I describe it a little more particularly. The full title, then, which stands on the first page is as follows : الجزء السَّابِع من كتَاب العِبَر وديوان المُبتدَا والخَبر في آيَّام العَرَب والعَجم والبَربَر

ومَن عَاصرَهُم من ذَوي السلطَان الاكبر تَاليف الشيخ الامَام العَالِم العَلَمَة ولي الدين ابي زيد عَبد

الرَّحمن بن الشيخ الامام العلامة ابي عَبد الله محمد بن خلدُون المالكي الحَضرمي i. e. The seventh

---

ᵉ كتاب يتيمة الدهر في محاسن اهل العصر لابي منصور الثعالبي .                    ᶠ السكردان لابن حجله .

ᵍ خلاصة تحقيق الظنون في شروح المتون .          ʰ كمال الدين ابو فتوح بن مصطفي بن كمال

الدين بن علي الصديقي .

part of the book of examples and of the Dīwān of the commencements * and accounts, on the times of the Arabs, Persians, Berbers, and others contemporary with them, who came into supreme power; a publication of the Priest and learned Sheikh the very learned Walī Oddīn Abu Zaid Abd El Rahmān, son of the Priest and very learned Abu Abd Allah Mohammed Ibn Khaldūn, of the sect of Ibn Mālik, and of the country of Hadramaut. The work is closely and accurately written in the Mogrebine hand in large quarto upon stout well polished paper. The history of the Berbers covers three hundred and sixty-nine pages; the remainder of the book, which contains seventy-seven pages, is an account of the family and life of the author, written by himself. This part is prefaced by these words, التعريف بابن خلدون مؤلّف الكتاب. On the last leaf of the book we have وكان الفراغ من تعليقه ثامن المحرم سنة ثمان والف i. e. The cessation from writing it out was on the 8th of Moharram, in the year 1008, A.D. July 21, 1599. This book does not belong to the University Library of Cambridge as some have supposed, but to the Rev. Richard Edward Kerrich, A.M., son of our late principal librarian, the Rev. Thomas Kerrich, A. M., who informed me that it had belonged to his father, which is no doubt the truth, as an engraving containing his arms and name, Samuel Kerrich, S. T. P., is pasted within the cover at the beginning of the book. Upon discovering to Mr. Kerrich, our Librarian, the character and rareness of this work, I was permitted to copy and translate it, upon tendering a bond of five hundred pounds, ensuring its safe return at the end of two years.

In writing the proper names of persons and places, I have generally retained the Oriental orthography, as I deemed it proper to preserve these as nearly as possible, rather than attempt to follow the varying models of different travellers. But, in order to know how these words ought to be pronounced, it is necessary I should explain my system of orthography. Consonants then will be pronounced as they generally are in English, excepting kh, which must be sounded like the German *ch*, i. e. as a deep guttural. The vowels thus : A as *a* in *America* : ā as *a* in *war, wall,* &c. : *u* as *oo* in

---

* The terms مبتدا and خبر signify the *subject* and *predicate* in grammar, as shewn by Dr. Nicoll in his continuation of Uri's Catalogue, after M. de Sacy, p. 114. M. de Sacy has, however, since changed his mind, as may be seen in the Second Edition of his Chrestomathie Arabe, and now thinks that the literal meaning is the true one. Dr. Nicoll has made a trifling mistake in giving in the title عاصوهم instead of عاصرهم, in which our copy agrees with that used by M. de Sacy. See Chrest. Arab., tom. ii. pp. ١٠٦, 290, &c. This work it is my intention to translate and publish with the original text as soon as circumstances will allow.

*good, stood*: *ū* as *oo* in *boot, root,* : *i* like *i* in *bid, rid,* : *ī* like the *i* of the Italians, French, &c. or like our *ee* in *meet, seek,* &c. : *O* as *o* in *rose* : *ai* and *ei* as *i* in *bite.* I have judged it expedient to mention this, because my orthography will stand for nothing, until readers know how it is intended to be pronounced.    I have also retained the orthography of proper names, throughout, in the Arabic character : and in representing the defi- nite article (الل) El, I have followed the example of Mr. Burckhardt, who always writes it *El.*   Some writers, indeed, follow the rules of the Arabic grammar, chang- ing the l (ل), whenever what is termed a solar letter follows, for such letter ; which, however, has the effect of so much obscuring proper names, when they happen to begin with one of these letters, that it requires some knowledge of the Arabic lan- guage, to be able to recognise them, *e. g.* in the word [i]*Elkhafīf,* I can easily see that it is a compound of El and Khafīf ; but in that of [k]*Ennöomān,* if I do not understand Arabic, and am told that a place was so called, because it was built by *Nöomān,* I shall be at a loss to conceive where the mark of connexion is to be found ; not to insist on another difficulty, in which the vowel belonging to this article is changed by the con- struction of the preceding word, making it at one time *Unnöomān,* at another, *Innöomān,* and at another, *Annöomān,* or *Ennöomān.* In a few very well known words, such as *Oddīn, Allah,* and the like, I have not thought it worth while to depart from the usual orthography. The text too I have divided into chapters, to which an abstract of the contents of each is prefixed, for the convenience of the reader.

---

[k] التعمان .            [i] الخفيف .

# ADDITIONS AND CORRECTIONS.

The passage alluded to in p. 18, note, is found in pp. 218-19 of Psalmanazar's (not Psalmeser, as there erroneously printed) valuable Essays, entitled " Essays on the following Subjects, &c. By a Layman in Town. London, 1753." The place mentioned by him, and to which I could not refer, because the book was not then accessible to me, is the following : " Hic populi numerosi habitavere Gergesæi, Jebusæi, aliáque habentes nomina Hebræis voluminibus memorata : qui quum inexpugnabilem conspicerent advenarum exercitum, patrios fines deserentes in Ægyptum vicinam migraverunt, ibique numero ac sobole excrescentes, quum non satis commodum tantæ multitudini locum invenissent, in Africam penetravere, ubi civitates quamplures habitantes omnem eum tractum usque ad Herculis columnas tenuerunt, semiphœnicia lingua ac catalecto utentes. Oppidumque Tingen situ munitissimum in Numidia ædificaverunt, ubi duo ex albo lapide columnæ prope magnum fontem constitutæ, in quibus Phœnicum lingua litteræ incisæ sunt hujuscemodi. Nos a facie fugimus Jesu prædonis filii Nave, &c." Procopius de Bello Vandilico, Lib. ii. p. 222. edit. 1531.—The edition of Dow's Hindustan quoted is the quarto of 1768.

## ERRATA.

| Page | line | read. | Page | line | read. |
|---|---|---|---|---|---|
| 4 | 19 | judice. | 100 | 22 | Dabistān. |
| 13 | 19 | Kalāwūn. | 112 | 18 | .لَلْمِش |
| 14 | 30 | Moniat. | | | |
| 16 | 13 | Sayyad. | 116 | 28 | Ferishta. |
| 17 | 24 | امَّا | 123 | 10 | Kālyūr. |
| 18 | 4 | Bejāh and. | 135 | 6 | Haita. |
| — | 23, 27 | Edrīsī. | 140 | 16 | Hejāz. |
| 24 | 3 | Yours is. | — | sæpe. | Methkāl. |
| — | 31 | Jawharī. | 145 | 21 | .بجائي |
| 25 | 35 | .ياحذون | 149 | 34 | Munshī. |
| 28 | 30 | .الربعي | 157 | 27 | .روز اول |
| 33 | 3 | midnight. | 178 | 8 | is a sea ... |
| 45 | 13 | Harawī. | 184 | 23 | .جبل سامي |
| 49 | 17 | Kānūn. | — | 24 | .ومنها |
| 50 | 23 | by her. | 187 | 35 | .بوزنه |
| 54 | 3 | Oddīn. | Ub. occ. lege Ghayāth pro Ghīath. | | |
| 55 | 32 | Makdishu. | 230 | 14 | .حماماتها |
| 69 | 26 | Khazir. | 232 | 14 | شرقي |
| 87 | 12 | .بشرقيه | 237 | 1 | Kābara. |
| 95 | 6 | Hanīfa. | — | 35 | .المغاربة |

# THE

# TRAVELS

OF

# IBN BATŪTA.

## CHAPTER I.

*Tanjiers—Tilimsān—Milyāna—Algiers—Bijāya—Kosantīna—Būna—Tūnis—Sūsa—Sajākus—*
*Kābis—Tripoli—Meslāta, &c.*

IN THE NAME OF THE COMPASSIONATE AND MERCIFUL GOD.

PRAISE be ascribed to God the lord of worlds; and the blessing of God be upon our Lord Mohammed, and upon all his posterity and companions. But to proceed: The poor, and needy of the forgiveness of his bountiful lord, Mohammed Ibn Fat,h Allah El Bailūnī states, that the following is what he extracted from the epitome of the Kātib Mohammed Ibn Jazzī El Kelbī (upon whom be the mercy of God), from the travels of the theologian "Abu Abd Allah Mohammed Ibn Abd Allah El Lawātī* of Tanjiers known by the surname of Ibn Batūta:† and, that he did not extract any

---

" ابو عبد الله محمد بن عبد الله اللواتي الطانجي المعروف بابن بطوطه .

---

* El Lawātī. We have in the geographical work entitled كتاب مراصد الاطلاع علي اسمآء الامكنة, &c. the following account of two places, to one of which this patronymic is undoubtedly to be referred. لواته بالفتح والتآء مثناة ناحية بالاندلس من قريش والواته قبيلة من البربر . Lawāta is a district of Karīsh in Spain. It is also the name of a tribe of the Berbers. According to the same work جَزّه Jazza is a place in Khorāsān موضع بالخراسان, to which the patronymic Jazzī is probably to be referred.

† Mr. Burckhardt writes this name Ibn Batouta, adopting the French pronunciation of *ou* I suppose. I have thought it more conformable with our orthography and pronunciation to write

thing except what was strange and unknown, or, known by report, but not
believed on account of its rarity, and the frequent carelessness of historians
in delivering down what has been reported, but what he himself considered
as true, in consequence of the fidelity of the Traveller, and because he had
written what he believed to be credible from histories of various nations and
countries; and, because that which has been reported by faithful witnesses,
generally receives credit and excites inquiry. Some of his statements,
indeed, are opposed to the statements of others; as, for instance, his
accounts of what he saw of the aromatic roots of Hindustan, which differ
from those given by the physicians : and yet his accounts are probably the
true ones.

The Sheikh Ibn Batūta, the author of these travels, left his native city,
ᵇTanjiers,* for the purpose of performing the pilgrimage in the 725th year

---

<sup>b</sup> طنجه .

---

Batūta. " There are two abridgments of these travels," says Mr. Burckhardt, " one by Ibn
Djezy el Kelby (ابن جزي الكلبي), the other by Ibn Fathallah el Beylouny (ابن فتح الله البيلوني)
printed by mistake البيلوني ابن فتح الله ); the latter I possess." He tells us in the same page
that he possessed two copies of this abridgment; but the fact is, there are three among his
books bequeathed to the University of Cambridge, all of which present the same text : the few
variations found have evidently originated in the mistakes of the transcribers. Mr. Burckhardt
writes *Djezy*, giving *Dj* for the Arabic ج. I have adopted Pococke's method of giving our j for
this letter, with which it exactly corresponds. In this word جزي some of the MSS. have جزّي
doubling the j z, which I have no doubt is the true orthography. From the extracts printed in
Germany by Professor Kosegarten and Mr. Apetz, it is quite certain that Mr. Seetzen's copy, which
they probably used, is nothing more than an abridgment of the great work of Ibn Batūta; and
although it presents some varieties with our copies, it is most likely a copy of the same abridgment.
I may remark here, once for all, that, as the proper names of places are extremely erroneous
in Mr. Burckhardt's abstract (Travels in Nubia, Appendix III), I shall not in future notice
them; but shall give such words in this work as correctly as I can from the documents in my
hands.

* The Arabian geographers divide Northern Africa into three parts, as given by Abulfeda in
the following extract وبلاد المغرب ثلاث قطع الغريب منها يعرف بالمغرب الاقصي وهو من ساحل
البحر المحيط الي تلمسان غربا وشرقا ومن سُبّته الي مراكش ثم الي سجلماسه وما في سمتها شمالا
و جنوبا والقطعة الثانية تعرف بالمغرب الاوسط وهي من شرقي وهران عن تلمسان مسيرة يوم وشرقيها
الي اخر حدود مملكة بجايه من الشرق والقطعة الثالثة الشرقية افريقيه ويمتد الي برقه الي حدود
ديار مصر . The regions of the west consist of three divisions, the most western of which is

of the Hejira (A.D. 1324-5). I shall mention here only the names of some of the districts through which he passed, although this may contribute but little towards impressing the reader with the greatness of his courage, his religious confidence, or his indefatigable perseverance, in overcoming the difficulties of passing deserts and of crossing mountains.

The first city, therefore, at which he arrived, was [c]Tilimsān*; the next [d]Milyāna; the next [e]El Jazāer (Algiers): the next [f]Bijāya; the next [g]Kosantīna†

قسنطينه . [g]     بجايه . [f]     الجزاير. [e]     مليانه . [d]     تلمسان . [c]

known by " the Extreme West." This part extends from the shores of the ocean to Tilimsān, considered in an eastward or westward direction: and again, from Subta to Morocco and thence to Sijilmāsa with the parts adjacent, considered from north to south. The second division is known by " the Middle West," and it extends from the east of Wahrān, which is one day's journey from Tilimsān eastward, to the boundaries of the kingdom of Bijāya. The third and eastern division is termed Africa, and this extends from Barca to the boundaries of Egypt. Abulfeda places Algiers in Bijāya, and states the longitude and latitude to be respectively 20° 58′, 33° 30′, reckoning the longitude eastward from the جزاير خالدات perpetual islands, i. e. from Ferro, the most westward of the Canary Islands 17° 52′ west of Greenwich. The قسنطينه Kosantīna of our traveller is by him written قسطينه Kosatīna, but the ن n has probably been omitted by the copyist. He makes the longitude and latitude, according to the Atwāl, 28° 30′, 31 30′; Ibn Saīd 24 40′, 33° 22′ respectively.

\* In the مراصد الاطلاع we have تنمسان يقول بعضهم والسين مهملة وسكون الميم بكسرتين تلمسان بالنون عوض اللّام بالمغرب مدينتان متجاورتان مسورتان بينهما رمية حجر احدهما قديمة والاخري حديثة &c. i. e. Tilimsān: some pronounce it Tinimsān with an n instead of the l: they are two walled and neighbouring cities in the west, between which there is the distance of a stone's throw: the one is ancient, the other modern.—The word is probably a dual. I notice this, because I find M. de Sacy writing it Telmisan.

† We have قسطينيه Kosantīnia, in the مراصد الاطلاع, with this account of the place, مدينه وقلعة يقال لها قسنطينيه الهوا وهي قلعة كبيرة عالية جدا لا يصلها الطير الا بجهد من حدود افريقية مما يلي المغرب وهي علي ثلثة انهار عظام تجري فيها السفن i. e. " A city and tower, the latter of which is termed Kosantīnia el Hawā. It is an extremely large and high tower, so that the birds cannot get to it without considerable effort. It is situated in the boundaries of Africa which limit the western parts, upon three large rivers navigated by ships." This place is also styled by El Harawi, in his book of pilgrimages, قسطنطينه الهوي Costantīna El Hawa, in which he says was a most wonderful bridge having only one arch, and that with a span of 150 paces: the only building like it was another in Khūzistān. مدينة قسطنطينه بها القنطرة من عجايب العمارات الا ان القنطره

the next <sup>h</sup>Būna; the next <sup>i</sup>Tūnis\*; the next <sup>k</sup>Sawsa; the next <sup>l</sup>Safākus.

---

<sup>l</sup> سفاقس .     <sup>k</sup> سوسه .     <sup>i</sup> تونس .     <sup>h</sup> بونه .

التي علي باب ارجان مما يلي خوزستان التي تنسب الي الديلمي طبيب الحجاج ليس في بلاد
الاسلام مثلها طوق واحد ما بين العمودين مقدار ماية و خمسين خطوة . In this place is a bridge,
to which there is no equal in the countries of Islamism for its wonderful construction : it consists
of one arch of 150 paces in extent between two piers, if we except that at the gates of Arjān
upon the borders of Khūzistān, which is referred to El Dailamī the physician of El Hejāj.

Of this other wonderful bridge we find some account in the work of Mr. Ulenbroek, taken from
Ibn Haukal (p. 44), as follows : واما انهار فارس فذاب مياه طيبة تخرج من حدود اصبهان وجبالها
فتظهر بناحية السردن بعد ممرها بنواحي البرج وانصبابها في نهر مسن وهو النهر الخارج من نواحي
اصبهان الي نواحي السردن ومجمعها عند قرية تدعي مسن ولا يزال ما يفضل عن حاجتهم جاريا
الي باب الرجان تحمت قنطرة ثكان وهي قنطرة بين فارس وخوزستان قليلة النظير وهي عندي اجل
which من قنطرة قرطبة من عمل بعض ثنا فارس فتسقي رستاق وشهر ثم يقع في البحر عند حد شينيز
he thus translates : " ad fluvios Persidis quod attinet, habet bonas aquas orientes in confiniis
Isphahanæ ejusque montibus, et apparentes in regione Al Sardan postquam transierunt tractum
Al Bordj. Sese exonerant in fluvium Masen, qui itidem e tractu Isphahanæ versus illum Sardani
procedit. Conjunguntur prope vicum Masen dictum ; neque desinit aqua fluere uberius quam
incolarum necessitates postulant, usque ad postam al Radjan sub ponte Tsakan ; qui pons inter
Persidem et Khouzistanum exstans paucos sibi pares habet, ita ut, me quidem judic, opere
præstantior sit ponte Condubæ et ex laudatissimis Persiæ rebus. Rigat pagum et urbem, deinde
incidit in mare prope confinia Schiniz." It may be remarked here, that the place termed ارجان
by El Harawī, is given by Mr. Ulenbroek رجان. The former, however, is the reading given in
the Calcutta edition of the Kāmoos, thus الارجان د بفارس, i. e. El Arjān, a district in Fārs.
Abulfeda gives ارجان, but says that it is also written ارغان with غ. Instead of شينيز too,
Abulfeda gives سينيز. (See also pp. 31, 88 in Mr. Ulenbroek's Translations).

\* In Abulfeda, تونس مدينة كبيرة محدثة بافريقية علي ساحل البحر عمرت من انقاض
قرطاجنه وهي علي ميلين منها وكان اسم تونس ترسيس قيل يحيط بسورها احد وعشرون الف ذراع
وهي الان قصبة بلاد افريقية وشربهم من ابار ومصانع يجتمع فيها ماء المطر والمينا في شرقيها . Tūnis
is a large modern city in Africa, situated upon the sea-shore. It was built from the ruins of
Carthage which is two miles from it. It has been called Tarsīs also. Its walls are said to enclose
twenty-one thousand cubits. It is now a village of Africa. They drink from wells and canals
supplied by rain water. The port is towards its eastern part. Upon the authority of the geographical work entitled the Moshtarik (المشترك) Carthage, says Abulfeda, بلدة من اعمال افريقية
قرب تونس خراب وبها اثار قديمة قال وقرطاجنه ايضا مدينة بالاندلس من اعمال تدمير غمرها
البحر فبادت. It is a town in the districts of Africa near Tūnis, but now in ruins : there are in
it many marks of ancient splendour. He also says, that this is the name of a city in Spain in
the district of Tadmīr, which was overflowed by the sea and destroyed.

Ibn Jazzi El Kelbi states, that on this place the following verses were written by ᵐIbn Habīb El Tenūkhī.*

> May showers enrich thy happy soil,
> Fair land, where fanes and towers arise:
> On thee let sainted pilgrims pour
> The richest blessings of the skies.
> The wave that round thy bosom plays,
> Conscious of its endeared retreat,
> When the rude tempest rocks thy domes,
> In sighs resigns its happy seat.
> Yet urged another glance to steal
> Of thy loved form so good so fair,
> Flies to avoid the painful view
> Of rival lovers basking thence.

And, on the other hand, ⁿAbu Abd Allah Mohammed Ibn Abī Temīm †
has said:

ᵐ ابن حبيب التنوخي .       ⁿ ابو عبد الله محمد بن ابي تميم .

* As the Arabic text of this work is not likely soon to be printed, I shall occasionally give, in notes, such portions as I may think necessary, either for the purpose of promoting farther inquiry, or to present the reader with such specimens of Arabian poetry as may occur. The original lines of the above verses are as follows:

ذات المصانع والمصلى       سقيا لارض سفاقس
تزوره اهلا وسهلا       بلد تكاد تقول حين
تارة عنه ويملاء       وكانه والبحر يحسر
صبّ يريد زيارة فـــــاذا رأي الرّقباء ولي

This verse is a species of that termed البسيط or *expanded*. See Clarke's Arabic Prosody, p. 51. The measure will be found at page 60, as follows, مستفعلن فاعلن فعولن, with its varieties. Tenūkh is the name of a tribe in Bahrein, from which this poet probably took his origin. I have not been able to find any particulars respecting him.

† The following are the original lines:

قد عاين البحر قبحا في جوانبيا       فكلّما ان يدنوا لها هربا

The verse is of the species termed البسيط, *expanded*, and may be measured by مستفعلن فاعلن مستفعلن فعلن, with its varieties. See Clarke's Prosody, p. 52.

The author is probably بو عبد الله محمد بن ابي علي التميمي المازري الفقيه المالكي المحدث given at n. 628 of Tydeman's Conspectus operis Ibn Chalicani. Lugd. Batav. 1809.

See the swelling angry tide,
Rage and beat against her side:
But, only ask a moment's stay,—
It hisses, foams, and rolls away.

The next city was that of °Kābis; the next ᵖTarābulus (Tripoli). Ibn Batūta has stated, that he then passed on to ᵠMeslāta and ʳMesurāta, and ˢKasūra Surt (or Palaces of Surt). We then passed, says he, the 'low grounds* (which may also mean the *Forest*), and proceeded to the palace of ᵘBarsīs the devotee, to the ᵛKubbat El Islām, and to the city of ʷAlexandria, where we saw one of its most learned men, the judge ˣFakhr Oddīn El Rīki, whose grandfather is said to have been an inhabitant of ʸRīka. This man was exceedingly assiduous in acquiring learning: he travelled to ᶻHejāz, and thence to Alexandria, where he arrived in the evening of the day. He was rather poor, and would not enter the city until he had witnessed some favour-

° قابس . ᵖ طَرَابُلُس . ᵠ مسلاته . ʳ مسراته . ˢ قصور سرت . ᵗ الغابة . ᵘ قصر برصيص .

ᵛ قبّة الاسلام . ʷ الاسكندرية . ˣ فخر الدين الريقي . ʸ ريقة . ᶻ الحجاز .

---

* In the مراصد الاطلاع we have, بحر علي ساحل ثم المهدية وسفاقس بين اطرابلس مدينة قابس . Kābis is المغرب من اعمال افريقية وبها مرفا السفن من كل مكان بينها وبين البحر ثلاثة اميال . a city situated between Tripoli and Safākus near El Mehdīyat, upon the shore of the western sea. In it is a station for ships from all parts: it is three miles distant from the sea.—El Harawī writes this name اطرابلس as above; and, in mentioning this place, stops to give an account of Etna as it was in his day, *i. e.* early in the thirteenth century. He says وبجزيرة اسقليه جبل النار مطل علي البحر شاهق في الهوي يري في النهار الدخان طالع منه وفي الليل النار وحدثني رجل من علماء البلاد انه راي حيوانا علي شكل السمان رصاصي اللون يطير من وسط هذه النار ويعود اليها وقال هو السمندل وانا فما رايت الا حجارة سودا مثقبة مثل حجر الرجل الحمام يقع من هذا الجبل الي ناحية البحر وقيل بفرغانه جبل مثله يحرق الحجارة ويباع رمادها ثلث اواقي بدرهم يبيّضون به الثياب . "In the island of Sicily is there a fiery mountain, which hangs over the sea. It is very high in the air, and during the daytime smoke is seen arising out of it, and in the night fire. One of the learned men of the country told me, that he saw an animal like a quail of a leaden colour fly out of the middle of this fire and again return to it. This he said was *a samandal* (salamandar). For my part, I saw nothing but black perforated stones, like the stone of the pes columbinus, falling from this mountain on the part near the sea. They say, that there is a similar mountain in Fargāna which burns stones, the ashes of which are sold three ounces for the dirhem, and with this they whiten their clothes." From this it should seem, that *salamandar* is a corruption of *samandal*, an Arabic compound signifying *quail-like*.

able omen. He sat, accordingly, near the gate, until all the persons had gone in, and it was nearly time for closing the gate. The keeper of the gate was irritated at his delay, and said to him ironically, enter Mr. Judge. He replied, yes, judge! if that be God's will. After this he entered one of the colleges, and attended to reading, following the example of others who had attained to eminence, until his name and reputation for modesty and religion reached the ears of the king of Egypt. About this time the judge of Alexandria died. The number of learned men in Alexandria who expected this appointment was large: but of these, the sheikh was one who entertained no expectations of it. The Sultan, however, sent it to him; and he was admitted to the office, which he filled with great integrity and moderation; and hence obtained great fame.

---

## CHAPTER II.

*Alexandria—Tarŭja—Damanhŭr—Fawwah—Fāriskŭr—Ashmŭn El Rommān—Samanŭd—Caïro.*

ONE of the greatest saints in Alexandria, at this time, was the learned and pious Imām, Borhān[a] Oddīn El Aaraj, a man who had the power of working miracles.* I one day went in to him, when he said, I perceive that you are fond of travelling into various countries. I said yes; although I had at that time no intention of travelling into very distant parts. He replied, you must visit my brother [b]Farīd Oddīn in India, and my brother [c]Rokn Oddīn Ibn Zakaryā in Sindia, and also my brother Borhān Oddīn in China: and, when you see them, present my compliments to them. I was astonished at what he said, and determined with myself to visit those countries: nor did I give up my purpose till I had met all the three mentioned by him, and presented his compliments to them.

---

[c] ركن الدين بنْ زكريا.     [b] فريد الدين.     [a] برهان الدين الاعرج.

---

* It is generally believed among the Mohammedans, that every saint has it in his power to perform miracles without laying claim to the office of a prophet. This kind of miracle they term karāmet ( كرامة ), *benevolent action.* See my Controversial Tracts on Christianity and Mohammedanism, p. 2, 352, &c.

Another singular man was the [d] Sheikh Yākūt, the Abyssinian, disciple of the Sheikh [e] Abu Abbās El Mursī.  This Abu Abbās was the disciple of the servant of God, [f] Abu El Hasan El Shādalī, &c. author of the [g] Hizb El Bahr,† famous for his piety and miracles.  I was told by the Sheikh Yākūt, from his preceptor Abu El Abbās El Mursī, that the Sheikh Abu El Hasan El Shādhalī performed the pilgrimage annually, making his way through Upper Egypt, and passing over to Mecca, in the month of Rejeb, and so remaining there till the conclusion of the pilgrimage : that he visited the holy tomb, and returned by the [h] great passage to his city.  On one of these occasions, and which happened to be the last, he said to his servant, Get together an axe, a casket, and some spice, and whatever is necessary for the interment of a dead body.  The servant replied : and why, Sir, should I do this?  He rejoined, you shall see [i] Homaitara.  Now Homaitara is situated in Upper Egypt; it is a stage in the great desert of [k] Aidhāb, in which there is a well of very pernicious and poisonous water.  When he had got to Homaitara the Sheikh bathed himself, and had performed two of

[f] ولي الله ابي الحسن الشاذلي .   [e] ابو عباس المرسي .   [d] الشيخ ياقوت الحبشي .

[k] عيذاب .   [i] حميتري .   [h] الدرب الكبير .   [g] حزب البحر .

* The title of Wali (ولي) seems to be applied to none but such as have attained to the very last degree of mystic excellence.  Jāmi tells us in the first chapter of the نفحات الانس, that the appropriation of this title belongs to those only, who have arrived at the last stage of mysticism, and may be said to be annihilated in the divine essence.  ولايت خاص مخصوص است بواصلان از ارباب سلوك وهي عبارة عن فناء العبد في الحق وبقائه به فالولي هو الفاني فيه والباقي به, &c. where also several other definitions, all tending to the same point, are adduced.  In the chapter في اصناف ارباب الولايت, given a little farther on, we have the different degrees of these worthies pointed out.

In the first volume of M. de Sacy's Chrestomathie Arabe (2d edit. p. 481), we have an account of the death of this Sheikh, taken from the Jahān Namā, a little different from this : and, what is the most curious part of it, the discovery of coffee is attributed to a communication made by him after his death to one of his disciples.  Works by this Sheikh are to be found in the libraries of both Cambridge and Oxford : but they appear to be of no great use.

† In a bibliographical work entitled the خلاصة تحقيق الظنون في الشروح والمتون preserved in Mr. Burckhardt's collection, we have, under the word, حزب ... حزب البحر للشيخ ابي الحسن الشاذلي اليمني : the Hizb El Bahr by the Sheikh Abu'l Hasan El Shādhalī El Jemenī.

‡ On this place see the " Index Geographicus in vitam Saladini " by Schultens under the word AIDABUM, and Burckhardt's Travels in Nubia, Appendix III. p. 519.

the prostrations of his prayers, when he died : he was then buried there. Ibn Batūta states that he visited the tomb, and saw upon it an inscription tracing his pedigree up to Hosain the son of Ali.

I heard, continues the Traveller, in Alexandria, by the 'Sheikh El Sälih El Aābid* El Munfik, of the character of Abu Abd Allah El Murshidī, and that he was one of the great interpreting saints† secluded in the Minyat of Ibn Murshed : and that he had there a cell, but was without either servant or companion. Here he was daily visited by emirs, viziers, and crowds of other people, whose principal object it was to eat with him. He accordingly gave them food, such as they severally wished to have, of victuals, fruit, or sweetmeats : a circumstance which has seldom taken place in any days but his. To him also do the learned come for patents of office, or dismissal. These were his constant and well-known practices. The Sultan of Egypt too, El Malik El Nāsir, often visited him in his cell.

I then left Alexandria (says the Traveller) with the intention of visiting this Sheikh (may God bless him), and got to the village of ᵐTarūja, then to the city of ⁿDamanhūr the metropolis of the Delta ; then to °Fawwah not far from which is the cell of the Sheikh Abu Abd Allah El Murshidī. I went to it and entered, when the Sheikh arose and embraced me. He then brought out victuals and ate with me. After this I slept upon the roof of

---

° فوّه .    ⁿ دمنبور .    ᵐ تروجه .    ¹ الشيخ الصالح العابد المنفق .

* This word designates an order of the religious, whose business, according to Jāmi in the نفحات الانس, is to attend constantly on the service of God, particularly on works of supererogation with a view to their final reward, while a complete Sūfī follows truth, purely from the love of it ; his words are : اما عبادان طايفه اند كه پيوسته بوظايف عبادات وفنون نوافل مواظبت وملازمت نمايند از براي نيل ثواب اخروي وأين وصف در صوفي موجود بود وليكن معزّا ومبرّا از شوايب علل واغراض چه ايشان حقرا براي حق پرستند نه براي ثواب اخروي

† الاوليا المكاشفين These seem to be nothing more than perpetuators of the ancient practices of divining mentioned so often in the Hebrew Bible. The influence these impostors still possess in the East is very great, as may be collected from the text in this place. It may not be uninteresting to the student of the Hebrew to find, that we have here the very word which is used to designate these pretenders in the Bible, namely, מְכַשֵּׁף or مكاشف discoverer, revealer. A curious note on the methods employed by diviners of this sort will be found extracted from Ibn Khaldūn, in the second volume of M. de Sacy's Chrestomathie Arabe, pp. 298–301. See also my Controversial Tracts on Christianity and Mohammedanism, p. 212.

his cell, and saw in a dream the same night, myself placed on the wings of a great bird, which fled away with me towards the temple at Mecca. He then verged towards Yemen; then towards the east: he then took his course to the south. After this he went far away into the east, and alighted with me safely in the regions of darkness (or arctic regions), where he left me.

I was astonished at this vision, and said to myself, no doubt the Sheikh will interpret it for me, for he is said to do things of this sort. When the morning had arrived, and I was about to perform my devotions, the Sheikh made me officiate; after this, his usual visitors, consisting of emirs, viziers, and others, made their calls upon him, and took their leave, after each had received a small cake from him.

When the prayer at noon was over he called me, I then told him my dream, and he interpreted it for me. He said, you will perform the pilgrimage, and visit the tomb of the Prophet; you will then traverse the countries of Yemen, [2]Irak, [3]Turkey, and [4]India, and will remain in these some time. In India you will meet with my brother [5]Dilshād, who will save you from a calamity, into which you will happen to fall. He then provided me with some dried cakes and some dirhems, and I bade him farewell. Since I left him, I experienced nothing but good fortune in my travels; but never met with a person like him, except my Lord 'El Walī Mohammed El Mowwalla, in India.

I next came to the city of [6]El Nahrāriat, then to [7]El Mohalla El Kobra (or the great station), from this I went to [8]El Barlas, then to [9]Damietta, in which is the cell of the Sheikh [10]Jamāl Oddīn El Sāwī, leader of the sect called [11]Karenders.* These are they who shave their chins and eyebrows.

---

[2] عراق . [3] ارض الترك . [4] بلاد الهند . [5] الولي سيدي [1]محمد المولّه . [6] النحرارية .
[7] المحله الكبري . [8] البرلس . [9] دمياط . [10] جمال الدين الساوي . [11] القرندرية .

---

* This, it should seem, is a sect of Sūfīs, who pay little regard to any thing, but persuading themselves that they stand well with the Almighty, as may be seen in an interesting note from Makrizi by M. De Sacy (Chrest. Arab., tom. i. p. 263, edit. 2). In one instance, however, the learned Frenchman has mistaken his author, which it is important to rectify. After stating that they fast and pray but little, Makrizi proceeds, ولم يبالوا بتناول شيء من اللذات المباحة which I translate thus: " they care nothing about the enjoyment of lawful pleasures:" but which stands thus in M. de Sacy: " ils ne font point de difficulté d'user des plaisirs licites:" by which I suppose he means, they make no scruple in indulging in lawful pleasures. In the extract from

It is said, that the reason which induced the Sheikh to shave off his beard and eyebrows was the following. He was a well made and handsome man; one of the women of ʿSāwah consequently fell in love with him; after this she was constantly sending to the Sheikh, presenting herself to him in the street, and otherwise soliciting his society : this he completely resisted. When she was tired of this, she suborned an old woman to stop him on his way to the mosque, with a sealed letter in her hand. When the Sheikh passed by her she said, Good Sir, can you read? Yes, he replied. She said, this letter has been sent to me by my son; I wish you would read it for me. He answered, I will. But when she had opened the letter she said, Good Sir, my son has a wife who is in yonder house; could I beg the favour of your reading the letter at the door, so that she may hear? To this he also assented; but, when he had got through the first door, the old woman closed it, and out came the woman with her slaves, and hung about him. They then took him into an inner apartment, and the mistress began to take liberties with him. When the Sheikh saw that there was no escaping, he said, I will do what you like : shew me a sleeping room. This she did : he then took in with him some water and a razor which he had, and shaved

---

° ساوه .

---

Makrizi, moreover, two sects of these are noticed; the last of which, termed ملامتي Melāmetī, pay very great regard to their actions and carriage in society.

The account given of these sects in the King of Oude's Persian Dictionary, entitled the Seven Seas, is as follows: The term Kalender (or Karender), signifies a being, perfectly relieved from the forms and objects of earthly usages, which do not confer happiness; and who is so far advanced in spiritual acquirements, as to be entirely freed from the restraints of custom or address. Having freed both body and soul from every person and thing, the Kalender seeks nothing but the beauty and glory of the Deity; and this he believes he obtains. But, such an one, feeling the least inclination to any thing existing, is termed a reprobate, not a Kalender. The difference between a Kalender, a Melāmetī, and a Sūfī, consists in this : the Kalender labours to be freed and removed from all forms and observances. The Melāmetī, on the other hand, conceals his devotions from others, as he does every thing else tending to virtue; while he conceals nothing that is bad and vicious. The Sūfī is that person, who allows his feelings to be affected by no created being, and has no liking or dislike to them. The degree of the Sūfī is the highest; for perfectly separated and simplified as they are from worldly concerns, they nevertheless obey their spiritual senior, and walk in the footsteps of him and of the prophet. See also d'Herbelot, Bib. Or., under the word *Calendar*, and d'Ohsson's Tabl. Emp. Ott., tom. ii. p. 315, as cited by M. de Sacy.

off his beard and both his eyebrows. He then presented himself to the woman, who, detesting both his person and his deed, ordered him to be driven out of the house. Thus, by divine providence, was his chastity preserved. This appearance he retained ever after; and every one who embraced his opinions also submitted to the shaving off of his beard and both his eyebrows.*

It is also said of the Sheikh Jamāl Oddīn, that after he had gone to Damietta, he constantly attended the burial-grounds of that place. There was at that time in Damietta a judge, known by the surname of Ibn Omaid, who, attending one day at the funeral of one of the nobles, saw the Sheikh in the burial-ground, and said to him, you are a beastly old fellow. He replied, And you are a foolish judge, who can pass with your beast among the tombs, and know at the same time, that the respect due to a dead man, is just as great as that due to a living one. The judge replied, worse than this is your shaving off your beard.† The Sheikh said, mark me: he then rubbed a little alkohol on his eye-brows, and lifting up his head, presented a great black beard, which very much astonished the judge and those with him, so that the judge descended from his mule.‡ The Sheikh applied the alkohol the second time, and, lifting up his head, exhibited a beautiful white beard. He then applied the alkohol the third time; and, when he lifted up his head, his face was beardless as before. The judge then kissed his hand, became his disciple, and building a handsome cell for him, became his companion for the rest of his life. After a while the Sheikh died, and was buried in the cell; and when the judge died, he was buried, as it had been expressed in his will, in the door-way of the cell, so that every one who should visit the tomb of the Sheikh, would have to pass over his grave.

---

* A very different account of the origin of this practice is given in a note from Makrizi, by M. de Sacy (Chrest. Arabe, tom. i. p. 264, 2d edit.), in which it is said, that it must have originated about four hundred years before Makrizi's time; but, as Ibn Batūta lived more than one hundred years before Makrizi, it is probable that his account is the true one. Makrizi, besides, cites no author in support of his opinion, and probably says only what he might have heard.

† From this, as well as from what is related above about this woman, it may be seen how exceedingly reproachful it is considered in the East to shave off the beard. Compare Leviticus, xix. 27; xxi. 5. 2 Sam., x. 5. 1 Chron., xix. 5.

‡ Rebecca, we find, alighted from her camel (Gen. xxiv. 64), in order to pay respect to her future husband Isaac, just as the Judge here did to the Sheikh.

I then proceeded from this place to the city of <sup>d</sup>Fāriskūr, then to<sup>e</sup>Ashmūn El Rommān, then to the city of <sup>f</sup>Samānūd, then to <sup>g</sup>Misr (Caïro), the principal city of its district. The Nile, which runs through this country, excels all other rivers in the sweetness of its taste,\* the extent of its progress, and the greatness of the benefits it confers. It is one of the five great rivers of the world, which are, itself, the <sup>h</sup>Euphrates, the <sup>i</sup>Tigris, the <sup>k</sup>Sīhūn, the <sup>l</sup>Jaihūn (or Gihon). Five other rivers too may be compared with them, namely, the river of <sup>m</sup>Sindia, which is called the<sup>n</sup> Panj āb (or five waters); the river of India, which is called the <sup>o</sup>Gung (or Ganges), to which the Indians perform their pilgrimages, and into which they throw the ashes of their dead when burnt: they say it descends from Paradise; also the river <sup>p</sup>Jūn (or Jumna): the river <sup>q</sup>Athil (Volga) in the desert of <sup>r</sup>Kifjāk, and the river <sup>s</sup>Sarv in Tartary, upon the bank of which is the city of <sup>t</sup>Khān Bālik,† and which flows from that place to <sup>u</sup>El Khansā, and thence to the city of <sup>v</sup>Zaitūn in China, of which we shall give accounts in their proper places. The course of the Nile, moreover, is in a direction from the south to the north, contrary to that of all other rivers.

When I entered Egypt the reigning prince was <sup>w</sup>El Malik El Nāsir Mohammed Ibn El Malik El Mansūr Kālāwūn.‡ The learned men then in Egypt were, <sup>x</sup>Shams Oddīn El Isphahānī,§ the first man in the world in metaphysics; <sup>y</sup>Rokn Oddīn Ibn El Karīa, one of the leaders in the same

---

<sup>h</sup> سيكون .   <sup>i</sup> الدجله .   <sup>h</sup> الفرات .   <sup>g</sup> مصر .   <sup>f</sup> سمانود .   <sup>e</sup> اشمون الرمان .   <sup>d</sup> فاريسكور .

<sup>r</sup> قنجاق .   <sup>q</sup> آثل .   <sup>p</sup> جون .   <sup>o</sup> الكنك .   <sup>n</sup> بنج آب .   <sup>m</sup> نهر السند .   <sup>l</sup> جايخون .

<sup>w</sup> الملك الناصر محمد   <sup>v</sup> الزيتون .   <sup>u</sup> الخنسا .   <sup>t</sup> مدينة خان بالق .   <sup>s</sup> نهر السرو .

<sup>y</sup> ركن الدين بن القريع .   <sup>x</sup> شمس الدين الاصفهاني .   ابن الملك المنصور قلاوون .

---

\* That the water of the Nile was commonly drunk as early as the times of Moses, we are informed in the book of Exodus, chap. vii. See also Diodorus Siculus, lib. i, p. 49, edit. Wesseling. The Arabs, too, generally term this river the *sweet sea* (البحر الحلو), in order to distinguish it from the Mediterranean, which they term the *salt sea* (البحر الملح). See M. de Sacy's Chrestomathie Arabe, tom. ii. p. 15.

† Pekin, as will be shewn hereafter.

‡ See D'Herbelot, under Nasser Ben Calaoun: Annales Muslem., tom. v. p. 116, 331, &c.

§ See D'Herbelot, under Schamseddin.

science :* and the Sheikh ᶻAthīr Oddīn Abu Haiān of Granada, the greatest grammarian.†

---

## CHAPTER III.

*Upper Egypt—Baush —Dilās —Bibā—Bahnasā Minyat Ibn Khasīb—Manlawi—Manfalūt—Esoyūt—Ekhmīm—Hawwa—Kanā—Kaus—El Aksar—Armanat—Esna—Edfū—Ajarnā El Fīl—El Atwānī—Dugain—Homaitara—Aidhāb—Caïro.*

THE traveller continues: I then left Cairo, with the intention to go on the pilgrimage by way of ᵃUpper Egypt, and came to the ᵇDer El Tīn (or monastery of clay). From this place I went to ᶜBaush, then to ᵈDilās, then to ᵉBibā, then to ᶠBahnasā, then to the ᵍMinyet of Ibn Khasīb,‡ which was formerly attached to the government of Cairo. It is said, that one of the Califs of the house of Abbas was displeased with the people of Egypt, and took it into his head to place over them one of the meanest of his slaves, by way of punishment, and that he might afford an example to others. At this time Khasīb was the lowest slave in the palace, and his business was to get the baths warmed. He was accordingly appointed to the government, with the hope that he would sufficiently punish them by his tyranny, as it is usual with those who have not been brought up for such a station. But when Khasīb was established in Egypt, his conduct was exemplary in the extreme; and, for this, his fame was spread far and wide : the consequence was, he was visited by the relations of the Calif, and other persons attached to the court, and these he loaded with presents. Upon one of these occasions the Calif missed some of his relations, and upon

---

ᵃ الصعيد .    ᵇ دير الطين .    ᶜ مدينة بوش .    ᵈ دلاص .    ᶜ ببا .    ᵃ اثير الدين ابو حيان .

ᶠ البهنسا .    ᵍ منية ابن خصيب .

---

\* Annales Muslemici, tom. v. p. 300-1.          † See D'Herbelot, under Abou-Haian.

‡ This place is noticed in an extract given in M. de Sacy's Chrestomathie Arabe, tom. ii, pp. ᵟ and 3 of the French translation; as also in the Annales Muslemici, vol. iii. p. 750, where, as well as in the Appendix to M. de Sacy's Rélations d'Egypt, by Abd el Latīf, the first of these words is written *Moniat* or *Monyet*. It could have been wished that M. de Sacy had, in his Chrestomathie, given his reasons for changing his orthography.

inquiry found, that one of them had absented himself. After a time this man presented himself to the Calif, who interrogated him as to his absence. The man replied, that he had been paying a visit to Khasīb in Egypt: he then told him of the gifts he had received, which were indeed of great value. This enraged the Calif so that he ordered the eyes of Khasīb to be put out, that he should be expelled from Egypt, and cast out into one of the streets of Bagdad. When the order for his apprehension arrived, it was served upon him by an artifice, at some distance from his palace. He had with him, however, a large ruby, which he had hidden by sewing it up in his shirt during the night. His eyes were then put out, and he was thrown out in a street of Bagdad. Upon this occasion a poet happened to pass by, who said, O Khasīb, it was my intention to visit thee in Egypt, in order to recite thy praises: but thy coming hither is the more suitable to me. Will you then allow me to recite my poem? How, said Khasīb, shall I hear it? You know what circumstances I am in. The poet replied, my only wish is that you should hear it: but as to reward—may God reward you, as you have others! Khasīb then said, go on with your verse. The poet proceeded:

> Thy bounties like the swelling Nile,*
> Made the plains of Egypt smile, &c.

When he had got to the end of the poem Khasīb said, open this seam. He did so. Khasīb then said, Take this ruby. The poet refused; but being

---

* The words of the original are:

انت خصيب وهذه مصر      فتدفقا فكلا كما بحر

Thou art khasīb (or plentiful year, for the word has this meaning), and this Egypt increases and abounds with plenty, like the Nile. The *point* of this distich seems to consist in the play upon the word khasīb, which could not be transfused into the English translation, unless by some such circumlocution as the following:

> Stores of the richest bounty! This thy name,
> Spreads like the Nile, at once its blessings and thy fame, &c.

I notice this merely to shew how difficult it is to preserve the spirit of this kind of poetry in a translation. The thirty-ninth story of the first book of Saadi's Gulistan (Persian Rose-garden) is founded on the history of this man. In some of the editions the name is erroneously pointed خصيب *Khosaib* for خصيب *Khasīb*.

The line above cited is of the species البسيط, and of the measure مستفعلن فعلن فعولن with its varieties. See Clarke's Prosody, p. 60.

adjured to do so, he complied; he then went to the street of the jewellers, and
offered it for sale.  He was told that such a stone could belong to none but
the Calif.  The account of it was accordingly carried to him, who ordered
the poet to be brought into the presence.  When he came there, he was
interrogated on the subject, and his answers developed the whole matter.
The Calif was then sorry for what he had done to Khasīb, and ordered
that he should be brought before him.  When he came, the Calif gave him
some splendid presents, and ordered that he should have whatever he might
wish.  Khasīb requested to have this Minyet given to him, which was
done; and he resided there till the time of his death.  After this his
descendants held it, until the family became extinct.—I then proceeded
to the city of [h]Manlawī, then to [i]Manfalūt, then to [k]Esoyūt, then to [l]Ekh-
mīm, and then to [m]Hawwa.  Here I visited the Sheikh, Sayyud [n]Abu Mohammed Obaid Allah El Hasanī, who was one of the great saints.  When he
asked me what my object was, I told him, that it was my wish to perform
the pilgrimage by way of [o]Judda.  He replied, you will not succeed in this,
upon this occasion ; you had better return, therefore : for, the first pilgrimage
you will perform, will be by the plain of [p]Syria.  When I left him, I made no
effort to follow his advice, but proceeded on my way till I arrived at [q]Aidhāb,
and found that I could not go on.  I then returned to [r]Cairo, and after that
to [s]Syria (or Damascus); and the way I took, in my first pilgrimage, was
just as the [t]Sherīf had told me, by the plain of Syria.

From Hawwa, therefore, I proceeded to [u]Kanā, then to [x]Kaus, then to
the city of [y]El Aksar, then to [z]Armanat, then to [a]Esnā, then to [b]Edfū,
then to [c]Ajarnā El Fīl, then to the village of [d]El Atwānī, in company with
a tribe of Arabs known by the name of [e]Dugaim.  Our course was through
a desert, in which there were no buildings, for a distance of fifteen days.
One of the stages at which we halted was [f]Homaitara, the place in which
the grave of [g]El Walī Abu'l Hasan El Shādhelī is situated.  After this we

---

[h] منلوي .  [i] منفلوط .  [k] اسيوط .  [l] اخميم .  [m] هوّ .  [n] ابو محمد عبيد الله الحسني .  [o] جدّه .

[p] الدرب الشامي .  [q] عيذاب :  [r] مصر .  [s] الشام .  [t] الشريف .  [u] قنا .  [x] قوس .

[y] الاقصر .  [z] ارمنت .  [a] اسنا .  [b] ادفو .  [c] اجرنا الفيل .  [d] العطواني .  [e] دغيم .

[f] حميترى .  [g] الولي ابي الحسن الشاذلي .

came to the city of [h]Aidhāb, the inhabitants of which are the [i]Bejāh,*
who are blacks. Among these people the daughter never succeeds to
property.

[h]عيذاب .          [i]البجاه .

---

* On these people see Hamaker's Liber de expugnatione Memphidis et Alexandriæ, pp. 57, 58.
Burckhardt's Travels in Nubia, pp. 192-228. In this part of Mr. Hamaker's work a notice
is given of the Berbers; and, as he seems to have mistaken its import, I may be excused in
transcribing and translating it. والبربر امة اخرى لهم ارض في بحر الجنوب بين بلاد الحبشة وبلاد
الزنج يقال لهم بربرة وهم سودان وهم الذين يجعلون مهر نسايهم ان يقطعوا ذكر رجل ويسترقون وهم
اشبه منهم بالادميين . (بالوحش (lego بالوحوش) The Berbers are another people whose country is
situated upon the southern sea, between the districts of the Abyssinians and those of the Zinj;
they are called Berbera. They are blacks, and are the people who make the dower for wives
(this) that they (the men, not the women, as Mr. Hamaker proposes, by inserting the reading
يقطعن ) shall cut off the virilia of a man (perhaps an enemy), and also steal. They are more
like beasts than men. Mr. Hamaker seems to have forgotten, that in the East, the person who
marries a wife must provide the dower, just as gentlemen in this country make the jointure.
Something like this seems formerly to have prevailed in Palestine; see 1 Sam., xviii. 25, 27;
2 Sam., iii. 14; and if these Berbers are actually of the same stock with those on the north of
Africa, which Mr. Hamaker thinks to be the case, it is not improbable that this custom was
brought with them from Palestine, as it is very probable these people are a part of those formerly
expelled that country by Joshua. No one, perhaps, has taken so much pains to examine this
question as Ibn Khaldūn has done; and his opinion decidedly is, that the Berbers are derived
from Palestine, and descendants of Canaan. He also affirms that they are brothers to the
Abyssinians, Copts, and Nubians; his words are: تما نسبهم بين البربر فلا خلاف بين نسابتهم انهم.
من ولد شانا واليه نسبهم واتا شانا فقال ابو محمد بن حزم في كتاب الجمهرة قال بعضهم هوجانا
بن يحيي .... بن بديان بن كنعان بن حام .... وهذا اصح .... ومنهم زناتة وغيرهم كما قدمنا لاكنهم
اخوة البربر لرجوعهم كلهم الي كنعان بن حام .... اتا ادخاله نسب جالوت في نسب البربر وانه من
ولد مادغيس وسقط فخطا وكذلك من نسبه من العمالقة والحق ان جالوت من بني فلسطين بن
كسلوحيم بن مصرايم بن حام احدى شعوب حام بن نوح وهم اخوة القبط والبربر والحبشة والنوبه
كما ذكرنا في نسب ابناء حام وكان يبقى بين فلسطين هولاء وبين بني اسرائل حروب كثيرة وكان بالشام
كثير من البربر اخوانهم ومن ساير اولاد كنعان . As to their genealogy (i. e. the Zenāta tribe) among
the Berbers, there is no discrepancy among the genealogists, that they are of the posterity of
Shānā; and to him is their origin referred. As to this Shānā, Abu Mohammed Ibn Hazim
has said, in the book called the Jamharat (or collection), some have affirmed that this person is
Jānā, son of Yahya, son of Bidyān, son of Canaan, son of Ham, which is the truest statement.
Of these are the tribe of Zenāta and others, as we have already said; but they are the brothers
of the Berbers because they all trace their descent up to Canaan the son of Ham. But, as to
his (a certain writer) entering the pedigree of Goliath in that of the Berbers, since he is of

At this time, two-thirds of the revenue of Aidhāb went to the king of the Bejāh, whose name was [k] El Hadrabī, the remaining third to the king of Egypt. The cause of our not proceeding thence to Judda, was a war that had broken out in these parts between the [l] Bejāh and [m] Barnau people. I accordingly returned with the Arabs to [n] Kaws in Upper Egypt, and descended by the Nile to Caïro, where I lodged one night, and then set out for Syria. This happened in the month [o] Shaabān in the year twenty-six (A. H. 726—A. D. 1326).

---

## CHAPTER IV.

*Balbīs—El Salihīa - El Sawāda—El Wārid—Katīa—Matīlab—El Arīsh—El Kharūba—Rafaj—Gaza—El Khalīl.*

AFTER this I arrived at [a] Balbīs,* then at [b] El Salihīa. From this place I entered the sands (Desert), in which are the stages [c] El Sawāda, [d] El Wārid,

---

الحدري . [k]    البجاه . [l]    البرنو . [m]    قوص . [n]    شعبان . [o]    بلبيس . [a]

الصالحية . [b]    السواده , [c]    الوارد . [d]

---

the posterity of Mādaghīs and Sakat, it is an error; and, in the same manner, is his tracing them to the Amalekites (also an error). For the truth is, Goliath is of the sons of Philistīn, son of Kaslūhīm, son of Misrāim, son of Ham, one of the nations of Ham the son of Noah: but these are the brothers of the Copts, Berbers, Abyssinians, and Nubians, as we have said in the genealogy of the sons of Ham. Between these Philistīns, however, and the children of Israel, there were many wars; for there were in Syria many of the Berbers, their (*i. e.* the Philistines) brothers, and of the rest of the descendants of Canaan. Ibn Khaldūn explodes the opinion held by Idrīsī (see part i. clim. 3) and others, that the Berbers are descended from the Himyarites of Arabia Felix. See an extract to the same effect in Pococke's Specim. Hist. Arab., by M. de Sacy, pp. 462, 540. A very curious article on this subject, too, is to be found [i]n the Descriptio Africæ by Leo Africanus (pp. mihi 12, 13), where he states the opinions of Idrīsī, and in almost the same words, of these people coming from Arabia Felix, as well as that held by Ibn Khaldūn of their coming from Palestine; adding, that they were driven out by the Assyrians, which must put every body in mind of the story of Phenician Dido. We are told somewhere in the discourses of Psalmezer, that an inscription formerly appeared on a column in one of the Barbary states, saying, that the people who had erected it had been expelled from Palestine by Joshua. It is highly probable, I think, that the Tuarick of Major Denham's Narrative are Berbers, as the letters he gives at page lxviii are, as far as they can be traced, evidently Phenician. (See also The Universal History, vol. xvii. p. 220, &c. ed. 1748.)

* This word is pronounced either Balbīs or Bilbīs; it is, according to the ومراصد الاطلاع ten farsangs from Fustat in Cairo, on the road to Syria. بلبيس مدينة بينها وبين فسطاط مصر عشرة

'Katīa, 'El Matīlab, *El Aarīsh,† *El Kharūba, and 'Rafaj. At each of
these there is an inn, which they call *El khān. Here the travellers put up
with their beasts: here are also watering camels, as well as shops, so
that a traveller may purchase whatever he may want either for himself or
his beast.

I next arrived at 'Gaza, and from thence proceeded to the city of *El
Khalīl Ibrahīm (*Abraham the friend*). In the mosque of this place is the
holy cave, and in this are the tombs of Abraham, Isaac, and Jacob, with
those of their wives. This cave I visited. As to the truth of these being
the graves of those persons, the following is an extract made by me, from
the work of Ali Ibn Jaafar El Rāzī, entitled El Musfir Lilkulūb, on the true
position of the graves of Abraham, Isaac, and Jacob;* and which rests on
a tradition from "Abu Horaira, who has said, It was related by the prophet,
that when he was on his night journey to Jerusalem, Gabriel took him by
the grave of Abraham and said, descend and perform two prostrations, for
here is the tomb of Abraham thy father. He then took him by Bethlehem

---

<sup>k</sup>الخان .     <sup>i</sup>رفيج .     <sup>h</sup>الخروبه .     <sup>g</sup>العريش .     <sup>f</sup>المطيلب .     <sup>e</sup>قطيا .

<sup>n</sup>ابو هريرة .     <sup>m</sup>الخليل ابرهيم .     <sup>l</sup>غزه .

---

فراسخ علي طريق‌الشام. See an interesting note on this place in Hamaker's Liber de expugnatione
Memphidis, &c., pp. 48, 49. The following from Makrizi I cannot forbear copying and translating:
ذكر مدينة بلبيس وسميت في التورية ارض جاسان (جاشان I read) وفيها نزل يعقوب عم لما قدم
اليى ولده يوسف فانزل الي ارض حاشان (جاشان) وهي بلبيس الي العلاقة من اجل مواشيهم قال
ابن سعيد واليها يصل حكمه الي الواردة وهي اخرحد مصر واليها ينتهي المعاملة بفضة السواد ويصير
الناس يتعاملون بالفلوس بعدها الي العريش وهي أول‌الشام وقيل هي اخرمصر. Balbīs is called, in
the law of Moses, Jāshān (Goshen), and is the place to which Jacob went down after he had
presented himself to his son Joseph. So he went down to the country of Jāshān (Goshen), which
is Balbīs, to the pasturage on account of their cattle. Ibn Saïd, who was governor of this place,
has said, that its territory extends to El Wāridat, which is the extreme limit of Egypt. To this
place is the common silver coinage current: but beyond it, and to El Arīsh, which is the first
place of Syria, but as some say, the last of Egypt, are the fulūs (*i. e.* a sort of small copper coin)
in circulation.

* On this place, which is the Rhinocorura or Rhinocolura of the ancients, see Hamaker's
Liber de expugnatione Memphidis et Alexandriæ, p. 15.

† The name of the author with the whole title runs thus: سماه كتاب علي بن جعفر الرازي الذي
المسفر للقلوب عن صحة قبر ابرهيم واسحق ويعقوب .

and said, perform two prostrations, for here was born thy brother Jesus. He then went on with him to El Sakhrat, and so on, as recorded in the tradition.

In the city of El Khalīl was the aged saint and Imām, °Borhān Oddīn El Jaabarī, him I asked respecting the truth of the grave of Abraham being there. He answered, Every learned man I have met with has considered it as the fact, that these three graves are the graves of Abraham, Isaac, and Jacob; and that the three graves opposite to them are those of their wives; nor does any one, continued he, think of contradicting accounts so generally received from the ancients, but the heretics.

## CHAPTER V.

*Jerusalem—Askelon—El Ramlah—Naplous—Bawād—El Ghaur—El Kosair—Acca—Tyre—Sidon—Tiberias—Bairūt—Tripoli—Emessa—Hamāh—Maarrat El Nöomān—Sarmīn—Aleppo—Tizīn—Antioch—Sahyūn—Jabala—Laodicea—Mount Libanus—Baalbek—Damascus.*

I THEN passed on to Jerusalem, and on the road visited the tomb of Jonas, and Bethlehem the birth-place of Jesus. But, as to the mosque of Jerusalem, it is said, that there is not a greater upon the face of the earth: and in sacredness, and privileges conferred, this place is the third. From Jerusalem I paid a visit to °Askelon, which was in ruins. In this place was the meshhed,* famous for the head of Hosain,† before it was removed to Egypt. Without Askelon is " the valley of bees," said to be that mentioned in the Koran. I next proceeded to °El Ramlah, then to °Naplous,‡ then to °Eglon. From this place I set out for the maritime parts of Syria, passing by the route of °Bawād between two mountains, and called °El Ghawr. Here was the tomb of the guardian saint of this people, °Abu Obeidat Aāmir Ibn El Jarāh, which I visited: and then passed by a village

---

° بوّاد .    ° عجلون .    ° نابلس .    ° الرمله    ° عسقلان .    ° برهان الدين الجعبري .

° ابو عبيدة عامر بن الجراح .    ° الغور

---

\* This word, which is often seen in maps, means a place of attestation, *i. e.* the assembly of persons to give attestation to some fact, and should be pronounced meshhed.

† This was one of the sons of Ali, who fell in the battle of Karbela.

‡ The principal town of the Samaritans.

called El Kosair, in which was the tomb of [h]Moādh Ibn Jabalī, which I also visited.

From this place I proceeded to [i]'Acca: in this is the tomb of [k]Sālih the prophet, which I visited. After this I arrived at the city of [l]Tyre, which is a place wonderfully strong, being surrounded on three sides by the sea. Its harbour is one of those which have been much celebrated. I next visited [m]Sidon, and from this place went into the parts of [n]Tiberias, which it was my wish to see. The whole was, however, in ruins, but the magnitude of it was sufficient to shew that it had been a large place. The place is wonderfully hot, as are also its waters.* The lake is well

---

[h] معاذ بن جبلي .    [i] عكا .    [k] صالح .    [l] صور .    [m] صيدا .    [n] جهة طبرية .

---

\* The baths, &c. of Tiberias are thus described by El Harāwi: حمّام طبرية التي يقال انها من عجايب الدنيا ليست هذه التي علي باب طبريه علي جانب بحيرتها فان مثل هذه كثير راينا في الدنيا وانما التي من عجايب الدنيا فهو موضع من اعمال طبريه شرقي قرية يقال لها الحسينية في وادي وهو عمارة قديمة قيل عمرها سليمن بن داود عليهما الصلاة والسلام وهو هيكل يخرج الماء من صدره وقد كان يخرج من اثنتي عشرة موضعا وكل عين مخصوصة بمرض من الامراض اذا اغتسل منها صاحب ذلك المرض يبرا باذن الله تعالي والماء اشد حرارة واصفي ما يكون واعذب واطيب رايحة وهذا الموضع يقصده اصحاب الامراض والعاهات والزمني والرياح فيغتسلون فيه وعيونه تصب في موضع كبير حسن يسبح الناس فيه ومنفعته ظاهرة وما راينا ما يشابهه الا الثرميا الذي في حد تخوم القسطنطانية &c. *i. e.* " The baths of Tiberias, which are said to be one of the wonders of the world, are not those which are near the gates of Tiberias and upon the side of the lake, for many like these are to be seen elsewhere; but those which are described as wonders are in a place to the east of the city called El Hosainiya, and situated in a valley. It is evidently an ancient structure, and is said to have been built by Solomon. It consists of a pile of building, from the front of which issues water. It came formerly from twelve places, each of which was appropriated to the cure of some disease, so that when any one thus afflicted washed himself, he recovered by divine permission. This water is excessively hot, and is very pure and sweet, both to the taste and smell. To this place come many afflicted persons, maimed, aged, or those affected with bad smells, and wash themselves in it. Its fountains run into a large and handsome place, and in this the people bathe. The advantages it affords are evident; nor have we ever seen any thing like it except the Thermæ (baths) which are in the confines of Constantinople." We are told a little farther on, that on the road from Tiberias to Acca is Kafar Manda, and that this is said to be Midian: and that the writer also visited Midian, which is to the east of Sinai; the words are: وايضا من طريق طبريه الي مدينه عكا يقال لها كفرمنده قرية قيل انها مدين والله اعلم وقد زرنا مدين شرقي طور سينا &c. That a Midian was formerly found in both these parts appears from the Hebrew bible; but whether they were connected, or if they were, how, I believe no one can tell.

known : its length is six parasangs ; its width three. In the town is a mosque, known by " the mosque of the prophets :" and in this is the tomb of °Shoaib (Jethro) which I visited. I also visited the well of Joseph, which is famous in these parts.

I next arrived at *Bairūt which is on the sea-shore, and then set out to visit the tomb of *Abu Yaakūb Yūsuf, who is supposed to have been one of the kings of the west. It is situated in a place called "Kark Nūh, and upon it is a cell endowed by the sultan *Salāh Oddīn Ibn Ayūb.* It is said, that this Abu Yaakūb lived by weaving mats : it is also said, that he was hired to keep some orchards in Damascus, for the sultan 'Nūr Oddīn the martyr, the preceptor of Salāh Oddīn. After he had been some time in this situation, Nūr Oddīn happened to come into the orchard, and to ask the keeper for a pomegranate. He brought several, one after another, each of which, however, had the appearance of being sour. It was said to him, have you been all this while in the orchard, and do not yet know a sweet pomegranate from a sour one ? He replied, I was hired to keep the orchard, not to eat the pomegranates. By this the sultan knew who he was, and sent for him accordingly : for he had had a dream, in which he thought he met Abu Yaakūb, and derived some advantage from him. When he was come, he believed he knew his countenance too, and said, are not you Abu Yaakūb ? He replied, I am. The sultan then rose and embraced him, and made him sit by his side. After this Abu Yaakūb took the sultan to his house, and entertained him out of his honest earnings : and with him the sultan remained some days. After this Abu Yaakūb escaped, and could no where be found. The weather was at that time exceedingly cold, and Abu Yaakūb had betaken himself to a village, where he was honourably enter- tained by one of the villagers. This man had a daughter whom he wished to dispose of in marriage, and on this account represented to Abu Yaakūb the difficulty he experienced in affording him support. Upon this he was ordered to bring together all the copper furniture he had provided for her dower, and moreover, to borrow as much as he could from his neighbours.

---

" كَرَكْ نوح . ُ   ُ ابو يعقوب يوسف .   ُ بيروت .   ُ شعيب .

ُ نور الدين الشهيد .   ُ صلاح الدين بن ايوب .

---

* This was Saladin, who distinguished himself so much during the Crusades.

The villager accordingly got together a considerable quantity of this metal. Abu Yaakūb then dug a pit and put the whole into it. Upon this he made a fire which fused the metal, he then took out some elixir which he had with him, and putting it upon the metal, the whole became pure gold. When the next morning had arrived, Abu Yaakūb wrote a letter to his host for Nūr Oddīn the martyr, telling him to take out of this gold as much as would make a handsome portion for the young woman; also to give as much as would be sufficient to her father, and to expend the remainder in pious uses. He then made his escape by night. With this gold Nūr Oddīn built the infirmary which is in Damascus.

I next arrived at "Tarābalas (Tripoli) in Syria, which is a large city, and may be compared with Damascus. From this place I went to the fortress of the Kurds, then to *Emessa, and visited the tomb of *Khālid Ibn El Walīd,* which is in its environs. I next arrived at the city of *Hamāh.†
—The epitomator Ibn Jazzi El Kelbi says that the following verses were composed on this place by *Abu'l Hasan Ibn Saïd of Granada.

> ‡ May heaven from the seat of fair Hamah divide
> The breath, thought, or glance, which may make her repine ;
> Wreak its vengeance on him who would part from her side,
> For the smiles of the fair or the juice of the vine.
> But when through her streets rolls triumphant along
> *Rebellion's foul tide*, all in current so fair ;
> Then who shall refrain from the glass and the song,
> When the banquet is spread and so plentiful there?
> Yet, when the full goblet goes round, let me view
> Her breasts flow with sweets for her children within :
> Mark the tear of the mother—then say O how true,
> How vile, yet how lovely's the city of *Sin!*

---

" طرابلس . * حمص . ” خالد بن الوليد . ° حماه . ° ابو الحسن بن سعيد الغرناطي .

---

\* The general who conquered Syria. See Ockley's History of the Saracens; Hamaker's Incerti Auctoris Liber de expugnatione Memphidis et Alexandriæ. Lugd. Batav. 1825, p. 13.
† The Hamath of Scripture.

وقفت عليها السمع والفكر والطرفا      حمي الله من شطّي حماة مناظرا

بها واطيع الكاس واللهو والقصفا      يلومونني ان اعصي الصور التي

احاكيه عصيانا واشربها صرفا      اذا كان فيها النهر عاص فكيف لا

واشدوا

The following too has been composed on the same place :

> \* Heroes of Hamah's happier days,
> Yours my theme, my tribute, praise :
> Of you, the recollections sweet
> Hang on my heart, and still we meet.
> And should forgetfulness despoil
> The flowret reared with so much pain,
> A *sinner's* tears shall drench the soil,
> And then 'twill sweetly bloom again.

The [b]Aāsī (sinner or rebel) is a river of Hamah.   I next went to the city of [c]Maarrat El Nöomān, the place from which the patronymic of [d]Abu El Alā El Maarī† is derived.   It was named Maarrat El Nöomān because [e]El Nöomān Ibn Bashīr the Ansār and companion of the Prophet, lost a son there, when he held the government of Emessa.   Before this time it was called [f]Dhāt El Kusūr (i. e. *endued with palaces*).   It is also said, that it is so

---

[f] ذات القصور .   [e] النعمان بن بشير .   [d] ابو العلا المعرّي .   [c] معرّة النعمان .   [b] عاصي .

---

واشربها رقصا واشربها غرفا          واشدوا لي تلك (a)النواعير شدوها

تهيم بمرآها ونشلها العطنا (b)          تئن وتذري دمعها فكاتّما

(a) With the نواعير or mills, they draw up water out of wells in order to supply gardens, &c. The word also means a vein pouring out blood; and hence the allusion in the text is not unlike Shakspeare's " life-rendering pelican." For some account of the author of these lines, see M. de Sacy's Chrestomathie Arabe, 2d edit., tom. i. p. 240-3.

(b) This verse is of the species termed الطويل *long*.   The measure with the usual varieties will be فعولن مفاعيلن فعولن مفاعيلن .   See Clarke's Prosody, p. 35, &c.

  \* The text is as follows :

ماحلت عن ثقتي وعن اخلاصي          يا سادة سكنوا حماة وحقكم

يجري المدامع طائعا كالعاصي          والطرف بعدكم اذا ذكر اللقا

Where the play is in these, as in the preceding lines, on the name of the river Aāsī (عاصي), which signifies *sinner* or *rebel*.

  † This was a very celebrated poet and commentator, named generally Abu'l Alā El Tenūkhī, and surnamed El Maarrī. Tenūkh is, according to Jurharī, the name of a tribe in Yemen, and this Soyūtī places in Bahrein. The author of the Kāmūs and Pococke say generally, that it is the name of a tribe. See Pococke's Sec. Hist. Arab. p. 42-141. Chrestom. Arabe, tom. iii. p. 89.

called from a mountain named ᵍNŏomān, which overhangs it. Without this place is the tomb of ʰOmar Ibn Abd El Azīz, commander of the faithful. After this I arrived at ⁱSarmīn, then at ᵏHaleb (Aleppo). Its citadel is large and strong; and within it is a meshhed, in which Abraham is said to have performed his devotions.* On this place El Khālidī, the poet of ˡSaif El Doulat Ibn Hamdān, has said :

> Land of my heart, extended wide,
> Rich in beauty, great in pride:
> Around whose head to brave the storm,
> The rolling clouds a chaplet form.
> Here 'tis the empyreal fires glow,
> And dissipate the gloom below.

ᵍ نعمان . ʰ عمر بن عبد العزيز . ⁱ سرمين . ᵏ حلب . ˡ الخالدي شاعر سيف الدوله ابن حمدان .

* In the كتاب الاشارات في معرفة الزيارات, *the book of intimations respecting the knowledge of the places of pilgrimage,* by علي بن ابي بكر الهروي Ali Ibn Abu Bekr El Harawī, who travelled during the times of the Crusades, and fell into the hands of the king of England, are the following notices of this place : وبقلعتها مقام ابرهيم الخليل عليه السلام وبه صندوق فيه قطعة من راس يحيى بن زكريا عليهما السلام ظهرت سنة خمس وثلثين واربعمائة In its (*i. e.* of Aleppo) citadel is the station of Abraham the friend (of God), and in it is also a chest in which there is a piece of the head of John the son of Zachariah. It was observed in the year 435, *i. e.* A.D. 1043. A little lower down we have an account of a custom, which will in some degree illustrate the homage, if not the idolatrous worship, formerly addressed to the pillars called in the Hebrew bible מצבות. The first account we have of these is in Gen. xxviii. 18, where we are told that Jacob set one of them up and poured oil on the top of it. Here, says the traveller, حجر ظاهر باب اليهود على طريق ينذر له و يصب عليه ما الورد والطيب وللمسلمين فيه اعتقاد والنصاري و يقال تحته قبر بعض الانبيا والاوليا والله اعلم (*i. e.* at Aleppo). Without the gate of the Jews there is a stone upon the road : to this vows are made, and upon it they pour rose-water and perfumes; both Mohammedans and Christians have faith in the practice. It is said that the grave of some prophet is under it; but God knows best. This work I shall occasionally cite. See a very interesting note on this subject in the Specimen Hist. Arab. by Pococke, ed. 1806, p. 102-3, where, l. 15, read وسمي الزحل *et appellabatur Saturnus,* not " وسمي الرجل *quo appellabatur vir iste."* This very learned writer, having been betrayed into the very mistake which he corrects at the foot of the page in De Dieu. Edrīsī mentions a similar custom as prevailing in the islands of the Indian sea, sect. vii. clim. i. His words are ... مدينة بروه وهي اخر بلاد الكفرة الذين لا يعتقدون شيا وانهم ياخذون الاحجار القايمة فيدهنونها بدهن السمك ويسجدون لها . The city Barwah is the last of those belonging to the infidels who believe in nothing, but who take stones which they set up on their ends, pour the oil of fish upon them, and then worship them.

About thy breast in harmless blaze,

The lightning too for ever plays;

And like the unveiling beauty's glance,

Spreads round its charms t'astonish and entrance.*

The following lines are by <sup>m</sup>Jamāl Oddīn Ali Ibn Abu Mansūb:

† Thy milky towers in proud array,

Stop in its course the galaxy:

When see, the children at thy side

Rise and sip the ambrosial tide:

See too thy flocks the glories share,

And crop the gems‡ that glitter there.

---

<sup>m</sup> جمال الدين علي بن ابي منصوب .

---

* The text is as follows, of the measure الطويل.    See Clarke's Prosody, pp. 35, 36, &c.

بمرقيها العالي وجانبها الصعب          وخرقآ قد تاهت علي من يرومها

ويلبسها عقدا بانجمه الشهب          بجر عليها الجو جيب غمامه

كما لاحت العذرآ من خلل السحب          اذا ما سري برق بدت من خلاله

For some account of Saif El Doulat, see M. de Sacy's Chrestomathie Arabe, tom. iii. p. 33. ed. 2, and the authorities there cited. But, as the countenance he afforded to the poets and other geniuses of his times, has not been mentioned by M. de Sacy, or the authorities referred to, I will give an extract on this subject here, from my own copy of the يتيمة الدهر by ابو منصور الثعالبي Abu Monsūr El Thaālabī. After stating that he was descended from noble ancestors, it is said

وحضرته مقصد الوفود ومطلع الجُود وقبلة الامال ومحط الرحال وموسم الادباء وحلبة الشعراء ويقال انه His" لم يجتمع بباب احد من الملوك بعد الخلفاء ما اجتمع ببابه من شيوخ الشعر ونجوم الدهر.

presence was the object of travel, and source of liberality; the temple of hope and the inn of the traveller; the concourse of the polite, and the banquet of poets. It is said that there assembled at the door of no king, since the times of the Califs, a number so great of the poets and geniuses of his time, as there did at his." From this, as well as other passages in this work, it should seem, that he was one of the greatest patrons of polite literature the world ever saw. He was himself a tolerable poet, and an excellent judge of the merits of those who attended at his court. The author of these verses, said here to be El Khālidī, (الخالدي) is probably one of the two poets mentioned by that name by M. de Sacy, Chrestomathie Arabe, tom. ii. p. 333, edit. 2.

† The verses are these, the measure of which is البسيط.    See Clarke, p. 52, &c.

تستوقف الفلك المحيط الدائرا          كادت لبون علوها وسموها

ورعت سوائمها النجوم الازهرا          وردت قواطنها المجرة منهلا

‡ The word star نجم, signifies also in Arabic any small plant, and hence the play upon the word here.

I then left Aleppo for "Tīzīn, and soon after came to °Antioch, before which is the river ᵖEl Aāsī. In this place is the tomb of ᵠHabīb El Najār, which I visited. After this I arrived at the fortress of ʳBugrās, next at that of ᵉEl Kosair, then at that of ᵉEl Shaghar. I next came to the city of "Sahyūn, then to the fortress of ᵗEl Kadmūs, then to that of ᵞEl Aaḷikat, next to that of ᵡEl Manīkat, next to that of ᵃMasyāf, then to that of ᵇEl Kahf. These fortresses all belong to a people called the ᶜIsmāīlīah; they are also called the ᵈFidāwīa. No person can go among them except one of their own body.* These people act as arrows for El Malik El Nāsir; and by their means he comes at such of his enemies as are far removed from him, as in Irāk and other places. They have their various offices; and, when the Sultan wishes to despatch one of them to waylay any enemy, he bargains with him for the price of his blood. If then the man succeeds and comes safely back, he gets the reward; but if he fails it is then given to his heirs. These men have poisoned knives, and with these they strike the persons they are sent to kill.

From the fortresses of the Fidāwīa I went to the city of ᵉJabala, where I visited the tomb of the Sheikh ᶠEl Walī El Sālih Ibrahim Ibn Adham,† who had not succeeded to the kingdom from the father's, but from the mother's side. The father was originally one of the pious wandering Fakīrs: his story of giving up the throne is generally known. I then proceeded to ᵍLaodicea, the king of which is said to seize by violence every ship within his power. I then proceeded to the fortress of ʰEl Markab, then to the mountain ᶦEl Akraa, then to ᵏMount Libanus, which is the most fruitful mountain in the world: and on which are various fruits, fountains of water, and leafy shades. Nor is it destitute of those who have retired from the

" تيزين . ° انطاكيه . ᵖ العاصي . ᵠ حبيب النجار . ʳ حصن بغراس . ᵉ حصن القصير
ᵉ حصن المنيقة . ᵡ حصن العليقه . ᵞ القدموس . ᵗ صهيون . " حصن الشغر .
" حصن مصياف . ᵇ حصن الكهف . ᶜ الاسماعيليه . ᵈ الغداويه . ᵉ جبله .
ᶠ الولي الصالح ابرهيم بن ادهم . ᵍ اللاذقيه . ʰ حصن المرقب . ᶦ الجبل الاقرع . ᵏ جبل لبنان .

* On this sect, which are sometimes termed *Assassins*, see the Dabistān, usually ascribed to Mohammed Mohsin Fāni, Calcutta edition, p. ٣٢٨. M. de Sacy's Chrest. Arabe, tom. i, pp. 89, tom. ii. pp. 92, 93; Journal Asiatique, numbers for May and June 1824, and De Guignes' Histoire générale des Huns, tome i. p. 341. † See the نفحات الانس a little from the beginning.

world and devoted themselves to God, numbers of whom I myself saw. From this place I proceeded to 'Baalbek, and thence to ᵐDamascus, in the month of Ramazān, and in the year twenty-six (*i. e.* A.H. 726, A.D. 1326). It has been said by the Epitomator, Ibn Jazzī El Kelbī, that ⁿSharf Oddīn Ibn Anīn wrote the following lines on this place :*

> Damascus ! though the slanderer fill
> Worlds with thy blame, I love thee still.
> Spot, where alone the trav'ller meets
> Balmy winds and pearly streets :
> Where tearful streamlets weave† their chains,
> Yet joy and freedom bless the plains :
> Where too the gales with lusty love
> Fan into bloom the fainting grove.

The following was written on the same place by the eminent judge, °Abd El Rahīm El Baisāni.‡

---

بعلبكَ .      ᵐ دمشق .      ⁿ شرف الدين بن عنين .      ° عبد الرحيم البيساني .

---

\* An extract from the works of this author will be found in the Annales Moslemici, vol. iv. p. 268, and some account of his life at p. 416, of the same volume. The lines mentioned by Ibn Batūta are the following :

دمشق فبي شوق اليا مبرح      وان لج واش او الج عذول
بلاد بها المحصبآ دروتر بها      عبير وانفاس الشمال شمول
(a) تسلسل منها ماؤها وهو مطلق      وصح نسيم الروض وهو عليل

† The orientals, instead of saying that a stream is rippling, say that *it links* or *forms chains ;* hence the comparison of the chaining of the rivers with the freedom of the plains.

‡ Some notice is taken of this writer in M. de Sacy's Chrestomathie Arabe, tome i. pp. 233, 505. The original verse is as follows, and is of the species البسيط See Clarke's Prosody, pp. 52, 53, &c.

يا برق هل لك في احتمال تحية      عذبت فصارت مثل مائك سلسلا
باكر دمشق بشق اقلام الحيا      زهر الرياض مرصعا ومكللا
واجور بجيرون ذ يولا واختصص      مغني تازر بالعلا وتسربلا
حيث الحيا الربعي محلول الحيا      والوابل الوبعي مفري الكلا

El Harawī says of this place. دمشق هي ذات العماد التي لم تخلق مثلها في البلاد وقيل بناها دماشق بن قابي بن مالك بن شام بن نوح وقيل بناها الصحاك وقيل هي كانت دار نوح Damascus abounds with high buildings, such as have not elsewhere been constructed. It was built by Dimāshik, son of Kābī, son of Mālik, son of Shām, son of Noah : it is also said that

Lightning! with thy pouring rain,
How dost thou befriend the plain?
Why, 'ere the morning's dawn arise,
Spread'st terror through Damascus' skies?
Is't that thy flames may bid her glow,
Or gild her flow'rets opening blow?
Or, that her plains refreshed be seen,
Filled with fruits, and clothed in green?
Yes, 'tis that blessings round may spring,
And verdure make the vallies sing.

The mosque of Damascus, termed ᵖ El Amawī, is too well known to need description here. Of its learned men, professors, and theologians, of the sect of Hanbal, ᵠTakī Oddin Ibn Tīmīa may be mentioned as one in great repute for his lectures, if we except a few of his peculiarities. The people of Damascus, however, think very highly of him. In many instances he has preached things to which the theologians have objected; and, hence an information was laid against him to ʳEl Malik El Nāsir, who sent for him to Egypt, and there imprisoned them. When in prison he published a commentary on the Koran in forty volumes, entitled ˢ El Bahr El Muhīt.* After this he was liberated; but, going again to Damascus, he returned to his old practices of preaching heterodoxy. I happened one Friday to be present when he was addressing a congregation from the pulpit, and this was one of his assertions: God came down, said he, to the heaven of this

---

ˢ البحر المحيط .   ʳ الملك الناصر.   ᵠ تقي الدين بن تيميه .   ᵖ الاموي .

---

Zohāk built it, and also that it was the residence of Noah. There is a passage in the book of Genesis (chap. xv. v. 2) in which our authorized version has " This Eliezer of Damascus," and which I believe to be erroneous. The original stands thus: דמשק אליעזר not אליעזר הדמשקי as the version gives it. My opinion is, that this is the proper name of Abraham's servant and nothing more: Damascus might, indeed, have been built by him, but of this we have no knowledge. A little farther on we are told, that there is a column in the mosque near the little gate, to which pilgrimages and vows are made: this is probably one of the ancient מצבה of which we so often read in the Hebrew bible. His words are these وعامود ... عند الباب الصغير في مسجد يزار وينذر له .

* This is probably the work noticed by D'Herbelot under the title *Bahar al Mohith*, although the name does not agree with that given here. Neither of them, however, has given the full name, and this will perhaps account for the discrepancy.

world, just as I now go down : and upon this he descended one of the steps of the pulpit. A theologian of the sect of Ibn Mālik, happening to be present, contradicted this ; for which he was beaten by the congregation. The opponent, however, lodged an information with El Malik El Nāsir, who again cited the Sheikh, and put him in prison, where he continued till his death. He was afterwards buried at Damascus.

Without the gate called ' El Jābiat are the tombs of " Om Habiba wife of the prophet, of her brother ˢ Moāwīa, of ᵛ Balāl the Moazin of the prophet, and of ˢ Awīs El Karanī.* The grave of the last, however, is said to be in a burying-ground between the city and Syria, in which there is no building. It is also said to be in ˢSiphīn with that of Ali. It is said by Ibn Jazzi El Kelbi the epitomator, that the latter is the truer opinion. Ibn Batūta proceeds : without Damascus on the way of the pilgrimage, is the " ᵇmosque of the foot," which is held in great estimation, and in which there is a stone having upon it the print of the foot of Moses.† In this mosque they offer up their prayers in times of distress. I myself was present at this mosque in the year 746 (A.D. 1345), when the people were assembled for the purpose of prayer against the plague : which ceased on that very day. The number that died daily in Damascus had been two thousand : but, the whole daily‡ number, at the time I was present, amounted

---

ᵇ سجد القدم .   ˢصفين .   ᵈ اويس القرني .   ᶜ بلال .   ᵇ معاويه .   ᵃ ام حبيبه .   ' باب الجابية .

* According to Ibn El Athīr, in his abridgment of patronymics from El Samaāni, entitled كتاب اللباب لابن الاثير الجزري , this patronymic (i. e. قرَني karanī), is derived from one *Karan* of the tribe of Morād ; he was the son of Ridmān, son of Nāhia, son of Morād. This Awīs was son of Aāmer of this family ; he was a great saint, and is said to have been killed among the infantry of Ali at Sifīn ; others say he died at Mecca, others at Damascus. The passage is this.

القرَني ... هذه النسبة الي قرن وهو بطن من مُراد وهو قرن بن رذمان بن ناحية بن مراد ينسب اليه اويس بن عامر القرني الزاهد روي عن عمرو قتل بصفين في رجّالة علي رضي الله عنه وقيل مات بمكة وقيل بدمشق

† There can be no doubt, I think, that these *marks of the foot*, whether we find them at Damascus, in Ceylon, among the Burmese, at Mecca, or wherever else, are nothing more than remains of Buddhaïsm. The best relique of this superstition to be seen in Europe is, perhaps, the mark of the foot of Buddha placed in the hall of the British Museum by Captain Marryat.

‡ The passage, which I suspect is erroneous, stands thus : ثم انتهي بحضرتي في كل يوم الي اربعة وعشرين الفا . The words في كل يوم *daily*, are perhaps adscititious.

to twenty-four thousand. After prayers, however, the plague entirely ceased. On the north of Damascus is the mountain ᶜ Kāsayūn, in which is the cave where Abraham was born. From this (cave) he saw the sun, moon, and stars.* There is also a village in ᵈ Irāk called ᵉ Burs, between ᶠ El Hilla and Bagdad, which is said to be the birth place of Abraham. This is the truer notion. On the farther part of the Kāsayūn is the ᵍ mount of flight and assistance,† the asylum of Jesus.

## CHAPTER VI.

*El Arūs—Nejd—El Kādesīa—Meshhed Alī—Basra—Khafāja—Khawārnak—Wāsit—El Oballa Abbādān—El Lār—Irāk—Māgūn—Rāmin—Tostar.*

WHEN things were ready, the Syrian pilgrims proceeded on their pil-grimage, and I myself with them, with the same intention. This turned out well; for, thank God, I duly performed the pilgrimage; and, then proceeded with the pilgrims of Irāk to the tomb of the prophet at Medīna. After three (days) we descended into the valley of ʰ El Arūs.‡ We then entered the territory of ⁱ Nejd, and proceeded on in it till we came to ᵏ El Kādisīa§ the place in which the remarkable event happened, by which the fire-worship of Persia was extinguished, and the interest of Islamism advanced. This was, at that time, a great city, but it is now only a small village. We next proceeded to the city of ˡ Meshhed Alī, where the grave of Ali is thought to be. It is a handsome place and well peopled; all

---

ᵍ الربوة ذات الفرار والمعين .   ᶠ المحلّه .   ᵉ برُص .   ᵈ العراق .   ᶜ قاسَيون .

ˡ مشهد علي .   ᵏ القادسيه .   ⁱ ارض نجد .   ʰ بواد العروس .

---

\* Alluding to a passage in the Koran.

† It is doubtful whether we ought to read ذات الفرار or ذات القرار, as the MSS. have both readings : if the latter, then *residence* must be substituted in the translation for *flight*.

‡ The name of a fortress in Yemen, according to the Kāmoos: but this can hardly be the place mentioned here.

§ A village near Kūfa where Saad, one of the generals of Omar, obtained a decisive victory over the Persians. See the Annales Muslemici, vol. i. p. 231.

the inhabitants, however, are of the Rāfiza (or Shīah) sect. There is no governor here, except a sort of tribune. The inhabitants consist chiefly of rich and brave merchants. About the gardens are plastered walls adorned with paintings, and within them are carpets, couches, and lamps of gold and silver. Within the city is a large treasury kept by the tribune, which arises from the votive offerings brought from different parts: for when any one happens to be ill, or to suffer under any infirmity, he will make a vow, and thence receive relief. The garden is also famous for its miracles; and hence it is believed that the grave of Ali is there. Of these miracles, the [m] "night of revival"* is one: for, on the 17th day of the month Rejeb, cripples come from the different parts of [n] Fārs, [o] Room, [p] Khorāsān, [q] Irāk, and other places, assemble in companies from twenty

[m] ليلة المحيا . [n] فارس . [o] روم . [p] خراسان . [q] العراق

* Mr. Wolfe, the missionary, when last in this country, reported that the ليلة المحيا or "night of revival," among the Yezīdī sect, is a night on which they worship the devil. I should doubt whether Mr. Wolfe did not misunderstand the accounts he might have heard of this matter. In the Book of Pilgrimages, by Ali Ibn Abubeker of Herāt, we have a similar account given of a place in the lieutenancy of Aleppo, his words are: براق قريه من اعمالها بها معبد يقصده الزمني والمرضي من الاماكن ويبيتون به فامّا ان يبصر المريض من يقول له دوآ لك في الشي الفلاني او يبصر من يمسح بيده عليه فيقوم وقد بري باذن الله تعالي كما ذكروا اهل الموضع . Borāk is one of the villages of its lieutenancy, in which there is a sacred place visited by the aged and infirm of various places, and in it they lodge. Now, if such person should see (in his dream) some one saying to him, such or such a thing is thy remedy; or if he should see him rubbing his hand over him, he will then be well, as the people of that place report." And further on where the city of Balat (مدينه بلط) is noticed, we are told, that this Author saw a man who had been lame many years, but had been recovered merely by bathing, according to the injunctions of Ali which he had received in a dream. His words are ورايت لهذا الموضع آية عظيمة وذلك انه كان بالموصل رجل فقاعي يمشي علي اغلاق من الخشب ونحو رجله خلفه كانهما خرق وبقي كذلك سنين عدة زمانا طويلا يشاهده الناس وهو معروف بالموصل فراي عليا بن ابي طالب رضي الله عنه في المنام وذكر انه قال له امض الي مشهد ولدي عمر بن الحسين لاظهر فيك آية فحملوه الي هذا الموضع فاغتسل من الما الذي به وزاره وعاد الي الموصل ماشيا علي قدميه وسموه عبد علي ولعله في الحياه والله اعلم . That such miracles (if such they may be called) can be performed, without any extraordinary effort being exerted, has long been known. A strong persuasion of the mind has always proved wonderfully efficacious: and to this the Mohammedan, as well as the Roman Catholic, hierarchy owes perhaps more than half its authority.

to thirty in number. They are placed over the grave soon after sun-set. People then, some praying, others reciting the koran, and others prostrating themselves, wait expecting their recovery and rising, when, about night, they all get up sound and well. This is a matter well known among them: I heard it from creditable persons, but was not present at one of these nights. I saw, however, several such afflicted persons, who had not yet received, but were looking forwards for, the advantages of this " night of revival."

I next arrived at ᵛBasra, and proceeded on with the Badawīn Arabs of ᵉKhafāja, for there is no travelling in these parts, except with them. We next came to ᶜKhawārnak, the ancient residence of ᵈEl Nōomān Ibn Mondhor, whose progenitors were kings of the tribe ᵉBeni Mā El Samā, (sons of heavenly seed). There are still traces of his palace to be seen.* It is situated in a spacious plain, and upon a river derived from the Euphrates. We left this place, and came next to the city of ᶠWāsit. It is surrounded by an extensive tract of country, and abounds with gardens and plantations. Its inhabitants are the best of all Irāk. From this place I set out to visit the tomb of El Walī El Aārif, my Lord Ahmed of ᵍRephāa†, which is

---

ᵃ البصرة .            ᵇ عربان خفاجه .            ᶜ خورنكْ .            ᵈ النعمان بن منذر.

ᵉ بني ماء السماء .            ᶠ واسط .            ᵍ احمد الرفاعي .

---

* Some notices of this person and his palace will be found in the Historia imperii vetustissimiJoctanidarum in Arabia Felice, by A. Schultens, p. 129. And in his Monumenta vetustiora Arabiæ, pp. 11, 39, 47.

† The following is an abstract of the account given of this devotee in the نفحات الانس Nafahāt El Ins, by Jāmī: the miraculous intercourse, &c. there ascribed to him, I have not thought it worth while to copy out. شيخٍ سيدي احمد بن اني (ابي) الحسن الرفاعي قدس الله تعالي .... ذو المقامات العليه ولاحول السنيه ضرق (خرق) الله سبحانه علي يديه العوايد وقلب له الاعيان واظهر العجايب ولكن اصحابه فقيم (ففيهم) الجيد والردي يدخل بعضهم النيران و يلعب بالحيات فهذا ما عرفه الشيخ ولا (ولي) الصلحا اصحابه نعون بالله من الشيطان وي از اولاد امام بزركوار موسي كاظم است عليه السلام ... ساكن ام عبيد بوده ... وتوفي رضي الله عنهم (عنه) يوم الخميس الثاني والعشرين من جمادي الاول سنه ثمان وسبعين وخمسماية . The Sheikh my lord Ahmed Ibn Abu El Hasan El Raphāī, may God sanctify (a word wanting). His rank as a saint and confessor was high. By him God performed many miracles, and converted to him many persons of distinction. He also did many wonders. Of his disciples, some are good, others bad. Some of them will enter fires, and play with serpents. This is what the Sheikh the head of saints taught them. God protect us from Satan. He was one of the sons of the great Imām Mūsa Kāzim, upon whom be peace. He resided at Om Obaida, and died on the Thursday the 22d of the first Jumāda, in the year (of the Hejira) 578, A. D. 1182.

situated in a village called "Om Obaida, at the distance of a day from Wāsit. At this place I arrived, and found that the grandson of the Sheikh, upon whom the dignity of Sheikh had also devolved, had come thither before me for the same purpose. He was also named Sheikh Ahmed, and held the dignity of his grandfather, which he exercised in the cell formerly occupied by him. In the afternoon, and after the reading of the koran, the religious attached to the cell got together a great quantity of wood, to which they set fire: they then walked into it, some eating it, others rolling in it, and others trampling upon it, till they had entirely extinguished it. Such is the sect called <sup>b</sup> El Re-phāïa, and this the custom by which they are particularized. Some of them too will take great serpents in their teeth and bite the head off. It happened that, when I was in a certain part of India, there came to me a company of the religious of the <sup>c</sup>Hydarīa sect,* having in their hands and about their necks iron chains. Their leader was a black of a filthy colour. They requested me to solicit the governor of the place to bring them some wood to which they may set fire, and then sing and walk into it. I did so, and he brought them ten bundles; they then set fire to it, and commencing their song, went into it: nor did they cease dancing and rolling about in it until they had extinguished it. The leader then asked me for a shirt. I gave him a very fine one, which he put on, and then proceeded to roll about in the fire, and to strike it with his sleeves, until he had put it out. He then brought me the shirt, upon which the fire had not made the least impression. At this I very much wondered.

After visiting this Sheikh I proceeded to Basra, a place much abounding with palms. The inhabitants are so friendly to strangers that a traveller has nothing to fear among them. We have here the mosque of Ali, in which prayers are said every Friday: it is then closed till the next. This was formerly in the middle of the town; but is situated two miles† from its

---

<sup>a</sup> ام عبيده .          <sup>b</sup> الرفاعيه .          <sup>c</sup> حيدريه .

* When we come to Khorāsān in this work, some account of the leader and practices of this sect will be given.

† As the term *mile* (ميل) will occasionally occur in this work, we shall here determine its extent. According to the Succardān of Ibn Hajila, a mile is = 1,000 bāas, a bāa = 4 cubits; a cubit = 24 digits; a digit = 6 barley-corns placed side by side: and a barleycorn = 6 hairs taken out of the tail of a mule. A Parasang = 3 miles; a barīd = 4 parasangs والميل الف باع

present population. In this is the koran which Othmān had sent (for the use of
the inhabitants), and in which he was reading when he was killed. The marks
of his blood are still visible in the words فسيكفيكم الله, &c. I then went on
board a ᵈSambūk (Turkish ᵉSenbūki) which is a small boat, and proceeded
to ᶠEl Oballa,* which was once a large city, but is now only a village;

---

ᶠالابلّه . ᵉسنبك . ᵈسنبوك .

---

والباع اربعة الذرع و الذراع اربعة و عشرين اصبعا والاصبع ست شعيرة توضع بطن هذه لظهر تلك
. والشعيرة ست شعرات من ذنب البغل و الفرسخ ثلثة اميال والبريد اربعة فراسخ   In Golius, sub
voce برد, we have "mensura itineraria XII. milliarium, seu III. parasangarum," where for III
we ought to read IV. Now, in order to determine the relative value of an Oriental with an
English mile, I take 18⅔ parasangs to the degree, as given in the preface to Koehler's Syria of
Abulfeda; and getting rid of the fractions the ratio will be, that of 112 to 139: and inverting this,
the Oriental mile will be to the English one, as 139 to 112; and, if this be correct, the Oriental
mile will contain 2,184⅔ English yards. From this the value of the other measures mentioned above
may be known. According to the author of the Kāmoos, however, the *mile* (ميل) is a perfectly
lax and vague measure, and differing just as the parasang did in ancient and times.

* Abulfeda says of this place الابلّه اطوال عد . ح . ل . نه قانون عد . ح . لا . نه that, according to the Atwāl the longitude is 74° 8′ lat. 30° 55′ and according to the Kānūn long. 74° 8′ lat
31° 55′. He then describes it, قال ابن حوقل والابلّه مدينة صغيرة حصونة عامرة وليا نهر الابله الي
البصره وحذاها الدجلة التي يتشعب منها هذا النهر عاطفا عليها وينتهي عمودها الي البحر و عبادان
و طول نهرها اربعة فراسخ بين البصرة والابله وعلي حافتي هذا النهر قصور وبساتين متصلة كانها بستان
واحد قد مرت علي خيط واحد وكان نخلها قد مدت علي خيط واحد وجميع بساتين تلك الناحية
معترفة بعضها الي بعض حتي انا جاءهم مد البحر تراجع الماء في كل نهر حتي يدخل نخيلهم
. وغيطانهم من غير تكلف فاذا جزر الما انحطت حتي تخلوا البساتين والنخيل   Ibn Hawkal states,
that Oballa is a small, strong, and well peopled city. Its river, the Oballah, after issuing from the
Tigris which is over against the city, makes its way to it, and thence to Basra. The channel of
this river reaches to the sea, and to Abbādān. The length of its course to Basra is four
parasangs, upon the banks of which are palaces and gardens, so close to each other, that they
appear to form one garden passing on in a direct line: its palms also spread out in like manner in
an extended line. All the gardens too of these parts are so situated one by another, that when
the tide of the sea comes out towards them, it passes into all the channels until it comes to their
palms, and into their valleys without the least difficulty: and, when it ebbs, it rolls back, leaving
the gardens and palm-plantations. The channels here mentioned are, according to Dr. Russell,
Nat. Hist. Aleppo, generally so contrived as to bring the water into the gardens, and then, out of
these still smaller channels are cut, which carry the water into the several parterres and
divisions of the gardens. The Psalmist seems to have had these channels in view when he speaks
of the " tree planted by the rivers of waters," better, the *divisions* of the waters, the original being

which, with its gardens about it, is about ten miles from Basra. I then sailed from El Oballa in an arm of the Persian gulf, and arrived the next morning at ⁵ Abbādān,* which is a village situated in a salt marsh. It was my intention to have gone to Bagdad; but a person at Basra advised me to go on to the country of ʰ El Lār, then to ⁱ Irāk El Ajam,† then to Arabian Irāk: and I did so. I then proceeded from Abbādān by sea; and after four days, arrived at the city of ᵏ Māgūn (or Māgūl, of the quantity Fā-ūl, with the *g* pronounced hard). This is a small town on the Persian gulf. I passed from this by land, during a journey of three days, through

---

ⁱ عراق العجم.    ʰ ارض اللور.    ⁵ عَبّادان.    ماجون and ماجول ᵏ.

---

פַּלְגֵי מָיִם, which exactly corresponds with Dr. Russell's description.—See also Asseman's Bi-blioth. Orient., tom. iii., P. 2, p. dccvi, and D'Herbelot under Obollah.

* According to El Harawī this is an island in the sea, in which there is a meshhed dedicated to the prophet. It also has Ali's well, and a meshhed sacred to El Khizr, and other establish-ments: the pious of which are much visited from other parts. His words are عتبادان جزيرة في البحر بها مشهد النبي صلي الله عليه وسلم وبها بير علي رضي الله عنه ومشهد الخضر عليه السلام وبها رُبُط مباركه وهي موضع شريف يُزار من الافاق به العباد والزهاد.
Abulfeda says this place is in the longitude 74° 30′, lat. 25° 20′ according to the Atwāl: but others give 75° 55′, and 75° 30′ longitude. He then thus describes it after Ibn Saïd. قال وعبادان علي بحر فارس وهو يدور بها فلا يبقي منها في البر الا القليل وتصب دجله هناك في جنوبي عبادان وشرقيها وقال غيره عبادان علي مصب دجله في بحر فارس من الجانب الشرقي ومنها الي الساحل الي مهروبان نحو اربع مراحل وعبادان عن البصرة مرحله ونصف قال وفي جنوبي عبادان و شرقيها الخشباب وهي علامات في البحر للمراكب تنتهي اليها ولا يتجاوزها خوفا من الجزر ليلا تلحق بالارض. He has said that Abbādān is on the sea of Fārs, which encircles it, leaving only a small part of land (or isthmus). On the south-east of this place the Tigris joins the sea. Others have said, that Abbādān is upon the mouth of the Tigris towards its east, and on the sea of Fārs. From it to the shores of Mehrūbān is about four stages. From Basra it is a stage and a half. It has been said too, that on the south and east of Abbādān are the *Khushbāb*, i. e. marks placed in the sea for the purpose of limiting the approach of vessels, and beyond which they never pass, lest upon the ebbing of the tide they should strike upon the ground. Khushbāb خشباب Castell tells us, are moderately sized ropes: if so, they are here so placed as to mark the places to which ships may safely come. See also Asseman's Biblioth Orient. tom. iii. P. 2. p. dccvi; Sir Wm. Ouseley's Oriental Geography, p. 11, &c.; and D'Herbelot sub voce Abadan.

† The geography of these parts has been well illustrated by Ulenbroek in his Iracæ Per-sicæ descriptio, &c. Lugduni Batavorum, 1822. See pp. 4 and 5. Asseman's Biblioth. Orient. tom. iii., P. 2, p. dccxlv.

a plain inhabited by Kurds, and came to the city of ' Rāmin,* a beautiful place abounding with fruit and rivers. I then proceeded on through a plain, in which were villages of the Kurds, and in three days arrived at the city of ᵐTostar,† which is at the extremity of this plain. On the first of the mountains there is a large and beautiful city, abounding with fruits and rivers, surrounded by a river, known by the name of ⁿ El Azrak the blue. This river is wonderfully clear, and is cold in the summer season.

---

## CHAPTER VII.

*Idhaj—El Lūr —Ushturkān —Fairūzān—Tashnia Fīrūz—Shīrāz —Kalīl— Yezd Khās—Majd Oddīn, founder of the College El Majdīa—Mohammed Khudā Banda becomes a Sunnī—Abu Is-hāk —His liberality—Abu Abd Allah Khafīf, the first Mohammedan who went from India to Ceylon—Kāzerūn—El Zaidain -- El Hawaiza—Kūfa.*

I THEN travelled for three days over high mountains, and found in every stage, in these countries, a cell with food for the accommodation of travellers. I then came to the city of ᵒIdhaj,‡ which belongs to the ᵖSultan Atābek Afrāsiāb.§ With these people the word Atabek means any one governing a district. The country is called ��El Lūr.‖ It abounds with high mountains and has roads cut in the rocks. The extent in length is seventeen days journey; in breadth ten. Its king sends presents to the king of Irāk, and sometimes comes to see him. In every one of the stations in this country, there are cells provided for the religious, enquirers, and travellers: and,

---

اللور.⁹ اتابك افراسياب.ᵖ ایذج.ᵒ الازرق.ⁿ تستر.ᵐ راسین.'

---

* This is perhaps the ذَعُکۡ *Romon* or ذَعُکۡ دَمۡ *Beth Raman*, of Asseman. See Biblioth. Orient. tom. iii., P. 2, p. dcclxxii, which he writes in Arabic بارامان:—or perhaps the راسسین or رامش of Mr. Ulenbroek, see p. 65, Arab. text.

† See Asseman's Biblioth. Orient., tom. iii. P. 2., p. dcclxxxi.

‡ See Ulenbroek Iracæ Pers. descriptio, p. 25, Arab. text.

§ This is probably the " Mudaffereddin Afrasiab, fils de Rokneddin," of De Guignes, who was the last of the dynasty of the Atabeks of Lāristān; according to him he died A. H. 740, A.D. 1339, a little after the time our traveller must have visited these parts.

‖ See Mr. Ulenbroek's " Iracæ descriptio," pp. 4 and 5, and Arab. text.

for every one who arrives, there are bread, flesh, and sweetmeats : I travelled for ten days in this country over high mountains, with ten other religious, one of whom was a priest, another a moazin (a person who calls the people to prayers), and two professed readers of the koran. The Sultan sent me a present, containing money for travelling expences, both for myself and my companions. Having finished the districts belonging to this king on the tenth day, we entered those of Isphahān, and arrived at the city of ˊUshtorkān : after this at ˊFairūzān,* the name of which had been ˊTashnīa Fīrūz : and then at Isphahān, one of the cities of Irāk El Ajam. This is a large and handsome city : I remained in it some days. I then set out for ˊˊShīrāz, between which and Isphahān there are twenty stations, with the intention of visiting the Sheikh Majd Oddīn, at that place. In my journey, I passed by the towns of ˊKalīl and ˊˊYezd Khās, the latter of which is small, and arrived at Shīrāz. It is an extensive, and well built city, though inferior to Damascus, in the beauty of its streets, gardens, and waters. The inhabitants are people of integrity, religion, and virtue, particularly the women. For my own part, I had no other object than that of visiting the Sheikh Majd Oddīn the paragon of saints and worker of miracles. I came accordingly to the college called ˊEl Majdīa, which had been founded by him. He was then judge of the city ; but, on account of his age, the duties of the office were discharged by his brother's sons.† I waited on him. When he came out, he shewed me great kindness, and, embracing

---

| كليل . | شيراز , | تشنية فيروز . | فيروزَان . | اشترکَان . |
|---|---|---|---|---|
| | المدرسة المجدية . | | يزد خاص . | |

---

* According to the مراصد الاطلاع, this is a village of Isphahān, and is a most beautiful and healthy place : the words are  فيروزان من قری اصبهان ... من احسن القری وطيبها هواءً .

† This man is mentioned in the Khulāsut El Akhbār, by Khondemir, as having great influence at this time at Shīrāz, so much so, that he succeeded in bringing about an accommodation between the Emīr Jūbānī, and the partizans of the Emīr Mohammed Mozaffer. His words are these آخر الامر بتوسط قاضي مجد الدين اسمعيل بن يحيي كه از جمله اكابر زهاد وفضلات ( فضلا ) بود صورت مصالحه روي نمود وامير پير حسين جوباني در غايت اقبال وكامراني بشیر در آمدد &c. At length, by the mediation of the Kāzī Majd Oddīn Ismāīl Ibn Yahya, who was one of the great saints and men of eminence, an agreement took place ; and the Emīr Pīr Hosāin Jūbānī entered the city in the greatest splendour and delight. This is related as taking place in the year of the Hejira 740.

me, asked me about different places: to which I gave suitable answers. I was then taken into his college. The Sheikh is much honoured by the Emīrs of these parts, insomuch, that when they enter his company, they take hold of both their ears, a ceremony of respect paid only to the king. They, therefore, pay him the respect due to their king. The reason of this is, that when the king of Irāk, ªMohammed Khudā Banda, received Islamism, he had a favourite of the Rāfiza (followers of Ali), named ᵇJamāl Ibn Mutahhar, who induced him to join the Shīah sect, which he willingly did. The king then wrote to Bagdad, Shīrāz,* and other places, inviting them to be of this sect. The people of Bagdad and Shīrāz, however, refused to do so, and continued to be of the sect of the Sonnee. He then commanded the judges of these districts to be brought to him: and the first who arrived was this of Shīrāz. The king ordered him to be thrown to some great dogs which he had, and which were kept with chains about their necks, for the purpose of tearing to pieces any one, with whom the Sultan should happen to be angry. When, therefore, the Kāzī Majd Oddīn was thrown to the dogs, they came, and looking upon him, began to wag their tails, making no onset upon him, nor, in any way molesting him. This was told to the Sultan ᶜKhudā Banda, who came running to him in a great fright. He then kissed his hands, and stripping off all his own robes put them upon the Sheikh. He then took him by the hand, and led him to his mansion. This, therefore, became the source of great dignity to the Sheikh, his children, and to all belonging to him: which is the case with every one, upon whom the Sultan puts all his robes. The king then gave up the Shīah sect, and became a Sonnee, and to the Sheikh he gave a hundred villages in the district of Shīrāz. Thus both the king and his courtiers bestowed the greatest honours upon the Sheikh and upon his successors. I also visited this Sheikh after my return from India, in the year 748 of the Hejira (A.D. 1347); and, for this purpose, I travelled a distance of five and thirty days. I once saw the Sultan of Shīrāz Abu ᵈIs-hāk holding his ears before him, by way of respect. The Sultan of

---

ª محمد خدا بنده.  ᵇ جمال بن مطهّر.  ᶜ خدا بندد.  ᵈ ابو اسحق.

---

* See on this place Asseman's Biblioth. Orient. tom. iii. P. ii. p. dcclxxv—vi.

Shīrāz, on my first arrival at that place, was Mohammed Abu Is-hāk Ibn Shāh Yanjū. He was one of the best of princes. His father Shāh Yanjū was governor of Shīrāz, under the King of Irāk:* but when he died, the government was put into the hands of another. When, however, the King of Irāk died, and left no issue, each of the governors assumed the government of the district over which he had been placed: and, in this way, the government of Shīrāz, &c. came under the control of Abu Is-hāk. He was a man much beloved on account of his courage and good conduct; and possessed a territory of a month and a half's journey, with an army of fifty thousand men.†

In liberality Abu Is-hāk imitated the king of India: for, on one occasion, he gave to a person, who had come before him, the sum of seventy thousand dinars. No one, however, can be compared to the king of India:* for he

---

\* According to Mīrkhond, the province of Fārs was committed to the care of the Emīr Mosāfar Ināk, A. H. 734, and the Emīr Mahmūd Shāh Anjū was, for years, the protector and assistant of the Emīr Jūbān, who was magistrate of those parts. His words are:

در سنه اربع وثلثین وسبعمایه سلطان ابو سعید بهادر خان حکومت ولایت فارس را بر امیر مسافر ایناق مسلم داشت وسالها امیر محمود شاه انجوبحمایت واهتمام امیر جوبان حاکم آن ولایت بود ودر ولایت شیراز وشبانکاره چندان املاک داشت که هر سال مبلغ صد تومان بوی واصل میشد .

And, that in the districts of Shīrāz and Shabānkāra, he had possessions to such an extent as to bring him in annually 100 tūmāns; which, he goes on to say, was the cause of his being brought into disgrace at the court of Abusaīd. A little lower down we are told that Abu Is-hāk was one of the sons of Mahmūd Shāh Anjū. پسران امیر محمود شاه از تبریز بکریختند.

امیر مسعود شاه بروم رفت وامیر محمود وامیر شیخ ابو اسحق بخدمت امیر علي پادشاه شتافتند .

The sons of Emīr Mahmūd Shāh fled from Tebrīz, the Emīr Mahmūd Shāh went to Room, and the Emīrs Mahmūd and Sheikh Abu Is-hāk betook themselves to the service of the Emīr Ali, the king. What power Abu Is-hāk exercised in Shirāz is not mentioned in the historians; but that he had great power there can be no doubt. In 742 he succeeded to the government of Isphahān, and in 743 he vigorously opposed the descent of Malik Ashraf upon Shīrāz, and by the help of the citizens forced him to retire. Khondemir, under this date. This author's account of Abu Is-hāk agrees exactly with that given by our traveller. His words are: امیر ابو

اسحق بوفور جود وکثرت مکارم اخلاق از حکام افاق امتیاز تمام داشت . The Emīr Abu Is-hāk was distinguished among the rulers of the world, by extreme liberality, and the politeness of his address.

† The accounts given of the liberality of Mohammed Shāh, who was the reigning emperor when Ibn Batūta entered India exceed all description. Dow (Hindustan, vol. i. pp. 313, &c.) has noticed some instances, and Ferishta many more. He also says, that nobles, learned men, and persons who had suffered shipwreck, came with the hope of relief from Khorāsān, Irāk, Māwara,

will give sums equal to this many times in the same day, particularly to those who come from the parts of Khorāsān. He once said to one of his courtiers, Go into the treasury and bring as much gold as you can carry at once. The courtier filled thirteen purses with gold; and, tying them on his shoulders, attempted to go out, but fell through the weight of the purses. The king then commanded him to take and weigh it, which he did, and found it to be thirteen [e]maunds of Dehli, the maund of Dehli being equal to five and twenty[f] ratls of Egypt. On another occasion, he placed one of his Emīrs, namely, [g]Sharf Ul Mulk Emīr Bakht of Khorāsān, in a pair of scales, putting gold in the opposite part, till the gold preponderated. He then gave him the gold and said, give alms out of this for your own salvation. He also appointed to the theologian and collector of traditions, [h]Abd El Azīz El Ardabīlī, for his daily expenses, the sum of one hundred dinars of silver: five and twenty of which are equal to the golden dinar. Upon one occasion the above mentioned Sheikh entered into the presence of the king, who rose; and, having kissed his feet, poured upon his head with his own hand a vessel full of gold, and said, both the gold and the vessel, which is gold, are thine.

The most famous meshhed of Shīrāz is that of Ahmed Ibn Mūsa, the brother of [i]El Rizā, which is indeed held in the highest estimation. In this is the tomb of the Imām [k]El Kotb El Walī Abū Abd Allah Ibn Khafīf,[*]

---

[e] مَنّ .     [f] رطلا مصريا .     [g] شرف الملك اميربخت .     [h] عبد العزيز الاردويلي and الاردبيلي .

[i] احمد بن موسي اخي الرضي .     [k] القطب الولي ابي عبد الله بن خفيف .

---

El Nahr, Arabia, and Turkey, to Hindustan. غطما وكبرا وهنروران و كشتي شكستكان باميد

عواطف ومراحم او از خراسان وعراق وماورا النهر وعربستان وتركستان بهندوستان مي آمدند

وزياده از آنچه تصور كرده بودند نوازشها مييافتند, &c. and received more than they had imagined they should. I cite this merely to show the minute accuracy of our traveller.

[*] This saint is frequently mentioned in the نفحات الانس by Jāmī as one of the first authorities in judging of matters peculiar to the Sūfīs; and is occasionally styled both Wali and Kotb, as here by Ibn Batūta.

In vol. i. p. 546, of the Transactions of the Royal Asiatic Society, I have made some allusion to this Sheikh, supposing it probable that his grave may be that of the person mentioned in an inscription there translated. The traveller, however, here says that his tomb is in Shīrāz: and, if that be the fact, there is an end to the probability; but we shall find, when we get to Ceylon, that there is a belief of his grave being in that country. We have no account, however,

who is the great exemplar of all the region of Fārs.   This Abu Abd Allah is
the person, who made known the way from India to the mountain of Seren-
dib, and who wandered about the mountains in the island of ʹCeylon.   Of
his miracles, his entering Ceylon, and wandering over its mountains in
company with about thirty fakeers is one : for when these persons were all
suffering from extreme hunger, and had consulted the Sheikh on the necessity of slaughtering and eating an elephant,* he positively refused and
forbade the act.   They, nevertheless, impelled as they were by hunger,
transgressed his commands, and killed a small elephant, which they ate.
The Sheikh, however, refused to partake.   When they had all gone to
sleep, the elephants came in a body, and smelling one of them, put him to
death.   They then came to the Sheikh, and smelled him, but did ·him no
injury.   One of them, however, wrapt his trunk about him, and lifting
him on his back, carried him off to some houses.   When the people saw
him, they were much astonished.   The elephant then put him down and
walked off.   The infidels were much delighted with the Sheikh, treated
him very kindly, and took him to their king.   The king gave credit to his
story, and treated him with the greatest kindness and respect.   When I

ˈ بجزيرة سيلان .

of his having founded a college or any thing of the sort ; although, from the estimation in which
he appears to have been held at court, he might have had it in his power to do so.   Upon turning
over the lives of the saints by Jāmī (نفحات الانس) I find that this Sheikh died A.H. 331 ; and
according to the inscription, this endowment was made in the year 317 ; and the inscription
itself written in 337.   So that he might have been in Ceylon in 317, and obtained the privileges
here adverted to, from the king : and if he died in 331, the inscription might have been written
in 337.   Jāmī, however, gives no such name as Khālid Ibn Abu Bakāya, &c.; he only tells us
that his name was Mohammed Ibn Khafīf Ibn Isfikshār El Zabī (under ابو عبد الله بن خفيف
الشيرازي Abu Abd Allah Ibn Khafīf of Shīrāz), where he says نام وي محمد بن خفيف بن
در سنه احدي وثلثين   The date of his death is given in these words. اسفكشار الصبي است.
وثلثمايه برفته از دنيا in the year 331 he left the world.   " A certain former king," says Knox, in
his Ceylon, " gave this temple (i. e. a mosque in Candy) this privilege, that every freeholder
should contribute a ponnam to it," p. 171.   I am disposed to believe, therefore, that my conjecture respecting this Sheikh is just ; and that he was the first who obtained security for the property of the Mohammedans in this island.

    * The elephant is unclean with the Mohammedans, so Saadi . الشاة نظيفة والفيل جيفة   " The
sheep is clean, but the elephant is carrion."—Gulistan, chap. i. tale iii.

entered Ceylon I found them still infidels, although they had given great
credit to the Sheikh. They also very much honour the Mohammedan
Fakeers, taking them to their houses and feeding them, contrary to the
practice of the infidels of India; for they neither eat with a Mohammedan,
nor suffer him to come near them.

I then left Shīrāz intending to make <sup>m</sup> Kāzerūn, situated at the distance
of two days' journey, in order to visit the tomb of the Sheikh <sup>n</sup> Abu Is-hāk
El Kāzerūnī.* This Sheikh is held high in esteem both in India and
China: and even the sailors, when labouring under adverse winds, make
great vows to him, which they pay to the servants of his cell, as soon as
they get safely to shore. I accordingly visited the tomb of the Sheikh.

I then left Kāzerūn and went to the city <sup>o</sup> El Zaidain (the city of the
two Zaids). It was so called, because <sup>p</sup> Zaid Ibn Thābet and <sup>q</sup> Zaid Ibn
Arkam,† two of the companions of the prophet, were buried there. I then
went to <sup>r</sup> El Huwaizā,‡ a small town inhabited by Persians, between
which and Basra is the distance of four days: but from Kūfa, that of
five. From this place I went to Kūfa through a desert, in which water was
only to be found at one of its stages. This is one of the mother cities of
Irāk: but, it is now very much in ruins. In the mosque is the oratory,

---

<sup>m</sup> كازرون .     <sup>n</sup> ابو اسحق الكازروني .     <sup>o</sup> الزيدين .     <sup>p</sup> زيد بن ثابت .

<sup>q</sup> زيد بن ارقم .     <sup>r</sup> الحويزا al الحويزا .

---

* This is, no doubt, the Abou-Ishak Alkarzouni of D'Herbelot; *vide* sub voce; and if he be
right, this word ought to be written الكارزوني. under *Carzuni*, however, he writes Cazruni and
Cazeruni. It is said in the مراصد الاطلاع that Kāzerūn is a city in Fārs, situated between the
sea and Shīrāz, and is said to be the Damietta of the Persians. Something not unlike kasab (or
fine Egyptian cloth), is made there from cotton. It abounds with palaces, gardens, and palms,
extending its palaces far to the right hand and the left (north and south), and is at the distance of three days from Shīrāz. The words are: كازرون ... مدينة بفارس بين البحر وشيراز يقال
هي دمياط الاعاجم يعمل بها من الكتان علي شبه القصب وهي كلها قصور وبساتين ونخيل ممتدة
عن يمين و شمال وبينها وبين شيراز ثلاثة ايام .

† Annales Muslemici, tom. i. p. 119.

‡ This name is given in the مراصد الاطلاع. El Huwaiza thus: الحويزة وهذا الموضع الحويزة تصغير الحوزد
بين واسط والبصرة وخوزستان في وسط البطائح . It is a place situated between Wāsit, Basra, and
Khūzistān, in the marshes.

in which Ali was killed by the vile ⁵Ibn Moljim. In the back part of the mosque, is the place in which Noah is said to have grown warm from the oven in the time of the ⁶deluge.*

---

⁶ التنور فار منه في طوفان نوح عم .       ⁵ ابن ملجم .

---

* This is one of the absurd and silly legends, of which the Orientals are so fond : but, as a knowledge of mankind consists in knowing the follies, as well as the wisdom, practised in the world, I may be excused, perhaps, if I give Mirkhond's edition of it.

از امیر المومنین علي عليه السلام نقل کرده اند که مراد از فوران تنور ظهور فجر وطلوع صبح است وبعضي کفته اند که مقصود از کلمه وفار التنور جوشیدن آبست از روي زمین قتاده کوید که هنوز موضعي عالي بود از زمین که آب از آنجا بجوش آمد و جمهور برانند که مراد از تنور تنور نان پزي است که زن با دختر نوح در آن نان مي پخت و بمیراث بنوح رسیده بود وآن تنور نزدیک باب الکنده بود از مسجد کوفه و نوح عم از آن جا در کشتي نشست مقاتل کوید که در شام بوده در موضعي که آن را عین الورد کویند قریب ببعلبک وباراضي هند نیز کفته اند وطایفه کفته اند که نوح عم بر در دکان خبازي ایستاده بود وخباز بر سبیل هزل کفت کجاست آن آبي که مارا از آن بیم میکردي واز کجا خواهد بود نوح کفت که از تنور تو وهماندم آب از تنور جوشیدن کرفت . They have related from Ali, the commander of the faithful, that the meaning of the oven's heat is, the appearance of the dawn of the morning. Some have said that the meaning of " and the oven became hot," is the boiling up of the water from the surface of the earth. Kotāda says, that it was a high place of the earth, from which the water boiled up. But generally it is held, that by " the oven" is meant the oven of a baker, in which the wife and daughter of Noah baked their bread, and which came to him by hereditary right. This oven was situated near the gate El Kenda of the mosque at Kūfa, and from this place Noah took his seat in the ark. Mokātel says that it was in Syria, in a place which they call " the Fountain of the Rose" near Baalbec; some say that it is in India; others, that Noah was standing at the door of a baker's shop, when the baker said by way of jest, where is the water you have been frightening us about, and from what place is it to come? Noah replied, from your own oven : and, at the same moment, water began to boil out of his oven. El Harawī gives a similar account under his mention of Kūfa, but it is not worth copying.

## CHAPTER VIII.

*El Hilla—Karbelā—Bagdad—Abu Saīd, now King of Irāk—Ibn Batūta accompanies his army—Sāmarrā—Tekrīt—Island of Ibn Omar—Nisībīn—Sinjār—Dārā—Mardīn—Bagdad—Mosul—Mecca.*

I NEXT arrived at the city of " El Hilla,* which runs far along by the side of the Euphrates. Its inhabitants are all followers of the twelve Imāms. We have here a mosque, over the gate of which is an extended veil of silk. They call it the Mosque of the last ᵛ Imām. It is said, that Mohammed Ibn El Hasan El Askarī entered this mosque, and became concealed in it. This person is, according to them, the Imām Mehdi (or leader), who has long been expected. It is a practice with them to come daily, armed to

---

ᵛ صاحب الزمان .        ᵘ الحِلَّة .

---

* Ann. Mosl. tom. iii. p. 716. This is very near the site of ancient Babylon. El Harāwī tells us that the Jews make pilgrimages to the graves of Ezekiel and Joseph, which they believe to be here. See Mr. Rich's Notice of the Ruins of Babylon; Les Mines de l'Oriente, tom. iii.

† The following is the creed of the Shīah on this subject, as given by the author of the Dabistān :

نزد امامیه مقرر است که امام محمد بن عسکری زنده است واو از نظر نهان وآنرا تعبیر بغیبت صغری وغیبت کبری کنند غیبت صغری که مدت آن هفتاد وسه سالست در زمان معتمد عباسی در سنه ست وستین ومایتین بود وغیبت کبری در عهد راضی ابن مقتدر عباسی بود وفرق درمیان این دو غیبت آنست که در صغری سفری ووکلا میان امام وصلحای امت واسطه بودند ودرکبری آمد وشد منقطع کردید وکیل اول عثمان ابن سید العمری بود وبعد ازو بحکم امام زمان به پسرش ابو جعفر محمد مفوض شد واو قریب به پنجاه سال کرد بعد ازو ابو القاسم حسین ابن روح ابن ابی بحر نوبختی واو بعد از خود بابو الحسن علی ابن محمد السمری وصیت کرد او اخر وکلاست چون بیمار شد شیعه سؤال کردند که بعد از تو وکیل ناحیه مقدسه که خواهد بود او توقیعی مشتملبر منع وصیت بیرون آورد وآن اینست . It is established among the Imāmīa (followers of the Imāms), that the Imām Mohammed Ibn Askarī is still alive, but that he is invisible. This they term the less, and greater concealment. The less concealment lasted seventy-three years, and happened in the times of Muatamid of the house of Abbās, in the year 266 (A. H.). The greater concealment happened in the time of Rāzī, the son of Muktadir, of the house of Abbās. The difference between these two conceal-ments is this : that in the less, a book and ministers were mediatorial between the Imām and the pious of the people : but in the greater, all communication was cut off. The first Wakeel was Othmān Ibn Saīd El Omarī; and, after him, by command of the Imām of his time, it was transferred to his son Abu Jaafar Mohammed, who executed the office about fifty years. After him Abu El Kāsim Hosain Ibn Rūh Ibn Abi Bahr Nawbakhtī, who after-wards left it by will to Abu El Hasan Ali Ibn Mohammed El Samarī; and he was the last

the number of a hundred, to the door of this mosque, bringing with them a beast saddled and bridled, a great number of persons also with drums and trumpets, and to say, Come forth, Lord of the age, for tyranny and base-ness now abounds: this then is the time for thy egress, that, by thy means, God may divide between truth and falsehood. They wait till night, and then return to their homes. I next came to $^w$Karbela, and there visited the meshhed of the Imām El Hosain, the son of Ali.* This is one of the greatest meshheds. The inhabitants are of the sect of the twelve Imāms.

---

$^w$ كربلا .

---

of the Wakeels. When he was sick the Shiah asked him, who should hold this sacred office after him; upon which he drew out an instrument forbidding a will, which is this:

بسم الله الرحمن الرحيم يا علي ابن محمد السمري اعظم الله اجر اخوانك فيك (وبك al)
فانك ميّت ما بينك وبيني ستة ايام فاجمع امرك ولا تعرض الي احد فيقوم مقامك بعد
وفاتك فقد وقعت الغيبة التامة فلا ظهور الا بعد اذن الله تعالي ذكره بعد طول الامد (الابد al)
وتسوا القلوب (بالقلوب al) وامتلاء الارض جورا وسياتي من شيعتي من يدعي المشاهدة الا فمن
يدعي المشاهدة قبل خروج السفياني والصيحة فهوكذاب مفتر ولا حول ولا قوة الا بالله العلي العظيم .
ودر منتصف شعبان سنة ثمان وعشرين وثلثماية وفات يافت

" In the name of the compassionate and merciful God. O Ali, son of Mohammed of Samaria, may God increase the reward of thy brethren by thee: but thou art a dead man: between me and thee are (only) six days. Arrange thy matters, therefore, and turn towards no one for supplying thy place after thy death: for now has happened the complete concealment: nor shall there be a revelation, except by the permission of God, whose memorial be reverenced, till after the duration of the age, and hearts shall be hardened, and the earth shall be filled with violence. But there shall come out of my people one who shall lay claim to a testimony. He, however, who shall lay claim to this before the outgoing of El Sofyānī and the shout, that man is the antichrist, the corrupter. There is no power or virtue except in the great God." He died in the middle of the month Shaabān, An. Hej. 328. See my Persian Controversies, p. 433. I have been the more particular in explaining this passage, in order to shew the great similarity there is, between the Shīah and our own Millenarians in this respect. The Shīah expect the Mehdi to appear, when Mohammed and Jesus are also to descend from heaven, and this is to happen at the end of an age or dispensation, when the world shall be filled with oppression and sin. Upon this occasion, they further tell us, there is to be a general resurrection of the wicked, and then a horrible slaughter is to ensue: and after this the earthly Paradise is to commence. It is my intention hereafter to shew, that the Mohammedans have retained this from the early heretics, as well as many other things peculiar to one or other of their sects.

* At this place Hosain was killed. Annales Moslem. tom i. pp. 389-391; and D'Herbelot under Kerbela.

I next arrived at Bagdad, which, notwithstanding the injuries it has sustained, is still one of the largest of cities. Its inhabitants are mostly of the sect of Hanbal. In this place is the grave of [x]Abu Hanifa, over which is a cell, and a mosque. Not far off is the grave of the Imām [y]Ahmed Ibn Hanbal :* as also that of [z]El Shibalī,† of [a]Sarī El Saktī,‡ of [b]Bashar El Hāfi,§ of [c]Dāūd El Tāī,‖ and of Abu Kāsim El [d]Jonaid,¶ all of them Imāms of the Sūfīs. When I entered Bagdad, the Sultan of the two Irāks and Khorāsān was [e]Abu Saīd Bahādur Khān, son of Mohammed Khudā

[b] بشر الحافي .      [a] سرى السقطي .      [z] الشبلي .      [y] احمد بن حنبل .      [x] ابو حنيفه .

[e] ابو سعيد بهادر خان .      [d] الجنيد .      [c] داؤد الطائ .

* Two of the leaders of the four principal sects of the Mohammedans, see D'Herbelot, sub vocibus, i. e. Abou-Hanifah, and Hanbal.

† Jāmī calls him ابو السعود بن الشبلي and tells us, that he was contemporary with Jonaid. In his history, which occurs in the last quarter of the نفحات الانس we have some very strange miracles recorded of him, which, however, are not worth copying out.

‡ This saint, according to the نفحات الانس, where his history will be found a little from the beginning, was the preceptor of Jonaid, and the rest of the enlightened of Bagdad. His full name was سري بن المفلس السقطي : his surname (كنيت) ابو الحسين. He was contemporary with the following.

§ The full name of this saint, according to the نفحات الانس a little from the beginning, where his history will be found, is بشر بن الحارث بن عبد الرحمن الحافي and the surname (كنيت) ابو نصر Bashar Ibn El Hārith Ibn Abd El Rahmān, surnamed Abu Nasr; he died A. H. 227—A. D. 841.

‖ See the Annales Muslem. tom. ii. p. 41. In the Itinerary of El Harawī, the graves of these worthies are placed بالشونيزية in the part of Bagdad termed Shūnīzīa, and they receive the titles of ابدال Abdāl, الاوليا Awliā, الصالحين pious persons, and شهدآء martyrs. In the مراصد الاطلاع we are told, that الشونيزية is the burying ground situated on the west side of Bagdad, and that several of the above-mentioned saints are buried there : and that there is a mosque and inn for the Sūfīs in this ground.

¶ This, according to Jāmī, is a saint of the second class: his surname was Abul Kāsim (قواريري زجاج و خزاز), his title Kawārīrī, Zajāj, and Khazāz (كنيت او ابو القاسم است), He was one of the three who flourished, A. H. 298-9 (A. D. 910-11) who in intellectual powers are without a fourth كفته اند ازين طبقه سه تن بوده اند كه ایشان را چهارم نبوده جنید ببغداد &c. (نفحات الانس)

Banda,* which last was one of those Tartar kings who embraced Islamism, and with his brother<sup>f</sup>Kāzān,† ruled in these parts.  When this Abu Saīd died, he left no issue, and the consequence was, his Emīrs, each claimed and exercised the rule in those parts in which he had been placed.‡  When Abu Saīd left Bagdad for his own country, I travelled for ten days with him, and saw the wonderful arrangement of their march, and their numerous army. I then went with one of his Emīrs to <sup>g</sup>Tebrīz, which is a large and beautiful city.§  In this I lodged one night; but, when an order came from the Sultan commanding the Emīr <sup>h</sup>Alā Oddīn's presence in the camp, he set out the next day, and took me with him.  The Sultan, however, became acquainted with my being there, and sent for me accordingly.  I presented myself to him, and was honoured with a dress and other large presents. The Emīr Alā Oddīn told him, that it was my intention to go on the pilgrimage; he accordingly ordered such conveyances and provisions for me as would be necessary for the undertaking.  He also wrote to the same effect to the Emīr of Bagdad.  I then returned to Bagdad, and claimed the royal bounty from the Emīr.  But, as the time for the pilgrimage was distant, I set out for <sup>i</sup>Mosul and <sup>k</sup>Diarbeker.  I then went from Bagdad to the city of <sup>l</sup>Sāmarrā,‖ which was in ruins.  There had been a <sup>m</sup>meshhed

---

<sup>m</sup> مشهد .　<sup>l</sup> سامرا .　<sup>k</sup> دياربكر .　<sup>i</sup> موصل .　<sup>h</sup> علا الدين .　<sup>g</sup> تبريز .　<sup>f</sup> قازان .

* According to De Guignes "Aldgiaptou Khan, surnommé Gaïathedin Khodabendeh Mohammed, meurt le 27 de Ramadhan, A. D. 1316."  And, "Abousaïd bahadur Khan, fils d'Aldgiaptou, regne 19 ans; mort le 12 de Rabi elakher, A. D. 1335.  Mogols de Perse, ou de l'Iran." Histoire Générale des Huns, tom. i. p. 282-3.  See also d'Herbelot under Algiaptu, and Abou-Said.

† See D'Herbelot, art. Gazan, and Annales Muslemici, tom. v. p. 190.

‡ So De Guignes and others.  "La puissance de ces Moguls finit avec le regne d'Abousaïd bahadour Khan.  Les princes de la Dynastie des Dgioubaniens mettoient sur le trône, et deposoient a leur gré les Khans ses successeurs." tom. i. p. 283.  See Mirkhond, vol. v. sub. an. Hej. 736, &c., and D'Herbelot sub voce Abou-Said.

§ See Asseman's Biblioth. Orient. tom. iii. p. ii. p. dcclxxxiv. and D'Herbelot, art. Tabriz.

‖ Abulfeda says, سرمر راي وهي سامر اطوال سطج لدح قانون سط مه لدن رسم سط مه لدح
قال في اللباب وسرمر راي مدينة بالعراق فوق بغداد وهي مشهورة فتخففها الناس وقالوا سامرا بنا المعتصم وخربت عن قريب من عمارتها قال في العزيزي ومن مدينة سرمر راي الي عكبرا اثنا عشر فرسخا قال وهي علي شاطي دجله الشرقي وهو بلد صحيح الهوا والتربة قال وليس فيها عامر اليوم سوي

in it, dedicated to the last Imām by the Rāfiza, as in [n] El Hilla. I then proceeded to [o] Tekrīt,* a large city; then, after many stages, to Mosul. This is an ancient and strong place. Its citadel [p] El Hadba is splendid. From this I went to the island of [q] Ibn Omar,† where I arrived after two days. This is a large city surrounded by a valley, and has thence been called the [r] Island. The greatest part of it is now in ruins. The inhabitants are well informed, and are kind to strangers. From this place I went to [s] Nisībīn,‡ where I arrived after a journey of two days. This is an ancient city; but is now mostly in ruins. It abounds in water and gardens, and is surrounded by a river as with a [t] bracelet. Rose-water incomparable in scent is made here.

I then went to the city of [u] Sinjār,§ a place abounding with fountains

---

[r] جزيرة .     جزيرة ابن عمر [q] .     الحدبا [p] .     تكريت [o] .     الحله [n]

ساجار [u].     انعطاف السوار [t] .     نصيبين [s] .

---

مقدار يسير كالقرية قال ابن سعيد بناها المعتصم واضاف اليها الواثق المدينة الهارونية والمتوكل المدينة الجعفرية فعظم قدرها. Sarmar Ray, also called Sāmar, has its longitude according to the Atwāl in 69° 8', lat. 34° 8'; according to the Kānān in 69° 45', 34° 50'; the Rasam 60° 45', 34° 8'. It is said in the Lobāb, that Sarmar Ray is a city in Irāk above Bagdad: it is a well-known place. People have abridged its name and called it Sāmarrā. El Moatasim built it, but it was soon destroyed. It is said in El Aazīzī that from Sarmar Ray to Okbara is twelve farsangs: it is also said to be on the eastern shore of the Tigris. The air and soil of this place are pure: but it is said to be now without inhabitants, except in a very few instances, like a village. Ibn Saïd says, that El Moatasim built it, and El Wāthik added to it the city El Harūnia, and El Mutawakkel the city El Jaafaria, and very much enlarged it. See also D'Herbelot under Samara. Annales Muslem. tom. ii. pp. 169, 205, 221.

* See Ulenbroek's Iracæ Persiæ descriptio. Proleg. p. 40 Asseman, Biblioth. Orient. tom. iii. P. II., p. dcclxxxiii.; and D'Herbelot sub voce Tacrit.

† "Le Geziret ben Omar," says De Guignes (tom. i. p. 257) "est une ville bâtie par les descendans d'Omar dans une isle du Tigre, au-dessus de Moussoul. Elle étoit de la dépendance du Royaume de Moussoul, sous le règne de Seïfeddin gazi." See D'Herbelot, art. Gezirat; Asseman, Bibl. Orient., tom. iii. P. II. p. dccli. "Qui Ibn-omar qualis fuerit non liquet," says Mr. Ewald in his Mesopotamia of El Wākedī.

‡ For an account of this place under the Christians, see Asseman's Biblioth. Orient., tom. iii. P. II, pp. dcclxvii-viii. El Harawī tells us, that there is a jujube tree here, about which strange things are said, and also a Greek inscription which will cure pains in the back, &c. ejusdem farinæ. See also D'Herbelot under Nassibin.

§ El Harawī says of this place: مدينة سنجار بها مسجد علي بن ابي طالب رضي الله عنه علي الجبل وبها تل قنبر. وقيل ان من جبلها ضرب سفينة نوح عليه السلام فثلمها فسميت

and rivers, much like Damascus.  The inhabitants are Kurds, a generous
and warlike people.  At this place I saw the Sheikh ᵛEl Sālih El Walī El
Aābid Abd Alla El Kurdī, the theologian : I met him with a party on the
highest part of the mountain.  They say, that he does not break his fast
of forty days,* except with a crust of barley-bread.  Many miracles are
ascribed to him.    I then went to the city of ᵂDārā ;† then to ˣMārdīn‡ in
which there is a very celebrated and strong citadel.  The Sultan of Mārdīn,
at the time I entered it, was El Melik El Sálih the son of ʸEl Melik El
Mansūr.§  This is a very generous prince, and much praised by the poets,
on whom he bestows splendid gifts.

    I now returned through Mosul to Bagdad, and there found the con-
veyances ready for the pilgrimage.  With these I proceeded, and arrived

---

ˣ ماردين .        ᵂ دَارَا .        ᵛ الشيخ الصالح الولي العابد عبد الله الكردي .

ʸ الملك الصالح ابن الملك المنصور

---

سنجارا انه جار عليها والصحيح انه بناها سنجار بن ملك بن الذعر فنسبت اليه وكذلك آمد نسبت

الي امد بن السميد لانه بناه وكذلك الرها نسبت الي الرها ابنة البليد بن ملك (بن) الذعر لانها

عمرتها والله اعلم .

"In the city of Sinjār is a mosque of Ali the son of Abu Tālib.  This is
upon the mountain, and within it is the hill of Kambar.  It is said that the ark of Noah struck
upon an eminence (tooth  سن) of the mountain, and thence received a fracture : the place was
hence called Sinjār, because he resided ( جار  jāra) upon it.    But the truth is, the city was
built by Sinjār, son of Malik, son of El Dhaar, and to him the name relates.  In like manner Amid
is named after Amid son of El Somaid, because he built it ; and Roha (Edessa) received its name
from Roha the daughter of Bolaid, son of Malik, (son) of El Dhaar, because it was built by him."
I have deemed it important to make this extract to shew among other things, that according to
the Orientals, places take their names from persons, and not the contrary, as some, with the great
Bochart at their head, have supposed.  See Asseman, Biblioth. Orient., tom. iii. P. II, p. dcclxxix,
and Mr. Ewald's Mesopotamia of El Wākedī, p. xv. Annal. Muslem., tom iii. p. 702.  D'Herbelot, art. Sangiar.

    * This fasting, which however continues only during the day, is one of the qualifications of a
saint in the East.

    † Here, according to El Harawī, are ruins to be seen, which may be referred to the times of
Darius . دارا الملك عهد من قديمة اثار (دارا مدينة) وبها    See Mr. Ewald's " Libri Wakedii de
Mesopotamiæ expugnatæ Historia," p. xiv.

    ‡ See Asseman's Biblioth. Orient., tom. iii. P. II, p. dcclxii.

    § It will be in vain to look into De Guignes for this and several other princes mentioned in
these travels.  The truth seems to be, Mr. De Guignes had not documents before him by any
means so ample as he felt necessary for his purpose : to supply these chasms is a consummation
devoutly to be wished.

at Mecca in the same year; and remained there during another. In the second year arrived the caravan from Irāk, with a great quantity of alms for the support of those who were staying at Mecca and Medina.

---

## CHAPTER IX.

*Mecca —Judda —Sawākin— Halī — Sarja —Zabīd—Ghasāna—Jabala— Tiazz— Senāa—Aden— Zaila — Makdashū —Mombasa—Kalwā— Zafār —Hadramaut —Ammān—El Ahkāf—Fruits, &c.—El Hāsik—The Island of Taïr—Kolhāt— Ammān—Nazwā.*

At this time, that is, in the year 729 (A.D. 1328), prayer was made, during the sermon, for the King of Irāk ᶻ Abu Saïd, and after that for ᵃ El Melik El Nāsir. I remained there during the third year also, and then left Mecca* with the intention of visiting Yemen. I arrived accordingly at

ᶻ ابو سعيد .    ᵃ الملك الناصر.

---

* The following account of the temple of Mecca, by El Harawī, as to its state both before and after its being destroyed and rebuilt by the Koreish, is well worthy the attention of the reader. من الجانب الغربي احد وثلثين ذراعًا ومن الركن الذي فيه الحجر الاسود الي الركن الذي تجاهه من جهة الجنوب اثنين وعشرين ذراعًا ومن الجانب الشمالي تجاهه عشرين ذراعًا فكان دورها مائة وخمسة اذرع ولم تزل كذلك الي ان هدمتها قريش وعمرتها في عهد رسول الله ... وصغروها عما كانت عليه اولًا وبقي منها في الحجر ستة اذرع ونصف وزادوا في ارتفاعها تسعة اذرع فصار ارتفاعها ثمانية عشر ذراعًا وكانت عمارتها سافا من خشب وسافا من الحجارة فكان الخشب خمسة عشر مدماكا والحجارة ستة عشر مدماكا وكان فيها ست سواري وكان بها صور الملايكة والانبيا عليهم السلام والشجر وصورة ابرهيم الخليل عليه السلام والازلام بيده وصورة عيسي ابن مريم وامه عليها السلام فلما كان عام الفتح امر رسول الله ..... فالتمست جميع الصور وكان بها قرني الكبش الذي ذبحه ابرهيم عليه السلام معلقة داخل الكعبه وبقيت كذلك الي عهد ابن الزبير فاحترقت .

" From the western side one and thirty cubits, and from the pillar in which the black stone is found, to that which is opposite to it on the south, were two and twenty cubits, and from the northern opposite part, twenty cubits. Its circumference was one hundred and five cubits, and thus it remained, until destroyed and rebuilt by the Koreish in the times of the prophet. They also made it smaller than it was at first, so that there remained six cubits and a half in its capacity (internal length and breadth I suppose). Its height they increased by nine cubits, so that it became eighteen cubits. Its building consisted of a layer of wood and another of stone; so

*b* Judda. From this place I went with a company of merchants who were going to Yemen ; but, as the wind changed upon us, we put into the island of
*c* Sawākin, the Sultan of which was *d* El Sharīf Zaid Ibn Abu Nomma,* son
of the Emīr of Mecca. Sawākin fell to him on the part of the *e* Bejā,† who
were nearly related to him, and from whom he had an army attending
upon him.   From Sawākin I set out for Yemen with the merchants, and
came to *f* Hali,‡ a large and handsomely built city.   The inhabitants are
aboriginal Arabs, governed by the Sultan *g* Aāmir Ibn Dhuwaib of the tribe
*h* Beni Kenāna.   He is one of the most elegant, generous, and poetical
geniuses (of his time) ; he took me with him and entertained me very hospitably for some days.   From this place I travelled with the merchants to

---

*f* حَلِي .        *e* البِجاة .        *d* زيد ابن ابي نُمَي .        *c* سواكن .        *b* جُدّةء .

*h* بني كنانه .        *g* عامر بن ذُوِيبــ .

---

that there were fifteen courses of wood, and sixteen of stone.  Within it were six columns, as
also images of the angels, the prophets, the tree, and of Abraham the friend, with the divining
arrows in his hand : there was also an image of Jesus and another of his mother Mary.   But in
the year of victory the prophet ordered them all to be destroyed.   There were also in it, the horns
of the ram which Abraham sacrificed (in lieu of his son).  They were hung up within the temple,
and thus they remained to the times of Ibn El Zobair, and then they were burnt."  That this
temple was at first the residence of some of the patriarchs seems to me extremely probable,
and as it was at first larger than it is now, it might then have been quite sufficient for all the
purposes of a shepherd. If, indeed, it contained an image of Abraham, the ram's horns, &c. as
here mentioned, a curious proof is afforded to the truth of the original history : and if there
was an image of our Lord and his mother, it should seem that the Christians of Arabia had
adopted images before the times of Mohammed, for from them the pagans must have taken
them.

* We are told by Abulfeda (Ann. Muslem., tom. v. p. 282-3, *i. e.* A. D. 1313) that Abul Ghaith
Ibn Abu Nami (as Reiske writes it) accompanied him to Mecca, in order to be put in possession of
the government of that place in lieu of his brother.  The appointment took place ; and it is probable that the person here mentioned was son to the same governor, who must have held Mecca
when our traveller visited it.

† See Ouseley's Oriental Geography, p. 13.

‡ Abulfeda puts this place, according to the Atwāl, in long. 66° 20′, lat. 13° 50′ ; according
to the Kānūn, long. 66° 50′.  He then says وحَلي من اطراف اليمن قال الادريسي ومن اراد أن
يركب البرية من تهامه الي صنعا فانه يسير من السرَّيْن نحو ست مراحل وبتلك الناحية مدينة
حلي .   Hali is one of the parts of Yemen : El Edrīsī says, that any one who wishes to pass
the desert from Tahāma to Senaä, let him go about six stages from Sirrain, and in those parts
(he will find) the city of Halī.

the town of [i] Sarja, a small place inhabited by merchants of Yemen, a liberal
and hospitable people. From this place I went to the city of [j] Zabīd,* where
I arrived in two days. This is one of the primary cities of Yemen; it is large
and handsome, and abounding with every commodity. The inhabitants are
generous, well-informed, and religious. In its environs the village of [k] Gha-
sāna† is the grave of El Wali El Sālih Ahmed [l] Ibn El Ojail El Yemenī.
The doctors of Zabīd told me of one of his miracles, which was this: The
doctors and great people of the Zaidia‡ sect once came to his cell. The
Sheikh sat without the cell, and received and returned their salutations. At
length a question arose on the subject of predestination; the Zaidia affirming, that there was no such thing, and that every man was the author of
his own actions. The Sheikh replied: If the matter be as you say it is,
get up from the place where you are now sitting. They all endeavoured to
rise, but not one of them could do so. The Sheikh left them in this situation, and went into his cell. They accordingly remained in this state, subject to the burning rays of the sun and lamenting their sad condition, till
after sunset, when some of the Sheikh's companions going in to him
told him, that the people had repented and turned from their corrupt
creed. He then came out to them; and, taking them by the hand, joined
them in their conversion to the truth, and dereliction of error. They
arose and entered the cell, where he hospitably entertained them, and
sent them home. I went to the village in order to visit the grave of the
Sheikh, which I did, and met his son [m] El Khāshia Ismāīl, who entertained me very hospitably. I then went to [n] Jabala,§ which is a small

---

[n] جَبَلَة . ‏‎ [m] الخَاشِع . ‏‎ [l] العُجَيِّل اليمني . ‏‎ [k] غسانه al عسانه al غشانه . ‏‎ [j] زبيد . ‏‎ [i] سَرجَة .

* See D'Herbelot under Zebid.

† This, according to the Marāsid El Itlāa (مراصد الاطلاع) is the name of several lakes in
Arabia, on one of which the Beni Māzin resided; of another at the obstruction of Māarab in
Yemen, which is said to be near Jahfa, and perhaps of another in Yemen, between .... and
Zabīd, غسان اسم ماء نزل عليه بنوا مازن بن الازد بن الغور قيل ماء بسد ءآرب باليمن ويقال
. هو ماء ... قريب من الجحفة وقيل ماء باليمن بين ... وزبيد

‡ See D'Herbelot art. Zeidiah, and Annales Muslem., tom. iii. p. 734.

§ This place, according to Abulfeda, is named Jubla (جبلَه), and is said after Abu Akūl to
be in long. 65° 8', lat. 13° 55' (نی not ني as in our copy, which is manifestly wrong). It is

town ; and from that to the city of *p*Tiazz,* the residence of the King of
Yemen.   This is one of the most beautiful and extensive cities of Yemen.
The Sultan of this place was El Malik El Mojāhid Nūr Oddēn Ali, son
of the Sultan *q* El Mawayyid Dāūd, son of *r*Rasūl,† (*sent or commissioned*).   The grandfather of these sultans was called *Rasūl*,‡ because one
of the Califs of the house of Abbās had *sent* or *commissioned* him as the
Emīr of Yemen, after which his descendants kept possession of his government.   I was introduced to the king with the Kāzī of the place.   Their

---

*r* رسول .          *q* المويد .          *p* تَعَزّ .

---

situated between Aden and Senaä, in the mountains.  It stands upon two rivers, and hence has
been called the city of the two rivers.  It is modern, and was built by the Sulaihī when they had
power in Yemen.  Some respectable travellers have stated that Jubla is less than a day from
Tiazz in an eastern direction, inclining a little to the north.  The passage is وجبله بين عدن

وصنعا في الجبال وهي علي نهرين ولذلك تسمي مدينة النهرين وهي محدثة بناها الصليحيون لما
استولوا علي اليمن... قال بعض الثقات جبله عن تعز دون يوم وهي عن تعز في الشرق بميله يسيرة
الي الشمال .

* Abulfeda pronounces this word Tiaz ( تعز ), and gives the longitude and latitude after the
different authors as follows : long. 64° 30′, lat. 13° 8′.  Ibn Saīd, long. 70° 8′, lat. 14° 30′.  Ana-
logy, long. 65° 30′, lat. 13° 40′, and says, that it was in his times the residence of the kings of
Yemen, was a fortress situated on the mountains overhanging the coasts and the country of
Zabīd.   Beyond Tiaz is a pleasure ground called Sahlah, to which water has been brought from
the mountains by the king of Yemen ; and in this he has erected some spacious and strong edifices
in the middle of a garden. وتعز في زماننا هذا هي مقر ملوك اليمن وهي حصن في الجبال مطال

علي التهايم وارض زبيد وفوق تعز منتزه يقال له صهله قد ساق اليه صاحب اليمن المياه من الجبال
التي فوقها وبنا فيها ابنية عظيمة في غاية الحصن في وسط بستان .

† We are told in the Annales Muslemici, tom. v. p. 348-9 that the father of this prince died
at Tiazz تعز which Reiske writes Teez) A.D. 1321 ; and, that on this occasion, his son, Ali
received the title of El Malik El Mojāhid Saif El Islām, and succeeded to his throne : but, as he
was very young and inexperienced, he was near losing it with his life more than once (p. 357,
361, &c.)  He nevertheless continued in power, and was, no doubt, king of Yemen when our
traveller was there.

‡ A title of this sort seems to have originated the *Prester John* of Abyssinia, of which the missionary accounts said so much.  A Tartar king seems also to have assumed this title, which
in Persian was translated فرشته جان Ferishta Jān, *John the Angel*, probably, because he had
received Christianity.  Hence the European Prester John : but, how this became ascribed to
the King of Abyssinia it is not easy to say, unless he had assumed the title mentioned here
by our traveller which belonged to the king of Yemen.  See Asseman's Biblioth. Orient. tom. ii.
P. II, p. 404.

custom in saluting their king is this: any person coming before him, first places his fore-finger on the ground, and then, putting it on his head, says, " May God perpetuate thy power." I was received very courteously, and then invited to a banquet.

After this I travelled to the city of ⁵Senaā,* the capital of Yemen. It is a large and well-built city. From this place I went to the city of ᵗAden,† which is situated on the sea-shore. This is a large city, but without either seed, water, or tree. They have, however, reservoirs, in which they collect the rain-water for drinking. Some rich merchants reside here: and vessels from India occasionally arrive here. The inhabitants are modest and religious. I then went from Aden by sea, and after four days came to the city of ᵘZaila.‡ This is a city of the Berbers, a people of Soudān, of the Shāfia sect. Their country is a desert of two months' extent. The first part is termed Zaila, the last ᵛMakdashū.§ The greatest part of the inha-

ᵛ مقدشو.    ᵘ زيلع.    ᵗ عَدَن.    ⁵ صنعا.

* See Asseman. Biblioth. Orient. tom. iii. P. II., p. dccdxxv., and D'Herbelot, under the word Sanaa.

† For an account of this place, see the geographical Index appended to the life of Saladin, by Schultens, sub voce *Adenum*, Asseman, Biblioth. Orient. tom. iii. P. II. p. dccvii, and D'Herbelot, sub voce Aden.

‡ On this place see Rinck's Tract, containing extracts from Makrizi and Abulfeda on Abyssinia, Lugd. Batav. 1790, p. 9, Arab. text, and p. 10 Lat. trans. Also p. 12, Arab. text from Abulfeda; also Eichhorn's Africa, p. 31, which I thus translate: Ibn Saīd has said, that Zaila is a well-known city of the Abyssinians. Its inhabitants are Moslems. It is situated upon a canal which comes from the sea, and is low: its heat is excessive. Its waters are sweet, and are got from wells. The people have no gardens, and know nothing of fruits. Zaila is said in the Kānūn to be a port of Abyssinia not far from Yemen; and to be a place of scarcity. It is situated between the equinoctial line and the first climate. Those who have seen it have stated, that it is a small city nearly the size of Aidhāb. It is situated upon the shore, and is governed by Sheikhs. Merchants frequent the place, who are treated with hospitality and traded with. See also D'Herbelot, art. Habasch.

§ Abulfeda, as given by Rinck and Eichhorn (Afr. p. 33) pronounces this word Mahdishū, and says, that it is situated on the Indian sea; that its inhabitants are Moslems. It has a large river like the Nile of Egypt, which swells in the summer season: it is said to be a branch of the Nile which issues from the lake of Kaurā, and runs into the Indian sea near Makdishū. Abul Majd of Mosul has said in the *Mazīl El Irtiāb*, that Makdishū is a large city, lying between the Zinj and Abyssinians. See also Sir Wm. Ouseley's Oriental Geography, p. 14. On the fruits, &c. of these countries see Rinck's Tract above-mentioned. Arab. text. pp. 11, 12, &c. It is worthy of remark, that Ibn Batūta affiliates these people with the *Berbers* of Sūdān; see note at p. 17. This is the Magadocia of the Portuguese navigators.

bitants of Zaila, however, are of the Rāfiza sect.  Their food is, for the
most part, camel's flesh and fish.  The stench of the country is extreme,
as is also its filth, from the stink of the fish, and the blood of camels which
are slaughtered in its streets.  I then proceeded by sea for fifteen days, and
came to Makdashu, which is an exceedingly large city.  The custom here
is, that whenever any ships approach, the young men of the city come out,
and each one addressing himself to a merchant, becomes his host.  If there
be a theologian or a noble on board, he takes up his residence with the
Kāzī.  When it was heard that I was there, the Kāzī came with his students to the beach: and I took up my abode with him.  He then took me
to the Sultan, whom they style *Sheikh*.  Their custom is, that a noble or
a theologian, must be presented to the Sultan, before he takes up his abode
in the city.  When, therefore, the Kāzī came to the palace, one of the
King's servants met him.  The Kāzī was then ᵂBorhān Oddīn El Misrī
(of Egypt), and to him he mentioned my having come.  The servant
then went to the Sultan, and informed him: but soon returned to us with a
basket of vegetables, and some ˣfawfel nut.  These he divided among us,
and then presented us with rose-water; which is the greatest honour done
among them to any one.  He then said: It is the command of the King,
that this person should reside in the student's house.  The Kāzī then took
me by the hand, and conducted me to it.  It was near the palace, was
spread with carpets, and prepared for a feast.  The servants then brought
meats from the palace.

Their meat is generally rice roasted with oil, and placed in a large wooden
dish.  Over this they place a large dish of elkūshān, which consists of
flesh, fish, fowl, and vegetables.  They also roast the fruit of the ʸplan-
tain, and afterwards boil it in new milk: they then put it on a dish, and
the curdled milk on another.  They also put on dishes, some of preserved ᶻlemon, bunches of preserved pepper-pods salted and pickled, as
also grapes, which are not unlike apples, except that they have stones.
These, when boiled, become sweet like fruit in ᵃgeneral, but are crude
before this: they are preserved by being salted and pickled.  In the same

<hr>

ʸ الموز .        ˣ الفوفل .         ᵂ برهان الدين الصدي or المصري .
              ᵃ كالفاكهة .         ᶻ من الليمون المصيّر.

manner they use the [b]green ginger. When, therefore, they eat the rice, they eat after it these salts and pickles. The people of Makdashu are very corpulent: they are enormous eaters, one of them eating as much as a congregation ought to do.

The Sultan then sent for me and for each of my companions a dress; after which I was presented to him. Their custom in giving a salute is the same with that among the kings of Yemen. I remained some days the King's guest, and then set out for the country of the [c]Zanūj,* proceeding along the sea-shore. I then went on board a vessel and sailed to the island of [d]Mambasa,† which is large, abounding with the [e]banana, the lemon, and the [f]citron. They also have a fruit which they call the [g]jammoon (jambu). It is like the olive with a stone except that this fruit is exceedingly sweet. There is no grain in this island; what they have is brought to them from other places. The people are generally religious, chaste, and honest, and are of the sect of Shāfia. After lodging there one night, I set out, by sea, for the city of [h]Kulwā, which is large, and consists of wooden houses. The greater part of the inhabitants are Zunūj of the sect of Shāfia, of religious and peaceful habits. The king of this place, at the time I entered it, was [i]Abu El Mozaffir Hasan, a person who had obtained great victories over the countries of the infidel Zunūj. He gave much away in alms. The greatest gift bestowed by the people of these countries is ivory, which is the elephant's tooth: they seldom give gold. I then proceeded to the city of [j]Zafār‡ by sea: this is the farthest city of Yemen,

---

[b] الزنجبيل الاخضر. [c] الزنوج. [d] مَتْبَسَى [e] الموز. [f] اترج. [g] الجَمّون.

[h] كُلُوآ. [i] ابو المظفر حسن. [j] ظفار al. ظغار.

---

* See D'Herbelot, under Zeng. From this word the Zanguebar of the maps seems to be derived. It is doubtful, however, whether our traveller proceeded so far south as to touch on those countries as there given.

† This is the Mombas of Hamilton. India, chap. i.

‡ Asseman's Biblioth. Orient., tom. iii. P. 2, p. dcclxxv.; and D'Herbelot under Dhafar. Abulfeda puts this place in the following longitudes and latitudes, viz. after the Atwāl in long. 66° 30′, lat. 13° 30′; the Kānūn, long. 67° 8′, lat. 13° 30′; Ibn Saïd, 73° 8′; the Rasam, 73° 8′. No reliance can be placed on the other numbers given, I therefore omit them. He then describes the place thus:

وظفار مدينة علي ساحل خور وقد خرج من البحر الجنوبي وطعن في البر جهة الشمال نحو ماية
ميل وعلي طرف هذا الخور ظفار ولاتخرج المراكب من ظفار في هذا الخور الا بريح البر ويقلع منها

and situated on the shore of the Indian sea. From this place they carry horses to India; and when the wind is fair they pass from it to the Indian shores in a full month. Between Zafār and Aden, by land, is the distance of a month; but between it and [k] Hadramaut * that of sixteen days; and between it and [l] Ammān † twenty days. This city of Zafār stands alone in a large plain, in which there is no other village or governed district. It is a filthy place, and full of flies on account of the great quantity of fish and dates which are sold there. They feed their beasts and flocks also with fish, a custom witnessed by me no where else. Their money is made of copper and tin: they bathe several times in the day on account of the heat of their country. Their diseases are generally the elephantiasis and hernia. The greatest wonder among them is, that they injure no one unless he have previously injured them. Many kings have attempted their country, but have been forced to return, with the effects of their devices upon their own necks. At the distance of half a day from this place is the city of [m] El Ahkāf,‡ the residence of the people of

---

[m] الاحقاف .      [l] عَمَّان .      [k] حضرموت .

في الخور المذكور الي الهند وظفار قاعدة بلاد الشجر ويوخذ في ارضها كثير من نبات الهند مثل النارجيل والتنبل وشمالي ظفار رمال الاحقاف وبين ظفار وبين صنعا اربعة وعشرون فرسخا وعن

بعضهم ظفار علي ساحل اليمن ولها بساتين , &c. Zafār is a city standing upon the margin of an estuary which stretches out from the southern sea, and makes an indenture into the land in a southern direction for about one hundred miles; upon a part of this estuary therefore is Zafār. No vessel leaves Zafār and this estuary but by a land breeze; but there clear out from it vessels for India. Zafār is a principal city of the districts of El Shajr, and in its lands are found many of the productions peculiar to India, such as the cocoa-nut and the betel leaf. To the north of Zafār are the sand banks of Ahkāf: between it too and Sanaä is a distance of twenty-four farsangs. According to some this place is on the shores of Yemen, and abounds with gardens, &c.

    * See D'Herbelot, under Hadhramout.

    † We have, in the Marāsid El Itlāa, this word pronounced Omān, and the place is said to be a westerly tract of land on the shore of the sea of Yemen, and on the east of Hajar; that it contains two towns; its heat is proverbial, and its inhabitants of the Ibāzia sect of heretics.

عمان بضم اوله وتخفيف ثانيه واخره نون اسم كورة غربية علي ساحل بحر اليمن في شرقي هجر تشتمل علي بلدان يضرب بحرها المثل واهلها خوارج اباضيه .

    ‡ This word means sand-hills or banks, as mentioned in the note on Zafār. The author of the Marāsid El Itlāa says on it والاحقاف المذكور في الاحقاف جمع حقف الرمل وهو الرمل المعوج

[n]Aād.* In this city there are many gardens, in which there is the large and sweet fruit of the [o]banana, the seed of one of which will weigh ten ounces.†
There is also the [p]betel-tree, and that of the [q]cocoa-nut, which are generally found no where else except in India, and to those of India may these be compared. I shall now describe both. With respect to the betel-leaf, its tree is supported just as that of unripe grapes generally is; they prop it up with reeds.‡ It is planted near the cocoa-nut, and is sometimes supported by it. The betel-tree produces no fruit, but is reared merely for its leaf, which is like the leaf of the [r]thorn, and the smallest are the best. These leaves are plucked daily. The people of India esteem it very highly, for whenever any one of them receives a visit from another, the present made is five of these leaves, which is thought to be very splendid, particularly if the donor happen to be one of the nobles. This gift is esteemed among them as being much more valuable than that of gold or silver. Its use is as follows: A grain of fawfel (which is in some respects like a [s]nut-meg) is first taken and broken into small pieces: it is then put into the mouth and chewed. A leaf of the betel is then taken, and when sprinkled with a little quick lime is put into the mouth and chewed with the fawfel. Its properties are to sweeten the breath, help the digestion, and to obviate the danger incident to drinking water on an empty stomach: it also elevates the spirits and stimulates to venery.

As to the [t]cocoa nut, it is the same with the [u]Indian nut. The tree is very rare and valuable. It is something like the palm. The nut is like a

---

[r] عُلَّيْق .    [q] التنبول و النارجيل .    [p] التنبول .    [o] الموز .    [n] عاد .

[u] جوز الهند .    [t] النارجيل .    [s] جوز الطيب .

---

الكتاب العزيز واد بين عُمَّان وارض مَهْرَة وقيل بين عمان الي حضرموت وهي رمال مشرفة علي البحر
El Ahkāf is the plural of Hikf, sand, and it is taken to signify a crooked sand-bank. But the Ahkāf which is mentioned in the Koran is a valley between Ommān (al. Ammān) and the country of Mahrat; it is also said to be between Ommān and Hadramout: they are sand-banks which approach the sea.

* A tribe mentioned in the Koran.

† As this passage appears obscure to me, I give the original تبلغ الحبة منه وزن اثني عشر اوقية.

‡ Knox says: " the tree that bears the betel-leaf, so much loved and eaten in these parts, grows like ivy, twining about trees or poles which they stick in the ground for it to run up by, and as the betel grows, the poles grow also." Ceylon, p. 34.

man's head; for it has something like two eyes and a mouth; and within, when green, is like the brains. Upon it too is a fibre like hair. From this they make cords with which they sew their vessels together, instead of iron nails. They also make great ropes for their anchors out of it.*

The properties of this nut are, to nourish and quickly to fatten the body, —to make the face red, and greatly to stimulate to venery. Milk, oil olive, and honey, are also made out of it. They make the honey thus: having cut off the tendril on which the fruit would be formed, leaving it, however, about the length of two fingers, they then suspend a larger or smaller pot to it, and into this a kind of water drops, which they collect morning and evening. They then expose it to the fire, just as they do dried grapes, and it becomes stiff, and exceedingly sweet, honey: out of this they make sweetmeats.† As to the making of milk, they open a side of the nut, take out the whole of the inside with a knife, and put it on a plate. This they macerate well in water. It then becomes milk, both as to taste and colour: and is eaten as such. The oil-olive is thus made: When the nut is ripe and has fallen from the tree, they peel off the bark and cut it

---

* According to Mr. Crawfurd, a species of this palm, called the *gomuti* in the islands of the Indian archipelago, produces a superior kind of cordage to that of the cocoa-nut: and while that of the cocoa-nut is most in use in the Maldives, Ceylon, &c., this prevails in the parts he is describing, vol. i. pp. 380, 398. It is curious enough to observe, that the same thing is said by Abu Zaid El Hasan, in his remarks on the Arab travellers of the ninth century, translated by Renaudot, when speaking of the ships of these parts; and that the editor doubts the truth of the statement. See Pinkerton's Voyages and Travels, vol. vii. pp. 207, 220, where the whole process of making is described.

† Mr. Crawfurd's description of the manner in which the *toddy* is extracted from the gomuti palm is so nearly allied to this, that I cannot forbear copying it, vol. i. p. 398: " The principal production of this palm is the *toddy*, which is procured in the same manner as from other palms, or in the following mode: one of the *spathæ*, or shoots of fructification, is on the first appearance of its fruit beaten for three successive days with a small stick, with the view of determining the sap to the wounded part. The shoot is then cut off a little way from the root, and the liquor which pours out is received in pots of earthenware, in bamboos, or other vessels......... When newly drawn the liquor is clear, and in taste resembles fresh must. In a very short time it becomes turbid, whitish, and somewhat acrid, and quickly runs into a viscous fermentation, acquiring an intoxicating quality. A still larger quantity is immediately applied to the purpose of yielding sugar. With this view the liquor is boiled to a syrup, and thrown out to cool in small vessels, the form of which it takes, and in this shape it is sold in the markets." The manner of making the oil is also mentioned by Mr. Crawfurd, pp. 381, 382.

into pieces; it is then placed in the sun, and when it is withered they heat it in a pot, and having extracted its oil, eat it with their breakfast and other meals. The Sultan of Zafār is [v]El Malik El Mogīth, uncle's son to the King of Yemen.

Leaving Zafār, I proceeded by sea towards [w]Ammān, and on the second day put into the port of [x]Hāsik; where many Arab fishermen reside. We have here the [y]incense tree.* This tree has a thin leaf, which when scarified produces a fluid like milk: this turns into gum, and is then called [z]lobān, or frankincense. The houses are built with the bones of fish, and are covered with the skins of camels.

Leaving this place, we arrived in four days at the mountain of [a]Lomaān, which stands in the middle of the sea. On the top of it is a strong edifice of stone, and on the outside of this there is a reservoir for the rain-water.

After two days I arrived at the island of [b]Taïr, in which there is not a house: it abounds with such birds as the [c]sparrow. After this I came to a large island, in which the inhabitants have nothing to eat but fish. I then arrived at the city of [d]Kulhāt,† which is situated on the top of a mountain. The inhabitants are Arabs, whose language is far from elegant, and who are, for the most part, [e]schismatics. This, however, they keep

---

[v] الملك المغيث . [w] عمان . [x] حَاسِك . [y] الكُندُر . [z] لُبَان . [a] جبل لُمَعَان .

[b] جزيرة الطير of birds, al.الطمير El Tamir . [c] كالشقاشق . [d] قَلْهَات . [e] خوارج .

---

* This is the χόνδρος of the Greeks. See the Phaleg. of Bochart, lib. ii. cap. 18, or, as appended to the Monumenta Vetustiora Arabicæ, by Alb. Schultens, pp. 25-6.

† This is written Kalhāt قَلْهَات by the author of the Marāsid El Itlāa, who says, ... قَلْهَات مدينة بعمان علي ساحل البحر عامرة اهلة واهلها كلّهم خوارج اباضية يتظاهرون بذلك A city in Ammān upon the sea shore, which is well inhabited and populous: the inhabitants, however, are all schismatics of the Ibāzīa sect, which they openly profess. As some further notices will occur of this sect, I will here give what the author of the Kāmoos with Jawharī says about it. والإباض ... عبد الله بن إباض التميمي نُسِبَ اليه الاباضية من الخوارج El Ibāz...Abd Allah Ibn Ibāz of the tribe of Beni Temīm, after whom the Ibāzīa schismatics are named. Jawharī's explanation is: والاباضية فرقة من الخوارج اصحاب عبد الله بن إباض التميمي i.e. " the Ibāzīa are a sect of the schismatics, the followers of Abd Allah Ibn Ibāz El Temīmī," who, as our traveller will presently tell us, is, according to them, the saint who is to put an end to error.

secret, because they are subject to the *f* King of Hormuz, who is of the Sonnee sect.

I then set out for the country of *g* Ammān, and after six days' journey through a desert, arrived there on the seventh. It abounds with trees, rivers, gardens, with palms, and various fruit trees. I entered one of the principal cities of these parts, which is *h* Nazwā.* This is situated on a hill, and abounds with gardens and water. The inhabitants are schismatics of the *i* Ibāzīa sect. They fall in with the opinions of the base *j* Ibn Moljam,† and say, that he is the saint who shall put an end to error. They also allow the Califats of Abu Beker and Omar, but deny those of Othman and Ali. Their wives are most base; yet, without denying this, they express nothing like jealousy on the subject.

The Sultan of Ammān is an Arab of the tribe of *k* El Azd,‡ named *l* Abu Mohammed Ibn Nahbān; but Abu Mohammed is with them a general title, given to any ruler, just as Atābek, and other titles are, to Sultans of other places.§ The inhabitants eat the flesh of the domestic *m* ass, which is sold in the streets, and which they say is lawful.

---

| *k* قبيلة الازد | *j* الشقي بن مُلْجم | *i* اباضيه | *h* نزوا | *g* عَمَّان | *f* هرمز |
| | *m* الحمار الانسي | *l* بن ينهان al. نهبان | | | |

---

* This is probably the نزوه of the Marāsid El Itlāa (مراصد الاطلاع) which is there said to be a hill in Ammān; there is, it is added, a number of large villages on the shore near it, the whole of which are called by this name. The inhabitants are of the Ibāzīa sect. نزوه بالفتح ثم السكون وفتح الواو جبل نعمان (بعمان) (I read ... بالساحل عنده عدة قري كبار يسمي مجموعها بهذا الاسم واهلها اباضيه . Our copy reads وليس بالساحل, but this I cannot understand, unless it means that there is not a number of large villages, *i. e.* a number of small ones. I prefer however, omitting ليس .

† See the Annales Muslemici, tom. i., pp. 332-3, &c.

‡ See D'Herbelot, under Azd.

§ So the Pharaohs of Egypt, (*i. e.* Pe Ouro. Copt.) the king: the Abimeleks of Gerar among the Philistines, &c. According to Abulfeda, the title of Atābek was first given by Malik Shāh to his Vizier Nizām El Mulk, A.D. 1052. Annales Muslemici, vol. iii., p. 226-7.

# CHAPTER X.

*Hormuz—Harauna—Janja Bāl—Kūzistan—Lār—Kaisa or Sīrāf—Fārs—Pearl Fisheries—Kosair and Hoair—El Kotaif—Hajar or Hasā—Yemāma—Rās Dawāir—Aidhāb—Egypt—Cairo—Syria—El Ramla—Tripoli—Jabala—Lādhikīa—Koom—El Alāyā.*

From this place I went to Hormuz,* which is a city built on the sea-shore; opposite to which, but within the sea, is [n] New Hormuz. This is an island, the city of which is called [o] Harauna. It is a large and beautiful place, and here the King resides. The island is in extent about a day's journey: but the greatest part of it consists of salt earth, and of hills of [p] Dārānī salt.† The inhabitants subsist upon fish and dates, the latter of which is brought from Basra or Ammān. They have but little water. The most strange thing I saw here, was the head of a fish, which might be compared to a hill. Its eyes were like two doors, so that people could go in at the one, and out at the other. The Sultan of Hormuz was at this time [q] Kotb Oddīn Tamahtas, son of [r] Tūrān Shah,‡ a most generous and brave prince. Under his control were the pearl fisheries.

From Harauna I proceeded to [s] Janja Bāl,§ for the purpose of visiting a

[n] هرمز الجديده . [o] حَرَوْن al. جَرَوْن . [p] الدراني al. الملح الداراني .
[q] تمهتر al. تمهتس . [r] طوران شاه . [s] جَنْج بال .

* See an excellent geographical article on this place in Asseman's Biblioth. Orient., tom. iii., P. 2, pp. dcclvii-viii.; also Sir Wm. Ouseley's Oriental Geography, pp. 12, 88, 138, 140, 141, &c.; and D'Herbelot, art. Hormouz.

† According to the author of the Kāmoos, this patronymic is irregularly formed, but refers to داريّاة *Darayyāt*, a town in Syria, vol. i. p. ٥٢٨, edit. Calcutta. Jāmi tells us in the نفحات الانس that it is referred to Dārā, one of the villages of Damascus: his words are: داراني ... از دارا كه دهي است از دههاي دمشق . See also Mr. Hamaker's "Liber de expugnatione Memphidis," &c., who derives it from دارايّا .

‡ De Guignes has given a list of the Kings of Ormuz (tom. i. p. 345), from Texeira, which he had some suspicion was not very correct. In this Touran Shah is placed in 1378: but our traveller places a son of this prince upon the throne before 1340, and gives him a name not to be found in Texeira's list; the suspicion of De Guignes is therefore well-founded.

§ This is, perhaps, the جرجنبان of Mr. Ulenbroek, see his Irac. Persic. descriptio, p. 65. In the Marāsid El Itlāa this place is given جَرْجَنْبان *Jargānbān*, and is said to be a large village between Sāwa and Aldī قرية كبيرة بين ساوه والدي .

certain saint.　I accordingly crossed the sea, and then hired some Turkomāns, who inhabit these parts, and without whose assistance there is no travelling, on account of their courage and knowledge of the roads.　We have now a waterless desert, four days in extent, over which the Badawīn Arab caravans travel.　In this the Somoom blows during the months of June and July, and kills every one it meets with, after which his limbs drop off.　Over this I travelled, and arrived at the country of 'Kauristān (Kūzistan), which is small.　From this place I proceeded for three days over a desert like the former, till I came to "Lār,* which is a large and beautiful city, abounding with rain water and gardens.　I now went to the cell of the holy Sheikh "Abu Dolaf, the person whom I intended to visit at Janja Bāl. In this cell was his son "Abd El Rahmān, with a number of Fakeers.　In the same place resides a Sultan, whom they call "Jalāl Oddin El Turkomānī.

I next went to the city of Janja Bāl, in which the Sheikh Abu Dolaf resided.　I went to his cell, and found him alone sitting on the side of it upon the ground, and clothed in an old woollen "garment.†　I saluted him; he returned the salute, and then asked me about my coming thither, and of my country.　He afterwards made me stay with him, and, by one of his sons, who is a pious, humble, abstemious, and very good man, he sent me meat and fruits.　This Sheikh is an astonishing man.　He has a very large cell, and bestows costly presents ; and moreover clothes and feeds all who visit him.　I saw no one like him in these parts, nor is it known whence his income is derived, unless it is brought to him by the brotherhood.‡　Most people, however, think that it is from miraculous operations.§ The people of these parts are of the sect of Shāfia.

---

<sup>ᵞ</sup> جبّة صوف .　<sup>ˣ</sup> جلال الدين التركماني .　<sup>ʷ</sup> عبد الرحمن .　<sup>ᵛ</sup> ابو دُلَف .　<sup>ᵘ</sup> لار .　<sup>ᵗ</sup> كُورِستَان .

---

* The capital of Laristān.

† *Jubbati Sūf.* Hence, as it is generally believed, the Sūfīs have received their name. See Tholuck's Ssufismus &c. Berolini, 1821, p. 26, &c.

‡ Of this brotherhood, or society, some notice will be taken hereafter.

§ The passage is ويزعم كثير من الناس انه ينفق من الكون, where كون is the only word which can create any difficulty.　It is generally defined to mean, " matter not existing from eternity, but produced in time," (چيزي حادث يغي نبوده وپيدا شده).　In this place it probably means money produced out of matter by some miraculous process.

I then bade farewell to the Sheikh, and travelled on to the city of [z]Kaisa, which is also called [a]Sīrāf.* It is situated on the shore of the Indian ocean, and near to the sea of Yemen. [b]Fārs is a good and extensive district: its gardens are wonderfully rich in scented herbs. The inhabitants are Persians: those, however, who dive for the pearls are Arabs. The pearl-fisheries which are between Sīrāf and [c]Bahrein are situated in a quiet gulf of the sea, not unlike a large valley. To this place comes a great number of boats, and in these are the divers, with the merchants of Fārs and Bahrein. When one of the divers intends to go down, he places something upon his face made out of tortoise-shell, and in this a place for the nose is cut out; he then ties a rope round his middle and goes down. The time they will remain under water varies; some will remain an hour, others two, others less. When the diver gets to the bottom of the sea, he finds the shells firmly fixed in the sand among trees (of coral). He then either tears them off with his hands, or cuts them away with an iron knife, and puts them into a leathern bag which hangs to his neck. When he begins to experience a difficulty of remaining under water, he shakes the rope, and the man who holds it draws him up, and puts him into the boat. The bag is then taken and the shells opened, and they find in each a piece of flesh, which being cut away with a knife and exposed to the air, hardens and becomes a pearl. After this both great and small are collected together, and one-fifth goes to the King: the rest are sold to the merchants present. To many of these merchants, however, the divers are generally in debt, and in this case the pearls are taken by way of payment.

I next proceeded from Sīrāf to the city of [d]Bahrein,† which is a large and handsome place, abounding in gardens and water. It is wonderfully hot, and so very sandy, that the houses will sometimes be overwhelmed with sand. There is at both the eastern and western side of it, a hill (or bank): the one they call [e]Kosair, the other [f]Hoair, and on these they

---

[d] البحرين .    [c] البحرين .    [b] الفارس .    [a] سيراف .    [z] قَيْس .

[f] عوير .al عُوَيْر .    [e] كُسَيْر .

---

* See Asseman's Bib. Or., tom. iii. P. 2, p. dcclxxix; Sir Wm. Ouseley's Oriental Geography, pp. 11, 82, 88, 104, 105, &c.; and Edrīsī, section 6 of the third Climate.

† See D'Herbelot, art. Baharein.

have an adage, and say : " Kosair and Hoair, and, indeed, every opponent brings advantage " * (كسير وعوير وكل غير خير).

I then travelled to the city of $^g$ Kotaif,† (as if it were a word of the diminutive form from $^h$ Kotf). It is, however, a large and handsome place, inhabited by Arabs of the Rāfiza sect, extremely enthusiastic, publishing their sentiments and fearing no one. From this place I proceeded to the city of $^i$ Hajar, which, however, is now called $^j$ El Hasā. We have here a greater abundance of dates than is to be found elsewhere, and which are used as fodder for the beasts. The inhabitants are Arabs of the tribe of $^k$ Abd El Kais. From this place I travelled to $^l$ Yemāma, which is also called $^m$ Hajr,‡ a beautiful and fertile city, abounding with water and gardens.

$^m$ هَجَر .    $^l$ اليَمامة .    $^k$ عبد القَيس .    $^j$ الحَسا .    $^i$ هَجَر .    $^h$ قَطَف .    $^g$ القُطيف

---

* Edrīsī, in his 6th sect. of the 2d climate, mentions these hills in the following manner :

مما يلي شط اليمن جبلا كسير و عوير ويحاذي هذين الجبلين المكان المسمي دردورا ويسمي بحر موضعه بحر عزرة والدردور موضع يدور فيه الماء كالرحي دورانا دائما من غير فترة ولا سكون فاذا سقط اليه مركب او غيره لم يزل يدور حتي يتلف .... وهو مضيق علي مقربة من جبلي كسير وعوير تسلكه السفن الصغار ولا تسلكه السفن الصينية وهذان الجبلان غايران تحت الماء لا يظهر منها شيء والبحارون والربانيون يعرفون مكانهما فيجنبونهما .     "The two hills Kosair and Hoair, are close to the shore of Yemen ; and opposite to these hills is the place called the *vortex*. The sea here is called the sea of Azrat. The vortex is a place in which the water continually whirls round like a mill-stone without the least remission or rest ; and should a vessel, or any thing else come into it, it would continue to whirl round until it would be lost .... This is a narrow place near the two hills (or banks) Kosair and Hoair, into which small ships may pass, but not the ships of China. These two hills, moreover, lie concealed under the water, so that no part of them is seen. The pilots know their places and avoid them."—The meaning of the adage seems to be, that public opposition tends to promote public good. Mention is made of these rocks by the two Mahommedan travellers of the ninth century.  Pinkerton, vol. vii. p. 185.

† Edrīsī says of this place, sect. vi. Clim. iii.  واما مدينة القطيف فانها مجاورة للبحر وهي في ذاتها كبيرة ومن القطيف الي الاحسا مرحلتان ومن القطيف الي حمص يومان وهي علي البحر الفارسي i. e. as to the city of Kotaif, it is close to the sea, and is in itself large. From Kotaif to El Ahsā are two stages, and from the same place to Hamas a distance of two days, and this place is also situated on the Persian Gulf.

‡ In speaking of this place Edrīsī says : ثم الي الاحسا مرحلة ثم حمص مرحلة ثم الي ساحل هجر مرحلة وهذه المراحل كلها مراس ومواضع لا ماء فيها .  Then to El Ahsā one stage, thence to Hamas one stage, thence to the shore of Hajar one stage ; and all these stages, &c. In the 6th sect. of the 2d climate this place is also mentioned, as is likewise Yamāma : the words are

The inhabitants are, for the most part, of the tribe [n]Beni Hanīfa; they are the ancient possessors of this district. From this place I went on pilgrimage and arrived at Mecca, in the year 733 of the Hejira (A. D. 1332). In this year the Sultan of Egypt El Malik El Nāsir, also performed the pilgrimage. After finishing the pilgrimage, I proceeded towards [o]Judda, intending to go by way of Yemen to India: but in this I failed. I then proceeded by sea towards [p]Aidhāb, but was driven by the wind into a port called [q]Ras Dawāir. From this place I travelled by land with the [r]Bejā, and passed over a desert, in which there was a great number of ostriches and gazelles, and some Badawīn Arabs subject to the Bejā. After a journey of nine days I arrived at [s]Aidhāb; and leaving this place, and

---

[s]عيذاب .    [r]البجاه .    [q]راس دَوَاير .    [p]عيذاب .    [o]جُدَّة .    [n]بني حنيفه .

---

..... ومع الشمال ارض اليمامه ومن مدنها هجر وهي الان خرابة وبها كانت اليمامة الملكة ساكنة في وقتها

ومن ساحل هجر الي البصرة طريق علي الساحل غير معمورة . And with the northern country of El Yemāma, and of its cities is Hajar, which is now in ruins. In this country resided the queen Yemāma in her times ...... From the shores of Hajar there is a road to Basra along the shore, but uninhabited. See also Annales Muslemici, tom. i., p. 173. Abulfeda, however, places El

Ahsā (الاحسا) in long. 73° (or 8) 30', lat. 22° 8', and says وماء كثيرة نُخيل ذات بليدة هي

جارية ومنابيعها حارة شديدة الحرارة والاحسا في البرية وهي عن القطيف في الغرب بميله الي الجنوب علي نحو مرحلتين ونخيلها بقدر غوطة دمشق مستدير عليها قال في المشترك والاحسا جمع حسا وهو رمل يغوص فيه الماء حتي اذا صار الي صلابة الارض امسكته فيحفر فيه العرب ويستخر جونه والاحسا علم لموضع في بلاد العرب وهي احسا بني سعد من هجر وهي دار القرامطة بالبحرين وقيل احسا بني سعد غير احسا القرامطة وليس للاحسا سور وبين الاحسا واليمامه مسيره اربع ايام واهل احسا والقطيف يجلبون الثمر الي الخرج وادي اليمامه ويشترون بكل راحلة من الثمر راحلة من الحنطة . This is a small city abounding with palms and running water: its springs are exceedingly hot. El Ahsā is in the desert, and is from Kotaif (Katīf) in a south western direction about two stages. Its palms are as numerous as those in the vale of Damascus, and they are all round it. It is said in the Moshtarik, that Ahsā is the plural of Hīsā, which means *sand*, into which the water sinks, and proceeds until it comes to the hard earth, which retains it. In this the Arabs dig and draw out the water. El Ahsā, therefore, has become the proper name of a place among the districts of the Arabs. This is the Ahsā of the tribe Beni Saad of Hajar, and is a residence of the Karāmata (heretics so called) in Bahrain. It is also said, that the Ahsā of the Beni Saad, is a different place from that of the Karāmata. El Ahsā has no walls. Between it and Yemāma is a distance of four days. The people both of Ahsā and Kotaif carry fruits to El Kharj, a valley of Yemāma, and for every camel-burden of fruit, they buy another of wheat.

passing through district after district in Upper Egypt, arrived at last at
Caïro, where I remained some days. Hence I proceeded to Syria, and
then to Jerusalem. From this place I went to [t]El Ramla, [u]Acca, [v]Tripoli,
[w]Jabala,* and [x]El Lādhikīā (Laodicea). And from this I went by sea to the
country of [y]Room, which has been so called, because it formerly belonged
to the Romans :† and, even now, they are here in considerable numbers,
under the protection of the Mohammedans. Here are also many Turko-
mans. I next arrived at [z]El Alāyā, which is a large city upon the sea
shore, inhabited by Turkomāns. The present Sultan is [a]Yūsuf Beg, son
of [b]Karmān. I was introduced to him. · Our meeting was pleasant, and
he furnished us with provisions.‡ ·

---

## CHAPTER XI.

*Anatolia—Burdūr—Sabartā—Akrīdūr—Akshahar—Karā Hisār—Lādhik—Fortress of Tawās
—Mīlās—Kūnia, the grave of Mawlānā Rūmī—Laranda—Aksarā—Nikda—Sīvās—Amāsia
—Sūnusa—Kumash—Arzanjān—Arzerrūm—Birki, remarkable piece of meteoric stone seen here—
Tīra—Ayāsaluk—Yazmīr—Magnesia—Bergama—Burūsa—Yaznīk—Bustunī—Būlī—Barlū
Kastamūnia.*

FROM this place I proceeded to the district of [c]Anatolia,§ which contains
some handsome cities. In all the Turkomān towns there is a Brotherhood
of [d]youths, one of whom is termed اخي (my brother, *i. e.* the word brother
اخ joined with the pronoun of the first person singular ي my). No people
are more courteous to strangers, more readily supply them with food

---

[z]العَلَايا ·   [y]الروم ·   [x]اللاذقيه ·   [w]جَبَلَة ·   [v]طرابلس ·   [u]عكا ·   [t]الرملة ·

[a]يوسف بيك ·   [b]ابن قرمان ·   [c]انطاليه ·   [d]الاخيه الفتيان ·

* See Annales Muslemici, tom. iii. p. 329, tom. iv. p. 109.

† See D'Herbelot, under the article Roum.

‡ Of this prince De Guignes gives us no account whatever.

§ According to the Marāsid El Itlāa علي شاطي بلاد الروم وهو حسن حسن مشاهير من كبير بلد
القسطنطينية خليج بقرب الاهل كثير الرستاق واسع منيع البحر, a large, well-known and handsome district of Room, situated on the sea-shore ; it is strong, contains many villages and inhabitants, and is near the gulf of Constantinople. See also Annales Muslemici, tom. iv. p. 220-1.

and other necessaries, or are more opposed to oppressors than they are. The person who is styled الاخي *the Brother* is one, about whom persons of the same occupation, or even foreign youths, who happen to be destitute, collect and constitute their president. He then builds a cell, and in this he puts a horse, a saddle, and whatever other implements may be wanting. He then attends daily upon his companions, and assists them with whatever they may happen to want. In the evening they come to him and bring all they have got, which is sold to purchase food, fruit, &c. for the use of the cell. Should a stranger happen to arrive in their country, they get him among them, and with this provision they entertain him; nor does he leave them till he finally leaves their country. If, however, no traveller arrive, then they assemble to eat up their provisions, which they do with drinking, singing, and dancing. On the morrow, they return to their occupations, and in the evening return again to their president. They are therefore styled " *the Youths*," their president " *the Brother*."

In this city I went to the college of its Sheikh, ᵉShahāb Oddīn El Hamāwī; and, on the second day, one of this society came to me. He was addressed by the Sheikh in Turkish. The Sheikh told me that this man came to invite us to a feast. I was much astonished, and said to the Sheikh, This is a poor man, how can he afford to feast us, who are many. The Sheikh was surprised at my reply, and said: This is one of the Brotherhood, a society consisting of two hundred silk merchants, who have a cell of their own. I consented, therefore, and went to the cell, and witnessed the astonishing attention, kindness, and liberality which they shewed their guests. May God reward them! The Sultan of Anatolia was ᶠKhāzir Beg Ibn Yūnus the Turkomān. I was presented to him. He was then sick. He behaved very liberally towards us, gave us provisions, and sent money for our travelling expenses.

I next proceeded to the town of ᵍBurdūr, which is small, and surrounded by trees and gardens. I first went to the house of the ʰKhatīb (the preacher), and there met the society of the Brotherhood, who invited us to their feast.

---

ᵍ بُرْدُور . ᶠ خضر بيك ابن يونس التركماني . ᵉ شهاب الدين الحماوي .
ʰ الخطيب .

---

\* No mention of this prince occurs in De Guignes.

The Khatīb refused to go : they therefore gave us a feast in a garden without the town.   I was truly astonished at their wish to shew us every respect and attention, although we were ignorant of their language, and they of ours.

From this place I went to the town of [i] Sabartā, which is handsomely built, and has good streets.   I next went to the city of [k] Akrīdūr, which is large, and abounding with trees and water.   A lake of sweet water adjoins it, over which vessels pass, in the space of two days, to the town of[l] Aksha-har, and to other places.   I here put up at the lecturer's, [m] El Fāzil Moslih Oddīn, who treated me very respectfully.   The Sultan of this place was [n] Abu Is-hāk Beg, one of the greatest princes of these parts.   He gave us protection in his district throughout the month of Ramadān.   During my residence I was introduced to him ; after this he sent me a horse and some money.   He is a condescending and excellent prince.

I then went to the city of [o] Karā Hisār.*   It is small, and surrounded by water on every side.   The Sultan is [p] Mohammed Chelebī.   He is the brother of Abu Is-hāk, King of Akrīdūr.   I was introduced to him, and he treated me with great respect, and gave me some provisions.   After this I proceeded to the city of [q] Lādhik, which is a large and fine city, abound-ing with water and gardens.   As soon as I had entered it, a number of persons who were in the streets got up and seized upon the bridles of our horses ; after which others came and contested the point with them.   We were much alarmed at this ; but a person coming up who could speak Arabic, said they were contending only as to who should entertain us, as they were of the society of Youths.   Upon this I felt safe.   They then cast lots, and we proceeded to the cell of the party on whom the lot fell, and on the day following, to that of the other.   Both the parties shewed us the greatest respect.   The Sultan [r] Yataj Beg, who is one of the greatest princes of these parts, hearing of us, sent for us and treated us with great respect.

---

[n] ابو اسحق بيك .   [m] الفاضل مصلح الدين .   [l] آق شهَر.   [k] اكريدُور .al اكريدور .   [i] سَبَرتا .

[r] ينج بيك .   [q] لَاذِق .   [p] محمد چلبي .   [o] قرَا حِصَار .

---

* According to the Marāsid El Itlāa, a large farm on the north of Aleppo : . مرج كبير من شمالي

الحلب

I then proceeded to the fortress of ⁵Tawās, then to the city of ᵗMīlās, which is large and beautiful. Its Sultan is "Urkhān Beg, ᵛIbn El Mantashā. When I was introduced to him he treated me with great respect: he is a very excellent prince.* I proceeded from this place to the city of ʷKūnia,† which is large and handsome, and abounds with water and gardens. This district belongs to the Sultan ˣBadr Oddīn Ibn Karmān; over which, however, the King of Irāk has occasionally had the rule, on account of its proximity to some of his states which are in these parts. I put up at the cell of its Kāzī, who is known by the name of ʸIbn Kalam Shāh. He is a member of the society of Youths. His cell is most beautiful; and he has a great number of disciples, who trace the authorities for their judicial decisions as high as Ali Ibn Abi Tālib. They are clothed as the Sūfīs are with the khirka,‡ and close trowsers.

In this place is the tomb of the holy Sheikh ᶻJalāl Oddīn, better known by the title of ᵃMawlānā§ (our Mawla). He is very highly esteemed. It is said, that he was at first a mere lecturing doctor who had a large number of pupils: but upon a certain day a stranger came into his lecture-room with a basket of sweetmeats, which he had for sale, upon his head; the Sheikh said to him, bring your basket here. The man took a piece of sweetmeat and gave it to the Sheikh, who ate it. He then went out, no one else having tasted the sweetmeat; the Sheikh became agitated and went out after him, giving up his reading, and leaving his pupils in a state of expectation. At length, however, they set out in quest of him, but failed to discover the place of his retreat. Some years after, he returned with his mind deranged, and speaking nothing but Persian verses. These

---

قونيه . ʷ  المنتشا . ᵛ  أورخان بيك . ᵘ  ميلاس . ᵗ  حِصن طَوَاس . ˢ

مولانا . ᵃ  جلال الدين . ᶻ  ابن قلم شاه . ʸ  بدر الدين قرمان . ˣ

---

\* According to De Guignes, this Ottoman prince reigned from 1326 to 1369 (tom. i. p. 271), and consequently he must have been living when our traveller was in these parts.

† Iconium.

‡ A coarse ragged garment worn by the religious beggars of the east.

§ See an interesting article on this writer in fourth Tabaka (طبقه چهارم) of Dawlatshah, art. مولانا جلال الدين رومي, and in the نفحات الانس by Jāmī, not far from the end.

his pupils, as they followed him, noted down and published under the title of the [b] Mathnavī, a book highly esteemed in these parts.

I next proceeded to the city of [c] Lāranda,* the Sultan of which is [d] El Malik Badr Oddīn Ibn Karmān, who makes this place his capital. I met him, and was entertained with the greatest kindness as his guest.

I then proceeded to [e] Aksarā, which is one of the finest districts of Room, and subject to the king of Irāk. I next went to the city of [f] Nikda, then to [g] Kīsarīa (Cæsarea), both of which are subject to the king of Irāk. I next proceeded to the city of [h] Sīvās, which is also subject to the king of Irāk. It is a large place, and now the rendezvous of the greater part of the king's army. I next went to the city of [i] Amāsia,† then to [j] Sūnusa, then to [k] Kumash, then to [l] Arzanjān, then to Arzerrūm; all of which are subject to the king of Irāk. In [m] Arzerrum I saw the *brother* [n] Tūmān, one of *the Society of Youths*, whose age exceeded one hundred and thirty years. He was still in possession of all his faculties, and could walk wherever he wished. After receiving his blessing I proceeded to the city of [o] Birkī, the king of which was Mohammed Ibn [p] Aīdīn; I was, in company with the lecturer of this place [q] Mohyī Oddin, one of the most celebrated and reputable men of his age, introduced to the presence.

The king one day said to me, have you ever seen a stone that came down from heaven?‡ I answered, No. He continued, such a stone has fallen in the environs of our city. He then called some men and ordered them to bring the stone, which they did. It was a black, solid, exceedingly hard, and shining, substance. If weighed it would probably exceed a [r] talent.§ He then ordered some stone-cutters to come in, when four came forward. He commanded them to strike upon it. They all struck together upon it

---

[e] اقصيراي .al اقصرا .    [d] الملك بدر الدين بن قرمان .    [c] لارنده .    [b] المثنوي .

[f] نكده .al تكده .    [g] قيصاريّه .    [h] سيواس .    [i] أماصيه .    [j] سوفسي .al سونُسي . سوقُسي .

[k] كُمش .al مكش .    [l] ارزنجان .al ارزنحان . اورزنجان .    [m] ارزالروم .    [n] طومان .

[o] بِرْكي .al بِرْكى .    [p] محمد بن آيدين .    [q] محيي الدين .    [r] تبلغ قنطارا .

---

\* See D'Herbelot, under the article Mathnaoui.

† See D'Herbelot, under Amasia.

‡ For some very interesting accounts of other phenomena of this sort, see the second edition of M. De Sacy's Chrestomathie Arabe, tom. iii. pp. 437-441.

§ According to some 112, to others 120 pounds weight.

accordingly with an iron hammer four successive strokes, which, however, made not the least impression upon it. I was much astonished at this. The king then ordered the stone to be taken to its place. He sent fruit and food to us during the time we remained there; and, when I had bidden him farewell, he sent me a thousand dirhems with one hundred mithkāls of gold, as also clothing, two horses, and a slave. He also sent for my companions some dirhems and clothing separately.

I then proceeded to the city of 's Tīra, which belongs also to this prince. It is large, and abounds with gardens and water. From this place I went to the city of 't Ayāsulūk, the Emīr of which is the Sultan "u Mohammed Ibn Aīdīn, son of the Sultan of 'v Birkī; then to the city of 'w Yazmīr, which belongs to the Sultan of Birkī; its Emīr is 'x Omar Beg, one of the Sultan's sons, and a most excellent prince. I then proceeded to the city of 'y Magnesia, the Sultan of which is called 'z Sārū Khān. I then went to the city of 'a Bergama (Pergamos), of which the philosopher Plato is said to have been an inhabitant. His house is still seen here. The Sultan of this place is styled 'b Bakhshī Khān. I next went to the city of 'c Bālī Kasra, which is large and beautiful. Its governor is called 'd Damūr Khān. I then went to the city of 'e Burūsa,* which is a large place, and governed by 'f Ikhtiyār Oddīn Urkhān Beg, son of 'g Othmān Jūk. This is one of the greatest, richest, and most extensive in rule, and commanding the greatest army of all the Turkoman kings. His practice is, constantly to be visiting his fortresses and districts, and to be inquiring into their circumstances. It is said that he never remained a month in any one place. His father had con-

---

<sup>s</sup> تِيرَه .    <sup>t</sup> أَيَاسُلُوق .    <sup>u</sup> محمد بن آيدين .    <sup>v</sup> بِرِكِي .    <sup>w</sup> برمير . al. يزمير .

<sup>x</sup> عمر بيك .    <sup>y</sup> مَغْنِيسِيَه .    <sup>z</sup> صاروخان .    <sup>a</sup> بَرْغَمَه .    <sup>b</sup> بخشي خان .    <sup>c</sup> بالي كسره .

<sup>d</sup> دمور خان .    <sup>e</sup> بُرُوسَه .    <sup>f</sup> اختيار الدين اورخان بيك .    <sup>g</sup> عثمان جوق .

---

* Mr. Kosegarten has here برصي which he writes Burssa. Our copies add مدينة عظيمة a great city: and again واكثرهم مالًا وبلادًا وعساكر وهوفي اكثر اوقاته لا يزال يطوف علي حصونه &c. and again و بلاده ويتفقد احوالها ويقال له انه لم يقم شهرا كاملا ببلد قط ووالده &c. This I notice to shew, that the copies differ considerably in some instances, and to warn the reader, that, where my translation differs from Mr. Kosegarten's, he must not immediately conclude that either of us is wrong.

quered the city of Burūsa, and had besieged that of [h]Yaznīk,* nearly twenty years, but did not take it; after this his son besieged it for twelve years and took it.   In this place I met him; he received me very respectfully, and provided me with a considerable number of dirhems. I next went to Yaznīk.   It has a large lake eight miles in length; the city is also surrounded with water and trees.   I then left this place, and after some days arrived at the city of [i]Bustūnī;† after this at the city of [j]Būlī, the king of which is [k]Shāh Beg.   I then went to the city of [l]Burlū, which belongs to the governor of [m]Kastamūnia.   I then went to Kastamūnia, which is a very large and beautiful city, abounding with every delicacy, which may be purchased at a very low rate.   I saw an aged Sheikh among its inhabitants, whose age, as I was told, amounted to that of one hundred and sixty-two years.   Its Sultan was [n]Suleimān Bādshaw, a splendid, but aged man; he is a respectable and respected person.   I was introduced to him, and received very honourably.

---

## CHAPTER XII.

*Sanūb—Crim—Kirash—The Desert of Kifjāk—El Kafā, subject to Mohammed Uzbek Khān—El Sarai—Azāk—El Mājar—Bish Tāg, the Camp of Mohammed Uzbek—Ceremonies observed here—Bulgār—Mode of travelling here—Astrachan—Permission to visit Constantinople— Ukak—Mountains of the Russians—Surdāk—Bābā Saltūk.*

I THEN went on to the city of [o]Sanūb, which is large, and belongs to the governor of Kastamūnia, Soleimān Bādshaw.   I remained here some time. Leaving this place I proceeded by sea for the city of [p]El Kiram (Crim),

---

[g] يزنيك .        [h] sea) بحيرة .      [i] (Bustūnī بسطوني al. Muturnī ‏مطرني‎‡ al. ‏بُسْطوني‎).

[j] بُولي al. بِرلي .      [k] شاه بيك .      [l] برلُو al. بورلي .      [m] قصطمُونيه .

[n] سليمان بادشاه .      [o] صَنُوب .      [p] القِرم .

---

* Mr. Kosegarten has ازنيك which he writes *Isnik*.

† So Mr. Kosegarten, which he writes *Materni*.

‡ Mr. K. بولي *Boli.*   Our MSS. present here large additions to that of Mr. Kosegarten.

but suffered considerable distress in the voyage, and was very near being drowned. We arrived, however, at length, at the port of [q] El Kirash, which belongs to the desert country of [r] Kifjāk.* This desert is green and productive: it has, however, neither tree, mountain, hill, nor wood in it. The inhabitants burn dung. They travel over this desert upon a cart, which they call [s] Araba. The journey is one of six months; the extent of three of which belongs to the Sultan [t] Mohammed Uzbek Khān;† that of three more to the infidels. I hired one of these carts for my journey from the port of Kirash to the city of [u] El Kafā, which belongs to Mohammed Uzbek. The greater part of the inhabitants are Christians,‡ living under his protection. From this place I travelled in a cart to the city of [v] El Kiram, which is one of the large and beautiful cities of the districts of the Sultan Mohammed Uzbek Khān. From this place I proceeded, upon a cart which I had hired, to the city of [w] El Sarai,§ the residence of Mohammed Uzbek. The peculiarity of this desert is, that its herbs serve for fodder for their beasts: and on this account their cattle are numerous. They have neither feeders nor keepers, which arises from the severity of their laws against theft, which are these: When any one is con-

---

| | | | |
|---|---|---|---|
| [t] مُحَمَّد اوزبك خان . | [s] عربة . | [r] قِفجاق . | [q] الكِرش . |
| [w] السَّرَاي . | [v] القِرم . | [u] الكَفَا . | |

* On the origin of this name and people, see D'Herbelot's very interesting article, under Cabgiak.

† " *Uzbek Khān*, fils de Toghtagou, meurt, selon les Russes en 1341." De Guignes, Hist. gen. de Huns, tom. i. p. 287. He must, therefore, have been living when our traveller visited these parts. In tom. iv. however, pp. 284-5, it is stated that he died in 1335 or 6, and what is still more decisive the author proceeds: " on remarque que l'époque de sa mort est celle de la naissance du fameux Tamerlan. Les Arabes ont désigné cette année par ce mot de leur langue *Loudh* qui signifie *refuge*, pour fair voir que les hommes avoient besoin d'asyle dans si grandes calamités. Les lettres qui forment ce mot, en les prenent selon leur valeur numérique, désignent l'année 736 de l'Hegire." He was descended of the Mogul dynasty of Kifjāk (De Guignes, Captchaq). For some account of the movements of this prince about this time, see D'Herbelot, art. Abou-Said, and of his successors, art. Uzbek.

‡ These Christians were generally Nestorians, and were well treated for the most part under Mohammed Uzbek Khān. See Asseman's Biblioth. Orient., tom. iii. P. 2, pp. ci. and cxxi, &c., where we have some very valuable notices respecting them. See also D'Herbelot, under the articles Crim, and Solgat.

§ See D'Herbelot, under Sarai.

victed of having stolen a beast, he is compelled to return it with nine others
of equal value. But, if this is not in his power, his children are taken.
If, however, he have no children, he is himself slaughtered just like a
sheep.

After several days' journey I arrived at [x] Azāk,* which is a small town
situated on the sea-shore. In it resides an Emīr on the part of the Sultan
Mohammed, who treated us with great respect and hospitality. From
this place I proceeded to the city of [y] El Mājar, which is a large and handsome place. The Turkish women of these parts are very highly respected,
particularly the wives of the nobles and kings. These women are religious,
and prone to almsgiving and other good works. They go unveiled, however, with their faces quite exposed.

I next set out for the camp of the Sultan, which was then in a place
called [z] Bish Tāg, or *Five Mountains*, and arrived at a station to which the
Sultan with his retinue had just come before us : at this place, which is
termed the urdū, or camp, we arrived on the first of the month Ramadān. Here we witnessed a moving city, with its streets, mosques, and
cooking-houses, the smoke of which ascended as they moved along. When,
however, they halted, all these became stationary. This Sultan Mohammed Uzbek is very powerful, enjoys extensive rule, and is a subduer of the
infidels. He is one of the seven great kings of the world; which are, the
Sultan of the West, the Sultan of Egypt and Syria, the Sultan of the two
Irāks, the Sultan of the Turks Uzbek, the Sultan of Turkistān and [a] Māwarā El Nahar, the Sultan of India, and the Sultan of China.

It is a custom with Mohammed Uzbek to sit after prayer on the Friday,
under an alcove called the " golden alcove," which is very much ornamented: he has a throne in the middle of it, overlaid with silver plate,
which is gilded and set with jewels. The Sultan sits upon the throne ; his
four wives, some at his right hand,† others at his left, sitting also upon the

---

[a] ماوراء النهر .    [z] بش طاغ .    [y] الماجر.    [x] أزاق .

---

* See D'Herbelot, under Azac.

† We have here a fine illustration of the regal pomp exhibited in the 45th Psalm, where we find
the queen also enjoying the honour due to her rank, very unlike the practice of the Mohammedans, among whom they are never allowed to appear in public. We shall hereafter find something
similar to this witnessed by our traveller in the island of Sumatra.

throne. Beneath the throne stand his two sons, one on his right, the other on his left; before him sits his daughter. Whenever one of these wives enters, he arises, and taking her by the hand, puts her into her place upon the throne. Thus they are exposed to the sight of all, without so much as a veil. After this, come in the great Emīrs, for whom chairs are placed on the right and left, and on these they sit. Before the King stand the princes, who are the sons of his uncle, brothers, and near kinsmen. In front of these, and near the door, stand the sons of the great Emīrs; and behind these, the general officers of the army. People then enter, according to their rank; and saluting the King, return and take their seats at a distance. When, however, the evening prayer is over, the supreme consort, who is Queen, returns; the rest follow, each with their attendant beautiful slaves. The women, who are separated on account of any uncleanness, are seated upon horses; before their carriages are cavalry, behind them beautiful Mamlūks. Upon this day I was presented to the Sultan, who received me very graciously, and afterwards sent me some sheep and a horse, with a leathern bag of kimiz, which is the milk of a mare; and very much valued among them as a beverage.

The wives of this King are highly honoured. Each one has a mansion for herself, her followers, and servants. When the Sultan wishes to visit one of them, he sends word, and preparation is made. One of these wives is a daughter of [b]Takfūr, the Emperor of Constantinople. I had already visited each of them, and on this account the Sultan received me: this is a custom among them; and whoever fails in observing it, suffers the imputation of a breach of politeness.

I had formerly heard of the city of [c]Bulgār,* and hence I had conceived a desire to see it; and to observe, whether what had been related of it, as to the extremity of the shortness of its nights, and again of its days, in the opposite season of the year, were true or not. There was, however,

---

[c] بُلْغَار.    [b] تَكْفُور.

---

* According to the مراصد الاطلاع &c. بُلْغَار مدينة الصقالبة شديدة البرد لا يكاد البرد يقلع عن
ارضهم صيفا ولا شتاء وبناوٌهم بالخشب. Bulgār is a city of Siberia, which is extremely cold; the cold scarcely ever leaves their country either in summer or winter. Their houses are built of wood.

between that place, and the camp of the Sultan, a distance of ten days. I requested the Sultan, therefore, that he would appoint some one who would bring me thither and back, which he granted.

When, therefore, I was saying the prayer of sun-set, in that place, which happened in the month of Ramadān, I hasted, nevertheless the time for evening prayer came on, which I went hastily through. I then said that of <sup>d</sup> midnight, as well as that termed <sup>e</sup> El Witr; but was overtaken by the dawn.* In the same manner also is the day shortened in this place, in the opposite season of the year. I remained here three days, and then returned to the King.

In Bulgār, I was told of the land of darkness, and certainly had a great desire to go to it from that place. The distance, however, was that of forty days. I was diverted, therefore, from the undertaking, both on account of its great danger, and the little good to be derived from it. I was told that there was no travelling thither except upon little sledges, which are drawn by large dogs; and, that during the whole of the journey, the roads are covered with ice, upon which neither the feet of man, nor the hoofs of beast, can take any hold. These dogs, however, have nails by which their feet take firm hold on the ice. No one enters these parts except powerful merchants, each of whom has perhaps a hundred of such sledges as these, which they load with provisions, drinks, and wood: for there we have neither trees, stones, nor houses. The guide in this country is the dog, who has gone the journey several times, the price of which will amount to about a thousand dinars. The sledge is harnessed to his neck, and with him three other dogs are joined, but of which he is the leader. The others then follow him with the sledge, and when he stops they stop. The master never strikes or reprimands this dog; and when he proceeds to a meal, the dogs are fed first: for if this were not done, they would become enraged, and perhaps run away

---

<sup>e</sup> الوِتْر .          <sup>d</sup> وصليت التراويح .

---

* On the prayers and times for performing them generally among the Mahommedans, see M. de Sacy's Chrestomathie Arabe, tom. i. pp. 161-168. Of the last (الوِتْر) he takes no notice: but in the lexicons we are told that it signifies prayer generally, and that which is not prescribed, but spontaneous.

and leave their master to perish. When the travellers have completed
their forty days or stages through this desert, they arrive at the land of darkness; and each man, leaving what he has brought with him, goes back to
his appointed station. On the morrow they return to look for their goods,
and find, instead of them, sable, ermine, and the fir of the *f* sinjāb.* If then
the merchant likes what he finds, he takes it away; if not, he leaves it,
and more is added to it: upon some occasions, however, these people will
take back their own goods, and leave those of the merchant's.† In this
way is their buying and selling carried on; for the merchants know not
whether it is with mankind or demons that they have to do; no one being
seen during the transaction. It is one of the properties of these firs, that
no vermin ever enters them.

I returned to the camp of the Sultan on the 28th of Ramadān; and,
after that, travelled with him to the city of *g* Astrachan, which is one of his
cities. It is situated on the banks of the river *h* Athal,‡ which is one of
the great rivers of the world. At this place the Sultan resides during the
very cold weather; and when this river, as well as the adjoining waters,
are frozen, the King orders the people of the country to bring thousands of
bundles of hay, which they do, and then place it upon the ice, and upon
this they travel.

When the King had arrived at Astrachan, one of his wives, who was daughter to the Emperor of Constantinople, and then big with child, requested to
be allowed to visit her father, with whom it was her intention to leave her
child and then to return: this he granted. I then requested to be permitted
to go with her, that I may see Constantinople; and was refused, on account
of some fears which he entertained respecting me. I flattered him, however, telling him that I should never appear before her but as his servant
and guest, and that he need entertain no fear whatsoever. After this he
gave me permission, and I accordingly took my leave. He gave me fifteen

<hr>

*h* أَثَلَ .        *g* الحاج تَرْخَان .        *f* سِنْجَاب .

<hr>

* See an interesting note by Mr. Kosegarten on this passage, p. 24.

† Mr. Kosegarten has a small addition here, which he translates: " Principes Sinenses bene ex
iis augurantur, et summopere eas appetunt, ita ut mille circiter dinaris ibidem æstimuntur."
Immediately after this our text presents a large addition.

‡ The Volga. See D'Herbelot, under the article Etel.

hundred dinars, a dress of honour, and several horses. Each of his ladies also gave me some pieces of bullion silver, which they call El Suwam (الصوم from the singular sawma ﺻَﻮْﻣَﺔ), as did also his sons and daughters.

I set out accordingly on the 10th of the month Shawāl, in company with the royal consort [i] Bailūn, daughter to the Emperor of Constantinople. The Sultan accompanied us through the first stage, in order to encourage her, and then returned. The Queen was attended in her journey by five thousand of the King's army, about five hundred of which were cavalry, as her servants and followers. In this manner we arrived at [j] Ukak,* which is a moderately sized town but excessively cold. Between this place and [k] El Sarāi which belongs to the Sultan, there is a distance of ten days. At the distance of one day from this place are the mountains of the Russians, who are Christians, with red hair and blue eyes, an ugly and perfidious people. They have silver mines : and from their country is the [l] suwam, i. e. the pieces of silver bullion brought. With these they buy and sell, each piece weighing [m] five ounces. After ten days' journey from this place we arrived at the city of [n] Sūdāk,† which is one of the cities of the desert of [o] Kifjāk, and situated on the sea-shore. After this we arrived at a city known by the name of [p] Bābā Saltūk. Saltūk, they say, was a [q] diviner. This is the last district (in this direction) belonging to the Turks ; between which, however, and the districts of Room, is a distance of eighteen days, eight of which are over an uninhabited desert without water : but as we entered it during the cold season, we did not want much water.

---

| | | | | |
|---|---|---|---|---|
| [m] خمسة اواقي . | [l] الصوم . | [k] السَّرَاي . | [j] اُكَّك . | [i] بَيلُون . |
| [q] رجل مكاشف . | [p] بابا سَلطُوق . | [o] قفجاق . | [n] al. سُرْداق. سوداق | |

---

* Mr. Kosegarten has اكل Ukal. Our copies here present a large addition.

† This is probably the Soudak of M. D'Herbelot.

## CHAPTER XIII.

ON the occasion of my preparing to enter this desert, I presented myself
before the Queen, and paid my respects to her both in the morning and
evening. She received me very graciously, and sent to me a good part of
every present which then came to her. I then made known to her my want
of some horses: and she ordered fifteen to be given to me. After this we
arrived at the fortress of 'Mahtūlī, which is the first in the districts belonging to Room, but between which and Constantinople is a distance of two
and twenty days.

Before this time, the news of her approach had reached her father, who
sent out ladies and nurses to meet her at this fortress, with a large army.
From this place to Constantinople they travel with horses and mules only,
on account of the unevenness of the roads; she, therefore, left her carriages behind her. The Emīr who attended her husband's troops returned
when we had arrived at this place, and she was now attended by her own
followers only. At this place I also dismissed my carriages, and a number
of my attendants and companions, recommending them (to the returning
party), who received and treated them courteously.

The Queen had with her a mosque, which she set up at every stage, just
as her husband used to do. In this she had daily prayers. She left it, however, at the fortress. After this the office of the Moäzin ceased: wine was
brought into the banquet and of this she drank. I was also told, that
she ate swine's flesh with them: nor did one who prayed remain with her;
some, however, of her Turkish servants daily prayed with us. Thus were
the tastes changed by entering into the territories of infidelity. The Queen,
however, ordered the officer who had come out to meet her, to pay every
attention and respect to me. When we had arrived within a day's journey
of the city, her younger brother came out to meet her, accompanied by

ʳ حصن مهتولي .

about five thousand cavalry, all in armour. He met her on foot, on account
of his being her junior. When she had kissed his head, he passed on with
her. On the next day her second brother, who is the heir-apparent, met
her, having with him ten thousand horse. Both parties in this case dis-
mounted; and after they had met they remounted and went on. When
at length she approached Constantinople, the greatest part of its inhabitants, men, women, and children, came out attired in their best clothes,
either walking or riding, beating drums and shouting as they proceeded.
The Sultan, also, with his queen, the mother of this lady, attended by
the officers of state and nobles, came to meet her. When the Emperor
drew near both the parties mixed, and such was the pressure that it was
impossible for me to pass between them. I was therefore obliged, at the
peril of my life, to see to the carrying of our lady and her companions. I
was told, that when she met her parents she alighted and kissed the ground
before them, as well as the hoofs of their horses.

We entered Constantinople about sun-set; they were then ringing their
bells at such a rate, that the very horizon shook with the noise. When
we came to the gate of the Emperor, the porters refused to admit us without a permission from the Emperor; some of her followers, therefore, went
and told her our case, and she requested permission of her father, stating our circumstances to him. We were then allowed to enter, and were
lodged in a house adjoining that of our lady, who sent our provisions
morning and evening. The King also granted us a letter of safe conduct,
permitting us to pass wherever we pleased about the city. On the fourth
day after our arrival, I was introduced to the ⁵Sultan Takfūr, son of
George, king of Constantinople. His father George was still living, but
had retired from the world, become a monk, and given up the kingdom
to his son.* When I arrived at the fifth gate of the palace, which

---

⁵ تكفور بن جرجيس .

* The retired Emperor must have been Andronicus the elder, the present one Andronicus
junior, his grandson. In Mr. Kosegarten's extract we have نكفور Nicephorus, perhaps: but
which, or whether either of these names, is the true one, I have not been able to determine.
It is not improbable, that the name of Nicephorus Gregoras has got in here by mistake.
Nor have I been able to find in any of the historians when or where this shameful marriage was contracted. I am much tempted to believe that the Byzantine writers have been
ashamed to mention it. Gibbon, indeed, mentions such a marriage as this brought about by the

was guarded by soldiers, I was searched, lest I should carry any wea-
pon with me; which is submitted to by every citizen, as well as stranger, who wishes to be introduced to the King. The same is observed by
the Emperors of India. I was introduced, therefore, and did homage.
The Emperor was sitting upon his throne with his Queen, and daughter,
our mistress; her brothers were seated beneath the throne. I was kindly
received, and asked, as to my circumstances and arrival; also about Jerusalem, the Temple of the Resurrection,* the Cradle of Jesus,† Bethle-

---

management of John Catacuzenus: but, then, this is said to have been of his own daughter. Vol. v.
p. 278, ed. 1826. We are told in Mr. Savage's abridgment of Knolls and Rycaut's Turkish
History, that Amurath the First married the Emperor of Constantinople's daughter, but this
must be a totally different affair. The death of Andronicus the elder is placed by Gibbon in
1332. As Mr. Ulenbroek has given a very interesting note on this subject in his Iracæ Descriptio, I may perhaps be excused in giving it in this place (p. 80, proleg.) " Hinc semel iterumque,
affinitate etiam ablata, Impp. Græci Principes Mohammedanos sibi devincire studuerunt. Sic
Imp. Andronicus Palæologus senior filiam suam obtulit Cazano Mogolorum (vel uti Græci agunt,
Tocharorum) Persicorum Khano, A. 1304. Cf. Pachymeres Andronici Hist. lib. v. c. 16. Fate-
mur interim dubitari posse, an Cazanus veris Moslemis sit annumerandus. Cf. de Guignes Hist.
des Huns, tom. iv. p. 267, 270. Græci certe illum Christianorum fautorem habuisse videntur. Cf.
Pachym. lib. vi. c. 1. At de Islamismo successoris Cazani fratrisque, Gaïatseddini Mohammedis
Khodabendeh, alias Kharbenda et corrupte a Pachymere χαρμπανταν appellati, nulla certe dubi-
tatio est. Huic tamen Maria Imperatoris soror A. 1308 desponsata fuit. Cf. Pachym, lib. vii. c.
33. Nec multo interjecto tempore nupserat etiam alia Maria filia notha Imp. Andronici Toghtagou Khano Mogolorum Kapschakensium Khano, Guignesio teste, tom. i. p. 350. Hujus quoque
successori filioque Mohammedi Uzbekkhano, Moslemicis sacris deditissimo, uxorem fuisse filiam
Andronici Junioris colligas ex Kosegarteni V. C. Commentatione de Mohammedis Ibn Batutæ
Tingitani itinerario...Hæc igitur acciderunt inter A. 1333 et 1341...Denique haud ita multo post,
decessorum exemplum imitatus Joannes Cantacuzenus, circa A. 1346, filiam suam Theodoram
sive Mariam...Orkhano uxorem dedit, &c." Hence Mr. Ulenbroek thinks it probable, that Mohammedan places of worship had been tolerated before and after this time at Constantinople. I
will merely remark, that if so, it is extraordinary that neither El Harawī, who visited this city
in the thirteenth century, nor Ibn Batūta, who visited it in the fourteenth, has made any mention of the fact.

* القمامة This church, according to Edrīsī, is large, and in his days was considered as a place
of pilgrimage. His words are الكنيسة العظمى المعروفة بكنيسة القيام ويسميها المسلمون قمامة وهي
والكنيسة المحجوج اليها من جميع بلاد الروم, &c. The great church, known by " the Church of
the Resurrection," but which the Mohammedans call Kamāma. This is the church to which
pilgrimages are performed from all the parts of Room, &c. Edit. Rosenmüller, Lipsiæ, 1828.

† This is, according to El Harawī, in a cave under the temple of El Aksa; his words are

وتحت الاقصى ... مغارة يقال بها مهد عيسى بن مريم عليه السلام .

hem, and the city of Abraham (or 'Hebron), then of Damascus, Egypt, Irāk, and the country of Room; to all of which I gave suitable replies. A Jew was our interpreter. The King was much surprised at my tale; and said to his sons: Let this man be treated honourably, and give him a letter of safe conduct, He then put a dress of honour on me, and ordered a saddled horse to be given me, with one of his own umbrellas, which with them is a mark of protection. I then requested that he would appoint some one to ride about with me daily into the different quarters of the city, that I might see them. He made the appointment accordingly, and I rode about with the officer for some days, witnessing the wonders of the place. Its largest church is that of "Saint Sophia.* I saw its outside only. Its interior I could not, because, just within the door there was a cross which every one who entered worshipped. It is

---

" ايا صوفيا αγια σοφια.          ‘ مدينة الخليل or Hebron.

---

* El Harawī, who visited Constantinople in the 13th century, thus speaks of it, and of this church. وبها الاصنام النحاس والرخام والعمد والطلسمات العجيبة والمناير التي تقدم ذكرها والاثار التي ليس في الربع المسكون مثلها وبها ايا صوفيا وهي كنيسة العظمي عندهم ذكر لي ياقوت بن عبد الله التاجر الموصلي قال دخلتها وهي كما ذكرت، وفيها ثلثمائة وستين بابا ويقولون بها ملك من الملايكة مقيم بها وقد عملوا داير مكانه درازين من الذهب وله حكاية عجيبة نذكرها موضعها وسنذكر ترتيب هذه الكنيسة وهيكلها وارتفاعها وابوابها وعلوها وطولها وعرضها والعمد التي بها وعجايب هذه المدينة واوضاعها وصفة السمك التي بها وباب الذهب والابرجة الرخام والافيله النحاس وجميع ما بها من الاثار والعجايب وما فعل الملك مانويل معي من الخير والاحسان في كتاب العجايب كما تقدم ان شاء الله تعالي وهذه المدينة اكبر من اسمها فالله تعالي يجعلها دار الاسلام بمنه وكرمه ان شاء الله تعالي. In this place are statues of brass and marble, pillars and wonderful talismans, as well as the minarets already mentioned, and other monuments (of greatness) to which no equal can be found in the habitable world. Here is also Ayia Sophia (Αγια Σοφια) which is the greatest church they have. I was told by Yākūt Ibn Abd Allah, the merchant of Mosul, that he had entered it, and that it was just as I had described it. In it are 360 doors, and they say, that one of the angels resides in it. Round about his place they have made fences of gold; and the story about him is very strange, which we shall relate in its place, when I shall speak of the arrangement of this church, its size, height, its doors and their height, its length, breadth, and the pillars that are in it: also of the wonders of the city, its order, the sort of fish found in it, the gate of gold, the towers of marble, the brazen elephants, and all its monuments and wonders: and all the kindness shewn me by the king Emanuel (which I shall do), in the book of wonders (كتاب العجايب) D. V. as already mentioned. This city, which is greater than its fame, may God of his bounty and grace make the capital of Islamism!

said, that this church is one of the foundations of [v]Asaf, the son of Barachias, and nephew of Solomon. The churches, [w]monasteries, and other places of worship within the city, are almost innumerable.

When it appeared to the Turks, who had accompanied our mistress, that she still professed the religion of her father, and wished to remain with him, they requested permission to return to their own country, which she granted. She also gave them rich presents, and appointed persons to accompany them to their homes. She also requested me, that she might commend these attendants to me, giving me, at the same time, 300 dinars, with 2,000 dirhems in money; likewise dresses both of woollen and cotton cloth, as well as horses, on the part of her father. I returned, therefore, after a stay in Constantinople of one month and six days, to the place where I had left my companions, carriages, and other goods: and, from this place we travelled upon these carriages, until we arrived at Astrachan, where I had formerly left the Sultan Mohammed Uzbek Khān. But here I found that he had gone with his court to [x]El Sarāi, to which I also proceeded. When I was admitted to his presence, he asked me of our journey, of Constantinople and its king, of all which I told him. He then reimbursed my travelling expenses, as is his usual custom. This city of [y]El Sarāi is very handsome and exceedingly large. Of its learned men is the Imām, the learned [z]Noömān Oddīn, [a]El Khavārezmī. I met him in this place. He is a man of the most liberal disposition, carries himself majestically with the king, but humbly with the poor, and with his pupils. The sultan visits him every Friday, sits before him, and shews him every kindness; while he behaves in the most repulsive manner.

I then travelled on to [b]Khavārezm, between which and this place is a journey of forty days, through a desert in which there is but little water and grass. There are carriages in it, which are drawn by camels. After ten days I arrived at the city of [c]Sarāi Jūk, which is situated upon the banks of a large and full river, which they call the [d]Ulū sū or great water. Over this is a bridge joining its nearest parts, like the bridge of Bagdad. From this place I travelled for three days with all the haste

---

[z] نعمان الدين .    [x] السراي .    [y] السراي .    [x] المانسترات .    [w] آصف . [v]

[d] الوصو .    [c] سَرَاي جوق .    [b] خوارزم .    [a] الخوارزمي .

possible, and arrived at Khavārezm. This is the largest city the Turks have, and is very much crowded, on account of the multitude of its inhabitants. It is subject to the sultan Uzbek Khān, and is governed on his part by a great Emīr, who resides within it. I have never seen better bred, or more liberal, people than the inhabitants of Khavārezm, or those who are more friendly to strangers. They have a very commendable practice with regard to their worship, which is this: When any one absents himself from his place in the mosque, he is beaten by the priest in the presence of the congregation; and, moreover, fined in five dinars, which go towards repairing the mosque. In every mosque, therefore, a whip is hung up for this purpose.

Without this city is the river 'Gihon, one of the four rivers which flow from Paradise. This river, like the Athal, freezes over in the cold season and remains frozen for five months, during which time people travel over it. Without this city also, is the grave of the Sheikh ᶠNajm Oddīn the Great, one of the great saints, over which there is a cell. Here also is the grave of the very learned ᵍJār Allah El Zamakhsharī.* Zamakhshar is a village at the distance of four days from Khavārezm. The prevailing sect at Khavārezm, is that of the ʰSchismatics.† This, however, they keep secret, because the Sultan Uzbek is a Soonnee.

They have in Khavārezm a melon to which none, except that of ⁱBokhāra, can be compared: the nearest to it is that of Isphahān. The peel of this melon is green, the interior red  It is perfectly sweet and rather hard. Its most remarkable property is, that it may be cut in oblong pieces and dried, and then put into a case, like a fig, and carried to India or China. Among dried fruits there is none superior to this. It is occasionally used as a present to their kings.

---

ᵉ جيحون .        ᶠالشيخ نجم الدين الكبير .        ᵍجار الله الزمخشري .

ʰالاعتزال .        ⁱبخاري .

---

* See D'Herbelot, under Zamackschar and Zamakschari.

† On the origin and peculiarities of this sect, see Pococke's Specimen Hist. Arab. pp. 20, 214, ed. 1806. M. de Sacy's Chrest. Arab. tom. i. p. 351. Their principal dogma is a denial of predestination, and a belief that man can do either good or evil just as he pleases. They are also termed Kadarites (قدريّة) because they deny predestination.

From Khavārezm I set out for [k] Bokhāra, and, after a journey of eighteen days through a sandy and uninhabited desert, arrived at the city of [k] Ei Kāt* which is but small, then at [l] Wabkana : then, after one stage, we came to Bokhāra, which is the principal city of the country beyond the Gihon.　After it had been ravaged by the Tartars, it almost entirely disappeared :　I found no one in it who knew any thing of science.

It is said that Jengiz Khān,[†] who came with the Tartars into the countries of Islamism and destroyed them,　was in his outset a blacksmith in the country of [m] Khotā.[‡]　He was a liberal-minded, powerful, and corpulent

---

[m] الْخَطَا .　　　[l] وَبَكَنَه al دبكسه .　　　[k] الكَات .

---

* This is, perhaps, the Kāth (كاث) of the Marāsid El Itlāa, which it thus describes :

كاث بلدة كبيرة من نواحي خوارزم من شرقي جيحون وليس بشرقيه من نواحي خوارزم غيرها .

Kāth is a large city of Khavārezm (or Kharezm), on the eastern parts of the Jaihūn (or Oxus), nor is there any other eastward of it in the districts of Khavārezm.

† Our copies constantly read جنكزخان not تنكزخان with Mr. Kosegarten's.　Whatever might have been the intention of the copyist in writing his, I think there can be no doubt, that our traveller did not intentionally write " porcorum regem," as he supposes, p. 25.

The accounts given of the origin of this extraordinary man by Abulfeda (Annales Muslemici, vol. iv. p. 278-9) and others, differ in many respects from this.　It is not improbable, however, that if we were in possession of all the particulars, they could be reconciled much easier than accounts of much later date, and of events which have taken place much nearer home.　See the Rauzut El Safä, vol. v.; the History of Ghengiz Khān, by Petis La Croix ; and D'Herbelot, under Genghizhan ; also Marco Polo's account, (Travels by Mr. Marsden, chap. xliv. p. 194, with the notes).　The accounts given by these travellers agree much better with one another, than either of them does with the historians.

For accounts of the battles between Jengiz Khān, Khavarezm Shāh, and his son Jalāl Oddin, see Abulfeda, vol. iv. pp. 294–5, 368–9, &c.　Histoire des Mongols, Paris, 1824 : liv. i. ch. v. &c.

‡ In the very valuable notes of Mr. Marsden, on the Travels of Marco Polo, he gives it as his opinion, that خطا, خطاي, or ختاي, Khota, Khotai, or Kotai, is the same with Chinese Tartary, and appeals to the Oriental geographers as being of this opinion.　I can only say from all I have seen of them, that they speak very vaguely on the situation of these places.　Abulfeda, for example, who is no mean geographer, says (Ann. Mus. vol. iv. p. 228) وكان وراء الخطاء في حدود الصين التتر . عبر النهر وسار الي الخطا . i. e. " he passed the river (Gihon) and went into Khota : and there was beyond Khota on the borders of Chinese Tartary," &c. which plainly marks the places as distinct.　Again, in our text, we have Khota and China mentioned as distinct places.　Edrīsī, too, speaks of Chinese Tartary, and the أرض الاتراك as distinct places, meaning the towns, &c. which are evidently to be found in Khota.

person.  His practice was, to assemble and feast the people ; who in consequence joined him in considerable numbers, and made him their leader.
He then conquered the district in which he lived ; and, with this accession
of strength and followers,  he next subdued  the whole country of [n] Khotā,
then China : after this the countries of [o] Khashak,  [p] Kāshgar, and  [q] Mālik.*
At this time  [r] Jalāl Oddīn Sanjar, son of  [s] Khavārezm Shāh, was king of
Khavārezm, [t] Khorāsān, and [u] Māwarā El Nahr, a powerful and splendid
prince.   Jengiz Khān, on account of an affair which had happened among
the merchants, and in which some property had been taken, invaded his territories.†  This is well known.  When, however, Jengiz Khān had entered
upon the frontiers of Jalāl Oddīn's countries, he was met by the king's army,
which, after some fighting, was put to the route.  After this Jalāl Oddīn
himself met him, and some such battles took place, as have never been witnessed among the Mohammedans.

   In the event, however, Jengiz Khān got  possession of Māwarā El Nahr,
and destroyed Bokhāra, Samarkand, and [v] El Tirmidh; killed the inhabitants, taking prisoners the youth only, and leaving the country quite deso-
late.  He then passed over the Gihon, and took possession of all [w] Khorāsān
and [x] Irāk, destroying the cities and slaughtering the inhabitants.  He then
perished, having appointed his son [y] Hūlākū to succeed him.  Hūlākū (soon
after) entered Bagdad, destroyed it, and put to death the [z] Calif El Mostaa-

---

[r] جلال الدين سنجر .   [p] كاشَجر .   [q] مالتی .   [o] البَحشَتق .   [n] India هند al خطا .

[w] خراسان .   [v] الترمذ .   [u] ماوراء التّهر .   [t] خراسان .   [s] خوارزام شاه .

[z] المستعصم .   [y] هولاكو .   [x] العراق .

---

Asseman seems to me to have determined this question justly.  Biblioth. Orient. tom. iii. P. II,
p. 512.  " Primo, provinciam *Mangi*, qua Abulpharagio *Manzi*, aliis عْنوم Masin,  ماشين
*Mascin*, et  ماحين *Macin* dicitur, Sinam esse propriè dictam, cujus notissimæ urbes *Nankin*,
et *Confu* Abulpharagio et Paulo memorantur," &c.  Secundo, Chatajæ Sinæque nomine à
Syris, Arabibus, Persis, Turcisque scriptoribus septentrionalem Sinam intelligi, hoc est, eam
Sinæ partem, quæ ad celeberrimum murum, quo Tartari à Sinis dividuntur, accedit.  Tertio,
*Chan-Balek* urbem, in qua Coblaius sedem regni fixit, quam M. Paulus *Cambalu* vocat, eandem
esse ac *Pekinum*, ut Herbelotius et Renaudotius rectè monent."

   * *Almalig*, dans le voisinage des hauts montagnes *Guenk* et de mont *Cout*, &c. Histoire des
Mongols, liv. ii. ch. i. p. 376-7.

   † See an account of this affair in the Histoire des Mongols, tom. i. liv. i. chap. v. p. 148-9,
&c.  Paris, 1824.

sem of the house of Abbās, and reduced the inhabitants.\* He then proceeded with his followers to Syria, until divine Providence put an end to
his career: for there he was defeated by the army of Egypt, and made
prisoner. Thus was their progress in the Mohammedan countries put an
end to.

The epitomator Ibn Jazzī El Kelbī states, that he has been told by the
Sheikh [a] Ibn El Hāji, who had heard it from [b] Abd Allah Ibn Roshaid,
who had met [c] Nūr Oddīn Ibn El Zajāj one of the learned men of Irāk,
with his brother's son in Mecca, and who told him as they were con-
versing together, that in the war with the Tartars in Irāk not fewer than
four and twenty thousand learned men perished; and that himself, and
that man, pointing to his brother's son, were the only learned men who had
escaped.

I next proceeded from Bokhāra for the camp of the Sultan [d] Alā Oddīn
Tarmashīrīn,† and, in my way, passed by [f] Nakhshab, the place to which
the patronymic of the Sheikh [f] Abu Turāb El Nakhshabī‡ is referred.

| | | | |
|---|---|---|---|
| <sup>d</sup> علاء الدين طرمشيرين . | <sup>c</sup> نور الدين بن الزجاج . | <sup>b</sup> عبد الله بن رشيد . | <sup>a</sup> ابن الحاج . |
| | <sup>f</sup> ابو تراب النخشبي . | | <sup>e</sup> نَخشَب . |

---

\* For particulars respecting the butchery here alluded to, see the Annales Moslemici, vol.
iv.p.550-1, &c.

† This is, probably, the *Tirim Siri Khan* (ترمسيرين خان) of Dow and Ferishta, who
invaded Hindustan A. H. 727, with a numerous army, but retired without making a conquest
of it, after receiving great wealth from Mohammed Shāh. Dow, vol. i. p. 314. See also the
extract from De Guignes a little lower down. Some account of the exploits of this prince in
the neighbourhood of Ghizna, is also to be found in the first volume of the مطلع السعدين by
عبد الرزاق السمرقدي under the date of 732 of the Hegira, A.D. 1331. This name is written
in the Tārīkhi Badāyūnī (تاريخ بدايوني) ترمه شيرين .

‡ A short account of this recluse is given in the نفحات الانس of which the following is an
extract: ابو تراب نخشبي قدس الله تعالي سره از طبقه اول است نام وي عسكر بن حصين است
وكفته اند كه عسكر بن محمد بن الحصين از جمله، مشايخ خراسانست بعلم فتوة وزهد وتوكل وبا
ابو حاتم عطار بصري وحاتم اصم صحبت داشته است استاد ابو عبد الله جلاد وابو عبيد الله بسروي
(بسري) است ابو تراب با سيصد ركوه دار در باديه شد دو تن با وي ماندند ابو عبد الله جلاد
وابو عبيد بسري و ديكر همه باز كشتند ووي كفته كه عارف آنست كه هيچ چيزي اورا تيره نكند
وهمه چيز باو روشن شود ..... وابو تراب در باديه در نماز بود باد سموم ويرا بسوخت يكسال بر

From this place I proceeded to the camp of the Sultan, the king of Māwarā El Nahr. This is a powerful prince, who has at his command a large army, and is remarkable for the justice of his laws. The territories of this king occupy a middle station among those of the four great kings of the world, who are, the king of China, that of India, that of Irāk, that of the Turks Mohammed Uzbek Khān: all of whom send presents to him, give him the place of honour, and very highly respect him. He succeeded to the kingdom after his brother Jagatai, who was an infidel, and had succeeded to his elder brother ⁸ Kobak, who was also an infidel: he was, nevertheless, just, and much attached to the Mohammedans, to whom he paid great respect.

It is said that this king Kobak was one day talking with the doctor and preacher ʰ Badr Oddīn El Maidānī, when he said to him: you say that God has left nothing unmentioned in his book. The preacher replied, it is even so. Shew me, then, said he, where my name is to be found. The reply was, In the passage (في اي صورة ماشا' ركبك) '' In which form he pleased hath he fashioned thee.''* This astonished him, and he said, ʲ Bakhshī, that is, well done! I spent some days in the camp of Tarmashīrīn. Upon a certain day, however, I went to the mosque, which was in the camp (the camp they call the Urdū) for I had heard that the Sultan was to be in the mosque. When the service was ended, I approached in order to pay my respects to him, as he had heard of my arrival. He was pleased with me, and treated me very respectfully. After this he sent for me. I went to

---

ʲ نبخشي يعني جيّد.    ʰ بدرالدين الميداني.    ⁸ كُبَك.

---

Abu Turāb . باي بماند در سنه خمس واربعين وماىتين درآن سال كه ذو النون برفت از دينا Nakshabī, may God sanctify his mystery, was (a saint) of the first class; his name was Askar Ibn Hasīn: they also say, that Askar Ibn Mohammed Ibn Hasīn was one of the Sheikhs of Khorāsān, famous for his knowledge of decisions, piety, and faith. He was associated with Abu Hātim Attār of Basra, and Hātim Asamm. He was also the preceptor of Abu Abd Allah Jallād, and of Abu Obeid Allah Basarī. This Abu Turāb went with three hundred Rukwah Dārs (i. e. I suppose, persons clothed in rags as religious). Two of these remained with him, namely, Abu Abd Allah Jallād, and Abu Obeid Basari, all the rest returned. It is one of his sayings: That is an enlightened man, whom nothing perplexes, and with whom every thing is clear. He was at his prayers in the desert, when he was scorched by the samoom, and remained for a whole year standing on his feet; this happened in the year 245, the year in which Dhu El Nūn departed this life.

* This passage occurs a few lines from the beginning of the 82d chapter of the Koran.

him, and found him in his tent, and there paid my respects to him. He then asked me of Mecca, Medina, Jerusalem, Damascus, and Egypt; as also of El Malik El Nāsir, the kings of Irāk, and Persia. To all of which I gave suitable answers, and received marks of distinction. One of the odd things that happened respecting him, was, that once when the hour of prayer had arrived, and the people were assembled in the mosque, the Sultan delayed. One of his young men coming in, said to the priest [k]Hasām Oddīn El Yāghī, the Sultan wishes you to wait a little. Upon this the priest got up and said: I ask, are prayers had here for the sake of God, or of Tarmashīrīn? He then ordered the Moazin to proclaim the prayers. So the Sultan came in after two prostrations had been performed, and went through his prayers at the extremity of the part in which the people stand, and which is near the door of the mosque where they usually leave their mules, and there went through what he had missed. He then came and seized the hand of the priest, who laughed heartily at him. He then sat down in the oratory, the priest by his side, and I by the side of the priest. He then addressed me. When, said he, you go back to your own country say, that a doctor of the Persians sat thus with the Sultan of the Turks (al. that a poor man of the poor of the Persians thus did with the Sultan of the Turks). This priest it was who succeeded in reducing the King to the observance of all the positive and negative commands. The Sultan very much respected, loved, and obeyed him. But the Sheikh accepted of no gifts from the King; nor did he eat any thing but what he acquired by the labour of his own hands. This King, when I wished to travel on, provided me with 700 dinars for my journey. We broke up our intercourse, therefore, and I set out accordingly.

This Tarmashīrīn (it may be remarked) had broken some of the statutes of his grandfather Jengiz Khān, who had published a book entitled [l]El Yasāk*, *the prohibition*, which enacted, that whosoever should oppose

---

[k] حسام الدين الياغي .   [l] اليساق .

---

* Makrizi mentions this work as containing the regulations of Jengiz Khān, and calls it
ياسا yāsā, and يسق yasak. From this word, according to him, originated the word سياسة Siyāsat,
now in use among the Arabs to signify *government*, or *punishment*. See the Chrestomathie
Arabe of M. de Sacy, tom. ii. pp. ٥٨-٥٩ and 160, edit. 2, where we have a short account

any one of these statutes, should be put out of office. Now, one of the statutes was this, that the descendants of Jengiz, the governors of the several districts, the wives of the nobles, and the general officers of the army, should assemble upon a certain day in the year which they call [m] El Tawa, *i. e.* the feast; and, that should the Emperor have altered any one of these statutes, the nobles should stand up and say, Thou hast done so and so upon such and such a day, and hast made an alteration in the statutes of El Yasāk (*i. e.* that which is not to be changed), and, therefore, thy deposition is a necessary consequence. They are then to take him by the hand, and remove him from the throne, and to place in it another of the descendants of Jengiz Khān. And, should any one of the nobles have committed any crime, he is to be duly adjudged on this occasion.

Now, Tarmashīrīn had entirely abolished the observance of this day, which gave very great offence. Some time, therefore, after we had left the country, the Tartars, together with their nobles, assembled and deposed him, appointing for a successor one of his relations : and to such an extent was the matter pressed, that Tarmashīrīn took to flight and was put to death.[*]

I then proceeded to Samarkand, which is a very large and beautiful city. Without it is the tomb of [n] Kotham, son of Abbās, who was martyred on the day the city was taken. After this I arrived at the city of [o] Nasaf,[†]

---

[m] الطوي .        [n] قثم .        [o] نَسَف .

---

of these regulations. See also tom. v. des Notices et Extraits des Manuscrits de la Bibliothèque du Roi, pp. 592, &c. The author of the Histoire des Mongols, Paris, 1824, says, tom. i. p. 296, " Ses statuts ne sont point parvenus jusqu'à nous; on n'en trouve que quelques extraits dans les auteurs de cette époque," &c.

[*] De Guignes (Hist. gen. des Huns, tom. iv. p. 311) gives us, under the date 1342, the following notice of this prince : " Après sa mort (Dgelaleddin) l'empire fut donné à Beghi, qui eut pour successeur Bougha-timour, ensuite à Doizi-khan fils de Barak. Après eux regnèrent successivement Kendgik, &c. et Daouatmour-khan, &c. Celui-ci eut pour successeur son frère Turmeschirin, qui se fit Musulman, et qui le premier ordonna à tous ses sujets d'embrasser cette religion, dont il ne se trouvoit plus de traces parmi les Mogols, depuis que Berrak-khan en avoit fait autrefois profession. Ce prince fut detrôné par son frère Butun-khan qui lui succeda, et qui éprouva un pareil sort de la part de son frère Zenkechi."

[†] This place, according to the Marāsid El Itlāa, is مدينة كبيرة الاهل والرستاق بين جاحون وسمرقند لها فهندر (قهندز) وربض وابواب اربعة وهي في مستواة والجبال منها علي فرسخين فيها

to which the patronymic of Abu Jaafar Omar El Nasafī is referred. I then went on to the city of ᴾ Tirmidh, to which is referred the patronymic of Abu Īsa Mohammed El Tirmidhī, author of the ᵠ Jāmia El Kebīr.* This is a large and beautiful city, abounding with trees and water. We then passed over the Gihon into Khorāsān; and, after a journey of a day and half over a sandy desert in which there was no house, we arrived at the city of ʳ Balkh,† which now lies in ruins. It has not been rebuilt since its destruction by the cursed Jengiz Khān. The situation of its buildings is not very discernible, although its extent may be traced. It is now in ruins, and without society.

Its mosque was one of the largest and handsomest in the world. Its pillars were incomparable: three of which were destroyed by Jengiz Khān, because it had been told him, that the wealth of the mosque lay concealed

---

ʳ بَلخ .    ᵠ الجامع الكبير .    ᵖ ترمد .

يلي كشر ولها قري كثيرة وليس بها نهر جار سوي نهر يجري في وسط المدينة وينقطع في بعض السنة a city great in inhabitants and independent villages, and situated وزروعهم وبساتينهم علي الابار between the Jaïhūn (Oxus river) and Samarcand. It has a citadel, suburbs, and four gates, and it is in a plain. The hills are about two farsangs from it, and adjoining Kashar. It has many villages but no river except one which runs through the middle of the city. It fails however in some seasons of the year. Their tillage and gardens are near wells.

* Among the several works bearing this title in Haji Khalfa, I find none ascribed to this author. He notices it, however, under the title جامع الصحيح . There appears also to be some notice of him in the نفحات الانس by Jāmī, under the name Abu Bekr El Warāk El Tirmidhī, which is as follows. ابو بكر الوراق الترمذي قدس الله تعالي سره از طبقه ثانيه است نام وي محمد بن عمر الحكيم الترمذي است باصل از ترمذ بود وقبر وي آنجاست اما بلخ بودي خال ابو عيسي ترمذي است صاحب مسند , &c. Abu Bekr El Warāk El Tirmidhī was (a saint) of the second rank. His name was Mohammed Ibn Omar El Hakīm El Tirmidhī. He was originally of Tirmidh (Termed of our maps), and his grave is now there, but was in Balkh. He was the paternal uncle of Abu Isa of Tirmidh, author of the Musnad (مسند or book of cases); which is probably the work styled الجامع الكبير by Ibn Batūta. A copy of this work is to be found at Oxford. See Uri's Catalogue, No. clxxxvii; D'Herbelot, art. Giame al. Kebir; and Ann. Muslem. tom. ii· p. 275.

† A well known city in Khorāsān, famous in history and for its wealth: between this place and Tirmidh is a distance of twelve farsangs. مدينة مشهورة بخراسان من اجلها واشهرها ذكرا واكثرها , &c. خيرا وبينها وبين ترمذ اثني عشر فرسخا - مراصد الاطلاع

under them, provided as a fund for its repairs. When, however, he had destroyed them, nothing of the kind was to be found; the rest, therefore, he left as they were.

The story about this treasure arose from the following circumstance. It is said, that one of the Califs of the house of Abbās was very much enraged at the inhabitants of Balkh, on account of some accident which had happened, and, on this account, sent a person to collect a heavy fine from them. Upon this occasion, the women and children of the city betook themselves to the wife of their then governor, who, out of her own money, built this mosque; and to her they made a grievous complaint. She accordingly sent to the officer, who had been commissioned to collect the fine, a robe very richly embroidered and adorned with jewels, much greater in value than the amount of the fine imposed. This, she requested might be sent to the Calif as a present from herself, to be accepted instead of the fine. The officer accordingly took the robe, and sent it to the Calif; who, when he saw it, was surprised at her liberality, and said: This woman must not be allowed to exceed myself in generosity. He then sent back the robe, and remitted the fine. When the robe was returned to her, she asked, whether a look of the Calif had fallen upon it; and being told that it had, she replied: No robe shall ever come upon me, upon which the look of any man, except my own husband, has fallen. She then ordered it to be cut up and sold; and with the price of it she built the mosque, with the cell and structure in the front of it. Still, from the price of the robe there remained a third, which she commanded to be buried under one of its pillars, in order to meet any future expenses which might be necessary for its repairs. Upon Jengiz Khān's hearing this story, he ordered these pillars to be destroyed; but, as already remarked, he found nothing.

In the front of the city is, as it is reported, the tomb of 'Akāsha Ibn Mohsin El Sahābī; who, according to what is related in the 'Athar (a book so called), entered paradise without rendering up an account (of his deeds).

After this I travelled from Balkh for seven days, on the mountains of "Kūhistan, which consist of villages closely built. In these there are

---

many cells of religious, and others who have retired from the world. I
next came to the city of [x]Herāt, which is the largest inhabited city in
Khorāsān. Of the large cities of this district there are four: two of these
are now inhabited, namely, Herāt and [y]Nīsābūr; and two in ruins, namely
Balkh and [z]Meraw. The inhabitants of Herāt are religious, sincere, and
chaste, and are of the sect of [a]Hānīfa. The King of Herāt was at this
time the Sultan, the great Hosain son of the Sultan [b]Giāth Oddīn El
Gaurī, a man of tried valour.* From Herāt I went to [c]Jām,† which is a
moderate sized city, abounding with water and plantations. From this
place I went to [d]Tūs, one of the largest cities of Khorāsān. In this the
Imām [e]Abu Hāmed El Ghazālī‡ was born, and in it we still find his tomb.
From this place I went to the Meshhed of [f]El Riza, i. e. of [g]Ali Ibn

---

[x]هراة . [y]نيسابور . [z]مَرَوْ . [b]المعظم حسين ابن السلطان غياث الدين الغوري . [a]حنيفه .

[c]الجام . [d]طوس . [e]الغزالي . [f]الرضي . [g]الكاظم .

---

* The dynasty, however, as such, ceased long before this time, according to Abulfeda, vol.
iv. p. 228-9. For the origin of it see Dow, vol. i. p. 143. This, however, is the " Malek
Azzeddin-houssaïn, fils de Gaïatheddin" of De Guignes, who reigned in Herāt from about 1331 to
1370. Hist. gen. des Huns, tom. i. p. 416; also tom. iv. p. 313, &c.; and D'Herbelot, under
Schamseddin. In the first volume of the مطلع سعدين *Matlai Saadain*, we have the following
account of this prince and his dependents: درسال واقعه بادشاهي ابو سعيد چهارسال بود كه ملك
معزالدين حسين حكومت هرات ميكرد بعد از واقعه سلطان حكام عراق وخراسان يكديكررا كردن
نمي نهادند ودر هر كوشه متغلبي سر بر آورد وهر جانب متعدي خيال در سر آورد اشراف اطراف
واعيان بلدان بآن وازه عدل واحسان روي بدار الامان هراة آوردند ودر ظلال مرحمت ملك معز
الدين حسين مرفيه احوال شدند حضرت معزي بسيرت حميده وخصلت پسنديده همه را در
پناه عاطف وظل رافت قرارداده از فيض مكرمت وسحاب موهبت او فيض سراب كشتند .&c , " In
the year of the death of Abu Saïd, it was the fourth in which the king Moïz Oddīn Husain
had reigned in Herāt. After the death of the Sultan (i. e. Abu Saïd), the Governors of Irāk and
Khorāsān refused submission to each other; and hence a pretender set up his head in every
corner, as did every ultra become vain in every part, and hence the nobles and gentry of
every district betook themselves to Herāt, a place where justice, kindness, and safety, was to
be found; and under the shadow of the king Moïz Oddīn Husain they were quiet. This
personage was of laudable and prepossessing manners, and protected and amply provided for all
who sought refuge with him." This confirms Ibn Batūta's account, see p. 48.

† The birth-place of the celebrated Jāmī, author of various Persian and Arabic works.

‡ A celebrated writer on the Mohammedan sects, often cited by the author of the Dabistān and
the learned Pococke. See Specimen Hist. Arab, p. 356, edit. 1806.

Mūsa El Kāzim son of Jaafar Sādik. It is a large and well peopled
city, abounding with fruits. Over the Meshhed is a large dome, adorned
with a covering of silk, and golden candlesticks. Under the dome, and
opposite to the tomb of El Riza, is the grave of the Calif Hārūn El
Rashīd.\* Over this they constantly place candlesticks with lights. But
when the followers of Ali enter, as pilgrims, they kick the grave of El
Rashīd, but pour out their benedictions over that of El Riza. From this
place I went to the city of [h] Sarakhas,† then to [i] Zāva, the town of the
Sheikh [k] Kotb Oddīn Haidar, from whom the Fakeers of the sect called the
Haidarīa,‡ take their name. These men place an iron ring on their hands
and their necks; and, what is still more strange, on their virilia, in order
to prevent intercourse with women.

From this place I went to [l] Nīsābūr, one of the four principal cities of
Khorāsān. It is also called *the Little Damascus*, on account of the abundance of its fruits. The city is handsome, and is intersected by four rivers.
I here met the Sheikh [m] Kotb Oddīn El Nīsābūrī, a learned and accomplished preacher, and he took me to his house. It happened that I had

[m] قطب الدين النيسابوري .   [l] نيسابور .   [k] قطب الدّين حيدر .   [i] زَاوَ .   [h] سَرَخَس .

---

\* He died in Tūs, during an expedition he had undertaken into those parts. His general
character is, that he was any thing but religious, but nevertheless a bigotted Soonnee.

† Written according to the مراصد الاطلاع Sarakhas and Sarkhas (سَرَخَس and سَرَخَس). It is,
it is added, an ancient and large city in Khorāsān, in the mid-way between Nīsābūr and Meraw.
It is much subject to drought, having only one river, which is dry a great part of the year. The
people generally drink water from wells. سرخس ... مدينة قديمة من نواحي خراسان كبيرة بين
نيسابور ومرو في وسط الطريق وهي مدينة معطشة ليس بها ماء الا نهريجري في بعض السنة وشربهم
عند انقطاعه من الابار العذيبية

‡ I have not been able to find any other particular account, either of this Sheikh or of his
sect. In M. de Sacy's Chrestomathie Arabe, we have an account of a Sheikh Haider, who
appears to have been the leader of a sect in Khorāsān, and who discovered the use of the intoxicating herb called the khashīsha; but it may be doubted whether this is the person meant by
Ibn Batūta, because we have a different name given here from that given by him. See
Chrest. Arabe, tom. i. p. ٧٧; *i. e.* in Ibn Batūta we have قطب الدين حيدر, but in M.
de Sacy الشيخ حيدر الاديب محمد بن الاعمى الدمشقي; if the title in the traveller is not a
mere epithet. M. de Sacy says in his notes (p. 244) that he has not been able to find any
particulars respecting the life of this sheikh.

purchased a slave. The Sheikh said to me: Sell him, for he will not suit you; and I sold him accordingly. I was told, after a few days, that this slave had killed some Turkish children, and had been executed in consequence. This was one of the Sheikh's great miracles.

From this place I proceeded to [n]Bastām, the town to which the patronymic of [o]Abu Yezīd El Bastāmī is referred.* His grave is also here, under the same dome with that of one of the sons of Jaafar Sādik. I next proceeded to [p]Kundus and Baghlān, which are villages with cultivated lands adjoining each other. In each of these is a cell for the sainted and recluse. The land is green and flourishing, and its grass never withers. In these places I remained for some time for the purpose of pasturing and refreshing my beasts.

After this I proceeded to the city of [q]Barwan,† in the road to which is a high mountain, covered with snow and exceedingly cold; they call it the [r]Hindū Kush,‡ i. e. Hindoo-slayer, because most of the slaves brought thi-

---

" بَسْطَام .  ° اَبو يزيد البِسْطَامِي .  P قُنْدُس وبَغْلَان .  q بَرْوَن al. بردن al. بَرْوَن .  r هِنْدو كُش .

* Some account will be found of this devotee in Pococke's Specimen Hist. Arab. p. 372, edit. 1806, and also in the نفحات انس of Jāmi, of which the following is an extract: ابو يزيد بسطامي قدس الله تعالي روحه از طبقهٔ اول است نام وي طيغفور (طيفور Pococke) بن عيسي بن سروشانست جد او كبري بوده مسلمان شده از اقران احمد بن خضرويه وابو حفص ويحيي معاذ است وشقيق بلخي را ديده بود وفات او در سنه احدي وستين ومايتين بوده ودر سنه اربع وثلثين نيز گفته اند وأول درست تر است واستاد وي كردوي بوده است وصيت كرده كه قبر من فروتر از استاد من نهيد حرمت استادرا ووي از اصحاب راي بوده ليكن ويرا ولايتي نيامد در آن بديد كشاد كه مذهب, &c. Abu Yezīd Bastāmī, may God sanctify his spirit, was (a saint) of the first class. His name was Taiafūr (Pococke *Taifūr*) Ibn Isa Ibn Sarūshān. His grandfather was a Guebre, but became a Mussulmān. He was contemporary with Ahmed Ibn Khizrawa, Abu Hafīz, and Yahya Maādh; and he saw Shakīki Balkhī. His death happened in the year 261. They also say in the year 234, but the first is the most correct. His preceptor was Kardawī. He mentioned it as his will, that his grave should be made deeper than that of his master; this was done out of respect to him. He was a man of opinion, and the leader of a sect, which however never became general. Notices of the other persons here mentioned occur within a page or two in the same work.

† Perhaps the *Budaoon* of Dow (vol. i. p. 157) and the بداون of Ferishta.

‡ This Mr. Burckhardt gives in his abstract of these Travels in Nubia, p. 535, *Hindwaksh*, where he has not only disregarded the vowels given in the MSS., but has shewn that he must have been an entire stranger to the Persian language, as accurately given and translated here by our traveller.

ther from India die on account of the intenseness of the cold. After this
we passed another mountain, which is called [s] Bashāi. In this mountain
there is a cell inhabited by an old man, whom they call [t] Atā Evliā, that is,
the Father of the Saints. It is said that he is three hundred and fifty years
old. When I saw him he appeared to be about fifty years old. The people of these parts, however, very much love and revere him. I looked at
his body : it was moist, and I never saw one more soft. He told me, that
every hundredth year he had a new growth of hair and teeth, independently
of the first, and that he was the Raja [u] Aba Rahim Ratan of India, who
had been buried at [x] Multān,* in the province of Sindia. I asked him of
several things ; but very much doubted as to what he was, and do so still.

I next arrived at the city of Barwan. In this place I met the Turkish
Emīr [y] Barantay, the largest and fattest man I had ever seen. He treated
me very respectfully, and gave me some provisions. I then went on to the
village of [z] El Jarkh, and thence to [a] Ghizna, the city of the warrior of the
faith, and against India, the victorious Mahmūd, son of [b] Subuktagīn.†
His grave is here. The place is exceedingly cold : it is ten (al. three) stages
distant from [c] Kandahār. It was once a large city ; but is now mostly in
ruins. I then went on to [d] Kābul, which was once a large city ; but is
now, for the most part, in ruins. It is inhabited by a people from Persia
whom they call the [e] Afghāns.‡ Their mountains are difficult of access,

---

[s] بُشَاي .    [t] اَطَا اَوْلِيَا .    [u] ابا رهم رتن .    [x] مِلتَان .    [y] بَرَنطِيه al. بُرنطِيه .

[z] الجَرْخ .    [a] غَزنَه .    [b] محمد بن سُبُكتِكِين .    [c] القَندَهَار .    [d] كَابِل .    [e] الافغَان .

---

* See a note on this place in Mr. Kosegarten, p. 27.

† An abridgment of Ferishta's reign of Mahmood will be found in Dow's Hindostan, vol. i.
p. 52, &c.

‡ These people, according to their own statements, are descended from the house of Israel,
and of the family of Saul the first Israelitish king. Ibn Shah Aālam of the tribe of Kot'h Khail,
author of the Kholāsut El Ansāb, himself an Afghān, and a most sedulous enquirer, as he tells
us, into their history, gravely affirms, that nothing can be more certain than that this is their
origin. He then goes on to say, that they originally resided on Solomon's mount in Syria ; but
upon some emergency migrated to Candahār, whence many of them made their way into Hindustan, and were of considerable use in assisting Mahmūd of Ghizna, to make his first conquest
in that country. He also tells us, that his ancestors, hearing in Candahār of the teaching of
Mohammed, sent a deputation to him into Arabia, to inquire whether he was or not, the last

having narrow passes. These are a powerful and violent people; and the greater part of them highway robbers. Their largest mountain is called the mountain of Solomon. It is said that when Solomon had ascended this mountain, and was approaching India from it, and saw that it was an oppressive country, he returned refusing to enter it. The mountain was therefore called after his name : upon this the king of the Afghāns resides.

We next left Kābul by the way of *Kirmāsh which is a narrow pass situated between two mountains, in which the Afghāns commit their robberies. We, thank God, escaped by plying them with arrows upon the heights, throughout the whole of the way. The next place we arrived at was *Shish Naghār, which is situated at the extremity of the Turkish dominions. From this place we entered the great desert, which is fifteen days in extent. In this no one can travel except in one season out of the four, on account of the Samoom, by which putrefaction takes place, and the body as soon as dead falls to pieces in its several members. We got to the *Panj Ab, (*i. e.* the five waters,) in safety. This is the junction of five different rivers, and which waters all the agriculture of the district. We were comfortable enough when we got on the river, which happened in the beginning of the month Moharram, A.H. 734, (A.D. 1332). From this place the informers wrote of our arrival to the court of the Emperor of India. It is a custom with them, that every one who enters India with a wish to see the Emperor, must be described in writing from this place, stating the particu-

---

*b* بنج آب .      *a* شِش نَغار .      *a* كَرْماش .

---

Prophet mentioned in the law and the gospels; and that, upon being assured of this, the whole nation at once received the faith. If there were the least possible approximation to truth in the story of their descent, it is reasonable to suppose, that their language would either be pure Hebrew, or a dialect very nearly approaching it : but the truth is, as far as I can learn, that nothing like this is the fact: but quite the contrary. This boasted descent is, therefore, a fable ; as very probably their early attachment to the faith of Mohammed is. Some, indeed, have been credulous enough to believe this story of descent ; and thence to imagine, that in them they had discovered the ten tribes of the house of Israel ; which, however, is more than the Afghāns themselves imagine. That part of all the twelve tribes of Israel returned from the captivity, except such has had become real heathens, the New Testament will not allow us for a moment to doubt. (See Acts xxvi. 7. James i. 1.) I do not, therefore, see the least probability of finding them either in Candahār or elsewhere. Some part of the modern history of the Afghāns may probably be true.

lars of his person and the objects he has in view, which is sent off by a
courier.  For no one is allowed to appear at court, unless the Emperor has
been previously acquainted with all the circumstances of his case.

---

## CHAPTER XIV.

*The River Sinde—Multān—Jarāi—El Sāmira a Hindū Sect—Sīvastān—Natural Productions
—Description of Couriers — Lahari —Bakār — Uja— The Bow  a measure of Strength—
Abūhar—Natural Productions of Hindūstān—Passes a Desert infested by Hindu Robbers—
Ajūdahan—The Custom of burning Widows—Drowning in the Ganges—Sarsatī—Masūd Abād
—Dehli, description of.*

THE river (just mentioned) is the Sinde : it is the greatest river in the
world, and overflows during the hot weather just as the Nile does; and
at this time they sow the lands.   Here also commence the territories of the
Emperor of Sindia and India, who was at this time Mohammed Shāh.
From this place also is the description of persons arriving sent in writing to
the Emīr of *c*Sindia to Multān.   Their Emīr, at this time, was one of the
Mamlūks of the Sultan *d*Mohammed Sar Tīz Shāh, *i. e. sharp-head,* by
name; who reviews the armies of the Emperor.   I next proceeded to the
city of *e* Janāi,* in which is a people called *f* El Sāmira.†   They never eat

---

ٱلسَّامِرِهْ *f* .          جَنَاي *e* .          سِرْ تِين .al سِرْ تِيز *d* .          مُلْتَان .al مُلْتَان *c* .

---

* I do not find any place in the geographers corresponding sufficiently near to this in name and
situation to determine where it is.

† The name of a sect of Hindoos, of which we find occasional mention in the Dahistān.  They
are perhaps called Sāmira, as being a sort of legalists, samārat (سمارت) according to the
Dabistān, signifying law شرع .  We are told by the author of that work, that he saw one of
them, and him he describes very nearly in the words of Ibn Batūta : وازين طايفه نامه نكار سري
منيرام برهمن را در دار السلطنت لاهور ديد كه از مسلمانان غذا در نپذيرفتي وبا بيكانه كيشان
Of  نفرمود وقبول داد بدو رويبه لك سه مسلمانان امراي از يكي وميكفتند نداشتي صحبت .
this sect, the writer saw Sri Manī Rāma the Brahman in the capital of Lahore, who would
take no eatable from a Mohammedan, nor would associate with any of another persuasion.  They
said too, that one of the Mussulmān Emīrs offered him three lacks of rupees, which, however,
he would not accept of.

with strangers, nor are seen eating by them : nor do they contract affinities, or suffer any one to contract affinities with them. It was here I met the Sheikh [g] El Sālih El Aābid the religious Bahā Oddīn El Korashī (see p. 7), one of the three, of whom the Sheikh El Walī Borhān Oddīn El Aahraj said in Alexandria, that I should meet them in my travels : and I certainly did meet them. May God be praised.

I then proceeded to the city of [h] Sīvastān, which is large. Without it is a desert, and in this is there no tree except the [i] Egyptian thorn, nor do they sow any thing on the banks of its river except the [j] melon. They generally live upon a sort of [k] millet, [l] peas, fish, and milk of the buffalo : for the buffalo is here in great abundance. The place is exceedingly hot : from Multān, the capital of Sindia, it is at a distance of ten days; but from Multān to Dehli, the residence of the Emperor of Hindūstān, is a distance of fifty ; which, however, will be traversed by the courier with his despatches in five.

There are in Hindūstān two kinds of couriers; horse and foot : these they generally term [m] El Wolāk.* The horse courier, which is part of the Sultan's cavalry, is stationed at the distance of every four miles. As to the foot couriers, there will be one at the distance of every mile, occupying three (consecutive) stations, which they term [n] El Davāh, and making (in the

ᵍالشيخ الصالح العابد الزاهد بهآ الدين القرشي . ʰسيوستان al. سيوستان . ⁱام غَيلان .

ⁿالدواه . ᵐالوُلاق . ˡالجلبان . ᵏالذره . ʲالبطيخ .

* i. e. *Quick, hasting*, &c. from the Arabic root ولق, properavit, &c. The Eastern couriers are generally some part of the King's forces, and when the despatches are important are officers of distinction, as it is the case in our own military affairs. These among the ancient Hebrews were generally termed רצים *runners*, a term perfectly synonymous with that used here, ولق or دواٴه (which is perhaps an erroneous reading for دوان the Persian word for *runner*.) This will elucidate an obscure passage in the 19th Psalm, v. 5. where we have " rejoiceth as a *strong man* to run a race." The word answering to *strong* man, is in the original גִּבּוֹר, which means *hero*. In the translation too we have *a race*; but, as we know of no races among the Hebrews, we are reduced to some difficulty as to what could here have been intended by the writer. In the original, however, we have אֹרַח, which means nothing more than a way, road, or path : and the sense is, rejoiceth as a hero to run the road; *i. e.*, to bear the despatches of his master with the greatest possible celerity and safety. This makes the whole passage easy and plain : it exhibits the sun as an officer honoured by the Almighty to bear the announcement of his powers, through every clime of his dominion, in a language silent but expressive, and equally intelligible to all.

whole) three miles: so that there is, at the distance of every three miles, an inhabited village; and without this, three sentry-boxes, in which the couriers sit, prepared for motion, with their loins girded. In the hand of each is a whip about two cubits long, and upon the head of this are small bells. Whenever, therefore, one of the couriers leaves any city, he takes his despatches in the one hand, and the whip which he constantly keeps shaking in the other. In this manner he proceeds to the nearest foot-courier; and, as he approaches, he shakes his whip. Upon this out comes another, who takes the despatches, and so proceeds to the next. For this reason it is, that the Sultan receives his despatches in so short a time. In Sīvastān I met the aged Sheikh Mohammed of °Bagdad,* who told me, that his age was then one hundred and forty years; and, that he was present when the Calif ᵖEl Mostaasem was killed by the Tatars in the environs of Bagdad.

I then proceeded by the Sinde to the city of ᵠLāharī,† which is situated upon the shores of the Indian sea, where the Sinde joins it. It has a large harbour, into which ships from Persia, Yemen, and other places put. At the distance of a few miles from this city, are the ruins of another, in which stones in the shape of men and beasts almost innumerable are to be found. The people of this place think, that it is the opinion of their historians, that there was a city formerly in this place, the greater part of the inhabitants of which were so base, that God transformed them, their beasts, their herbs, even to the very seeds, into stones; and indeed stones in the shape of seeds are here almost innumerable.

I next proceeded to ʳBakār,‡ which is a handsome city, divided by an

---

ʳ بَكَّار .      al. لَاهَرِي al. الَاهَرِي      ᵠ الَاهِوِي      ᵖ المُستعصم .      ° محمد البغدادي .

---

* Instead of this we have in Mr. Kosegarten, " Et in ea incidi in illius loci concionatorem cui nomen Esscheibâni. Exhibuit mihi litteras quibus fidelium princeps Omar ben abd el asis Ommavida, quodam illius ab avo concionatoris Ssciwestanici munus contulit. Posteri hereditario jure munus retinent, litteras servant faustaque sibi ex iis augurantur."

† This is, no doubt, the Larry Bundur of Major Rennell, see his map of Hindustan, with the Memoir, pp. 285, &c. Mr. Kosegarten has لَاهَرِيَة Lahariat.

‡ Of this place we have no notice in Major Rennell, either in the Memoir or the map. It may have been destroyed, however, since the times of Ibn Batūta, and the name only survive in the Puckar river, one of the arms of the Sinde which meets the sea in those parts, and which may have run through the town when our traveller was there.

arm of the river Sinde. Here I met the religious and pious Sheikh ʿShams Oddīn Mohammed of Shīrāz. This was one of the men remarkable for age. He told me that he was something more than one hundred and twenty years old. I then proceeded on to the city of ᵗUja,* which is a large city, situated on the Sinde. The governing Emīr, at the time of my arrival, was ᵘEl Malik El Fāzil El Sharīf Jalāl Oddīn El Kabjī, a very brave and generous prince. Between myself and him a friendship arose and was confirmed. After this we met in Dehli. I next travelled on to ˣMultān, which is the principal city of Sindia, before the Emīr of which the Sultan's soldiers are obliged to appear.

This Emīr had always before him a number of bows of various sizes, and when any one, who wished to enlist as a bowman, presented himself, the Emīr threw one of these bows to him, which he drew with all his might.†
Then, as his strength proved to be, so was his situation appointed. But when any one wished to enlist as a horseman, a drum was fixed, and the man ran with his horse at full speed, and struck the drum with his spear.
Then, according to the effect of the stroke, was his place determined.

There were many persons, Emīrs, nobles, and learned men, who came to this place before us, and with us, all intending to be presented to

---

ᵘ الملك الفاضل الشريف جلال الدين الكبجي .  ᵗ اوجد al. أوجه .  ˢ شمس الدين محمد الشيرازي .  ˣ مُلتان .

---

* The Outch of Major Rennell, probably; Mr. Kosegarten has أَوجَه Aja.

† We find an allusion to this custom in the 18th Psalm, where David says that his arms can *break a bow of steel*. The word, however, rendered steel, means in the original *copper* (נְחוּשָׁה), and, probably, should be understood only as a part of the bow, either the middle limb, to which pieces of horn, or of any other elastic substances were fastened, or the firula, or clasps, by which this and the horn, &c. were combined.

The bow was among our own ancestors considered as a criterion of strength, as we find in one of the songs in Robin Hood's Garland: vol. ii. London, 1795, p. 13.

...... That ever a boy so young,
Should bear a bow before our king,
That's not able to draw one string.
See also Bishop Hall's preface to his " Revelation unrevealed."

That the strength of a man was thus measured among the ancient Arabians, may be seen in the " Historia imperii vetustissimi Joctanidarum in Arabia Felice," by A. Schultens, pp. 133–5.

the Emperor.    After a few days, therefore, one of the chamberlains of the
Sultan arrived here, in order to conduct these persons to the presence.    We
then hasted on to Dehli, between which and Multān there is a distance of
forty days ; throughout which, however, are many contiguous houses, and
at these we were honoured by being invited every morning and evening to
feasts, prepared by those who came out to meet such as were proceeding
to be presented to the Emperor.    The first city we entered belonging to
Hindūstān was ᵞ Abūhar, which is the first Indian city (in this direction).
It is small and closely built, and abounds with water and plantations.

There are not in Hindūstān any of the trees peculiar to our country, if
we except the ᶻ lote tree, which, however, is larger in the trunk than it is
with us ; and, its seeds are like those of a great ᵃ gall apple, exceedingly
sweet.    They have likewise large trees not known among us.    Of their
fruit trees, the grape* is one, which resembles the orange tree, except that
its stem is larger, and its leaves more numerous.    Its shade, too, is extensive and very dense, and is apt to affect with fever those who sleep under it.
The fruit is about the size of the large ᵇ Damask prune†, which when green
and not quite ripe they take, of those which happen to fall, and salt and
thus preserve them, just as the lemon is preserved with us.    In the same
manner they preserve the ginger while green, as also the pods of pepper :
and this they eat with their meals.    When the grape is ripe, which is in
the autumn, its seed becomes yellow, and this they eat like the apple : it
is sweet, but during mastication acquires some acidity.    It has rather a
large stone, which they sow like the orange seed, and from this a tree
grows up.

Of their fruits are those termed the ᶜ Shakī‡ and Barkī, the trees of which

---

ᶜ الشِيكِي al. الشَكِي وَالبَرِكِي .         ᵇ الانجاص الكبير .         ᵃ العفض .         ᶻ النبق .         ᵞ أبوهر .

---

* (العنبا) This is probably the mango.                          † So Mr. Kosegarten.

‡ This is commonly called the jack, or bread-fruit.  Crawfurd says, in his History of the
Indian Archipelago, vol. i. p. 422 : " of the *jack* fruit (autocarpus integrifolia) two species
occur in the Indian islands, the common jack and the Chămpădak.  These two fruits of
monstrous size grow, unlike most others, from the trunk and larger branches of the tree.
The first grows often to an enormous size : the taste, though too strong to be agreeable to
Europeans, is remarkably suited to the native palate.  Containing a large quantity of saccharine
and glutinous matter, the jack is highly nutritious."  He tells us a little lower down, that its

are [d] high, and their leaves are like the Jawz (or Indian nut): the fruit grows out from the bottom of the tree, and that which grows nearest to the earth is called the Barkī; it is extremely sweet and well flavoured in taste; what grows above this is the [e] Shakī. Its fruit resembles that of the [f] great gourd, its rind the skin of an ox (leather?) When it grows yellow in the autumn, they gather and divide it: and in the inside of each is from one to two hundred seeds. Its seed resembles that of a cucumber, and has a stone something like a large bean. When the stone is roasted, it tastes like a dried bean. These, *i. e.* the Shakī and Barkī, are the best fruits found in Hindūstān.

They have another sort of fruit, which they call [g] El Tand: this is the fruit of the [h] Pipercula. Its [i] seed is the size of that of an [j] Armenian peach, to which its colour may also be compared; it is exceedingly sweet. They also have the [k] Jummūn,† which is a high tree: the fruit resembles that of the olive, and is black; as does likewise its stone. They have also the sweet orange in great abundance; but the acid orange is more esteemed They also have one between the sweet and sour, which is exceedingly good. They have too the fruit called the [l] Mahwa: the tree is tall, and the leaves

---

[h] ابَنوس . التِنَد al. التِنه al. التِينة [g] . القرع [f] . الشيكي or الشكي [e] . عادية [d]

[l] المهوي . الجُمُّون [k] . المشمش [j] . حبات [i]

---

name in the archipelago is probably a corruption of the Telinga *jaka:* our word شكي Shakī (or shaka, perhaps) seems to be another corruption of the same word. Mr. Kosegarten has شَكي

*Shakī.* Mr. Marsden adds, in his History of Sumatra, p. 99: " The outer coat is rough, containing a number of seeds or kernels (which, when roasted, have the taste of chesnuts) inclosed in a fleshy substance of a rich, and to strangers, too strong a smell and flavour, but which gains upon the palate." The Chămpădak of Mr. Crawfurd is, probably, the Barkī (بركي) of our traveller: the name, however, is preserved in Knox's Ceylon, in the word *Warracha.* " Before they be full ripe," says he, " the inhabitants call them *Cose*; and when ripe *Warracha* or *Kellas:* but with this difference,.that the *Warracha* is hard, but the *Kellas* as soft as pap, both looking alike to the eye, but they are distinct trees." p. 26, edit. 1817.

\* Mr. Kosegarten also reads El Tand التَند p. 18.

† This is, probably, the *Jambu* (Eugenia) of Mr. Crawfurd. See History of the Indian Archipelago, vol. i. pp. 428-9. See also Marsden's Hist. Sumat. p. 99. Mr. Kosegarten has here الجَوَز, which he gives *Dschauk.* It is, no doubt, an error.

are like those of the [m]Jawz, except that there is a mixture of yellow and red in them. The fruit resembles the small [n]prune, and is very sweet. Upon the head of each of its berries is a small seed, not unlike the grape both in shape and taste; but they who eat it generally experience the head-ache. When dried in the sun, its taste is like that of the fig. This berry they call [o]El Angūr. The grape, however, is seldom found in Hindūstān, and then only in Dehli and a few other places. It produces fruit twice in the year. The fig is not found in Hindūstān.

They also have a fruit, which they call [p]Kosaf,* which is round and very sweet. About the tree they dig (and heap) the earth, just as they do about the chesnut. They also have in India fruit common with us which is the pomegranate, and which bears fruit twice in the year. The grain which they sow for subsistence, is sown twice in the year; and, that which is for the autumn, about Midsummer when the rains fall, which they reap in sixty days from the time of sowing it. Of this grain one is termed the [q]Kodrū, which is a sort of [r]millet. This is the most plentiful grain in use among them; and of it are the [s]Kāl and the [t]Shāmākh, the latter of which is smaller than a bean. The Shāmākh however often grows without culture, and is the food of the religious, the abstemious, the fakeers, and the poor generally, who go out and gather what thus grows spontaneously, and live upon it the year round. When this is beaten in a wooden mortar, the rind falls off, and then the kernel, which is white, comes out. This they boil in the milk of the buffalo, and make it into a stew, which is much better than when baked. Of their grain, one is the [u]Māsh,† which is a sort of pea:

| | | | | |
|---|---|---|---|---|
| [q] الكُدرُو . | [p] كُسَف . | [o] الانكور . | [n] الإجاص الصغير . | [m] جوز . |
| | [u] الماش . | [t] الشاماخ . | [s] القال . | [r] دخن . |

---

\* Mr. Kosegarten has here كسِرا kasirä, which he writes kessira doubling the s.

† To the valuable note of M. de Sacy on this vegetable (Relat. de l'Egypte, p. 119), the following may be added from the medicinal dictionary of Hosain. ماش مج خوانند وبشيرازي بتوماش خوانند وبتوسياد كويند جوهر وي نزديك بباقلي بود ونفخ وي كمتر وفاضلترين وقت استعمال كردن آن تابستان بود نيكوترين بود آن سبز بزرك آن فربه بود وطبيعت آن سرد بود در اول ومعتدل وپوست جون مقشر كنند وكويند خشك بود دراول كيموس وي محمود بود وزودتر از باقلا بكذرد وخاصهٔ جون مقشر وي جهت درد اعضا ضماد كردن نافع بود . The *māsh* they also call *maj*, but in the Shirāzi (dialect) *bitūmāsh*, and *bitusiyāh*. They say that its matter is nearly allied to

and of this the [x] Munjam* is a species. The seed is oblong, and of a clear green colour. This they cook with rice, and then eat it with oil. It is called [y] El Koshira and taken daily for breakfast. Another species of this is the [z] Lūbiā,† and another the [a] Murut, which resembles the Kodrū, except that its seed is smaller, and is used for fodder for cattle : it is pulse. They also feed the beasts with the leaves of the māsh, instead of green corn. All these are their autumnal grains. And when they cut these, they sow the spring grain, which consists of [b] wheat, [c] barley, [d] lentiles, and [e] pulse,‡

---

[c] الشعير .    [b] القمح .    [a] المرت .    [z] اللوبيا .    [y] الكشري .    [x] المنجم

[e] الحمّص .    [d] العدس .

---

that of the bākila (bean) but is less flatulent. The best time to use it is the summer : and the best of it, are those which are large, green, and plump. Its nature is cold at first, but moderate. Of its skin they make the *chŭn mukashshar*, and say that it is dry at first. The chyle produced by it is good ; and it digests sooner than the bākila (or bean). The property of its *chŭn mukashshar* is, to be advantageous in poulticing for pains in the limbs, &c. The term *chŭn mukashshar*, means *like something barked* or *peeled* : but here seems to be applied as a compound word, as the name of something, but what it is I have not been able to discover. Nor am I quite certain about the syllables *bitu*, in *bitusiyāh*, as the diacritical points in the MS. are not very plainly written : but as I could find nothing else so suitable, I have taken that, which according to Meninski means *exposed to the sun*, &c.

* We find in Golius, under ﺞﻣ Pers. ماش .... *Lusitanis* MUNGO. Is not this mungo the منجم *munjam* of Ibn Batūta ?

† To M. de Sacy's notes on the Loubia (Relat. de l'Egypte, p. 38, &c.) may be added the following from the dictionary of Hosain. لوبيا ولوبا نيز كويند وثامر وآن ترازماش سهل هضم شود وبيرون آيد و نفتخ (نفح) وي كمتر از باقلا بود ونيكوترين آن سرخ بود كه نخورده بود وطبيعت وي كرم در اول ومعتدل بود در تري وخشكي وكويند سرد وخشك بود ... خاصة سرخ وي دوم نفاس پاك كند وبول براند وبدن فربه كند وسينه وششرا نافع بود بود The lūbiā, which they also call lūbā and *thāmar*, is easier of digestion and ejection than the māsh. It is less productive of flatulency than the bākila (bean). The best of it is that which is red, but is not eaten. Its nature is warm at the first, but in moisture and dryness is moderate. They also say, that it is cold and dry .... The second property of the red sort is, that it assists in puerperal complaints, expels the urine and makes the body plump. It is also valuable in pulmonary diseases.

‡ Of this, according to Hosain, there is, the white, the black, the karsanī, the wild, and the garden, pulse. The wild is the most scarce, and the garden pulse is eaten. حمص بپارسي نخورد كويند سفيد و سرخ وسياه و كرسني بود وبري وبستاني بود بري كمتر بود .... وبستاني غذاي نيكو دهد &c. Then follow its medicinal properties.

on the ground from which the autumnal grain had been gathered. The soil of the country is exceedingly good.

As to the rice, they sow it three times during the year on the same ground: it is much in use among them. The sesamè and sugar-cane they cultivate along with the autumnal grain.

I at length left the town of Abūhar, and proceeded for one day through a desert enclosed on both sides by mountains upon which were infidel and rebel Hindoos. The inhabitants of India are in general infidels; some of them live under the protection of the Mohammedans, and reside either in the villages or cities: others, however, infest the mountains and rob by the highways. I happened to be of a party of two and twenty men, when a number of these Hindoos, consisting of two horsemen and eighty foot, made an attack upon us. We, however, engaged them, and by God's help put them to flight, having killed one horseman and twelve of the foot.

After this we arrived at a fortress, and proceeding on from it, came at length to the city of [f] Ajūdahan* which is small. Here I met the holy Sheikh [g] Farīd Oddīn El Bodhāwondī, of whom the Sheikh El Walī Borhān Oddīn El Aaraj had spoken to me in the port of Alexandria, telling me that I should meet him. I therefore did meet him, and presented him with the Sheikh's salutation, which surprised him; He said, I am unworthy of this. The Sheikh was very much broken by the temptations of the Devil. He allowed no one to touch his hand or to approach him; and, whenever the clothes of any one happened to touch his, he washed them immediately. His patronymic is referred to [h] Bodhāwond, a town of [i] El Sambal.

In this part, I also saw those women who burn themselves when their husbands die.† The woman adorns herself, and is accompanied by a

---

[i] السَنْبِل .      [h] بزاوند .al بُذَاوَنْد .      [g] فريد الدين البُذَاوُنْدِيّ .      [f] أَجُودَهَن .

---

* The *Adjodin* of Major Rennell.

† It will not be necessary here to notice what has been written on this inhuman practice by more modern travellers, or by our own countrymen resident in Hindūstān: but, as some curious matter is found in the Dabistān, a Persian book not yet translated, it may not be amiss here to give an extract on this subject: آورده اند که زني که پس از مرك شوهرستي شود كناهان زن وشوهر ايزد تعالي ببخشد وبسا هنكام در بهشت مانند واكر شوهر دوزخي بود چنانكه ماركيرماررا از سوراخ بزور بيرون مي آرد آنزن شوهررا از دوزخ بر آورده به بهشت رساند وهر آن زني كه ستي

cavalcade of the infidel Hindoos and [k]Brahmans, with drums, [l]trumpets, and men, following her, both Moslems and Infidels for mere pastime. The fire had been already kindled, and into it they threw the dead husband. The wife then threw herself upon him, and both were entirely burnt. A woman's burning herself, however, with her husband is not considered as absolutely necessary among them, but it is encouraged; and when a woman burns herself with her husband, her family is considered as being ennobled, and supposed to be worthy of trust. But when she does not burn herself, she is ever after clothed coarsely, and remains in constraint among her relations, on account of her want of fidelity to her husband.

The woman who burns herself with her husband is generally surrounded by women, who bid her farewell, and commission her with salutations for

---

[l] انفار .     [k] البراهمه .

---

شود دیگر به نشاء مونثی در نیاید واکر تعلق بتن کیرد مرد باشد وجون ستی نشود وبه بیوکی بسر برد اصلا از نشاء زنی نرهد زنرا باید با شوهر خود در آتش سوزنده در آید الا زن آبستن وباید زن برهمن با شوهر در یك آتش ستی شود ودیکران علیحده وبستم زنرا در آتش انداختن نا رواست وهمچنین زنی که خواهد ستی شود اورا باز داشتن جایز نیست ومحققین کفته اند مراد از ستی شدن آنست که زن بعد از شوهر جمیع خواهشهارا با شوهر بسوزاند وپیش از مردن بمیرد چه در زبان رمز زن شهوت است یعنی شهوترا بر اندازد نه آنکه خودرا مرده در آتش افکند چه آن ناستوده است . "They say, that the woman who becomes a Sattee after the death of her husband, obtains pardon both for her own and her husband's sins, so that they may both remain long in paradise: and even if the husband should have gone to hell, just as a snake-catcher draws out a snake from his hole, so would the woman draw her husband out of hell, and place him in paradise. Every woman, too, who becomes a Sattee, should she again have a body, would have that of a man, not that of a woman. But, if she did not become a Sattee, but remain a widow, she would never in the metempsychosis have any other body but that of a woman. It is considered the duty of a woman to enter the fire in which her husband is burning, unless she be pregnant. A Brahman's wife must burn with her husband in the same fire, and so become a Sattee: others may burn elsewhere. It is not considered right, however, to force a woman into the fire: and, in like manner, a woman desiring to become a Sattee, is not to be kept back from her purpose. The doctors have said, that the original intention of becoming a Sattee was this: that a woman should, after the death of her husband, consume all her desires, and thus die (to the world) before her natural death: for in the language of mysticism *woman* means *desire;* and the intention is, that she should cast away her desire, not that she should throw herself as a dead carcase into the fire, which is abominable," The word Sattee (in the Sanscrit सती ) means *saint,* &c.

their former friends, while she laughs, plays, or dances, to the very time in which she is to be burnt.

Some of the Hindoos, moreover, drown themselves in the river Ganges, to which they perform pilgrimages; and into which they pour the ashes of those who have been burnt. When any one intends to drown himself, he opens his mind on the subject to one of his companions, and says: You are not to suppose that I do this for the sake of any thing worldly; my only motive is to draw near to [m]Kisāī, which is a name of God with them. And when he is drowned, they draw him out of the water, burn the body, and pour the ashes into the Ganges.

After four day's journey, I arrived at the city of [n]Sarsatī*. It is large and abounds with rice, which they carry hence to Delhi. And after this at [o]Hānsī,† which is a very beautiful and closely built city, with extensive fortifications. I next came to [p]Masūd Abād,‡ after two days travelling, and remained there three days. The Emperor Mohammed, whom it was our object to see, had at this time left his residence in Dehli, and gone to Kinnoje,§ which is at the distance of ten days from that place. He sent his Vizier, however, [q]Khāja Jahān‖ Ahmed Ibn Ayās, a native of Room, with a number of kings, doctors, and grandees, to receive the travellers, (an Emīr is with them termed king.) The Vizier then so arranged the procession, that each one had a place according to his rank.

We then proceeded on from Masūd Abād till we came to Dehli, the capi-

---

[m] كِسَائِي . [n] سَرْسَتِي . [o] حَانسي al. حاشِي . [p] مَسْعُود آباد .

[q] خواجه جهان احمد بن اياس الرومي الاصل .

---

* The *Suruste* of Major Rennell.

† Perhaps the Hassengur of Rennell, or the هانسي of Ferishta, which is certainly near the river Suruste, mentioned in the account of the battle between Shahāb Oddīn and the Hindoo chiefs, A. H. 588. Dow writes it Hafsi, p. 169: (A. H. 752).

‡ This place I do not find in the maps.

§ This is, probably, the expedition noticed by Dow, Hindustan, vol. i. p. 322.

‖ *Chaja Jehan* was, according to Dow, high in power with Mohammed Shāh at this time. Hindustan, vol. i. p. 318; and Ferishta says, that Ahmed Ayāz received the title of Khāja Jahān, and was made commander of the forces of Guzerat upon the king's accession. واحمد ايازرا خواجه جهان خطاب كرده سپهسالار كجرات كردانيد.

tal of the empire. It is a most magnificent city, combining at once both beauty and strength. Its walls are such as to have no equal in the whole world. This is the greatest city of Hindūstān; and indeed of all Islamism in the East. It now consists of four cities, which becoming contiguous have formed one. This city was conquered in the year of the Hejira 584 (A.D. 1188).* The thickness of its walls is eleven ʳcubits. They keep grain in this city for a very long time without its undergoing any change whatever. I myself saw rice brought out of the treasury, which was quite black, but, nevertheless, had lost none of the goodness of its taste. The same was the case with the kodrū, which had been in the treasury for ninety years. Flowers, too, are in continual blossom in this place. Its mosque is very large; and, in the beauty and extent of its building, it has no equal. Before the taking of Dehli it had been a Hindoo temple, which the Hindoos call ˢEl Bur Khāna (But Khāna†); but, after that event, it was used as a mosque. In its court-yard is a ᵗcell, to which there is no equal in the cities of the Mohammedans; its height is such, that men appear from the top of it like little children. In its court, too, there is an immense pillar, which they say, is composed of stones from seven different quarries. Its length is ᵘthirty cubits; its circumference eight: which is truly miraculous.‡ Without the city is a reservoir for the rain-water; and out of this the inhabitants have their water for drinking.§ It is two miles in length, and one in width.

---

" ثلاثون ذراعًا .    ᵗ صومعة .    ᵘ البت خانة al. البرخانه .    ⁴ احد عشر ذراعًا .

---

* According to Ferishta, however, it was not conquered by the Mohammedans before A. H. 588. His words, which I do not find in Dow, are these: وچون پتهورا در معركه سلطان شهاب الدين مقتول كرديد دهلي چنانكه بيايد در اواخر سنه ثمان وثمانين وخمسمايه از تصرف كفار بر آمده . در حوزه ديوان ملوك غور واتباع ايشان انتقال كرفت ... When Pithūrā was slain in the field of battle of Shahāb Oddīn, Dehli, as will hereafter appear, in the latter part of the year 588 passing from the power of infidels, went into the government of the kings of Ghaur and their followers. According to the Aīni Akbarī, however, Dehli was first taken by Mahmood of Ghizna:

† This sort of temple is constantly termed But khāna (بت خانه, a but house or house of Budda) by Ferishta.

‡ Is it the pillar of Firozshāh?

§ The waters of the Jumna, it should seem, are so impregnated with natron as to be unfit for drinking. Col. Fitzclarence tells us, in his " Journal or Route across India, through Egypt to

About it are pleasure-gardens to which the people resort. (al. the nobles of the city.)

---

## CHAPTER XV.

*Conquest of Dehli—Abstract of the History of Hindūstān, from this time to that in which Ibn Batūta visited this place.*

THE city of Dehli was conquered by the Emīr ˣKotb Oddīn Aibak, one of the Mamlūks of the Sultan ˣShahāb Oddīn Mohammed Ibn Sām El Ghaurī* king of Ghizna and Khorāsān, who had overcome ʸIbrahim Ibn Mahmood Ibn Subuktagīn† the beginner of the conquest of India. This Emīr Kotb Oddīn resided here as governor, on the part of Shahāb Oddīn : but when Kotb Oddīn died, his son, ˣShams Oddīn Lalmish,‡ became governor. After this, Shams Oddīn became possessed of the kingdom here, having been appointed thereto by the general consent of the people ; and he governed India for twenty years. He was a just, learned, and religious prince. After his death, his son, ᵇRokn Oddīn, took possession of the throne ; but polluted his reign by killing his brothers, and was,

---

ˣ الامير قطب الدين ايبك .   ʸ شهاب الدين محمد بن سام الغوري .   ˣ ابراهيم بن محمود

بن سبكتكين .   ᵃ شمس الدين لَّمِش .   ᵇ ركن الدين .

---

England," (p. 236) that "the water of the Jumna, and of the wells, which they are now obliged to drink (*i. e.* the inhabitants of Delhi) is so much impregnated with natron, otherwise called soda, as to prove at times very injurious." Our traveller was in India before the time of Shāh Jahān, and consequently before the canal for supplying purer water (mentioned in the same page by the Colonel) had been made : and hence the necessity for this reservoir.

* The taking of Dehli by Kotb Oddīn Aibak (قطب الدين ايبك) who was then a servant of Shahāb Oddīn, is placed by Ferishta in the year of Hegira 588. See Dow, vol. i. p. 156 ; where we are also told that Kotb Oddīn made Dehli the seat of his government.

† An outline of these events will be found in Dow, vol. i. pp. 146-7-8.

‡ This is, no doubt, a mistake of the copyist : Shams Oddīn Altamish شمس الدين التمش was, according to Ferishta, the name of this king ; see Dow, p. 176. And by this account he reigned twenty-six years. The word for six, however, might have been omitted by our traveller's copyists.

therefore, killed himself.* Upon this, the army agreed to place his sister
*El Malika Razīa, upon the throne, who reigned four years. This woman
usually rode about among the army, just as men do. She, however, gave
up the government, on account of some circumstances that presented themselves.

After this, her younger brother, ᶜNāsir Oddin,† became possessed of
the government, which he held for twenty years. This was a very religious
prince; and so much so, that he lived entirely on what he got by writing
out and selling copies of the Koran. He was succeeded by his Nawāb,
ᵈGhīāth Oddīn Ahmed, one of his fathers' Mamlūks, who murdered him.‡
This man's name was originally ᵉBalaban; his character had been just,
discriminating, and mild: he filled the office of Nawāb of India, under
Nāsir Oddīn, for twenty years: he also reigned twenty years.§ One of his

---

ᵉ بلبن .   ᵈ غياث الدين احمد .   ᶜ ناصر الدين .   al. الملكه رضيه راضيه ᵇ

---

* The account of this reign is found in Dow, p. 182; and in p. 183 commences the account
of his sister's reign noticed by Ibn Batūta, and perfectly agreeing with it. The Emperor,
according to Ferishta, said of her: رضيه اكرچه بصورت زن است اما معني مرد است
" Although Razīa is a woman in form, she is a man in understanding."

† A similar account of him is given by Dow from Ferishta, where (p. 203) we have an
anecdote about one of the copies of the Koran, which in his industry he had copied out; and
another in which we are told, that his queen (for he had but one, and no concubines) one day
complaining of her hands being injured (دارد آزار من دستهاي) which Dow translates, " burnt her
fingers, " in baking his bread, and requesting to have a maid to help her, was told, "that he was
only a trustee of the state, and that he was determined not to burthen it with needless
expenses. He therefore exhorted her to proceed in her duty with patience, and God would
reward her in the end." Two reigns, according to Ferishta and the Tabakāti Akbari, intervene
here, of which Ibn Batūta makes no mention: the reason probably is, that they possess no particular interest.

‡ Nothing of this is mentioned in Ferishta.

§ According to Ferishta he ascended the throne A. H. 664 and died in 685. See Dow,
p. 208-221. At the outset of this section, we have an abstract of his origin according to the historians of Hindūstān, which differs in some respects from that of our traveller. Here, as already
remarked, he is erroneously named *Balin* for *Balaban*. Ferishta thinks, that as several persons
of the name of Balaban occur in history, it probably may be the name of a Turkish tribe. His
words are: وچون در تواريخ چند كسرا بلقب بلبن ذكر كرده اند ميتواند بود كه بلبن طايفه از
تركان باشند It is curious enough, that in the Tabakāti Akbari, which was composed before the
times of Ferishta, Balaban is said to have been called *Balaban the Dwarf*: the words are

pious acts was, his building a house which was called the *ᶠ House of Safety* ;*
for whenever any debtor entered this, his debt was adjudged; and
in like manner, every oppressed person found justice; every man-slayer
deliverance from his adversary; and every person in fear, protection.
When he died he was buried in this house, and there I myself visited his
grave. The history of his beginnings is surprising, which is this : When a
child he lived at Bokhāra in the possession of one of the inhabitants, and
was a little despicable ill-looking wretch. Upon a time, a certain Fakeer
saw him there, and said: "You little ᵍTurk!" which is considered by them
as a very reproachful term. The reply was : I am here, good Sir. This
surprised the Fakeer, who said to him : Go and bring me one of those pomegranates, pointing to some which had been exposed for sale in the street.
The urchin replied : Yes, Sir; and immediately, taking out all the money
he had, went and bought the pomegranate. When the Fakeer received it, he
said to Balaban : We give you the kingdom of India. Upon which the boy
kissed his own hand, and said : I have accepted of it, and am quite
satisfied.

It happened, about this time, that the Sultan Shams Oddīn sent a
merchant to purchase slaves from Bokhāra and Samarkand. He accordingly bought a hundred, and Balaban was among them. When these
Mamlūks were brought before the Sultan, they all pleased him except
Balaban, and him he rejected, on account of his despicable appearance.

---

ᵍ يا تركك .        ᶠ دار الامن .

---

در سنه أربع وستين وست مائة الغ خان كه بلبن خورد كفتندي جمله أمرا وملوك شهر در قصر
سبيد برتخت سلطنت اجلس دادند . "In the year 664 Aligh Khān, whom they called
*Balaban the Dwarf*, the whole of the Emirs and Governors of the city placed upon the throne of
empire, in the white palace." This appellation is not given to him by Ferishta, but must have been
fresh in memory in the times of our traveller, and perhaps when the Tabakāti Akbari was
composed.

* In a note p. 42, some notice will be found of an inscription brought from Ceylon by Sir
Alexander Johnston and translated by me. Upon referring to that inscription it will be found,
that an asylum is spoken of : the passage alluded to in our text in this place, seems to me to
signify an institution perfectly similar to that in the inscription, and appears to be confirmatory of the view there taken of the inscription. We have no account of this establish-
ment in Dow : but in the Tabakāti Akbari and Ferishta, it is said در دار الامان مدفون كشت
" He was buried in the *House of Safety*."

Upon this, Balaban said to the Emperor: Lord of the world! why have you bought all these slaves? The Emperor smiled, and said: For my own sake, no doubt. The slave replied: Buy me then for God's sake. I will, said he. He then accepted of him, and placed him among the rest; but, on account of the badness of his appearance, gave him a situation among the cup-bearers.

Some of the astrologers, who were about the king, were daily in the habit of saying to him: " One of the Mamlūks will one day overcome thy son, and take the kingdom from him. To this the Emperor, on account of the justice and excellency of his own character, paid no regard, till they also told it to the Queen-Mother; who soon made an impression on his mind respecting it. He accordingly summoned the astrologers before him, and said: Pray can you tell which of the Mamlūks it is, who is to take the kingdom from my son, if you see him? They said, we have a mark whereby we can distinguish him. The Emperor then ordered all the Mamlūks to be present; who came accordingly, station after station, as commanded. Upon these the astrologers fixed their eyes; but did not discover the person looked for, until* the day began to draw towards the close. At this time the cup-bearers said one to another, we are getting rather hungry, let us join and send some one into the street to buy us something to eat. They did so; and Balaban, as the most despicable, was sent to make the purchase. Balaban accordingly sallied forth, but could find nothing in that street which would suit him; he then went on into another, during which time the turn of the cup-bearers came on to be presented. But, as Balaban was not forthcoming, they took a little pitch and whatever else was necessary for their purpose, and daubing it over a child, took him with them in the place of Balaban; and when his name was called over, this child was presented; and the business of the day was closed, without the astrologers finding their mark upon any one; which was a providential circumstance for Balaban.

---

* The force of the particle حتّى (until) is worth remarking in this place, as it is obvious that no inference whatever can here be drawn, that the circumstance hinted at did afterwards take place. The same often takes place in the scriptural usage of the terms αχρις, עַד כִּי &c. very unlike the usage of our particle *until*. See Noldius, p. 534, edit. 1734.

At last Balaban made his appearance; but not till the business of the day was over. The cleverness of Balaban was afterwards noticed, and he was made head of the cup-bearers. After this he was placed in the army, and soon became a general officer. After this the Sultan Jālāl Oddīn married his daughter, which was before he had been made king. But when he was, he appointed Balaban to the office of Nawāb or Viceroy, which he filled for twenty years. He then killed his master, and seized the empire. This Balaban had two sons; one of these, namely, [h]El Khān El Shahīd, he appointed as his own successor, and governor on his part in the provinces of Sindia: he resided at Multān. He was killed, however, in an affair with the Tartars,[*] leaving two sons, Kaikobād[†] and [i]Kaikhosrū. Balaban's second son, named [k]Nāsir Oddīn, was appointed to govern the districts of [l]Laknoutī and [m]Bengal. When, however, the heir-apparent El Khān El Shahīd had been killed, Balaban appointed El Khān El Shahīd's son Kaikhosrū, his successor, passing over his own son Nāsir Oddīn.

Nāsir Oddīn, however, had a son named [n]Moïzz Oddīn residing at the court of his grandfather at Dehli, the person who eventually became successor to Balaban. This at length came to pass on account of Giāth Oddīn Balaban's dying in the night, when his own son Nāsir Oddīn was out of the way in the district of Laknoutī. On this occasion he appointed Kaikhosrū his grandson, the son of El Khān El Shahīd, as already mentioned.

The king, however (or chief) of the Emīrs and Nawāb to the Sultan Balaban, happened to have conceived a strong enmity against Kaikhosru,

---

[h] لخان الشهيد .   [i] كيقباد وكيخسرو .   [k] ناصرالدين .   [l] اللكنوتي .   [m] بنجاله .   [n] معزالدين .

* In Dow, vol. i. p. 226, we have the same account.

† The Tabakāti Akbarī and Farishta give the name of Kaikobād to the son of this Nāsir Oddīn, and who is here termed Moïzz Oddīn. All agree, however, in making the son of Nāsir Oddīn eventually to succeed to Balaban in the empire. Which of our writers is correct in the other particulars I have not the means of determining, nor is it of much importance; but, from the accounts given below by Ibn Batūta, and no where else to be found, I am disposed to believe, that he had access to documents not in existence in the times of the historians referred to: and if so, his story bids the fairest for being the true one. The title of Balaban's second son Bagherā Khān (بغرا خان) as given by Ferishta and Dow, is constantly in the Tabakāti Akbarī Bakerā Khān (بقرا خان).

on this account he had recourse to a stratagem, which gained him his end:
it was this: He forged a letter in the name of the Emīrs, stating that they
had declared Moïzz Oddīn son of Nāsir Oddīn, king. With this he goes
to Kaikhosrū by night, as if wishing to advise with him, and says: The
Emīrs have proclaimed thy uncle's son; and I very much fear for thy
safety. The reply was: What am I to do? He said, save thyself by
escaping to the districts of Sīndia. But, replied he, how am I to get through
the gates of the city, which are already barred. The keys, answered the
Emīr, are here in my possession. I will open the gates for you. The
young man thanked him for this, and then kissed his hand. The Emīr
said: Mount immediately. He accordingly did, with his nobles and slaves;
and the Emīr opened the gates, let them out, and immediately closed them
again.

He next went to Moïzz Oddīn, son of Nāsir Oddīn, and asked permission
to enter; which being granted, he proclaimed him Emperor. "But, how
is this," replied Moïzz Oddīn, "since Kaikhosrū my uncle's son was
appointed successor?" The Emīr told him of his stratagem, and how he
had got rid of Kaikhosrū. Moïzz Oddīn thanked him for this, and then
took him to the palace; where, sending for the rest of the Emīrs and
nobles, they invested him with the supreme authority during the night.
In the morning this was confirmed by the people generally; and Moïzz
Oddīn took possession of the throne.

His father, however, was living at this time in the provinces of Bengal
and Laknoutī: and, when the news of his son's being made Emperor
reached him, he said: I am heir to the crown, how then can my son
exercise this authority during my lifetime? He accordingly set out with
his army for Dehli, in order to make war upon his son Moïzz Oddīn. Moïzz
Oddīn too marched out with his troops to give battle to his father. They
both arrived at the same time at the city of °Karrā,* which is situated on
the banks of the Ganges, took their stations on opposite sides of the river,
and prepared for the onset. It was the will of divine Providence, however, to spare the blood of the faithful; and hence the heart of the father

ه كَرَّا °

---

* The Currah of Major Rennell.

Nāsir Oddīn began to relent towards his son; for he said to himself, surely
as long as my son is king, I shall partake of his glory. Moïzz Oddīn too
felt in his mind that someting of submission was due to his father. Each
of them, therefore, as if by instinct, left his army and rode directly into
the middle of the river and met there. Here the Emperor kissed the feet
of his father, and asked his forgiveness. His father replied, I give you my
kingdom; and so invested him with the authority of Emperor. He then
wished to retire to his districts; but his son said: Nay, but you must come
with me to mine. He accordingly accompanied him to Dehli; and,
entering the palace, seated his son upon the throne, and took his own station before him. This day is therefore called, *the day of meeting;* because
they had this happy rencontre in the middle of the river, no blood being
shed, and the kingdom mutually given and accepted.*

After this, Nāsir Oddīn returned to his districts; where after two years he
died, leaving a family behind him. The kingdom was thus confirmed to
Moïzz Oddīn, which continued for four years, during which the inhabitants

* The account of this transaction is given in a manner somewhat different in the Tabakāti
Akbarī, Ferishta, and after the latter, by Dow, vol. i. p. 225, &c., the former, stating, as Ferishta does, that Nāsir Oddīn did not think of leaving Luknouti for Dehli for two years, until he
had heard of the great profligacy of his son, proceeds thus: سلطان بسخن ملك نظام الدين با
لشكرها آراسته واسباب سلطنة ولوازم حشمت بجانب اوده حركت فرمود چون سلطان ناصر الدين
بريى مطلع شد دانست كه باعث اين امر ملك نظام الدين است ونيز با لشكرو فيلان وحشم
از لكهنوتي بجانب پسر روان شد هر دو لشكر بر كنار آب سرو بر دو جانب فرود آمدند سه روز
بمراسلات ومكاتبات تحريك سلسلة ملاقات نمودند ودر باب چگونكي ملاقات سخنان كذشت
آخر قرار يافت كه پسر بر تخت نشيند وسلطان ناصر الدين از آب كذشته شرائط تعظيم بجا آورده
پسرا بر تخت ملاقات نمايد &c. "The Sultan, at the instigation of the Vizier Nizām Oddīn, pro-
viding himself with an army, and other appurtenances of royalty, set out for Oude. When the
Sultan Nāsir Oddīn was acquainted with this, knowing that the Vizier Nizām Oddīn had originated it, he also set out with an army, elephants, and great pomp towards his son. Each of the
armies took its station on each side of the Sirve (Soorjew or Gogra). When three days were spent
in sending and receiving letters, as to how the meeting was to be arranged, it was at length
agreed, that the son should retain the throne; and that Nāsir Oddīn should pass the river, and
do homage to his son upon it." I make this extract, because Dow introduces certain matters
into the account not to be found either in Ferishta or the author cited. Such as the armies
waiting for some days in hourly expectation of an action; the old man finding his army inferior
to that of his son, and the like: when the fact seems to be, that a negociation was set on foot immediately, and that the father had no intention or wish to give his son battle. What authority
our traveller had for placing this meeting upon the Ganges it is not easy to say.

may be said to have enjoyed a continual holiday. After this he was affected by a complaint, by which one of his sides became quite withered,* and for which the physicians could find no remedy. At this time, his Nawāb, ᴾJalāl Oddīn Fīroz Shāh El Khilajī, revolted, taking his station upon a high mount without the city. Moïzz Oddīn sent his Emīrs for the purpose of giving him battle; but they all, one after another, joined him, and proclaimed him Emperor. Jalāl Oddīn then entered the city, and enclosing Moïzz Oddīn within his palace for three days, overcame him, put him to death, and took possession of his kingdom.† This Jalāl Oddīn was a mild and well-informed prince; he governed India for two years. He had a son and a daughter. The daughter he married to his brother's son Alā Oddīn, a daring, bold, and powerful man. His wife, however, so much harassed him, that he was obliged to complain to her father, in order to have an end put to their disputes.‡

The uncle had given him the government of ᑫKarrā and Manikbūr,§ containing two of the most populous districts in India. Alā Oddīn, how-ever, had an eye to the kingdom. The only difficulty he had to contend with was, his want of money; for he had none, except what he got by his sword in making new conquests. Upon one of these expeditions, his horse happened to stumble against a stone as he went along, and from this a kind of ringing noise proceeded. He immediately ordered his men to dig; and here they found an immense quantity of wealth.‖ This he divided among his followers, and hence acquired considerable power. It happened that his uncle undertook an expedition against him, and summoned him before him, but he refused to appear. The uncle then prepared to go to

ᑫ كرا ومَانِكبُور.     ᴾ جلال الدين فيروز شاه الْخِلَجِي.

---

* Dow, ib. p. 229.

† Here the Khilijī dynasty originated, and that of Ghaur ended. Dow, ib. pp. 229-231.

‡ Noticed by Dow, p. 243.

§ The *Currah* and *Manicpoor* of Major Rennell.

‖ This wealth seems to have been acquired in an expedition into the Deccan. Dow, ib. p. 245 and 247. In countries like those of the East, however, subject to a perpetual change of masters, it is not at all to be wondered at, that much treasure is often buried; and, perhaps, this will in some measure account for the stories we so often meet with, of great treasures being found in the earth.

him; for he said, This young man is as my son, I will therefore go to
him. The nephew accordingly met him, which happened upon the banks
of the Ganges, in the very place where Moïzz Oddīn and Nāsir Oddīn had
formerly met: and, like them, each rode into the middle of the river.
Alā Oddīn, however, had commanded his followers, that, at the time he
should embrace his uncle Jalāl Oddīn, they were to kill him. When,
therefore, the parties met, and the nephew was in the act of embracing
the uncle, the followers of the nephew killed him, which put Alā Oddīn
in possession of his uncle's army, and all proclaimed him Emperor.*
After this he governed Hindūstān for twenty years. He was just, and
looked to the affairs of his subjects in person. Now he also had a nephew
named °Soleimān Shāh, and as he was one day engaged in the chase,
this nephew conceived the intention of destroying him, just as *he* had of
destroying his own uncle. He shot him, accordingly, with an arrow in an
unguarded moment, and the uncle fell from his horse.† The nephew was

---

° سليمان .

---

* Ferishta's account of this transaction will be found in Dow, vol. i. pp. 252-254. But here
the Persian historians represent the affair as having taken place in the Ganges: and, as Ibn
Batūta says, it took place where the former one did, he must have written الكنك *the Ganges*,
on that occasion.

† Dow, ib. pp. 267-269. But here the name of *Akit Khān* occurs: if, however, we turn
to Ferishta, we shall find Soleimān Shāh, just as we have it in our traveller: and as we have
another variety, it may not be amiss to cite the passage: سلطان در غضب رفته بنفس نفيس
با کوکبه بادشاهي از بلده دهلي بدانجانب نهضت فرمود چون به تبت (تل پهت .al) رسيد آنجا
چند روز مقام کرده هر روز بصحرا ميرفت وشکار قمرغه مي نمود روزي برسم معهود بشکار رفته بود
چون بکاه (بیکاه .al) شد نتوانست بلشکر رسید بیرون ماند روز دیکر پیش از طلوع آفتاب فرمان
داد که مردم بقمرغه مشغول شدند وخود با چند کس بکوشه رفت وبر بلندي بنشست که چون
قمرغه طیار شود شکار کند ناکاه سلیمان شاه برادر زاده سلطان علاو الدین که الیخان خطاب داشت
و وکیل دربود وهمان قصه سلطان جلال الدین وعلاو الدین بخاطر آورده با چند سوار نو مسلمان که
چاکر قدیم او بودند سیر کنان درآمد وقصد سلطان نمود چون سلطانرا به تیر کرفتند سلطان از بلندي
آمده بته , &c. " The Sultan was enraged, and in his own person proceeded towards that part
in regal pomp. When he arrived at *Tibet* (according to the Tabakāti Akbarī at *Til Phut*), and
had resided there a few days, and went daily into the desert to hunt the kamurgah, upon one
of these he happened to have lost time, so that he could not get to the army, but remained out.
On the next day, before sun-rising, he ordered the hunting to commence, while he, with a

about to make up to him, when he was told by his slave that he need not do so, as he was quite dead. He left him, therefore, and returned to the palace, and took possession of the government. A little while after Alā Oddīn, recovering from his stupor, got up and mounted a horse, which the army perceiving joined him. He then entered the city, and besieged his nephew Soleimān Shāh in the palace; who, feeling his weakness, betook himself to flight, but was taken and put to death by his uncle Alā Oddīn. After this he never rode a hunting, to divine service, or to the celebration of any public holiday.

He had five sons, the younger of whom were ⁵Shahāb Oddīn and Kotb Oddīn: the eldest he had, during his life time, ordered to be kept in prison.* When taken with his last sickness (the anger of the young man on account of his imprisonment not having abated), and when the disease was making rapid advances, he sent for this son in order to name him as his successor; but, he delaying to come in consequence of this irritation, the Mamlūks, the head of whom hated this son, together with the principal Nuwāb, placed the younger son Shahāb Oddīn upon the throne, as soon as the Emperor was dead: and the appointment was confirmed by the people. The three elder children, however, were ordered to be imprisoned and their eyes to be put out: and thus was the government established.

---

⁵ شهاب الدين وقطب الدين .

---

few others, went aside and sat upon a height, so that when the Kamurgah should be started he might engage in the hunt. All on a sudden, however, Soleimān Shāh the Sultan's nephew, who was styled Alīkh Khān, and was keeper of the Door, having in his mind the affair of Jalāl Oddīn and Alā Oddīn, with a few horsemen who were his old servants and had lately become Mohammedans, parading as it were for his amusement, made for the Sultan; who, when they had attacked him with their arrows, fell from the height, &c." The place where this occurred is called *Jilput*, by Dow, which is, perhaps, an error of the press for Tilput, as found in the Tabakāti Akbarī. Of the Vakeel Muttaluk, as in Dow, we have in both histories وكيل در Vakīli Dar.

* This, we have, I suppose, in the temporary banishment mentioned by Dow, vol. i. p. 292. Ferishta, however, mentions it not as a command, as given by Dow, but merely as a permission to go to Amrohe, on a hunting excursion: his words are, خضر خان را بجانب امروهه He gave جهت سير و شكار رخصت داده كفت هركاه مرا صحت شود ترا طلب خواهم داشت . permission to Khazir Khān to make a hunting excursion to Amrohe, saying, when I shall have recovered my health, I will send for you. See also *ib.* p. 293, where Ferishta does not say one

Upon this the Queen sent for two of the most powerful of her husband's Mamlūks, the name of one of whom was 'Bashīr, that of the other, "Mubashshir, and with tears complained of the conduct of the principal Nuwāb towards her children, soliciting their assistance, and stimulating them to put the chief Nuwāb to death ; and affirming, that it was his intention to murder her younger son Kotb Oddīn.   They accordingly agreed to kill him, which they did by stratagem while he was in his house.*   They then brought forth Kotb Oddīn to his brother Shahāb Oddīn, who held the reins of government.   Kotb Oddīn remained for some time in the situation of his Nuwāb, but at length deposed his brother, and took possession of the kingdom ;  which he held for some time.

After this he took a journey to ˣDawlat Abād, between which and Dehli is a distance of forty days.   The road is from first to last inclosed with ʸwillow and other trees, so that a traveller seems to be in a garden throughout all this distance.†   Besides, there are at the distance of every three miles the stations of the foot couriers, at which there are also inhabitants, as already mentioned.   From this place to El Telingāna,‡ and ᶻEl Maabar,§ is a distance of six months.   In all these stations there is a

---

ᶻ التكتك والمعبر .            ʸ صفصاف .            ˣ دولة آباد .            " مبشر .            ' بشير .

---

word about trying his affections or seeing him weep, as stated by Dow, but that the Emperor embraced him affectionately, and allowed him to go into the haram to see his mother, &c.

* In pp. 295-6. The account of the Queen's proceeding differs a little in Ferishta from that in Ibn Batūta : and here Dow is incorrect.   " The mother of Mobārick Shaw .... acquainted Shech Nizam ul Dien," &c. ; but Ferishta says it was the Sheikh Najm Oddīn شيخ نجم الدين .   And a little lower down he tells us, just as our traveller does, that this affair was communicated to both the Mubashshir and the Bashīr : his words are باز كشتند وقصهرا بمبشر وبشير كه سردار بابكان بودند كفته &c. i. e. they returned and told the affair to the Mubashshir and the Bashīr, who were the heads of the Eunuchs. Where we also learn that these are names of office.

† We are told by Ferishta, and after him by Dow, Hind. vol. i. p. 319, that the emperor planted both sides of the road from Dehli to Dawlatabād with trees, for the purpose of shading the inhabitants when passing from the one place to the other.

‡ This is, no doubt, the تلنك of Ferishta and *Tilling* of Dow ; the reading of our MSS. تكتك is evidently wrong.

§ It will scarcely be necessary to add any thing to the valuable notes of M. de Sacy and Mr. Marsden on this place ; Relat. de l'Egypte, p. 112, and Travels of Marco Polo, p. 626. But as a few notices of it are to be found in Abulfeda's Geography, not mentioned by them, I shall here give them. قال ابن سعيد المعبر المشهور علي الالسن ومنها يجلب اللانس (اللاس) وبقصارتها يضرب

lodging for the Emperor, with cells for his suite, and for travellers generally. There is no necessity, therefore, for a poor man's carrying any provisions with him on this road.

When, therefore, the Sultan Kotb Oddīn was on this journey, and had with him [a]Khazir Khān, the son of his elder brother who was in prison, some of the Emīrs formed a conspiracy, by which it was their intention to depose the Emperor, and to proclaim this son of his elder brother. But the Emperor discovering this, instantly put his nephew and his nephew's father to death, as well as his other brothers, who were then confined in the fortress of [b]Kālīyūr.*

This fortress is situated on the top of a high hill, and seems as if it had been cut out of the rock: opposite to it is no other mount. Within it are reservoirs filled with rain-water; and about it are numerous walls,

---

[b] كاليور .        [a] خضر خان .

---

المثل وفي شماليها جبال متصلة ببلاد بلهرا ملك ملوك الهند وفي غربيها يصب نهر الصوليان في
البحر والمعبر شرقي الكولم بثلثة ايام او اربعة وينبغى ان يكون بميله الي الجنوب عنها. Ibn Saīd
has said, that the Maabar is well-known and often mentioned. From it is brought the Lās (un-washed silk), on the washing of which a proverb has been formed. On the north of this place are the mountains adjoining the districts of Balharā king of the kings of India. On the west of it does the river Sūliān discharge itself into the sea. The Maabar is to the east of Kawlam (Coulan), about three or four day's journey : to the south of which it must be necessarily placed. Again, the longitude and latitude are said to be, according to Ibn Saīd, east 142° 8'; lat. 17° 45'. Where the first, allowing about 17° west for the difference of calculation, is evidently too great. And if any reliance can be placed on the last, the conjecture of M. de Sacy, that the Maabar probably extends as far north as the mouths of the Ganges, cannot be true. If we could ascertain where the districts of بلهرا Balharā commence, we may, probably, be able to determine this question. The reader should be informed, that in many cases in which Ferishta has معبر Maabar, Col. Dow not knowing, I suppose, what to make of the word, has translated it by Malbar. Hist. Hind. vol. i. p. 300, &c. Again, it is said, قال واول بلاد المعبر من جهة المنيبار
(المليبار) راس كمهري بضم الكاف وسكون الميم وضم الها وكسر الرا المهمله ثم يا اخر الحروف. He
has said, the first (part) of the districts of El Maabar, on the part of Manībār (Malabar), is Cape Komhori (Comorin), with o after k, m without any vowel, o after h, i after r, &c. In this case Cape Comorin is the southern limit, and the latitude given above, the northern.

* The Gwalior of Rennell. Some account of this expedition, mutiny, and murder of the king's brothers, is to be found in Dow, vol. i. pp. 298-9. An abstract of the history of this cele-brated fortress will be given from the Gwalior Nāmah (كواليار نامه) in an Appendix to this chapter.

upon which warlike engines are planted. This is their strongest fortress : beneath it, is a small town.

When, however, Kotb Oddīn had killed his brothers, and so purified his kingdom that no one seemed left to contend with him, divine Providence gave the supreme power to one of his most powerful and choice friends, namely, <sup>c</sup>Nāsir Oddīn Khosrū Khān, who killed him, and took possession of the empire: but this he held only for a short time.* The reason was, that when he had taken possession of the throne, he sent dresses of honour to the governors of the several provinces ; which they all put on, as a mark of obedience, if we except <sup>d</sup>Toglik Shāh, father of the present Emperor of Hindūstān Mohammed Shāh. This person was then governor of <sup>e</sup>Debālbūr,† and would neither put on the dress, nor tender his obedience. The consequence was, an army was sent against him, which he put to flight. The Emperor then sent his brother against him : him also he routed, and put to death : and so far did matters proceed, that Toglik also slew Nāsir Oddīn Khosrū Khān and seized his empire.

This Nāsir Oddīn had originated some great abominations during his reign,‡ of which the forbidding oxen to be slaughtered is one, and which is one of the regulations of the infidel Hindoos. For among them, no one is allowed to slaughter an ox ; and, in case he should do so, he is ordered to be stitched up in its skin, and to be burnt. The reason is, they so much esteem the ox that they drink its urine, both to promote prosperity and to recover health. They also daub their walls with the dung of these ani-

---

<sup>e</sup> دَبَالبور.al. دَبَالبور.    <sup>e</sup> دبَالبور .    <sup>d</sup> تغلق شاه .    <sup>c</sup> ناصر الدين خسرو خان .

---

* The rise of this wretch will be found in Dow, pp. 300-4; and at p. 307 we are told, that his reign continued only five months; but according to my copies of Ferishta his reign was some days short of this. چند روزکم پنجماه.

† The province of this name. We have in Dow, vol. i. p. 305, the first intimation of this, where we are told, that this chief was governor of Lahore and Debalpūr; and that his son was appointed master of the horse in Dehli, as noticed by our traveller a little lower down. Toglik, however, is styled in Dow, Ghazi Malluk.

‡ Nothing is said in Dow of this; but in Ferishta some intimations of it are found, viz. "He began بهندوان بت پرستي آغاز نهاده مصحفـرا بجاي کرسي کار فرمودند وبالاي ان نشسته . to practise idolatry with the Hindoos, so that the Korān was occasionally placed as a stool and sat upon."

mals. Hence it was that Nāsir Oddīn became so hateful to the Mohammedans, that they stimulated ᶠ Toglik Ghiāth Oddīn, to put him to death,
and to take possession of the kingdom.

This Toglik was originally descended from the Turks who inhabit the
mountains in the district of Sindia.* He was very poor; but, betaking
himself to the cities of these parts, he got employment in feeding cattle.
After this he became a foot soldier, and then a horse soldier: in the next
place, as his abilities appeared he was made a ᵍ commanding officer.
After this the Emperor Kotb Oddīn appointed him governor of Debālbūr;
and his son, who is now Emperor, keeper of the horse. Toglik was
brave, warlike, honourable, and just: and, as his son was stationed at
Dehli as keeper of the horse, when the father had determined to rebel,

---

ᶠ تغلق غياث الدين ‪.‬ ᵍ امير ‪.‬

---

* Ferishta tells us, that he could find nothing upon which he could rely as to the origin of
Toglik Shāh. His words are these: كشته غافل ومتاخرين متقدمين از هندوستان مورخان
قاسم محمد اوراق اين ومسعود اند نكردانيده تحقيق قلم مرقوم تغلقشاهرا ونسبت اصل هيچيك
عادل ابراهيم سلطان عصر پادشاه جهانگير محمد الدين نور عهد اوائل در چون فرشته
هندوستان بادشاه تاريخ بخواندن رغبتي ايشانرا كه انجای مردم بعض از رسيد لاهور ببلدۀ شاه
ايم نديده كتاب هيچ در صريحا خبر نيز ما كفتند نمود تغلقشاهيه دودمان ونسب اصل استفسار بود
غلامان سلك در تغلقشاه الدين غياث سلطان پدر تغلق ملك كه دارد شهرتي ملك درين اما
دختر كرده وصلت اند ملك اين يوميه كه جت مردم با و داشت انتظام بلبن سلطان ترك
آمده وجود از زو الدين غياث وسلطان كرفت ايشان از " The historians of Hindustan, both
ancient and modern, have neglected to give any particular account of the origin and descent of
Toglikshāh. Mohammed Kāsim Ferishta, however, the writer of these pages, when he arrived at
Lahore, during the times of the Emperor Nūr Oddīn Mohammed Jahāngīr, on the part of the
Sultan of his time Ibrahīm Aādil Shāh, enquired of the persons of that place, whose desire it was
to investigate the history of the Kings of Hindustan, what was the origin and descent of the family
of Toglikshāh. They said: We have found no clear account of it in any book whatever. In this
State, however, there is a report, that the King Toglik, father of the Emperor Ghiāth Oddīn
Toglikshāh, obtained a situation among the Turkish slaves of the Sultan Balaban: and contract-
ing an intimacy with the Jit tribe, who are stipendiaries upon this kingdom, married a daughter of
one of them; and from him descended the Sultan Ghiāth Oddīn." We have a sketch of
this in Dow, vol. i. p. 308, where, instead of *Balaban* we read *Balin*. My two copies of Ferishta,
however, the Tabakāti Akbarī, and Ibn Batūtu, are constant in giving بلبن *Balaban*, which is
undoubtedly the true reading: and, as Ibn Batūta lived much nearer the time of Toglikshāh than
Ferishta did, it is very likely that his account of his origin is the true one.

he corresponded with this son, who cajoled the Emperor Khosrū Khān; sŏmetimes, for example, appearing at his post without the city, and then returning to his father. Aîter some days, however, he waɜ missing till after sunset, which giving some suspicion to Nāsir Oddīn, he sent for him, but could not find him : on this occasion he had escaped, and taken all the best of the Emperor's horses to his father.*

The Emīr of Multān, [h] Kashlū Khān, joined Toglik in his rebellion, in order to avenge Kotb Oddīn, son of Nāsir Oddīn, their common master. When, however, the two conspirators entered Dehli, and Nāsir Oddīn had betaken himself to flight with only a few Hindoo fakeers, Toglik said to Kashlū Khān : You shall be Emperor. But he refused; and Toglik took possession of the government. After this, Nāsir Oddīn was taken and put to death; and the kingdom was purged, and remained so for four years.

After this the Emperor sent his son, who is now Emperor, to reduce the provinces of Telinga,† which are at the distance of three months from

---

[h] كشلو خان ٠

---

* This is Dow's Malleck Fuchir ul Dien Jonah. Ferishta tells us, that the escape of this young man to his father, was the first thing that awakened this king to the danger of his situation : and, as his words very much confirm the account given by Ibn Batūta I shall here give them : دربین اثنا

بعد از دو ماه و نیم ملك جونا نیم شبي فرصت یافته با دو سه کس معتمد سوار شد واز دهلي بایلغار راه دیبالپور کرفت خسروخان از خواب غفلت بیدار شده از زوال دولت خویش اندوهناك کردید

&c. In the mean time, after two months and a half, Jūnā, finding an opportunity in the middle of the night, mounted with two or three confidential friends, and took the road from Dehli to Debal-pūr with all haste. Khosrū Khān being (thus) awakened from his sleep of negligence, became anxious as to the decline of his power, &c. The particulars, however, differ a little.

† Our MSS. here read التكتك which is a manifest mistake of the copyist, for تلنك the orthography of Ferishta, and which Dow writes, *Tilling*, vol. i. p. 309, where we have an abridgment of the account given by Ferishta of this rebellion. But as Dow's mode of writing the proper names, &c. differs very materially from that found in my MSS. it may not be amiss to notice it. Ferishta's words are these, وملك فخر الدین جوناله (جونا .al) پسر بزرك بود ولي عهد كردانیده سرشرا باعطاي چتر بآسمان رسانید والفخان خطاب داده " But Malik Fakhar Oddin Jūnāla (al. Jūnā) his eldest son, he appointed as his successor, and lifted his head almost to the skies, by giving him a royal umbrella. He also gave him the title of Alif Khān." With this my MSS. agree; Dow, however, gives Aligh Khān, (he probably read الغ where I have الف).

For some account of *Telingāna*, (occasionally written تلنكانه by Ferishta) the place here meant, see Rennell's Memoir to his Map of Hindustan, p. cxi. &c.

Dehli; but when he had arrived at a certain part of the way, one of the courtiers thought proper to rebel, and to possess himself (if possible) of the kingdom. For this purpose he circulated a report, that the Emperor was dead; supposing that the Emīrs would now immediately proclaim him king. When they heard this, however, every one of them struck his drum, and betook himself to his own part (*i. e.* to rebellion):* so that the prince was left with his particular friends alone.† The Emīrs, moreover, intended

---

* This appears to be equivalent to the scriptural expression, " Every man to his tent, O Israel," which seems to have been the watch-word for rebellion.

† As the account of this mutiny is not given correctly by Dow (vol. i. p. 309, &c.) I shall here give it in the words of Ferishta. درين اثنا در ارد از ممر عفونت وناسازي آب وهواي آن

دیار و بیماریهاي گوناکون بهمرسیده وخلقي بیحساب واسپ وفیل بیشمار بمعرض تلف شدند

ومردم لشکر بتنك اراجیف خبر غیر مکرر في انداختن مقارن آن حال بواسطهٔ سد طریق چون

قریب یکماه از دهلي خبر (نه) رسید وحال آنکه در هفته دو مرتبه بدانك چوکي از دهلي مي

آمدند شیخزاده دمشتي (دمشقي) وعبید شاعر که در آن حین بهند آمده ملازمت الف خان

مي بودند وکمال تقرب داشتند از شوخي طبیعت آوازهٔ دروغي انداختند که سلطان غیاث الدین

تغلقشاه فوت شده و پادشاه دیگر برتخت نشسته در دهلي خللي وفتنهٔ عظیم حادث کشته وباین

اکتفا نکرده هر دو مفتن بمنزل ملك تیمر وملك مل افغان وملك کافور مهردار وملك تکین که

عمدهٔ امراي لشکر بودند رفته کفتند که احوال دهلي برین نهج است والف خان چون شمارا از

کبار ملوك سلطان علا الدین وشریك ملك خود میداند قرار داده که هرچیار کسرا در یکروز بکیرد

وکردن زند ایشان از استماع این سخن مضطرب شدند وهراس عظیم در لشکر افتاده هرکس سرخود

کرفته رو بکریز نهاد &c. During this interval, from the corrupt state of the water and air of those parts, and as various diseases had appeared, a great number of men, horses, and elephants, perished; and, besides, the soldiers had circulated false reports. At the same juncture, as the roads had been stopped up, and no news had arrived from Dehli for about a month (two couriers usually arriving weekly) the Sheikh Zāda Dimashkī, and Obeid the Poet, who had lately come to Hindūstān, and waited on the prince's person, raised an insolent and false report, that the Emperor Toglik Shāh was dead, that another king was already upon the throne, and that the greatest confusion was prevailing in Dehli; but not content with this, the two insurgents went to the quarters of Malik Timūr, Malik Mal Afghān, Malik Kāfūr, the keeper of the seals, and Malik Tagīn, who was chief in command, and said: The affairs of Dehli are in this state; and, as Alif Khān knows you to have been the great men of Alā Oddīn, and participators in his rule, he has made up his mind to seize upon you all four in one day, and to strike off your heads. When they heard this, they were much alarmed; and, as great fear already existed in the army, each of them made up his mind and fled. The account given in the Tabakāti Akbarī agrees with this as to matter, except that it gives الغ خان Aligh Khān, for الف خان Alif Khān.

to kill him ; but from this they were diverted by one of the great men of
their body, whose name was <sup>i</sup>Timūr.  The prince then fled to his father
with ten of his friends, whom he styled <sup>k</sup>Yārān (*i. e.* friends in the Persic);
but, when he came to him, was immediately sent back on his journey with
a large army.  Upon this, the Emīrs, who had intended to put him to
death, fled; but some of them were taken, and put to death.  Thus the
matter terminated, and he returned to his father.

The father himself then undertook an expedition against the province of
<sup>l</sup>Laknoutī,* in which resided at that time the Sultan Shams Oddīn son of Ghiāth
Oddīn Balaban : to whom had fled the Emīrs of Toglik, as just mentioned.
About this time, however, Shams Oddīn died, having first bound his son,
Shahāb Oddīn (by contract), who accordingly took possession of the
throne.  His younger brother, however, <sup>m</sup>Ghiāth Oddīn Bahādur Būra,
overcame him, and seized upon the kingdom.  He then killed all the rest
of his brothers, except Shahāb Oddīn, who had been bound to mount
the throne, and Nāsir Oddīn : for they fled to Toglik imploring assistance.
He allowed them, therefore, to march with his army, in order to give battle
to Ghiāth Oddīn.  Toglik had also appointed his son Mohammed to the
office of Nuwāb in Dehli during his own absence on this expedition.  He
proceeded therefore, and gained possession of the province of Laknoutī,
having put Ghiāth Oddīn to the rout, after which, however, he took him
prisoner, and carried him to Dehli.

---

<sup>m</sup> بهادر بوره .          <sup>l</sup> اللكنوتي .          <sup>k</sup> ياران .          <sup>i</sup> تمور .

* Some account of this expedition is given by Dow, vol. i. p. 311, where we also find the
appointment of the Emperor's eldest son to the office of Nuwāb of Dehli.  Ferishta places this
expedition in the year of the Hejira 724, A.D. 1324, and as Dow's account is in some respects
inaccurate, I shall give Ferishta's words : سنه اربع عشرين وسبعمائة عرایض از لكهنوتي وسنارکانو
آمد که امرا وحکام آنجا دست دراز کرده بيداد بسيار ميکنند سلطان تغلقشاه لشکر جمع
کرده الف خان را در دهلي به نيابت خود نکاه داشته بجانب شرق هندوستان نهضت فرمود
&c. وجون به ترهت رسيد سلطان ناصر الدين ولد سلطان غياث الدين بلبن "In the year 724
accounts came from Lakhnoutī and Sanārgānw, stating that the Emīrs and magistrates of
that place were exercising great cruelties and injustice upon the inhabitants.  Upon this the
Emperor Toglikshāh getting an army together, and appointing Alif Khān for his Viceroy in Dehli,
set out for the eastern parts of Hindūstān: and when he arrived at Turhat, the Sultan Nāsir
Oddīn, son of the Sultan Ghiāth Oddīn Balaban, &c.

When he had got near to Dehli, he sent to his on Mohammed, requesting him to build him a "kushkā, that is, a palace, which he did, and constructed one, well built of wood, in the space of three days. But Mohammed the son made an agreement with the geometrician who planned it, that the steps leading to it should be made sufficiently broad to allow the elephants * to ascend them, in order to their being presented to the

---

" كشكا .

---

* We read in Dow (vol. i. p. 311) that forty elephants had been sent from Jagenagur, by Alif Khän, for the Emperor; and it is probable these were the elephants intended to be presented on this occasion, if there is any truth at all in this part of the story. In p. 312 of Dow, vol. i, we have a very short account of this event; but there the scene is placed at Afghänpoor, a place of which Rennell gives no account, but which must be very near Dehli. This has been taken from Ferishta, whose words are as follows : متوجه دار السلطنت شده در طي منازل ومراحل داد

سعي داد غافل از آنکه اجل کریبان او کرفته مي کشد الف خان چون شنید که پدر بطریق ایلغار متوجه است کوشکي قریب افغانپور در مدت سه روز احداث کرد که هرکاه سلطان آنجا رسد شب در آنجا توقف کرده صباح بعد از آنکه شهر آراسته کرده باشند وجمیع اسباب سلطنت آماده شده باشد بکوکبه تمام بشهر در آمد سلطان آنجا رسید سبب احداث عمارت بخاطر آورده در آنمقام نزول نمود ... وروز دیکر الف خان وسایر امراي دهلي بسعادت انامل پادشاد سرافراز شده باجماعه که باستقبال او آمده بودند در آن قصر نشست ومایده خاص کشیدند چون طعام برداشتند ومردم دانستند که سلطان بسرعت سوار خواهد شد دستها نا شسته بر آمدند سلطان بتقریب دست شستن آنجا بماند درین اثنا سقف خانه افتاد وسلطان با پنج نفر در ته رفته بجوار حق پیوست در بعضي تواریخ مذکور است که چون قصر نو ساخته وتازه بود فیلاي که سلطان تغلق از بنکاله همراه آورده بود بر کرد قصر دوانیدند از صدمهٔ آن زمین قصر نشست کرده فرو ریخت وبعضي از مورخان کفته اند که از ساختن این قسم قصرکه هیچ ضروري نبود بوي آن میآید که الف خان قصد پدر نموده باشد .  " He made for his capital, using every possible endeavour to expedite his progress, not at all aware that his end was so near. When Alif Khän had heard that his father was coming in great haste, he erected a palace for him near Afghänpür, in the space of three days; so that when the Sultan should have arrived at that place, he might lodge there for the night; and in the morning, when the city should be adorned, and every thing prepared to receive him, he should enter it with great pomp. The Sultan accordingly arrived there, and believing the reason given for erecting this palace to be the true one, he took up his lodging there. On the day following Alif Khän, with the rest of the Emïrs of Dehli, happy at the intimation of the king's arrival, with the company who came to welcome him sat down in the palace to a feast. When the eatables were removed, and the company was aware that the Sultan would soon mount, they got up, not waiting even to wash their hands. The Sultan, however, delayed as long as washing his hands would require,

Emperor Toglik.   A place also was so constructed, that when the foot of
the elephant should come in contact with it, the whole palace should fall
down upon all who may happen to be in it.   When, therefore, the Emperor
arrived at his palace, he had it carpetted and furnished, and took up his
residence within it.   Now, the Emperor had a second son, who was a
great favourite with him.   In consequence of this, the elder brother,

---

but during this time the roof of the palace fell in, and the Sultan with five others perished.
In some of the histories it is said, that since the palace was new and fresh built, and as some
persons made the elephants which the Emperor had brought with him from Bengal race round
it, as the weight of the elephants made the ground sink, the palace on this account fell.
Others say, that this useless palace was built merely because Alif Khān had a design upon his
father." This opinion, however, Ferishta rejects as improbable, and inclines to another, given
by the Hāji Mohammed of Kandahār, that the palace was struck by lightning.   The author
of the Tabakāti Akbarī, however, who is followed by the Farhat El Nāzirīn (فرحت الناطرين)
after giving the same account with Ferishta of this circumstance, concludes by ascribing it to
the same cause with Ibn Batūta.   His words are : از که نباشد پوشیده بصیرت ارباب برضمایر

ساختن این قصر که هیچ ضروری نبود آن می آید که الغ خان قصد پدر نموده باشد وظاهر است
وصاحب تاریخ فیروز شاهی چون در عصر سلطان فیروز تصنیف نموده وسلطان فیروز نسبت سلطان
محمد, اعتقاد مفرط بود از ملاحظهٔ آن ننوشته واین فقیر این معنی را مکرر از ثقات شنیده &c.
It will not be concealed from the minds of intelligent men, that the making of this otherwise
useless palace, was for the purpose of furthering a scheme which Aligh Khān had devised against
his father, and which is evident enough. And, as the author of the Tārīkhi Fīroz Shāhī, published
his work in the time of Fīroz Shāh, who had a very unreasonable faith in Mohammed Shāh, it is on
this account, as I have often heard from credible persons, that he said nothing about this circumstance.   Abul Fazl speaks of this event in the following terms : مهمات بنکاله انتظام داده بدهلی

آمد محمد خان پور او در سر کروهی دهلی در سه روز کوشکی بر ساخت وبخواهش فراوان سلطان را
بدان سر منزل برد سقف خانه فرود آمد وکارش سپری شد اگرچه ضیا برنی در نیکنامی او میکوشد
لیکن منزل بدان ساني ساختن وبچنان خواهش غزیری را مهمان بردن یاد بد کوهری دهد.
" Having arranged matters in Bengal, he came to Dehli.   Mohammed Khān, his son, at the
head of a party in Dehli, built a palace in three days, and with much solicitation got the Sultan
to come to it.   The roof, however, fell in, and his matters were brought to a conclusion ; and
although Ziä Barnī labours to give a good name to this prince, yet to have built such a
receptacle, and to have used such diligence to get the Sultan to it, must bring to mind the
badness of his character." (A-ini Akbarī.)  This Ziä Barnī, it should be remembered, was
a favourite with Mohammed Shāh, and wrote his history under the immediate inspection of
Mohammed's son Fīroz Shāh, as the author of the Tabakāti Akbarī has judiciously remarked.
There can be no doubt, therefore, that Ibn Batūta's account of this event is the true one.  An
account of this transaction, similar to those above given, is also found in the مآثر رحیمي
Maāthari Rahīmī, by Abd El Bākī.

Mohammed, very much feared lest he should be appointed successor to the throne. When, therefore, the different orders, as well as those who had come to welcome the Sultan, had concluded the banquet, the elephants were presented before him: but, when the elephant's foot came in contact with the place appointed, down came the palace upon the head of the Sultan Toglik, his favourite son, and the courtiers who were assembled before him, and all perished. Mohammed, the present Emperor, accordingly took possession of the throne, having been proclaimed by the Emīrs and people, and thus was the kingdom purged of his enemies.

---

# APPENDIX.

## *An Abstract of the History of the Fortress of Gwalior, from the Gwalior Nāmah of [o]Herāman Ibn Kardhar Dās the Munshī.*

As this fortress* is one of the greatest curiosities in Hindūstān, I may perhaps be excused in giving some extracts from a book entitled the [p]Gwalior Nāmah respecting its history and governors.

The hill, it is said, was originally called [q]Kūmatat, and that its neighbourhood abounded in wild beasts. Upon the hill a devotee named [r]Gawālī Pā made his residence, just thirty-two years before the reign of Bikramājīt. Some time after this a Zemindār named Sūraj Sīn, happening to come to this place while engaged in the chase, applied to the devotee for water to drink, which was granted. Upon this and some other occasions, the powers of these waters turned out to be so wonderfully beneficial, that the Zemindār requested to be permitted to enlarge the well, and to build a fortress on the hill, which was also granted. The Darvesh, after blessing the Zemindār, and giving him a casket, which had the supernatural property of supplying him with gold, gave him the name of Sūraj Pāl, adding, that as long as his descendants retained the name of Pāl, so long would they hold this fortress, and succeed in reducing their neighbours to

---

[o] هيرامن بن كردهر داس منشي . [p] كواليار نامه . [q] كومتت . [r] كوالي پا .

---

* For some good views of this fortress, see Colonel Fitzclarence's Journey overland from India; and Bernier's Voyage to Hindustan, in Pinkerton's Collection of Voyages and Travels, vol. viii. p. 64.

their obedience. The consequence of which was, this Zemindār and his posterity became the proprietors of all the neighbouring country: and, after him, the well [r]Sūraj Kund received its name.

After this King, eighty-four of his posterity reigned in the fortress of Gwalior: the fourth of whom, [s]Bhīm Pāl, built the pagoda called [t]Bhīm Absar: the seventh [u]Bhūj Pāl built, the pagoda called [x]Chatar Bhūj Rāe at the top of the fortress: the eighth, [y]Padam Pāl, built the pagoda of [z]Lachhmī Narāyan: the ninth, [a]Anang Pāl, skilled, as it should seem, in the chemical art, struck golden ashrafs of five tola in weight. Nothing remarkable is recorded of the rest until we come to the last, who received the name of [b]Yataj Karan, and who, conformable with the prophecy of the Hindū sage, lost the government of the fort, together with that of the adjacent countries. The account of this event is shortly this.

A neighbouring Raja, named Rhan Mal, had no son, and only one daughter; this prince therefore of the Pāl family offered himself as her suitor, and was accepted. Before he could return to Gwalior, he was adopted son and successor to the Raja Rhan Mal; and, as this Raja's dominions were greater than his own, he was easily persuaded by his Viceroy, Rām Deo, whom he had left at Gwalior, to make over the government of the country and fortress to him.

Seven of Rām Deo's successors held the fortress accordingly, until the time of the Sultan Shams Oddīn, who was originally a slave of Turkish extraction, belonging to the Sultan Kotb Oddīn Aipak. This king, when returning from an expedition to the Deccan, saw, for the first time, this singularly strong fortress; and, upon finding that none of its governors had paid tribute to the Emperors of Dehli, swore upon the Koran that he would subdue it; which he soon after accomplished.

Upon this occasion, which happened A.H. 630, A.D. 1232, a mosque was erected in the fort, and prayers offered up in the name of the Sultan. Some time after, the Sultan surveying the place, found that it contained only two wells of water, and that the part at which he had entered was rather weak; he ordered a wall, therefore, to be built, joining it to the hill; and in the area he made eight wells, and [c]nine bādries; all of which are still in being. One of these wells is very famous for its waters, which are carried to a great distance, and are found very useful to invalids.

After the Sultan had made all his arrangements he returned to Dehli, leaving the fortress in the hands of one [d]Bahādur Khān. From this time to that of the Sultan Alā Oddīn, no officer had been sent from Dehli to Gwalior; some time after his accession, however, it was given to two Rājpūts of the [e]purgunna of Dandarūlī, as a reward for faithful service. These men, however, being much envied by their neighbours, the Rāj-

---

[r]سورج کُنڈ ۔   [s]بھیم پال ۔   [t]بھیم ابسر ۔   [u]بھوج پال ۔   [x]چتر بھوج رای ۔

[y]پدم پال ۔   [z]لچهمي نراین ۔   [a]اننك پال ۔   [b]ینج كرن ۔   [c]نه بادري ۔

[d]بهادر خان ۔   [e]از پرکنه دندرولي ۔

pūts of Tūnūr, were at length invited to a feast, at a little distance from the fortress, and killed by treachery. The fortress then fell into their hands; and eight persons of that tribe held it in succession. Several wells, pagodas, and bowers, were made by this race; the last of whom was Bikramājīt. The fortress then reverted to the Moslems.

From this time to the reign of Ibrāhīm, grandson of the Sultan Bhalūl Lūdī, the fortress was held by Bikramājīt, upon paying tribute to the kings of Dehli. Ibrāhīm, however, forced the power, not without considerable loss, out of the hands of Bikramājīt, who being sent to the presence a prisoner, received the jāgīr of Shams Abād; the government of the fortress then fell into the hands of Aazam Humāyūn, Ibrāhīm's general.

Some time after this, Ibrāhīm suspecting the fidelity of his nobles, and thinking it particularly dangerous to retain Aazam Humāyūn, who had a large and powerful circle of friends, had him suddenly put to death; upon which Selīm Khān, son of the murdered general, rebelled, and betook himself to the east of Hindūstān; but was taken and put to death by Daryā Khān, who had been appointed Governor of the province of Bahār.

Soon after, the Lūdī family fled to the Panj Ab, and presented themselves and their services to Zahīr Oddīn Mohammed Bāber, in Kābul; here they represented the perturbed state of Hindūstān, and formed a treaty with him, which ended in its final subjugation; for soon after a battle took place, in which Ibrāhīm was slain, with Bikramājīt fighting at his side. Khāja Rahīm Dād, one of Bāber's servants, was now appointed to the government of Gwalior, but in a little time got out of favour; when a Rājpūt named Dahar Mankad, a Zemindār of that quarter, became Governor of the fortress.

Upon this occasion, [f] Sheikh Mohammed Ghauth, a man of considerable influence, represented to the king the great impropriety of an infidel's holding this fortress, under a sovereign who professed the true faith; and Khāja Rahīm Dād was restored to the government; which he held but a short time, and was succeeded by [g] Abul Fath, who held it till the death of Bāber.

When Mohammed Humāyūn succeeded to the throne, he took up his residence for some time in the fortress of Gwalior; and at that time built the [h] Humāyūn temple, a place commanding an extensive prospect, and enjoying the most wholesome air. He then returned to his capital.

When [i] Shīr Shāh came to the throne, he took up his residence for some time at Gwalior, and then built the [k] Shīr temple, and also constructed a large tank in its area.

After the death of Shīr Shāh, which happened at this place, his son [l] Jalāl Khān, succeeded to the throne, and took the name of [m] Islām Shāh. He also took up his residence in this fortress, and in it he died.

During the next reign, which was short and troublous, the possession of the fort of

---

[f] شیخ محمد غوث.    [g] ابو الفتح.    [h] همایون مندر.    [i] شیر شاه.

[k] شیر مندر.    [l] جلال خان.    [m] اسلم شاه.

Gwalior remained in the hands of [n]Bahbal, a slave of Shīr Shāh, who held it until Akbar came to the throne.

The Rājpūts, however, desirous of regaining their ancient ascendancy in these parts, with Rām Sāh, a son of Bikramājīt, assembled a large force and attacked the fortress. Upon this occasion, [o]Kayā Khān, one of Akbar's generals, was despatched to relieve and take possession of it. When Kayā arrived at Gwalior, he was met by the forces of [p]Rām Sah, and an obstinate battle of three days' continuance ensued, but which ended in favour of Akbar's troops. After this Bahbal remained to be subdued, and the fort to be taken, which after a short siege was completed. The servants of Akbar held the fortress after this for fifty years.

When Jahāngīr came to the throne, the government of Gwalior was put into the hands of his servants, who seem to have advised him to destroy the building termed the *Shīr Mandar*, to erect another in its place, and to name it the *Jahāngīr Mandar*, which is said to be very beautiful.

When [q]Shāh Jahān succeeded to the empire, the government of Gwalior fell to the lot of one of his greatest favourites and bravest generals, Muzaffir Khān, who, on this occasion, received the title of Wālā Khāni Jahān; and in his hands it remained during a space of nineteen years.

This Governor was a great encourager of good and learned men, and very remarkable for his justice and liberality to all. He is said to have had an elephant so powerful and courageous, that he would destroy whole ranks of the enemy at once; which he did so effectually upon a battle happening with the house of Lūdī, that he was the principal cause of the victory, and for which the Governor obtained the title of Khāni Jahān. On this and other accounts he had a statue of this elephant carved in stone, and set up at the north gate of the fort. Near the same spot he erected and peopled a village; and this he called, after his former name, Muzaffir Pūr. In the vicinity of this he planted a garden, and here he made two wells, and erected some seats for the accommodation of the inhabitants. A few trees of this garden still remain.

Besides this, be built a lofty mansion for himself, containing some large rooms of state, with other apartments: in the court of which he made a deep tank, and in the front of this court four gardens. In this mansion the Governors of the fort still reside. It is also said, that during this man's government, his son Mansūr planted a garden on the banks of the river [r]Sūn Rīgh, which he called after his own name, and which still is used as a promenade for the town; he built too four walls of stone, in the middle of which seats were constructed. He also built and peopled the village Mansūr Pūr, which he called after his own name; and this still remains.

After the expiration of nineteen years, Khāni Jahān took a journey to Lahore, and there died. Upon this occasion Sayyad Sālār Khān, who had been his confidential servant, asked for, and obtained the government of the fort of Gwalior. He then resided in it for two years : after this his brother governed the fort, and he himself was appointed to the government of the provinces. This brother, named Sayyad Aãlam, held the fort for five years, during which time he made and beautified a garden near the Sarai of [s] Meher Ali ; and in the ground known by the name of Kīsū Pūr, he built and peopled the village Shāh Kunj. It is said, that at that time the foundations of the gates of the fort, called [t] Bādal Kadda and [u] Hiata Pūl, had become much decayed, and that he repaired them, covering the gates with iron, and so firmly nailing them, that the rush of an elephant would not make the least impression on them.

Soon after this, he was put out of office for some crime which had better not be mentioned (as our author tells us), and was succeeded by [x] Loharhāsp Khān, son of Muhābat Khān, who appointed [y] Karshāsp Khān his lieutenant; but after two years took up his residence himself in the fortress. He is said to have been a brave and liberal man, charitable to the poor, and most anxious for information, both from travellers and others. He erected a court of justice without the gate called Bādal Kaddah, and close to the northern wall of the fort, in which, on certain days, he administered justice to the people. The kettle-drum of royalty, which formerly was placed at the gate termed Haita Pūl, he removed to the east of the fort, and nearer to the city, where it still remains. He commenced the removal of the [y] Shāh Kunj to the east of the fort, but left the work unfinished. He also erected a lofty state-room in the [a] Arwāhī, and made two wells of exceeding good water in its court-yard. After the space of six years, however, he was sent on an expedition into the Deccan, from which he returned with success. He then presented himself before the Emperor in Dehli, who appointed him to the government of the Sūbah of Kābul. Upon this occasion, his lieutenant at Gwalior was a person named Akhairāj, an officer in whom he placed great confidence. This happened A. H. 1067 ; A.D. 1656.

During the sickness of the reigning king, which happened at this time, and the troubles which arose on account of the rebellion of Dārāh Shikōh and his brothers, we hear scarcely any thing of the fortress of Gwalior; because, perhaps, it happened to lie almost entirely out of the scene of action; it remained, however, for some time in the hands of Akhairāj ; but as he had the imprudence to close it on one occasion against the royal standard, it was at length given to [b] Obaid Allah Khān; and soon after this, several of the rebels falling into the king's power, were put into confinement in the fortress, and there kept.

In the next year, i. e. A. H. 1068, A. D. 1657, Dārāh Shikōh was carried prisoner to Dehli, and there lost his life ; and upon this, his son, [c] Sipehar Shikōh, with several of his friends, were all placed in the fortress of Gwalior, in the custody of Obaid Allah Khān. The fort was now closely guarded, and no stranger permitted to enter it

---

[x] لهراسپ خان بن مهابت خان ۰    [u] هَیْته پول ۰    [t] بادل کده ۰    [s] مهر علي ۰

[c] شپهر شکوه ۰    [b] عبید الله خان ۰    [a] ارواهي ۰    [z] شاه کنج ۰    [y] کرشاسپ ۰

About this time a great scarcity took place, probably in consequence of the preceding wars, when Obaid Allah Khān made a provision, for the first time, for the pious, for travellers, and the poor; this was given in the court-house built by the former Governor, where Mohammed, a Sherīf and Mansabdār, presided.  Soon after, several other of the rebels, namely, Mohammed Sultan, Soleimān Shikōh, and several nobles, their friends, fell into the hands of the Emperor, and were consigned to the Governor of Gwalior, who now was Muatamid Khān, Obaid Allah having been commanded to give up the fortress to him.  Soleimān Shikōh, however, soon after died; and Morād Bakhsh, one of the nobles, was put to death by the law of retaliation.  The graves of both are on the top of the fort.

The first two years of the government of Muatamid Khān in the fortress of Gwalior, were marked with the utmost liberality and regard to public good; particularly so, as a great scarcity prevailed during this time.  He also erected a lofty hall for the transaction of public business, adjoining the Shāh Jahān Mandar, as also a bath which was a great public convenience.  A wall too, which had long ago been commenced, stretching out before the gate termed Bādal Kadda, and which had been intended to obstruct a ready egress from the fort, was completed by him; to which he added another, somewhat higher than the gateway, and joining the walls of the castle.  A sixth gateway, leading from the fort to the plain, was also constructed by him; and this received the name Aālamgīr.  Upon both angles of the wall he likewise erected a lofty tower, and over the gates of each of these, a [d] Chhaterī.  On the left side of the gate Bādal Kadda, a large hall of justice was also built, in which the business of state was ever after to be transacted; from all of which, the appearance and strength of the fort were greatly augmented.  The inscription then written on the Aālamgīrī gate, was this :

در زمان خجسته عالم کیر        ❊    که زفیضش زمانه یافت مراد

معتمد خان زفطرت عالي        ❊    در دولت بروي قلعه کشاد

گفت هاتف زسال تاریخش        ❊    باد دایم مکان فیض آباد

> In the happy times of Aālamgīr,
> From whose bounty time was blest,
> Muatamid Khān from his lofty mind,
> Opened a door of prosperity upon the face of the fortress.
> Hātif said, on the year of its date,
> " Let the place long remain the residence of plenty."

The sum of the letters, according to the Abjad, found in the last line of these verses will give the date of the Hejira in which this event took place, which is A.H. 1071, A.D. 1660.

The Mandui, looking towards the city eastward, and commenced by Muhābat Khān, was completed by this Governor, and called Awrang Kunj Abād.  He also constructed

---

[d] چهتري .

the shops which run in both directions, and in which the business of the city and markets is carried on. Over this place he constructed a high wall which joins the fort, and which received the name of [e] " The fort, the asylum of the city." Encompassing this is the [f] Nūri Kunj Abād, also erected by him for the reception and support of the pious. He also repaired, and very much strengthened, the court of the Kachharī : and, as the inhabitants of this part were very much in want of water, he obtained leave from the court to construct three stone cisterns, with seats, gates, and whatever else was necessary to promote the convenience and pleasure of the people : all of which he completed ; and the following is the inscription which was placed over one of the gates at this time.

در خلافت خديو عالم كير ۞ كه زعدلش زمانه معمور است

معتمد خان بناي منيع كرد ۞ كه زآبش شفاي رنجور است

سال تعميرش از خرد جستم ۞ كفت هاتف كه چشمهٔ از نور است

During the reign of the great prince Aālamgīr,

From whose justice the world is peopled,

Muatamid Khān erected a strong building,

From the water of which the sick are healed.

By wisdom, says Hātif, I sought the year of its erection ;

It is a fountain of light. (*i. e.* the sum of the letters in the four last words, which is, A.H. 1073—A.D. 1662.)

The tank, which stood in the way to the fort, and was situated near the Bhairūn Pūl, growing old, was by the heavy rains which fell about this time utterly destroyed ; and the stones of which it had been built were carried to some distance. This Governor thoroughly repaired it ; and the idol-temple standing near it, which had originally belonged to Gawālī Pā, and was now much frequented by the Hindoos, he converted into a mosque for the use of strangers and travellers. The following is the inscription which was then fixed upon it :

مشنوي

در زمان خديو عالمكير ۞ نوربخش جهان چو بدر منير

لله الحمد كين خجسته مقام ۞ معتمد خان زصدق كرد تمام

بود بتخانهٔ كوالي زشت ۞ مسجدي ساخته چو كشك بهشت

خان روشن دل وسراپا نور ۞ نور حق كرد روشن چو ظهور

كرد مسمار خانهٔ طاغوت ۞ آفرين شد زملك تا ملكوت

نور چون دور كرد ظلمت دير ۞ كفت هاتف كه نور باد بخير

In the reign of the great prince Aālamgīr,

Like the full shining moon, the enlightener of the world,

Praise to God, that this happy place,

[e] قلعه شهر پناه .     [f] نور كنج آباد .

Was by Muatamid Khān completed, as an alms.

It was the idol-temple of the vile Gawālī.

He made it a mosque like a mansion of Paradise.

The Khān of enlightened heart, nay light (itself) from head to foot,

Displayed the divine light like that of mid-day.

He closed the idol-temple:

Exclamations (of surprise), rose from earth to heaven.

When the light put far away the abode of darkness,

Hātif said, let the light be a blessing.

N.B. The sum of the letters composing the three last words, counted according to the Abjad, (see Sir William Jones's Persian Grammar, p. 14, edit. 9), amounts to 1075, and this gives the year of the Hejira in which this took place—A.D. 1664.

He also repaired and deepened a tank in the grounds called the Khabūtar Khāna, or Pigeon-house; and to this he gave the name of Nūri Sākir. Another tank, too, situated on the top of the fort, and near the Shāh Jahān Mandar, which had grown so much out of repair as to lose its water, notwithstanding its having been cut out of the solid rock, he thoroughly repaired, and enclosed with a wall firmly built with brick and mortar, so that not a drop of its water was lost. To each of these last a copy of verses was attached, giving the date of the repairs, and the name of the Khān; which I do not think it worth while to copy out and translate.

The same Governor, it is said, so adorned and planted the [g]Arwāhī, which appeared like a girdle about the mount, that it presented fountains, tanks, a [h]chabūterah, grapes, melons, and other fruits; such, that many of the fruits were, on account of their superlative excellence, frequently sent to the Presence at Dehli. The melons were occasionally so large, that some of them exceeded fourteen of the ser of Shāh Jahān Abād, in weight.

Besides this, a mosque was erected in the [i]Chok Bāzar, with three immensely high towers and some minarets, having also a tank of water with other fountains always filled with water, and surrounded with seats for the convenience of ablution. Before this is an area with a very high gate, on the top of which is a [k]Bankla, and on both sides two beautifully constructed halls. Another tank was also made, and named after his son, [l]Jamāli Sarūr, which was surrounded by stone walls, and provided with seats.

In the year 1078 of the Hejira, A. D. 1667, an order came from the court, commanding Muatamid Khān to give up the fort, together with the prisoners it contained, which were then three, to Khidmatgār Khān, and to proceed to the Presence, in order to receive the government of Akberābād. With this the Khān complied, and proceeded to Shāh Jahān Abād, where he was loaded with favours, and dismissed to his station. And, as the writer of this history, Herāman Ibn Kardhar Dās, the Munshī, was a servant of Muatamid Khān, his account of Gwalior closes with the removal of his master from that place.

---

[g]ارواهي ۰    [h]چبوترہ ۰    [i]چوک بازار ۰    [k]بنکله ۰    [l]جمال سرور ۰

## CHAPTER XVI.

*Ibn Batūta arrives at the Queen Mother's Palace—His Daughter's death and funeral—The Emperor's return to Dehli—Appoints Ibn Batūta Judge of Dehli—Character of the Emperor—Quarrels with the Inhabitants of Dehli, and commands them to quit the city for Dawlatabād—Emīr of Fargāna put to death—The Kāzī Jalāl Oddīn and others put to death—Cruelties of the Emperor—Arabic panegyric composed by our traveller for him—In danger of losing his life—Gives up his office, and joins the Religious.*

LET us now return to the description of our arrival Dehli. When we arrived at this place, the Vizier having previously met us, we came to the door of the Sultan's haram, to the place in which his mother, [m]El Makhdūma Jahān* resides, the Vizier, as also the Kāzī of the place, being still with us. These paid their respects at the entrance, and we all followed their example. We also, each of us, sent his present to her, which was proportionate to his circumstances. The Queen's secretaries then registered these presents, and informed her of them. The presents were accepted, and we were ordered to be seated. Her viands were then brought in ; we received the greatest respect and attention in their odd way. After this, dresses of honour were put upon us, and we were ordered to withdraw to such places as had been prepared for each of us. We made our obeisance and retired accordingly. This service is presented, by one's bowing the head, placing one of the hands on the earth, and then retiring.

When I had got to the house prepared for me, I found it furnished with every carpet, vessel, couch, and fuel, one could desire. The victuals which they brought us consisted of flour, rice, and flesh, all of which was brought from the mother of the Emperor. Every morning we paid our respects to the Vizier, who on one occasion gave me two thousand dinars, and said : This is to enable you to get your clothes washed. He also gave me a large robe of honour ; and to my attendants, who amounted to about forty, he gave two thousand dinars.

---

[m] المخدومة جهان .

---

* This, according to the Tabakāti Akbarī and Ferishta, was the name of the Emperor's mother, and to her was consigned the care of the household.

After this, the Emperor's allowance was brought to us, which amounted
to the weight of one thousand Dehli-Ritls of flour, where every Ritl * is

---

* This word, which accordingto the author of the Kāmoos, &c. may be pronounced either Ritl or
Ratl (رِطْل or رَطْل) is constantly given by M. de Sacy Rotl (as if written رُطْل) for what reason
I know not.  As it is important that the reader should have some idea of the value of this measure
of weight, I shall here put down what the author of the Kāmoos has said about it (sub voce
مَكّ) and, as it is here connected with several others, I shall copy the whole of the article.

المَكّوكُ كتنّورِ طاسٌ يشربِ به ومِكيالٌ يَسَعُ صاعاً ونِصفاً او نِصفَ رِطلِ الى ثَمانِ اواقِ او نِصفُ

الوَيبةِ والوَيبةُ اثنانِ وعشرونَ او اربعةٌ وعشرونَ مُدّاً بمُدِّ النبي ... او ثلثُ كَيلجاتٍ والكَيلَجةُ مناً

وسبعةُ اثمانِ مناً والمنا رطلانِ والرِطلُ اثنتا عشرةَ اوقيّةً والاوقيّةُ اِستارٌ وثُلثُ اِستارٍ والاِستارُ اربعةُ مَثاقيلَ

ونِصفُ والمِثقالُ دِرهمٌ وثُلثةُ اسباعِ دِرهمٍ والدِرهمُ سِتّةُ دَوانيقَ والدانِقُ قيراطانِ والقيراطُ طَسّوجانِ

والطَّسّوجُ حبّتانِ والحَبّةُ سُدسُ ثُمنِ دِرهمٍ وهو جزءٌ من ثمانيةِ واربعينَ جزءٌ من دِرهمٍ [a]   The
Makkūk, of the form Tannūr, is a cup out of which one drinks: it is also a measure containing
a sāa and a half, or (which is the same thing) from half a ritl to eight ounces; or, half the waibat.
And the waibat contains either two and twenty or four and twenty modds, according to the
modd of the prophet (i. e. of Hegāz), or three kailajes; and the kailaj containsthe maund and
seven-eighths of a maund; and the maund contains two ritls, a ritl twelve ounces, and an ounce
contains an istar and two-thirds, and an istar contains four mathkāls and a half; a mathkāl equals
a dram and three-sevenths of a dram; and a dram six dāniks; and a dānik contains two kīrāt
(carats); and a kīrāt two tassūjes; and a tassūj two grains; and a grain the sixth of the eighth
of a dram; which is a part of forty-eight parts of a dram.  Tabularly thus:

| | | |
|---|---|---|
| 1 Makkūk = 1 Sāa + $\frac{1}{2}$ = 1 $\frac{\text{Ritl}}{2}$ to 8 ozs. | 1 Mathkāl = 1 Dram + $\frac{3}{7}$ | |
| $\qquad$ = 1 $\frac{\text{Waibat}}{2}$ | 1 Dram $\quad$ = 6 Dāniks | |
| 1 Waiba $\;$ = 22 or 24 Modds = 3 Kailajes | 1 Dānik $\quad$ = 2 Kīrāts | |
| 1 Kailaj $\;$ = 1 Maund + $\frac{7}{8}$ | 1 Kīrāt $\quad$ = 2 Tassūj | |
| 1 Maund = 2 Ritls | 1 Tassūj $\;$ = 2 Grains | |
| 1 Ritl $\quad$ = 12 Ounces | 1 Grain $\quad$ = $\frac{1}{6}$ of $\frac{1}{8}$ of a Dram | |
| 1 Ounce $\;$ = 1 Istär + $\frac{2}{3}$ | $\qquad$ = $\frac{1}{48}$ of a Dram | |
| 1 Istär $\quad$ = 4 Mathkāl + $\frac{1}{2}$ | | |

The ounce, I believe, is our ounce troy, and hence the value of any other of the weights
may be found.  The value of weights, jewels, and metals, as used in Hindustan, are thus given

---

(a) Since writing this, I find that it has been also extracted by M. de Sacy in his Chrestomathie,
tom. i. p. 36, edit. 2.  But, as his extract is without a translation, and otherwise incomplete,
I shall retain it.

equal to five and twenty Ritls of Egypt.   We also had one thousand Ritls

in the Tijārat Nāmah : (تجارت نامه). دانكه آنرا در باشد كه سرخ حبه يك برنج هشت ... دانكه
هندي رتي خوانند وهشت حبه يكماشه باشد وسه ونيم ماشه درم باشد وچهارو نيم ماشه يك
مثقال وچهار جو يك دانك ودوازده ماشه توله وشانزده ماشه دام باشد نيم سير ومن يكسير
فلزات مخصوص باشد ...... Know   that 8 rice grains make 1 red grain, which in the Hindee is
called a Ratti: 8 of these grains make 1 Māsha; 3½ Māshas, 1 Dram; 4½ Māshas, 1 Mathkāl; 4
barley corns, 1 Dāng; 12 Māshas a Tōla; 16 Māshas, 1 Dām; 1 Ritl is equal to half a Sēr; 1 Maund
to 1 Sēr.   See also Shakespear's Hindūstānī Dictionary under تولا, ماشه, رتي, سير, and من :
and Hamilton's India.

The following are the names and values of measures used in Hindustan, in measuring grain
and other heavy substances, as given in the Tijārat Nāmah. چهتانك يك سير حصه شانزدهم
باشد ودوچهتانك نيم پاو وسه چهتانك پون پاو وچهار چهتانك يكپاو باشد ودو پاو نيم اثار و سه
پاويك اثار پاوكم و چهار پاو يكسير و پنج اثار پسيري باشد وهشت پسيري يكمن وآن چهل سير
بود وسير هرجا مختلف الوزان (الوزن) است چنانچه در شاه جهان آباد سير هشتاد روپيه سكه
نقد در اكبر آباد سير هشتاد روپيه سكه در فرخ آباد سير هشتاد ودو سكه بابت كرانه وبابت غله
سي ودو تنكه پخته در لكهنو سير نود وششش روپيه سكه در مرزاپور سير نود (و) هفت روپيه سكه در
بنارس سير هفتاد (و) دو روپيه سكه در عظيم آباد سير هفتاد وششش روپيه سكه در مرشد آباد
سير هشتاد يكروپيه پاوكم در دهاكه سير هشتاد يكروپيه پاوكم در كلكته سير اشتاد (هشتاد) دو
روپيه سكه در جنوب اكثر سير هشتاد روپيه سكه ودر بيروبجات كيل باشد يعني پيمانه
ودر شمال نيز اوزان مختلفه وپيمانه است ودر بيروبجات اين بلاد هم اوزان مختلفه است
يكي مقرر نيست   i. e. a sixteenth of a sēr makes one chhatānk; two chhatānks, half a pāo;
three chhatānks, a pāo, minus one-fourth; four chhatānks, one pāo: two pāos will be half an
athār: three pāos will be an athār, minus one-fourth: four pāos will be one sēr: five athārs, one
pasērī; eight pasērī, one maund, which will contain forty sēr.   But the sēr every where varies, so
that in Shāh Jahān Abād the sēr will be equal to eighty current rupees; in Akbar Abād, eighty
sicca rupees; in Farakh Abād, it will equal eighty-two sicca rupees in heavy articles; but in
grain, to two and thirty takkas (تخت.)   In Luknow the sēr is equal to ninety-six rupees; in
Mirzapūr, to ninety-seven sicca rupees; in Benares it is equal to seventy-two rupees.   In Aazīm
Abād the sēr equals seventy-six sicca rupees; in Mūrshed Abād it equals eighty-one rupees,
minus one-fourth; in Dakka eighty-one rupees, minus one-fourth; and in Calcutta, the sēr
equals eighty-two sicca rupees.   In the South, the sēr is, for the most part, equal to eighty sicca
rupees.   But in country places it is taken as a measure, not as a weight.   In the North also it
varies in weight, and is also used as a measure.   In the country places of these parts (Farakh
Abād) also the weights vary, no one having been established.   According to Mr. Shakespear,
the Calcutta rupee was by an order of the English government in India, in 1793, fixed to the
weight of 179⅝ grains (troy) : but, whether our writer reckons by this standard or not, it is more
than I can positively say : it is most likely that he does, as the work was written for a servant
of the Company (مستر رابت باترس) Mr. Robert Bātiras? perhaps Patterson) in 1806.

of flesh; and of fermented liquors, oil, oil-olive, and the betel-nut, many Ritls; and also many of the betel-leaf.*

During this time, and in the absence of the Emperor, a daughter of mine happened to die, which the Vizier communicated to him. The Emperor's distance from Dehli was that of ten stages; nevertheless, the Vizier had an answer from him on the morning of the day, on which the funeral was to take place. His orders were, that what was usually done on the death of any of the children of the nobility, should be done now. On the third day, therefore, the Vizier came with the judges and nobles, who spread a carpet and made the necessary preparations, consisting of incense, rose-water, readers of the koran, and panegyrists. When I proceeded with the funeral, I expected nothing of this; but upon seeing their company I was much gratified. The Vizier, on this occasion, occupied the station of the Emperor, defraying every expense, and distributing victuals to the poor, and others; and giving money to the readers, according to the order which he had received from the Emperor.

After this, the Emperor's mother sent for the mother of the child, and gave her dresses and ornaments, exceeding one thousand dinars in value. She also gave her a thousand dinars in money, and dismissed her on the second day. During the absence of the Emperor, the Vizier shewed me the greatest kindness, on the part of himself, as well as on that of his master.

Soon after, the news of the Emperor's approach was received, stating that he was within seven miles of Dehli, and ordering the Vizier to come and meet him. He went out, accordingly, accompanied by those who had arrived for the purpose of being presented; each taking his present with him. In this manner we proceeded till we arrived at the gate of the palace in which he then was. At this place the secretaries took account of the several presents, and also brought them before the Emperor. The presents were then taken away, and the travellers were presented, each according to the order in which he had been arranged. When my turn came, I went in and presented my service in the usual manner, and was very

---

* ورق التنبول . Of this the King of Oude's Persian Dictionary says: در که باشد برگي هندوستان پان كويند . It is a leaf which in Hindūstān they call pān, and which they eat with the betel-nut and quick lime.

graciously received, the Emperor taking my hand, and promising me every kindness. To each of the travellers he gave a dress of honour, [n] embroidered with gold, which had been worn by himself, and one of these he also gave to me. After this, we met without the palace, and viands were handed about for some time. On this occasion the travellers ate, the Vizier, with the great Emīrs, standing over them as servants. We then retired. After this, the Emperor sent to each of us one of the horses of his own stud, adorned and caparisoned with a saddle of silver. He then placed us in his front with the Vizier, and rode on till he arrived at his palace in Dehli. On the third day after our arrival, each of the travellers presented himself at the gate of the palace; when the Emperor sent to inquire, whether there were any among us who wished to take office, either as a writer, a judge, or a magistrate; saying, that he would give such appointments. Each, of course, gave an answer suitable to his wishes. For my own part, I answered, I have no desire either for rule or writership; but the office both of judge and of magistrate, myself and my fathers have filled. These replies were carried to the Emperor, who commanded each person to be brought before him, and he then gave him such appointment as would suit him; bestowing on him, at the same time, a dress of honour, and a horse furnished with an ornamented saddle. He also gave him money, appointing likewise the amount of his salary, which was to be drawn from the treasury. He also appointed a portion of the produce of the villages, which each was to receive annually, according to his rank.

When I was called, I went in and did homage. The Vizier said: The Lord of the world appoints you to the office of judge in Dehli. He also gives you a dress of honour with a saddled horse, as also twelve thousand dinars for your present support. He has moreover appointed you a yearly salary of twelve thousand dinars, and a portion of lands in the villages, which will produce annually an equal sum. I then did homage according to their custom, and withdrew.

We shall now proceed to give some account of the Emperor Mohammed son of Ghiāth Oddīn Toglik: then of our entering and leaving Hindūstān.

This Emperor was one of the most bountiful and splendidly munificent men (where he took); but in other cases, one of the most impetuous and

---

[n] مزركشة .

inexorable : and very seldom indeed did it happen, that pardon followed
his anger.   On one occasion he took offence at the inhabitants of Dehli, on
account of the numbers of its inhabitants who had revolted, and the liberal
support which these had received from the rest ; and, to such a pitch did
the quarrel rise, that the inhabitants wrote a letter consisting of several
pages, in which they very much abused him : they then sealed it up, and
directed it to the Real Head and Lord of the world, adding, " Let no other
person read it."   They then threw it over the gate of the palace.   Those
who saw it, could do no other than send it to him ; and he read it accordingly.   The consequence was, he ordered all the inhabitants to quit the
place ; and, upon some delay being evinced, he made a proclamation
stating, that what person soever, being an inhabitant of that city, should be
found in any of its houses or streets, should receive condign punishment.
Upon this they all went out.*   But, his servants finding a blind man in

---

* We have no mention of this circumstance, either in the Tabakāti Akbarī, Ferishta, or any
other history accessible to me.   Dow ascribes the intention of making Deogīr (afterwards called
Dawlatābād) the seat of government, to the Emperor's being pleased with its *situation* and
*strength*, of which Ferishta, &c. take no notice.   Ferishta, however, states that his reason was
its being more central than Dehli, and farther removed from the Persians and Tartars : but of
its strength nothing is said, except that the Emperor set about fortifying it as soon as he had
settled himself in it.   That Dehli was desolated on this occasion all attest, and from the manner
in which the author of the Tabakāti Akbarī mentions the migration, there is reason to suppose
that something more than the central position of Deogīr was the cause.   His words are these :

واین امر باعث استیصال برایا وتمرد رعایا کردید وکار زراعت معطل ماند وامساك باران نیز باین
حالت وقوع یافت قحطی عظیم در دهلی افتاده چنانچه اکثر خانها بر افتاد وجمیعتها مختل شد
وکار پادشاهي تزلزل تمام راه یافت اندیشه دیکر این بود که دیوکیر را که وسط ممالك پنداشته بود
دولتاباد نام کرده ودار الملك خود سازد از این جهت دهلي را که کشك (رشك) بغداد ودمشق
بود ویران کرده متوطنان اورا که باب وهوا خو کرده بودند حکم فرمود که باهل وعیال خود انتقال
نموده بدیوکیر روند وخرج راه و بهای خانه هریك را از خزانه داد .   " And this matter (*i. e.* the
arrangements made in the Doāb) became the cause of ruin and destruction to the inhabitants.
Hence agriculture was neglected ; and a drought happening at the same time, a terrible famine
appeared in Dehli ; so that the greater part of its houses fell off (from their allegiance) and
such confusion took place that the kingdom was shaken.   Another of his whims was to name
Deogīr Dawlatābād, and as it was central, to make it the seat of empire.   Hence Dehli, which
was the rival of Bagdad or Damascus, he entirely ruined, commanding its inhabitants, to whom
its air and water had become almost a second nature, to proceed with their families to Deogīr,
furnishing them with expenses for a house and for travelling out of the treasury."   And again,

ضابطۀ چند که بتفصیل مذکور خواهد شد وضع نمود تا مردم عاجز آمدند وجمعي که بي استطاعت

one of the houses, and a bed-ridden one in another, the Emperor commanded the bed-ridden man to be projected from a °balista, and the blind
one to be dragged by his feet to ᴾDawlatābād, which is at the distance of
ten days, and he was so dragged; but, his limbs dropping off by the
way, only one of his legs was brought to the place intended, and was
then thrown into it: for the order had been, that they should go to this
place.  When I entered Dehli it was almost a desert.  Its buildings were
very few; in other respects it was quite empty, its houses having been
forsaken by its inhabitants.  The King, however, had given orders, that
any one who wished to leave his own city, may come and reside there.*
The consequence was, the greatest city in the world had the fewest inhabitants.

Upon a certain occasion, too, the principal of the preachers, who was
then keeper of the jewellery, happened to be outwitted by some of the
infidel Hindoos, who came by night and stole some jewels.  For this he
beat the man to death with his own hand.

---

ᴾ دَوْلَةُ آبَادِ .         ° فِي الْمَنْجَنِيقِ .

---

بودند خراب ونابود كشتند وجماعتي كه في الجمله قوت داشتند رو از اطاعت كردانيده بتمرد قرار
دادند وچون سلطان محمد بد خو وزشت مزاج بود وقتل مردم طبيعي وجبلي او شده بود درکشتن
وسياست نمودن توقف وتاءل نميكرد وبواسطه آنكه احكام نفاذ يافت عالم را در ته تيغ
ميكشيد وعرصات‌را از خلق خدا خالي ميساخت تا كار نجائي رسيد كه اكثر ممالك منبوط از
قبضهٔ تصرف او بر آمد بلكه در دهلي كه تختكاه بود نيز تمرد وعصيان شايع شد ودر آمد خراج از
اطراف منقطع كشت وخزائن خالي ماند .  " He made some regulations, which will be particularly mentioned, by which those who had but little wealth were entirely ruined; and those who
had power sufficient to do so, rebelled openly.  And, as Mohammed was naturally a bloody and
fierce man, he made no hesitation whatever in punishing and slaughtering (all such), and as his
commands were enforced, vast numbers were put to death, and the country almost desolated;
in so far, that he lost a great part of the kingdom: nay, in Dehli itself, which was then the
capital, there was open rebellion.  The revenues from other parts were stopped, and the treasury
remained empty."  Immediately after this follows the above extract, which seems to put the
matter out of all doubt, that the account given by our traveller, although not mentioned by
Ferishta, is the true one, as it respects the cause of Dehli's being deserted.  Ferishta, indeed,
gives a similar account of the evacuation, and states that not so much as a slave was left
behind; but in such words as not to favour the reason ascribed by Ibn Batūta: I have, therefore, been induced to give these extracts from an earlier historian.

* The same is said both by Ferishta and the author of the Tabakāti Akbarī. See Dow, p. 333.

Upon another occasion, one of the Emīrs of ⁹Fargāna came to pay him a temporary visit. The Emperor received him very kindly, and bestowed on him some rich presents. After this the Emīr had a wish to return, but was afraid the Emperor would not allow him to do so; he began, therefore, to think of flight. Upon this a whisperer gave intimation of his design, and the Emīr was put to death: the whole of his wealth was then given to the informers. For this is their custom, that when any one gives private intimation of the designs of another, and his information turns out to be true, the person so informed of is put to death, and his property is given to the informer.

There was at that time, in the city of ʳKambāya,* on the shores of India, a Sheikh of considerable power and note, named the Sheikh Alī Haidarī,† to whom the merchants and seafaring men made many votive offerings. This Sheikh was in the habit of making many predictions for them.ˢ But when the Kāzī Jalāl Oddīn Afgānī rebelled against the Emperor, it was told him that the Sheikh Haidarī had sent for this Kāzī Jalāl Oddīn, and given him the cap off his own head. Upon this the Emperor set out for the purpose of making war upon the Kāzī Jalāl Oddīn, whom he put to flight. He then returned to his palace, leaving behind him an Emīr, who should make inquiry respecting others who had joined the Kāzī: the inquiry accordingly went on, and those who had done so were put to death. The Sheikh was then brought forward; and when it was proved that he had given his cap to the Kāzī, he was also slain. The Sheikh Hād, son of the Sheikh Bahā Oddīn Zakaryā, was also put to death, on account of some spite which he would wreak upon him. This was one of the greatest Sheikhs. His crime was, that his uncle's son had rebelled against the Emperor, when he was acting as governor in one of the provinces of India. So war was made upon him, and being overcome, his flesh was roasted with some rice, and thrown to the elephants to be devoured: but they refused to touch it.‡

Upon a certain day, when I myself was present, some men were brought

---

⁹ فرغانه .        ʳ كنباية .        ˢ كان يكاشف باحوالهم .

---

* The Cambay of Rennell.        † One of the Haidaree sect, already noticed.

‡ None of the matter given here is to be found in Ferishta, or any other historian to whom I have access.

out who had been accused of having attempted the life of the Vizier. They were ordered, accordingly, to be thrown to the elephants, which had been taught to cut their victims to pieces. Their hoofs were cased with sharp iron instruments, and the extremities of these were like knives. On such occasions the elephant-driver rode upon them : and, when a man was thrown to them, they would wrap the trunk about him and toss him up, then take him with the teeth and throw him between their fore feet upon the breast, and do just as the driver should bid them, and according to the orders of the Emperor. If the order was to cut him to pieces, the elephant would do so with his irons, and then throw the pieces among the assembled multitude : but if the order was to leave him, he would be left lying before the Emperor, until the skin should be taken off, and stuffed with hay, and the flesh given to the dogs.*

On one occasion one of the Emīrs, *viz.* the Ain El Mulk, who had the charge of the elephants and beasts of burden, revolted, and took away the greater part of these beasts and went over the Ganges, at the time the Emperor was on his march towards the Maabar districts, against the Emīr Jalāl Oddīn. Upon this occasion the people of the country proclaimed the runaway emperor : but an insurrection arising, the matter soon came to an end.†

Another of his Emīrs, namely 'Halājūn, also revolted, and sallied out of Dehli with a large army. The Viceroy in the district of "Telingāna also rebelled, and made an effort to obtain the kingdom ; and very nearly succeeded, on account of the great number who were then in rebellion, and the weakness of the army of the Emperor ; for a pestilence had carried off

---

' هلاجون .    " التكتك .

---

* Ferishta tells us, on one occasion, of a man having been flead alive, which is mentioned in Dow : but as Ferishta, the Tabakāti Akbarī, and perhaps all the rest of the historians of Hindustan, generally follow the accounts of Ziā El Barnī (ضيا البرني), who wrote for Fīroz Shāh, son of this Emperor, it is probable that he did not record half the cruelties of this man.—Knox tells us that the kings of Ceylon also use elephants as executioners, and that on these occasions, " they have sharp iron with a socket with three edges, which they put on their teeth at such times." Ceylon, p. 44.

† An account of this insurrection will be found in Dow, vol. i. pp. 327-8. This happened about A.H. 746.

the greater part. From his extreme good fortune, however, he got the victory, collected his scattered troops, and subdued the rebellious Emīrs, killing some, torturing others, and pardoning the rest. He then returned to his residence, repaired his affairs, strengthened his empire, and took vengeance on his enemies.—But let me now return to the account of my own affairs with him.

When he had appointed me to the office of Judge of Dehli, had made the necessary arrangements, and given me the presents already mentioned, the horses prepared for me, and for the other Emīrs who were about his person, were sent to each of us, who severally kissed the hoof of the horse of him who brought them, and then led our own to the gate of the palace; we then entered, and each put on a dress of honour; after which we came out, mounted, and returned to our houses.

The Emperor said to me, on this occasion, Do not suppose that our office of Judge of Dehli will cost you little trouble: on the contrary, it will require the greatest attention. I understood what he said, but did not return him a good answer. He understood the Arabic, and was not pleased with my reply. I am, said I, of the sect of Ibn Mālik, but the people of Dehli follow Hanafi;* besides, I am ignorant of their language. He replied, I have appointed two learned men your deputies, who will advise with you. It will be your business to sign the legal 'instruments.† He then added: If what I have appointed prove not an income sufficient to meet your numerous expenses, I have likewise given you a cell, the bequests appropriated to which you may expend, taking this in addition to what is already appointed. I thanked him for this, and returned to my house.

A few days after this he made me a present of twelve thousand dinars. In a short time, however, I found myself involved in great debts, amounting to about fifty-five thousand dinars, according to the computation of India,

---

ᵉ علي العقود .

---

* Two of the celebrated leaders who are at the head of the four larger sects of the Mohammedans. They differ from one another, however, only in some legal points.

† On the office and requirements of such persons, see the Chrestom. Arabe of M. de Sacy, tom. i. pp. 38-41, edit 2. These officers, which are there called عدول Justices, are styled by Abul Fazl مير عدل officers of justice. (آئین اكبري.)

which with them amounts to five thousand five hundred ʸ tankas;* but which, according to the computation of the west, will amount to thirteen thousand dinars. The reason of this debt was, the great expenses incurred in waiting on the Emperor, during his journies to repress the revolt of the Ain El Mulk (p. 147). About this time, I composed a panegyric in praise of the Emperor, which I wrote in Arabic, and read to him. He translated it for himself,† and was wonderfully pleased with it: for the Indians are fond of Arabic poetry, and are very desirous of (being memorialized in) it. I then informed him of the debt I had incurred; which he ordered to be discharged from his own treasury, and said: Take care, in future, not to exceed the extent of your income. May God reward him.

Some time after the Emperor's return from the Maabar districts, and his ordering my residence in Dehli, his mind happened to change respecting a Sheikh in whom he had placed great confidence, and even visited, and who then resided in a cave without the city. He took him accordingly and imprisoned him, and then interrogated his children as to who had resorted to him. They named the persons who had done so, and myself among the rest; for it happened that I had visited him in the cave. I was conse- quently ordered to attend at the gate of the palace, and a council to sit within. I attended in this way for four days, and few were those who did so, who escaped death. I betook myself, however, to continued fasting, and tasted nothing but water. On the first day I repeated the sentence,

---

ʸ تنكه .

---

* On the value of the dinar, direm, &c. of Arabia, see the notes to Professor Carlyle's Maured Allatafet, p. 3. The king of Oude's Persian Dictionary tells us, that the tanka (or rather تنگَه tangah) is a certain quantity of gold or money, according to the technical usage of any place; and that they call two fulūs a tangah: his words are, تنگَه مقداري از زر و پول باشد باصطلاح Mr. Shakespear says in his Hindūstānī Dictionary تنگا هرجائي ونيز دو فلوس‌را تنگه کويند. tangā (see تنگا) two paisās.

† According to Ferishta this Emperor either had, or was proud to be thought to have, consider- able pretensions to learning in the Arabic and Persic. His words are: ودر تقرير فصيح وكلام شيرين ضرب المثل بود ومكاتبات ومراسلات عربي وفارسي بربديهه چنان نوشتي که دبيران ومنشيان در آن حيران ماندندي. For the encouragement of polite literature he was quite proverbial. His Arabic and Persian letters were so elegant, that the regular scribes and mūnshīs were all astonishment.

" God is our support, and the most excellent patron,'"* three and thirty
thousand times; and after the fourth day, by God's goodness was I delivered;
but the Sheikh, and all those who had visited him, except myself, were put
to death.

Upon this I gave up the office of Judge, and bidding farewell to the
world, attached myself to the holy and pious Sheikh, the saint and phœnix
of his age, "Kamāl Oddīn Abd Ullah El Gāzī, who had wrought many open
miracles. All I had I gave to the Fakeers; and, putting on the tunic of
one of them, I attached myself to this Sheikh for five months,† until I
had kept a fast of five continued days; I then breakfasted on a little rice.

---

<sup>b</sup> كمال الدّين عبد الله الغازي .        <sup>a</sup> حسبنا الله ونعم الوكيل .

---

\* El Koran, Surat III.

† As the mystical nonsense to which the religious of the East pay so much regard is but
little known, and, perhaps, less understood in this country, I have thought that it might not be
unacceptable here to give some account of it, which I shall do, from a work of great authority
by the very celebrated poet Jāmī, viz. the نفحات الانس Nafahāt El Ins. The mysticism which
is termed by them Sūfīism, is treated just like any science. It has its various ranks and degrees,
and when one has gone through them all, he is supposed to have become an integral part of the
Deity, which they hold, indeed, that he always was: but that now he is not only assured of this,
but is endued with powers sufficient to give proof of it. They generally set out with fastings,
mortifications, and silence, just as the ancient Pythagoreans did, which seems to be the state in
which our traveller had placed himself; and in these they persevere till they have fully persuaded
themselves, that heaven and earth are entirely at their command. According to Jāmī, then, the
degrees of this science (or unity توحيد) are four, viz. اوّل توحيد ايماني دوم توحيد علمي سيوم
توحيد حالي چهارم توحيد الهي . امّا توحيد ايماني آنست كه بنده بتفرد وصف الهيت و توحيد
استحقاق معبوديه حق سبحانه وتعالي را بر مقتضاي اشارات آيات واخبار تصديق كند بدل واقرار دهد
بزبان واين توحيد نتيجهٔ تصديق مخبر واعتقاد صدق خبر باشد و مستفاد بود از ظاهر علم و تمسك بان
خلاص از شرك جلي وانخراط در سلك اسلام فايده دهد و متصوفه بحكم ضرورت ايمان با عموم مؤمنان
در اين توحيد مشارك اند و بديكر مراتب متفرد وبمخصوص . i. e. " The first is a oneness of faith;
the second, of assurance; the third, a oneness of circumstance; and the fourth, the oneness of the
Almighty. The oneness of faith is that, by which the servant of God believes in his heart, and
confesses with his tongue, the unity of the divine character of God, and the sole right which he
possesses to divine worship, as derived from the intimations of holy writ. This ascription of the
divine oneness is the medium whereby belief is placed in the revealer, and faith in the thing
revealed, which derives its proof from (the next stage, or) open assurance. The embracing of
this, therefore, effectually liberates the believer from manifest idolatry, and hastens his introduction to the true religion. The candidate, however, for Sūfīism is necessarily situated as

# CHAPTER XVII.

*Sent on an Embassy to China—Embassy from China to the Emperor—Gold Mines on the mountain of Kora—Sets out on the Embassy—Arrives at Biāna—Kūl—War with the Hindoos—Taken prisoner —Brought back to Dehli—Returns to Yūh Būra—Merwa—Gwālior—Barūn—Account of the Jogies—Witch burnt—Juggling of the Jogies—Arrives at Kajmara—Chandēri—Description of Gwalior—Dawlatābād—Nazar Abād—Mahrattas—Sāgar—Kambāya—Goa—Bairam—Kūka— Dankūl—Sindabūr—Hinaur—King of Hinaur not subject to the Emperor of Dehli—Malabar, customs—Kings of Malabar—Law of Succession—Account of the growth of Pepper.*

AFTER this, the Emperor sending for me, I went to him in my tunic, and he received me more graciously than ever. He said, It is my wish to

---

others are in holding the (divine) unity; it is in other respects that he is particular, and stands alone. As to the next degree, it is said: اما توحید علمی مستفادست از باطن علم که آنرا علم یقین خوانند وآن چنان بود که بنده در بدایت طریق تصوف از سر یقین بداند که موجود حقیقی وموثر مطلق نیست الا خداوند عالم جل جلاله وجملهٔ ذوات وصفات وافعال را در ذات وصفات وافعال او ناچیز داند هر ذاتی را فروغ از نور ذات مطلق شناسد وهر صفتی را پرتوی از نور صفت مطلق داند چنانکه هرکجا علمی وقدرتی وارادتی وسمعی وبصری یابد آنرا اثری از آثار علم وقدرت وارادت وسمع وبصر الهی داند, &c. It receives its proof from inward *assurance*, which is called *the assurance of knowledge*; and it is said, that the candidate knows from the beginning of his entering Sūfīism *assuredly*, that there is no real *being* or *agent* except the Lord of the world: that all essences, attributes, and works, are nothing with him (or end with him); that every existence is but a ray of light from him, and every attribute an emanation of those which in him are absolute; so that wherever he finds knowledge, power, will, the faculties of hearing or of sight, he recognizes the vestiges of that assurance, power, will, faculty, and the like, which centre in the divinity. The third stage is thus described: اما توحید حالی آنست که حال توحید وصف لازم ذات موحد گردد وجملهٔ ظلمات رسوم وجود الا اندك بقیهٔ در اشراق نور توحید متلاشی ومضمحل شود ونور توحید در نور حال او مستتر ومندرج گردد بر مثال اندراج نور کواکب در نور آفتاب شعر ۞ فلما استبان الصبح ادرج ضوء ۞ باسفارهٔ اضواء نور الکواکب ۞ ودرین مقام وجود موحد در مشاهدهٔ جمال وجود واحد چنان مستغرق عین جمع کرد که جزء ذات وصفات واحد در نظر شهود او نیاید تا غایتی که این توحید را صفت واحد بیند نه صفت خود واین دیدن را هم صفت او بیند وهستی او بدین طریق قطره وار در تصرف تلاطم امواج بحر توحید افتد وغرق جمع گردد. " The *oneness of state* is that, by which an *union of state* must be a character of the person to be united (with the Deity), and in this all the black characters of human existence, excepting the small part still remaining (*i. e.* I suppose those to be abolished by still further approximations) are to vanish and be lost in the rising of the light of the divine unity; and the light of the divine oneness

send you as ambassador to the Emperor of China, for I know you love
travelling in various countries. I consented ; and he sent dresses of honour,
horses, money, &c., with every thing necessary for the journey.

---

is to be enclosed and concealed in the light acquired by this his state, just as the light of the stars
is lost in the light of the sun : verse,

> When the bright morn renews its fires,
> Every twinkling star expires.

And, at this stage, the essence of the person thus united, witnessing the essential beauty of the
only one, becomes so overwhelmed in the very ALL IN ALL, that nothing but HIS being and
attributes meet his perception, or call forth his testimony, (and this) to such a degree, that he
considers this oneness as an attribute of the ONLY ONE, and not of self. This very perception
too he believes to be one of HIS attributes : and his existence, thus given up to the agitations of
the waves of the sea of unity, falls away, and becomes overwhelmed in the ALL IN ALL.

The last stage is thus described. امّا توحيد الٓهي آنست كه حق سبحانه در ازل آزال
بنفس خود نه بتوحيد ديگري هميشه بوصف وحدانيّة ونعت فردانيت موصوف بود وممنعوت كان
الله ولم يكن معه شئٌ واكنون همچنان بر نعت ازلي واحد وفرد است والا ان كما كان وتا ابد الابان
هم برين وصف خواهد بود &c. " As to the *Divine Unity*, it is that property by which the True
Object of worship has been characterized and described from all eternity, as contained within
himself and without union with any other, viz. ' God was, and with him did nothing exist.' So
even now, by his eternal attributes, he is ONE and ALONE, or (in other words) even as he was,
so shall he for ever be."

The following extract will shew what powers and privileges those are supposed to possess, who
arrive at the state of saintship here mentioned. القول في اصناف ارباب الولايه قدس الله تعالي
اسرارهم في كتاب كشف المحجوب خداوند سبحانه وتعالي برهان نبوي را باقي كردانيده است واوليا را
سبب اظهار آن كرده تا پيوسته آيات حق وحجّت صدق محمد صلي الله عليه وسلم ظاهر ميباشد
وهر ايشان را واليان عالم كردانيده تا مجرد مرخدمت ويرا كشته اند وراه متابعت نفس را در نوشته
از آسمان باران بركات ايشان آيد واز زمين نبات بصفاء احوال ايشان رويد بر كافران
مسلمانان نصرت بهمت ايشان يابند وايشان چهار هزار اند كه مكتومان اند وهر يكديكر را نشناسند
وجمال حال خود ندانند واندر كل احوال از خود وخلق مستور باشند واخبار بدين وارد است
وسخن اوليا بدين ناطن (ناطق) ومراد خود اندرين معني بمحمد الله خبر عيان كشتست وامّا آنانكه اهل
حل وعقد اند وسرهنكان درگاه حق اند سيصد اند كه هر ايشان را اخيار خوانند وچهل ديكر از ايشان را
ابدال خوانند وهفت ديكر از ايشان را ابرار خوانند وچهار ديكر اند كه ايشان را اوتاد خوانند وسه
ديكر اند كه ايشان را نقبا خوانند ويكي كه ويرا قطاب وغوث خوانند ... صاحب كتاب فتوحات مكّه
رضي الله عنه در فصل سي ويكم از باب صد ونود وهشتم از آن كتاب رجال هفتكانه را ابدال
كفته است ودر آنجا ذكر كرده كه حق سبحانه وتعالي زمين را هفت اقليم كردانيده وهفت تن از
بدكان خود بركزيده وايشان را ابدال نام نهاده ووجود هر اقليمي را بيكي از ان هفت تن نكاه

The Emperor of China had, at this time, sent presents to the Sultan, consisting of a hundred Mamlūks, fifty slave girls, five hundred dresses of [b]El Kamanjah, five hundred maunds of musk, five dresses wrought with jewels, five quivers wrought with [c]gold, and five swords set with jewels. His request with the Emperor was, that he should be permitted to rebuild an

---

[b] الكمنجه .          [c] تراكيش مزر كشه .

---

ميـي دارد وكفته است كه من در حرم مكه بايشان جمـع شدم وبر ايشان سلام كفتم وايشان بر من
سلام كفتند وبا ايشان سخـن كفتم فما رايت فيما رايت احسن سمتا منهم ولا اكثر شغلا منهم بالله .

" On the different classes of the Awlia or Saints. The Lord who is the object of worship has, in the revelation, made the proof of Mohammed's mission permanent; and to shew this have the saints been constituted, and that this proof should be constantly apparent. These he has in the Scripture appointed to be Lords of the World, so that they are set apart entirely for his service, and for following up the requirements of the soul. It is to bless their tracks that the rains of heaven descend, and to purify their state that the herbs of the earth spring up; and it is from their care, that the Moslems obtain victory over idolaters. Now these, which are invisible, are four thousand; of each other they know nothing, nor are they aware of the dignity of their own state. In every case, too, they are concealed from one another and from mortals. To this effect have relations been given, and to the same have various saints spoken; and for this, to the praise of God, have sages instructed. But of those who have this power of loosing and binding, and are officers of the court of the true God, there are three hundred whom they style AKHYAR. Forty others of them they call ABDAL, seven others ABRAR, four others AWTAD, three others NOKABA, and one whom they name KOTB and GHAUTH.... The author of the Fatūhāti Mecca, chap. 198, sect. 31, calls the seven-stated men ABDAL, and goes on to shew, that the Almighty has made the earth consisting of seven climates, and that seven of his choice servants he has named ABDAL; and, further, that he takes care of these climates by one or other of these seven persons. He has also stated, that he met them all in the temple at Mecca; that he saluted them, and they returned the salute; and conversed with them, and that he never witnessed any thing more excellent or more devoted to God's service." From what has here been said, I think there cannot remain the least doubt, that the mysteries of Sūfiism are those of Heathenism. These matured saints agree so perfectly with the Daimones (Δαιμονες) of the Greeks, the Boodhas of the Boodhists, the inferior deities of the Hindoos, the angels of the ancient Persians and Chaldeans, and the Powers (Δυναμεις, &c.) of the ancient heretics, that it is scarcely possible, they can have any other than a common origin. The same, perhaps, may be said of the Druzes on Mount Libanus, who worship one of the Sultans of Egypt as their favourite Avatar. And generally, it is impossible to read the works of Irenæus and Epiphanius on the heresies, with the accounts given of Sūfiism by the Arabs and Persians, without being convinced that Gnosticism and Sūfiism present one and the same thing, a mere continuation of the idolatry of Chaldee and Egypt, wrapt up just as that was, in the scarcely intelligible jargon of a wretched philosophy; and I may perhaps here remark, that wherever a similar mysticism presents itself, we are to look for its origin in the same source.

idol-temple in the country about the mountain of [d]Korā, on which infidel
Hindoos resided, on the top of which and on the heights was a plain
of three months' journey, and to which there was no approach. Here,
too, resided many infidel Hindoo kings. The extremities of these parts
extend to the confines of Thibet, where the musk gazelles are found.
There are also mines of gold on these mountains, and [e]poisonous grass
growing, such, that when the rains fall upon it, and run in torrents to the
neighbouring rivers, no one dares in consequence drink of the water during
the time of their rising : and should any one do so, he dies immediately.
This idol-temple they usually called the [f]Bur Khāna.   It stood at the foot
of the mountain, and was destroyed by the Mussulmāns, when they became
masters of these parts.   Nor were the inhabitants of the mountain in a condition to fight the Mohammedans upon the plain.   But the plain was necessary to them for the purposes of agriculture; they had, therefore, requested
the Emperor of China to send presents to the King of India, and to ask
this favour for them.   Besides, to this temple the people of China also
made pilgrimages.   It was situated in a place called [g]Samhal.   The reply
of the Emperor was, that this could not be permitted among a people who
were Mohammedans; nor could there exist any church whatsoever, in
countries subject to them, except only where tribute was paid; but if they
chose to do this, their request would be complied with : for the place in
which this idol-temple was situated had been conquered, and had, in
consequence, become a district of the Mohammedans.   The Emperor also
sent presents much more valuable than those he had received, which were
these following, namely : one hundred horses of the best breed saddled
and bridled; one hundred Mamlūks; one hundred Hindoo singing slave-
girls; one hundred [h]Bairamī dresses,* the value of each of which was a
hundred dinars; one hundred silken dresses; five hundred saffron coloured
dresses; one hundred pieces of the best cotton cloth; one thousand dresses
of the various clothing of India; with numerous instruments of gold and

---

ثوب بيرميه . [h]   . سمهل [g]   . (Butkhāna ? بتخانه)[f]   . حشايش مسمومة [e]   . جبل قرا [d]

---

*  بيرم according to Meninski, is a species of silk ; and in the King of Oude's Persian Dictionary it is said to be نوعي ازپارچ ريسماني باشد شبيه بمثقالي عراق ليكن از آن باريك تر و
نازكتر است a sort of thread-cloth like the Methkāli of Irāk, but finer and softer than it.   I find
no mention whatever of this kind of cloth among those given in the A-īni Akbarī.

silver, swords and quivers set with jewels, and ten robes of honour wrought with gold, of the Sultan's own dresses, with various other articles.

The Emperor appointed the Emīr [i]Zahīr Oddīn El Zanjānī one of the Ulemā, with [k]El Fatī Kāfūr, with whom the present was entrusted, to accompany me. These were favourite officers with the Emperor. He also sent with us a thousand cavalry, who were to conduct us to the place at which we were to take shipping. The servants of the Emperor of China, who amounted to about one hundred, and with whom there was a great Emīr, also returned with us. So we left the presence of the Emperor on the 17th day of the month Safar, in the year seven hundred and forty-three (A.D. 1342), and, after a few days, arrived at the city of [l]Biāna,* which is large. We next arrived at [m]Kūl,† which is a beautiful city, the greatest part of the trees of which are vines. When we had arrived here, we were informed that the infidel Hindoos had besieged the city [n]El Jalālī, which is seven days from Kūl. The intention of these infidels was, to destroy the inhabitants; and this they nearly effected. We made such a vigorous attack upon them, however, that not one of them was left alive. But many of our companions suffered martyrdom in the onset, and among them was El Fatī Kāfūr, the person to whom the presents had been confided. We immediately transmitted an account of this affair to the Emperor, and waited for his answer. During this interval, whenever any of the infidel Hindoos made an attack on the places in the neighbourhood of El Jalālī, either all or a part of us, gave assistance to the Moslems. Upon a certain day, however, I turned into a garden just without the city of Kūl, when the heat of the sun was excessive: and while we were in the garden, some one cried out, that the Hindoos were making an attack upon one of the villages: I accordingly rode off with some of my companions to their assistance. When the infidels saw this they fled; but the Moslems were so scattered in pursuing them, that myself and only five others were left. Some of their people saw this, and the consequence was, a considerable number of cavalry made an attack

---

[n] الجلالي .    [m] كول .    [l] بيانه .    [k] الفتي كافور .    [i] ظهير الدين الزنجاني .

* The Biana of Rennell.

† No trace of this place is to be found in any of the maps, although frequently occurring in books written in Hindustan. According to the A-īni Akbarī آئين اكبري it is a sircār, and has a citadel built of brick قلعه خشتي دارد

upon us. When we perceived their strength we retreated, while they pursued us, and in this we persevered. I observed three of them coming after me, when I was left quite alone. It happened at the same time that the fore-feet of my horse had stuck fast between two stones, so that I was obliged to dismount and set him at liberty. I was now in a way that led into a valley between two hills, and here I lost sight of the infidels. I was so circumstanced, however, that I knew neither the country, nor the roads. I then set my horse at liberty to go where he would.

While I was in a valley closely interwoven with trees, behold! a party of cavalry, about forty in number, rushed upon me and took me prisoner, before I was well aware of their being there. I was much afraid they would shoot me with their arrows. I alighted from my horse, therefore, and gave myself up as their prisoner. They then stripped me of all I had, bound me, and took me with them for two days, intending to kill me. Of their language I was quite ignorant: but God delivered me from them; for they left me, and I took my course I knew not whither. I was much afraid they would take it into their heads to kill me; I therefore hid myseif in a forest thickly interwoven with trees and thorns, so much so, that a person wishing to hide himself could not be discovered. Whenever I ventured upon the roads, I found they always led, either to one of the villages of the infidels, or to some ruined village. I was always, therefore, under the necessity of returning; and thus I passed seven whole days, during which I experienced the greatest horrors. My food was the fruit and leaves of the mountain trees. At the end of the seventh day, however, I got sight of a black man, who had with him a °walking-staff shod with iron, and a small water vessel. He saluted me, and I returned the salute. He then said, What is your name? I answered, Mohammed. I then asked him his name: he replied, °El Kalb El Karīh (i. e. the wounded heart). He then gave me some °pulse, which he had with him, and some water to drink. He asked me whether I would accompany him. I did so; but I soon found myself unable to move, and I sunk on the earth. He then carried me on his shoulders; and as he walked on with me, I fell asleep. I awoke, however, about the time of dawn, and found myself at the Emperor's palace-gate. A courier had already brought the news of what

---

<sup>q</sup> حمصا .      <sup>p</sup> القلب الفريح .      <sup>o</sup> عكاز .

had happened, and of my loss, to the Emperor, who now asked me of all the particulars, and these I told him. He then gave me ten thousand dinars, and furnished me for my return. He also appointed one of his Emīrs ͬEl Malik Sumbul* to present the gift. So we returned to the city of Kūl. From this we proceeded to the city of ˢYūh Būrah; and then descended to the shores of a lake called "ᵗthe water of life." After this we proceeded to ͧKinoj, which is but a small town. Here I met the aged Sheikh Sālih of Fargānah. He was at this time sick. He told me, that he was then one hundred and fifty years old. I was informed that he would constantly fast, and that for many successive days.

We next arrived at the city of ˣMerwa, which is a large place, inhabited for the most part by infidels, who pay tribute to the Emperor. We next arrived at the city of ʸKālyūr,† which is large, and which has a fortress on the top of a high mountain. In this the Emperor imprisons those of whom he entertains any fear. We next arrived at the city of ᶻBarūn, which is small, and inhabited by Moslems: it is situated in the midst of the infidel districts. In these parts are many wild beasts, which enter the town and tear the inhabitants. I was told, however, that such as enter the streets of the town are not wild beasts really, but only some of the magicians called ͣJogees, who can assume the shape of wild beasts, and appear as such to the mind. These are a people who can work miracles, of which one is, that any one of them can keep an entire fast for several months.‡

---

ͣ مروه .    ͧ قنوج .    ᵗ آب حياة .    ˢ يوح بوره .    ͬ الملك سمبل .

ͣ الجوكية .    ᶻ برون .    ʸ كاليور .

---

* This is probably a name of office. In the beginning of the reign of Shahāb Oddīn Khilijī, as given by Ferishta, speaking of the promotions, it is said: منصب سنبل را ملك اول وز On the first day he gave the office of Bārbegī (or Master of the Ceremonies according to Dr. Wilkins) to Meliki Sumbul (perhaps the Master of the Spikenard or perfumes generally.) But Sumbul is also a district of Hindūstān, and this might have been this officer's sūba or district. I do not find this officer mentioned in the A-īni Akbarī.

† Gwalior of Rennell, of which some account has already been given.

‡ We are often told of the wonders done by the Jogees in the popular tales of Hindūstān, of which some specimens may be seen in the tales published in the Nāgarī character by Mr. Professor Shakespear (in his Muntakhabāti Hindī). The author of the Dabistān gives, perhaps,

Many of them will dig houses for themselves under ground, over which any one may build, leaving them only a place for the air to pass through.

---

the best account of them, tracing their creeds and practices up to their original sources. It is

this : جوكيان طايفه اند معروف وجوك در لغت سهنسكرة هند (al. سمسكرت) پيوستن را كويند واين كروه خودرا واصلان حق كيرند وخدارا يك كويند وباعتقاد ايشان بركزيده حق وبلكه عين او كوركهنات است وهمچنين مجهندرنات وحورنكي نات (al. جورنكي نات) از بزركان سدّان يعني كاملاند ونزد ايشان برهما وبشن و مهيش از فرشتكانند امّا شاكردان ومريدان كوركهنات اند چنانچه الحال بعضي خودرا بهريكي از ايشان منعوت (منسوب) دارند واين طايفه دوازده پنت اند بدينكونه ... c&. پنت فرقهرا كويند وبزعم ايشان جميع خداوندان اديان وملل ومذهب از انبيا واوليا شاكرد كور كهنات اند آنچه يافته اند از او يافته اند وعقيدهٔ اين طايفه آنست كه محمد صلوة الله .... هم پروردهٔ شاكرد كور كهنات بوده .... وجمعي از ايشان نزد مسلمانان مقيد بصوم وصلوت باشند وپيش هندوان بدين آنكروه عمل كنند وهيچ چيز از محرمات در كيش آنكروه چه خوك خورند براٰئين هنود ونصارا وكاو بدين مسلمان وغيرهم وآدمي را نيز بكشند وبخورند .... وشراب اشامند بر آئين كبران ودر ايشان هستند كه بول وغايط خويش باهم آميخته از پارچه كذرانيده بياشامند وكويند عامل اين عمل بر كارها بزرك توانا بود وغريب چيزها داند وعامل اين طريقرا انيلا كويند وبر عقيدهٔ اين فرقه اكرچه همه از اينها از كوركهنات متشعب شده اند وبهر كيشي توان بكورك پيوست وپي راه نزديك آنكسان رفتند كه بيكي از دوازده سلسله جوكيه پيوستند ودر طريق ايشان كرفتن دم بسيار است چنانچه در پارسيان آذر هوشنك چه پادشاهان آنكروه حبس نفس كردندي ... ودر هنكام كشيدن درچپ تصور ماه كند يعني درجانب چپ قرص ماه را پديد داند وسوي راست آفتاب را بعضي از سناسيان در هر مرتبه از مراتب هفكانه تصور يكي از ستاركان روان كرده اند واين عمل نزد هنود فايق بر جميع عبادات وخيرات است كويند عامل اين تواند پريدن وبيمار نشود واز مرك برهد وكرسنه وتشنه نكردد .... ومحققين كفته اند چون اين عمل بكمال رسد بيم مرك بر خيزد وتا در تن بود خلع بدن تواند كردن وباز بتن پيوستن وبيمار نشود وقادربود بر جميع كارها ... ودر جوكيان مستمر است كه چون مرض برايشان برترين يابد خويش را زنده دفن نمايند وطريق ايشان آنست كه چشم كشاده در ميان دوابرو كمارند تا پيكري مرئي كردد واكر بي دست وپي يا بي عضوي ديكر باشد هركدامي را قراري داده اند كه علامات زيستن چند سال وچند ماه وچند روز است وچون بيسر ببيند بيكمان دانند كه از عمر جز قليلي باقي نمانده بنابرين نشانها چون ببينند خودرا دفن كنند c. i. e.& , The Jogees are a

well known class of people. The word *jog* they use in the Sanscrit (language) to signify *joining, adhering.* This people suppose themselves to be united with God, whom they believe to be One. The select, or rather the person himself, of God, they hold to be Kúrkhanát. Majhan-darnát and Hírankúnát are also great saints (سدان) or perfect beings. With them, Brahma, Vishnu, and Mahísh, are angels, but also pupils or disciples of Kúrkhanát, and some of them do now name themselves after one or other of these. Now this class of people consists of

In this the Jogee will reside for months without eating or drinking any
thing. I heard, that one of them remained thus for a whole year. I saw

---

twelve Pantas, as follows, ...... &c., and Pant signifies a class or tribe. According to their persuasion, the authors of every religion, sect, and belief, whether prophets or saints, were disciples
of Kūrkhanāt; and that whatever these persons might have known, they must have known
from him. It is also their belief, that Mohammed was brought up by a disciple of Kūrkhanāt.
Many of them will, when with the Mohammedans, attend to prayer and fasting, which they also
do with the Hindoos. None of the things forbidden for food, are considered so among them; for
they will eat swine's flesh after the manner of the Hindoos and Christians, as well as beef, as
the Mohammedans and others do. They will also kill and eat a man ...... and will drink wine
like the Guebres. There are too among them, those who will mix their urine and dung together,
which they will then pass through a cloth and drink. The person who does this, they say, will be
able to perform great feats, and to know wonderful things. Such persons they term Anīlā. In the
belief of this people, although they hold all to be derived from Kūrkhanāt, and that those of
every religion may finally be united with Kūrk, still they proceed in the path of one of those
persons, who have been united by one or other of the twelve links of Jogeeism. In their belief it
is considered of great importance to be able to hold the breath; just as it is among the Parsees of
Adhar Hoshenk: for the kings among them would constantly hold their breath. ...... When one
draws (his breath), he will picture the moon towards the left, i. e. he will consider the moon's
disk as visible on his left side, and that of the sun on his right. Some of the Sanāsī in each
of the seven stages, will thus picture one or other of the planets, which, with the Hindoos,
exceeds every other species of worship or alms; for they say, that he who does this will
be able to fly, never to be sick, to free himself from death, and never to be subject to
either hunger, or thirst....... Those who have been thoroughly initiated, say, that when
this work is perfectly performed, the fear of death is no more felt; and that as long as such an
one is in the body, he will be able to put it off, and again to put it on, never to be sick, and to
have power to do all things....... Among the Jogees, it is constant, that when disease runs high,
they bury themselves alive. It is also one of their practices, to open the eyes, and fix them
in a direction between the eyebrows, until they see a figure. If the image appear without a
hand or foot, or any other member, for each one of these they lay it down, that he has now a
sign how many years, months, or days, he shall live. But if it appear without a head, they have
no doubt, that but little of life remains: and on the strength of this, they will bury themselves
alive,",&c.—These Jogees will, according to some, commit themselves occasionally to the flames,
for no other end, perhaps, than to gratify the strongest of all passions, vanity. The following
statement is taken from the Heft Iklīm (هفت اقليم), a very interesting collection of geographical and biographical notices in the Persic. This extract is taken from the notice
of Hindūstān, and is there given on the authority of one Mohammed Yūsuf of Herāt.

در يكي از پركنات هند بودم شنيدم كه جوكي پيدا شده ميخواهد خودرا در نظر راجه آن محل
بسوزد وراجه آن پركنه سه روز بسور وسرور پرداخت وروز چهارم علي الصباح كه جوكي آفتاب
از شيرستان مغرب سر بر آورده بر نطع خاكستر متمكن كرديد خلق عظيمي از ارباب اسلام
واصحاب اصنام جمع كشت وجوكي مزبوررا از هستي بي بقا كريخته ودر نيستي بي فنا آويخت

too, in the city of [b]Sanjarūr, one of the Moslems who had been taught by them, and who had set up for himself a lofty cell like an obelisk.   Upon the top of this he stood for five and twenty days, during which time he neither ate nor drank.   In this situation I left him, nor do I know how long he continued there after I had left the place.   People say, that they mix certain seeds, one of which is destined for a certain number of days or months, and that they stand in need of no other support during all this time.   They also foretel events.

The Emperor of Hindūstān very much respects them, and occasionally sits in their company.   Some of them will eat nothing but herbs : and it is clear from their circumstances, that they accustom themselves to abstinence, and feel no desire either for the world or its show.   Some of them will kill a man with a look : but this is most frequently done by the women.   The woman who can do so is termed a [c]Goftār.   It happened when I was Judge of Dehli, and the Emperor was upon one of his journies, that a famine took place.*   On this occasion, the Emperor ordered, that

---

. (Pers. كفتار speech, perhaps.) [c]          سنجرور [b]

---

كسوف فنا در بر وكلاه ترك بر سر در برابر راجه آمد ومراسم تعظیم ولوازم تسلیم بجا آورد وعنچه وار
لب از تكلم بسته ونرکس صفت چشم بر پشت پا داشته به ایستاد وبارشاد وی ملازمان راجه فضلهٔ
كوسفند وكاو نرم ساخته .... بدامن بار کردن گرفتند تا آتش از همه طرف دست بهم دارد وهنگامه
کرم کردید در وقتی که شمع وار آتش تا کلوی آن سوخته رسید بجانب راجه توجه نمود وحرفی
چند بر زبان راند, &c.   " I was (says he) in one of the purgunnas of India, when I heard that a Jogee had appeared, and wished to burn himself in the presence of one of the Rājas of that district.   The Rāja employed three days in banqueting and pleasure (upon this occasion).   On the morning of the fourth, when the sun of the Jogee had arisen, having left the regions of the west, and risen in power over the carpet of the dust, a great company of the professors of Islamism, as well as of the followers of idolatry, came together, when the afore-mentioned Jogee escaping from the instability of being, clung to the annihilation which is incorruptible.   Having the eclipse of annihilation on his breast, and the cap of retirement upon his head, he came up to the Rāja; and having paid his respects with lips closed like the rose-bud, and with eyes on his feet like the narcissus, he stood still; and then, by his signal, the Rāja's servants collecting sheep and cow's dung set it on fire, until the flames arose from every part.   When he grew warm, and the fire, like the flame of a taper, approached his neck, he turned towards the Rāja and uttered something."—A similar account of men burning themselves is given in the Commentary of Abu Zaid El Hasan, in the two Arabian Travellers, translated by Renaudot.   Pinkerton's Voyages, &c. vol. vii. p. 216.

* Perhaps the famine noticed by Dow, vol. i. pp. 322-3.

the poor should be divided among the nobles for support, until the famine should cease.  My portion, as affixed by the Vizier, amounted to five hundred.  These I sustained in a house which I built for the purpose.  On a certain day, during this time, a number of them came to me, bringing a woman with them, who, as they said, was a Goftār, and had killed a child, which happened to be near her.  I sent her, however, to the Vizier, who ordered four large water vessels to be filled with water, and tied to her. She was then thrown into the great river (the Jumna).  She did not sink in the water, but remained [d]unhurt: so they knew that she was a Goftār. The Vizier then ordered her to be burnt, which was done; and the people distributed her ashes among themselves, believing that if any one would fumigate* himself with them, he would be secure from the fascinations of a Goftār for that year.  But if she had sunk, they would have taken her out of the water: for then they would have known that she was not a Goftār.

I was once in the presence of the Emperor of Hindūstān, when two of these Jogees, wrapt up in cloaks, with their heads covered (for they take out all their hairs, both of their heads and arm-pits, with powder), came in.

---

[d] وشافت ؟

* Fumigations for the purpose of driving away, or otherwise invalidating the power of evil spirits, seem to have been used in very ancient times, and hence, perhaps, Tobit's use of the fish.  See Tobit, vi. 8, 18; and the use of perfumes, &c., as alluded to by Pliny, for performing cures.  Plin. Nat. Hist. lib. 24 cap. xi.

† That some of our own supposed witches have been treated very nearly in the same manner, is too well known to need proof.  There has generally been a story current in Europe, too, that Mohammed's coffin was suspended in a temple at Medina, by a loadstone placed in the roof for that purpose.  It is curious enough to remark, that they have a similar story in the East relating to St. Peter.  It is thus told by El Harawī: سمعون الصفا في مدينة رومية الكبرى في كنيستها ... "Simon Cephas (the rock) العظمي في تابوت ... من الفضة معلق بسلاسل في سقف الهيكل والله اعلم . is in the city of great Rome, in its largest church, within an ark of silver which is suspended by chains to the roof.  But God knows best."  The following account of " the man in the moon," I had from the mouth of a New Zealander : " A man named Celano once happened to be thirsty, and coming near a well by moonlight he intended to drink, but a cloud coming over the moon prevented him.  He then cursed the moon, because it refused to give him its light: but upon this the moon came down and took him up forcibly, together with a tree on which he had laid hold; and there he is now seen, continued the Zealander, with the tree, just as he was taken up! I would merely remark, that it is by no means surprising that vulgar credulity should be much the same all the world over; but, that it should arrive at almost precisely the same results, is curious enough.

The Emperor caressed them and said, pointing to me, This is a stranger, shew him what he has never yet seen. They said, we will. One of them then assumed the form of a cube and arose from the earth, and in this cubic shape he occupied a place in the air over our heads. I was so much astonished and terrified at this, that I fainted and fell to the earth. The Emperor then ordered me some medicine which he had with him, and upon taking this I recovered and sat up: this cubic figure still remaining in the air just as it had been. His companion then took a sandal belonging to one of those who had come out with him, and struck it upon the ground, as if he had been angry. The sandal then ascended, until it became opposite in situation with the cube. It then struck it upon the neck, and the cube descended gradually to the earth, and at last rested in the place which it had left. The Emperor then told me, that the man who took the form of a cube was a disciple to the owner of the sandal: and, continued he, had I not entertained fears for the safety of thy intellect, I should have ordered them to show thee greater things than these. From this, however, I took a palpitation at the heart, until the Emperor ordered me a medicine which restored me.

We then proceeded from the city of Barūn to the stage of [e]Kajwarā,* at which there is a lake about a mile in length; and round this are temples, in which there are idols. At this place resides a tribe of Jogees, with long and clotted hair.[f] Their colour inclines to yellow, which arises from their fasting. Many of the Moslems of these parts attend on them, and learn (magic) from them.

We next came to the city [g]Genderī,† which is large; after this to that of [h]Tahār, between which and Dehli is a distance of twenty-four days; and from which leaves of the betel-nut are carried to Dehli. From this place we went to the city of [i]Ajbal, then to [k]Dawlatābād, which is a place of great splendour, and not inferior to Dehli. The lieutenancy of Dawlatābād extends through a distance of three months. Its citadel is called

---

ʰ طهار .          ᵍ جندري .          ᶠ لبدت شعورهم وطالت .          ᵉ كجورا .

ᵏ دولت آباد .          ⁱ اجبل .

---

* The Kitchwara of Rennell is a province, and seems to be too far to the south-west to be the place here intended. Gajara, or Kurrera, seems more immediately in the route of our traveller.

† Perhaps the Chanderee of Rennell, and چنديري of the Tabakāti Akbarī.

*[l]* El Dawīgīr.* It is one of the greatest and strongest forts (in India). It is situated on the top of a rock which stands in the plain. The extremities are depressed, so that the rock appears elevated like a mile-stone, and upon this the fort is built. In it is a ladder made of hides; and this is taken up by night, and let down by day. In this fortress the Emperor imprisons such persons as have been guilty of serious crimes. The Emīr of Dawlatābād had been tutor to the Emperor. He is the great Emīr *[m]* Katlūkhān.† In this city are vines and pomegranates which bear fruit twice in the year. It is, moreover, one of the greatest districts as to revenue. Its yearly taxes and fines amount to seventeen *[n]* karōrs. A karōr is one hundred lak; and a lak one hundred thousand Indian dinars. This was collected by a man (appointed to do so) before the government of Katlūkhān; but, as he had been killed, on account of the treasure which

---

كرور. *[n]* · قطلوخان. *[m]* · الدويغير. *[l]*

---

* This citadel is mentioned by Dow, vol. i. p. 320. The word here used is, no doubt, the ديوكير *Deogīr* of the Persian historians, the author of the Tabakāti Akbari, Ferishta, &c. An extract from the history of this fortress (Gwalior) has already been given.

† This person is named in the Tabakāti Akbari قتلغ خان, and in Ferishta قتلقخان, which last is read by Dow " Cuttilich Chan" (vol. i. p. 313) Ferishta says on this subject كه قتلقخانرا

پیش او مصحف وبعضی کتب فارسی خوانده بود وخط از او آموخته بون وکیلدری ارزانی فرمود

Cuttilich Khän (adopting the orthography of Dow), who had read the Korān and some Persian books to him, and from whom he had learned to write, he appointed to the office of deputy Vizier. It is curious enough, however, that Ferishta gives the name of a tank called after him قتلو, *Katlū,* where he tells us, that the last letter has been changed to و. His words are كه درین

عصربحوض قتلومشهور است تبدیل العین (الغین؟) تبدل واو. We are not quite certain, therefore, whether قتلو as given by Ibn Batūta, is not the correct mode of writing this name, as it is not so likely that the name given to a place would change in the mouths of the inhabitants, as that the scribes should vary in their mode of writing out the copies of Ferishta, &c. in Hindūstān. It seems certain, however, that this word did in Ferishta's time end in غ, otherwise, he could not have said, that غ had been changed into و : but even this change might have been made before his time, and the true pronunciation of the word have been retained in the name of the place, as given above. As no good explanation of the term وکیل در is given in the common dictionaries, I shall here give one from the King of Oude's. After giving the vowels it is said, بمعنی وکیل دربار

آمده و نایب مناب را نیز کویند. It is used in the sense of minister of the court, whom they also call the Näïbi Munäb, or deputy of the deputed (*i. e.* of the prime minister). Meninski, indeed, gives us " administrator, gubernator, præfectus," but this only leaves us where it found us.

was with him, and this taken out of his effects after his death, the government fell to Katlūkhān. The most beautiful market-place here is called the [o]Tarab Abād, in the shops of which sit the singing women ready dressed out, with their slave girls in attendance; over these is an Emīr, whose particular business it is to regulate their income.

We next came to the city of [p]Nazar Abād. It is small, and inhabited by the [q]Mahrattas, a people well skilled in the arts, medicine, and astrology: their nobles are Brahmins. The food of the Mahrattas consists of rice, green vegetables, and oil of sesamè. They do not allow either the punishing or sacrificing of animals. They carefully wash all their food, just as one washes after other impurities; and never intermarry with their relations, unless separated by the interval of seven generations at least. They also abstain from the use of urine.

Our next place of arrival was the city of [r]Sāgar which is large, and is situated on a river of the same name. Near it are mills which are worked for their orchards, *i. e.* to supply water. The inhabitants of this place are religious and peaceable.

We next arrived at the city of [s]Kambāya,* which is situated at a mouth of the sea which resembles a valley, and into which the ships ride: here also the flux and reflux of the tide is felt. The greatest part of its inhabitants are foreign merchants. We next came to [t]Goa, which is subject to the infidel king [u]Jālansī, king of [x]Candahār who is also subject to the Emperor of Hindūstān, and to whom he sends an annual present. We next came to a large city situated at a mouth of the sea, and from this we took shipping and came to the island of [y]Bairam, which is without inhabitants. We next arrived at the city of [z]Kūka, the king of which is an infidel, named [a]Dankūl, and subject to the Emperor of Hindūstān.

After some days we came to the island of [b]Sindabūr, in the interior of which are six and thirty villages. By this we passed, however, and dropped anchor at a small island near it, in which is a temple and a tank of water. On this island we landed, and here I saw a Jogee leaning against the wall of the temple, and placed between two idols; he had some marks about

---

[o] طرب آباد . [p] نذر اباد . [q] المرهته . [r] صاغر. [s] كنبابه. كنبايه ? [t] كاوه .
[u] جالنسي . [x] قندهار. [y] بيرم . [z] قوقه . [a] دنكول . [b] سندبور.

him of a religious warfare.* I addressed him, but he gave me no answer. We looked too, but could see no food near him. When we looked at him, he gave a loud shout, and a cocoa-nut fell upon him from a tree that was there. This nut he threw to us : to me he threw ten dinars, after I had offered him a few, of which he would not accept.† I supposed him to be a Moslem ; for, when I addressed him, he looked towards heaven, and then towards the temple at Mecca, intimating that he acknowledged God, and believed in Mohammed as his prophet.

We next came to the city of <sup>c</sup>Hinaur, which is situated at an estuary of the sea, and which receives large vessels. The inhabitants of this place are Moslems of the sect of <sup>d</sup>Shāfia, a peaceable and religious people. They carry on, however, a warfare for the faith by sea, and for this they are noted. The women of this city, and indeed of all the Indian districts situated on the sea-shores, never dress in clothes that have been stitched, but the contrary. One of them, for example, will tie one part of a piece of cloth round her waist, while the remaining part will be placed upon her head and breast. They are chaste and handsome. The greater part of the inhabitants, both males and females, have committed the Korān to memory.

<sup>d</sup> شافعية .          <sup>c</sup> هنور .

* Mr. Apetz translates this passage, " cui castigationum vestigia impressa erant. The original is اثر المجاهدة وعليه in his copy and mine. Mr. Apetz seems to have thought, that this Jogee had felt the effects of the religious wars of the Mohammedans. It is my opinion, that, as Ibn Batūta believed him to be a Mohammedan, as he says he did, he thought he recognized in him those characters or marks, which are common to those who are thus engaged. It is not necessary, however, that there should be scars, wounds, or the like, but a *promptness*, *fitness*, &c. to contend for the faith, as well by *argument* as by the *sword :* and hence, Mohammedan professors of theology are sometimes termed Mujtahids مجتهدون . This word, too, is occasionally used in the same connexion with رياضت abstinence, as in the Tārīkhi Aālam Arāi, when speaking of the education of the Sheikh Safī Oddīn it is said, قدم در وادي مجاهده ورياضت نياد he placed his foot in the valley of *abstinence* and *religious warfare.* See also M. de Sacy, Chrest. Arab. tom. i. p. 169, edit. 2. I think, therefore, that Mr. Apetz is wrong.

† According to the author of the Dabistän, it is a rule with the Jogees to accept of no presents whatever. His words are : چيزي از كسي نخواستن واكرنا خواسته آرند نكرفتن : not to ask any thing of any one, and when offered unasked, not to accept of it.

The inhabitants of *Malabar* generally pay tribute to the King of *Hinaur, fearing as they do his bravery by sea. His army too, consists of about six thousand men. They are, nevertheless, a brave and warlike race. The present king is *Jamāl Oddīn Mohammed Ibn Hasan. He is one of the best of princes; but is himself subject to an infidel king, whose name is *Horaib.

We next came into the country of Malabar, which is the country of black pepper. Its length is a journey of two months along the shore from *Sindābūr to *Kawlam. The whole of the way by land lies under the shade of trees, and at the distance of every half mile, there is a house made of wood, in which there are chambers fitted up for the reception of comers and goers, whether they be Moslems or infidels. To each of these there is a well, out of which they drink; and over each is an infidel appointed to give drink. To the infidels he supplies this in vessels; to the Moslems he pours it in their hands. They do not allow the Moslems to touch their vessels, or to enter into their apartments; but if any one should happen to eat out of one of their vessels, they break it to pieces. But, in most of their districts, the Mussulmān merchants have houses, and are greatly respected. So that Moslems who are strangers, whether they are merchants or poor, may lodge among them. But at any town in which no Moslem resides, upon any one's arriving they cook, and pour out drink for him, upon the leaf of the *banana; and, whatever he happens to leave, is given to the dogs. And in all this space of two months' journey, there is not a span free from

<sup>h</sup> هريب .      <sup>g</sup> جمال الدين محمد بن حسن .      <sup>f</sup> هنور .      <sup>e</sup> المليبار .

<sup>l</sup> الموز .      <sup>k</sup> كولم .      <sup>i</sup> سندابور .

---

* In the account of Malabar translated and published by Mr. Apetz, we have this word written مَلِيبَار Molaibār. In the King of Oude's Persian Dictionary, however, it is directed to be read مَلِيبَار Malībār, after which we have this account of it and its inhabitants. ولايتي است بر كنار

درياي عمان ومردم آن ولايت همه ديوث اند چه زنان ايشان هر يك از ده شوهر زياده كنند

وفرزندي كه بهم رسد بعد ازيكسال همه يكجا جمع ميشوند وهريك چيزي بردست ميكيرند وآن

طفلرا مي طلبند بجانب هر كدام كه مرتبهٔ اول متوجه شود از آن شخص است واو تربيت ميكند .

It is a country situated on the shore of the sea of Ammān, all the men of which have no respect whatever for the chastity of their wives, every one of whom will have more than ten husbands. When a child is born, and has arrived at the age of one year, they all assemble in one place, each taking something in his hand; they then call the child, and that man towards whom he first turns is considered as his father, and therefore undertakes the charge of his bringing up.

cultivation. For every body has here a garden, and his house is placed in the middle of it; and round the whole of this there is a fence of wood, up to which the ground of each inhabitant comes. No one travels in these parts upon beasts of burden; nor is there any horse found, except with the King, who is therefore the only person who rides. When, however, any merchant has to sell or buy goods, they are carried upon the backs of men, who are always ready to do so (for hire.)

Every one of these men has a long staff, which is shod with iron at its extremity, and at the top has a hook. When, therefore, he is tired with his burden, he sets up his staff in the earth like a pillar, and places the burden upon it; and when he has rested, he again takes up his burden without the assistance of another. With one merchant, you will see one or two hundred of these carriers, the merchant himself walking, But when the nobles pass from place to place, they ride in a dūla* made of wood, something like a box, and which is carried upon the shoulders of slaves and hirelings. They put a thief to death for stealing a single nut, or even a grain of seed of any fruit, hence thieves are unknown among them; and, should any thing fall from a tree, none, except its proper owner, would attempt to touch it.

In the country of Malabar are twelve kings, the greatest of whom has fifty thousand troops at his command; the least, five thousand or thereabouts. That which separates the district of one king from that of another, is a wooden gate upon which is written: " The gate of safety of such an one." For when any criminal escapes from the district of one king, and gets safely into that of another, he is quite safe; so that no one has the least desire to take him, so long as he remains there.†

Each of their kings succeeds to rule, as being sister's son, not the son

---

* في دولة من خشب Mr. Apetz says, دولة per ferculum redidi. In Lexicis non reperitur, &c. The word is Hindūstānī, and therefore not very likely to occur in the Arabic Lexicons. Dow says, Hind. vol. i. p. 280 ...... " concealed themselves in doolies or close chairs, in which women are always carried." And, in Gilchrist's Vocabulary we have, " Dola (ee) litter, and in Mr. Shakespear's Dictionary دولَا dola, and دولی dolī, a kind of sedan (for women)." Mr. Apetz is very right, therefore, for it is a mere palanquin, or, as it is called in Hindustani, a pālkī or dolī.

† This custom seems nearly allied to that which obtained among the Israelites, by which the man who happened to kill another accidentally, saved his life by escaping to one of the cities of refuge, and remaining there until the death of the high priest.

to the last. Their country is that from which black pepper is brought; and this is the far greater part of their produce and culture. The pepper tree resembles that of the dark grape. They plant it near that of the cocoa-nut, and make frame-work for it, just as they do for the grape tree. It has, however, no tendrils, and the tree itself resembles a bunch of grapes. The leaves are like the ears of a horse; but some of them resemble the leaves of a $^m$ bramble. When the autumn arrives, it is ripe; they then cut it, and spread it just as they do grapes, and thus it is dried by the sun. As to what some have said, that they boil it in order to dry it, it is without foundation.

I also saw, in their country and on the sea-shores, aloes like the seed-aloe, sold by measure, just as meal and millet is.*

---

$^m$ العليق .

---

\* This passage is very imperfect in the edition of Apetz. The words are : وقد رايت في بلادهم
وسواحلهم صبرا كصبر الحبوب يباع بالكيل كالقمح والذرة .    Of the aloe, according to the Medical
Dictionary of Ibn El Hosain of Bagdad, there are three sorts. His words are : صبر سه نوع است
" Of the aloe there are three sorts, the    . اسقوطيري وعربي وهمجنا بهترين وي سقرطيوي بود
Socotrine, the *Arabic*, and the *Humjana.*" The two first are well known, but what the last is,
it is out of my power to say. I suspect, however, that the proper word has been omitted by
the transcriber, and the وهمجنا for وهمجنان, *and thus :* for he goes on to say, the Socotrine
is the best. We are then told, that Alexander colonized this island from Greece, for the
purpose of cultivating the aloe, by people who are horribly addicted to magic, &c. We are then
told, that the best of the Socotrine is that which is of the colour of liver, and which smells like
myrrh, and is shining.    ونيكوترين صبر اسقوطيري آن بود كه لون آن ماند جكربود وبوي ماند مُر
بود وبراق باشد .   We then have the methods of making up and using it, which need not be
detailed here.

Of the millet he says : ذره جاورس هنديست وبشيرازي آنرا زرت خوانند وآن دو نوع است
i. e. Dhora is the Indian millet, which, in the dialect of    سفيد وسياه بهترين وي سفيد بود. &c.
Shīrāz, they call *zorat.* It is of two sorts, the white and black : but the white is the best.

## CHAPTER XVIII.

*Arrival at Abi Sardar—Kākanwar—Manjarūn—Mohammedan merchants here—Hīlī—Jurkhannan —Dadkannan—Miraculous Tree—Fattan—Fandarainā—Kālikūt—Chinese Junks—Embassy goes on board, and is wrecked—Proceeds to Kawlam after his property; arrives at Kanjarkarā; returns to Kālikūt—Joins an expedition against Sindābūr—The place carried by assault— Arrives at Hinaur—Fākanaur—Manjarūr—Hīlī—Jarafattan—Badafattan—Fandarainā— Shāliāt; returns to Sindābūr, and sets out for the Maldive Islands.*

THE first town we entered in the country of Malabar was that of ⁿAbi Sardar which is small, and is situated on a large estuary of the sea. We next came to the city of ᵒKākanwar, which is large, and also upon an estuary of the sea. It abounds in the sugar-cane. The Sultan is ′an infidel. He sent his son as a pledge to our vessel, and we landed accordingly, and were honourably received. He also sent presents to the ship, as marks of respect to the Emperor of India. It is a custom with them, that every vessel which passes by one of their ports shall enter it, and give a present to its Sultan; in this case they let it pass, but otherwise they make war upon it with their vessels, they then board it out of contempt, and impose a double fine upon the cargo, just in proportion to the advantage they usually gain from merchants entering their country.

We next arrived at the city of ᵖManjarūn, which is situated upon a large estuary of the sea, called the "�q*estuary of the wolf*," and which is the greatest estuary in the country of Malabar. In this place are some of the greatest merchants of Persia and Yemen. Ginger and black pepper are here in great abundance. The king of this place is the greatest of the kings of Malabar, and in it are about four thousand Mohammedan merchants. The king made us land, and sent us a present.

We next came to the town of ʳHīlī, which is large and situated upon an estuary of the sea. As far as this place come the ships of China, but they do not go beyond it; nor do they enter any harbour, except that of this place, of ˢKālikūt, and of ᵗKawlam.*

ᵗ كولم . ˢ قالقوط . ʳ هيلي . q خور الذيب . ᵖ منجرون . ᵒ قاكنور . ⁿ ابي سردر .

---

* This name often appears in our MSS. as well as in that of Mr. Apetz, thus: كوكم *Kawkam*. It is given correctly by Abulfeda الكولم, and in the long. قلب, ح 132° 8'; lat. يب, ح 12° 8';

The city of Hīlī is much revered both by the Mohammedans and infidels,
on account of a mosque, the source of light and of blessings,* which is
found in it. To this seafaring persons make and pay their vows, whence
its treasury is derived, which is placed under the control of the principal
Moslem. The mosque maintains a preacher, and has within it several
students, as well as readers of the Korān, and persons who teach writing.

We next arrived at the city of ᵘJurkannan, the king of which is one of
the greatest on these coasts. We next came to ˣDadkannan, which is a
large city abounding with gardens, and situated upon a mouth of the sea.
In this are found the betel leaf and † nut, the cocoa-nut and colocassia.‡
Without the city is a large pond for retaining water; about which are gardens. The king is an infidel. His grandfather, who had become Mohammedan, built its mosque and made the pond. The cause of the grandfather's receiving Islamism was a tree, over which he had built the mosque.
This tree is a very great wonder;§ its leaves are green, and like those of
the fig, except only that they are soft. The tree is called *Darakhti Sha-
hādet* (the tree of testimony), *darakht* meaning tree. I was told in these

<hr>

ˣ ددكن .          ᵘ جركن .

<hr>

by Ibn Saïd; and in the Atwāl قي , ح . ح, ل *i. e.* long. 110° 8′; lat. 18° 30′. It is the *Coulan*
of the maps.

\* I am not at all satisfied with my own translation of this passage. It stands thus
in the original مشرق النور عظيم البركة .MSS in two of the : بسبب جامع بها مشرق النور والبركة .
Nothing of this occurs in the edition by Mr. Apetz. I have given, however, the only tolerable
sense I can find in it.

† This, according to the Medical Dictionary of Ibn El Hosain, ثمري است در قوت مانند
صندل سرخ درخت وي مانند درخت تاركيل بود ووي سرد بود بقوت ويابس, &c. It is a fruit
in power something like the red sandal-wood. Its tree is like that of the cocoa-nut; it is in its
nature cold and dry, &c.

‡ القلقاس

§ Mr. Apetz thinks he finds a description of the banyan tree here; his words are: " arborem
istam vere singularem jam veteres mirati sunt;" after which we have a citation from Strabo in
the words of Onesicritus, and another from Pliny, and then we are told, that it is the Bengal
fig-tree (Ficus Bengalensis), &c. How Mr. Apetz got to this conclusion it is extremely difficult
to say, unless he supposed the wonder of our traveller to have risen from the same cause with
that of the ancients: but, as the ground of his wonder is explained to be the leaf's changing its
colour, &c. there appears to be very little reason for supposing, that this is the tree mentioned by
Onesicritus and Pliny.

parts, that this tree does not generally drop its leaves; but, at the season of autumn in every year, one of them changes its colour, first to yellow, then to red; and that upon this is written, with the pen of power, " There is no God but God; Mohammed is the Prophet of God;" and that this leaf alone falls. Very many Mohammedans, who were worthy of belief, told me this; and said, that they had witnessed its fall, and had read the writing; and further, that every year, at the time of the fall, credible persons among the Mohammedans, as well as others of the infidels, sat beneath the tree waiting for the fall of the leaf: and when this took place, that the one half was taken by the Mohammedans, as a blessing, and for the purpose of curing their diseases; and the other, by the king of the infidel city, and laid up in his treasury as a blessing; and that this is constantly received among them. Now the grandfather of the present king could read the Arabic; he witnessed, therefore, the fall of the leaf, read the inscription, and, understanding its import, became a Mohammedan accordingly. At the time of his death he appointed his son, who was a violent infidel, to succeed him. This man adhered to his own religion, cut down the tree, tore up its roots, and effaced every vestige of it. After two years the tree grew, and regained its original state, and in this it now is. This king died suddenly; and none of his infidel descendants, since his time, has done any thing to the tree.

We next came to the city of ᵞFattan (Pattan), the greater part of the inhabitants of which are Brahmins, who are held in great estimation among the Hindoos. In this place there was not one Mohammedan. Without it was a mosque, to which the Mohammedan strangers resort. It is said to have been built by certain merchants, and afterwards to have been destroyed by one of the Brahmins, who had removed the roof of it to his own house. On the following night, however, this house was entirely burnt, and in it the Brahmin, his followers, and all his children. They then restored the mosque, and in future abstained from injuring it; whence it became the resort of the Mohammedan strangers.

After this we came to the city of ᶻFandarainā, a beautiful and large place, abounding with gardens and markets. In this the Mohammedans have three districts, in each of which is a mosque, with a judge and preacher.

---

ᶻ فندرينا .    ᵞ فتن .

We next came to "Kālikūt, one of the great ports of the district of Malabar, and in which merchants from all parts are found. The king of this place is an infidel, who shaves his chin just as the [b]Haidarī Fakeers of Room do. When we approached this place, the people came out to meet us, and with a large concourse brought us into the port. The greatest part of the Mohammedan merchants of this place are so wealthy, that one of them can purchase the whole freightage of such vessels as put in here; and fit out others like them. Here we waited three months for the season to set sail for China: for there is only one season in the year in which the sea of China is navigable. Nor then is the voyage undertaken, except in vessels of the three descriptions following: the greatest is called a [c]junk, the middling sized a [d]zaw, the least a [e]kakam. The sails of these vessels are made of cane-reeds, woven together like a mat; which, when they put into port, they leave standing in the wind. In some of these vessels there will be employed a thousand men, six hundred of these sailors, and four hundred soldiers. Each of the larger ships is followed by three others, a middle-sized, a third, and a fourth sized. These vessels are no where made except in the city of El Zaitūn in China, or in Sīn Kīlān, which is Sīn El Sīn.* They row† in these ships with large oars, which may be compared to great masts, over some of which five and twenty men will be stationed, who work standing. The commander of each vessel is a great Emīr. In the large ships too they sow garden herbs and

---

<sup>e</sup>كَكَم .        <sup>d</sup>زَوْ .        <sup>c</sup>جُنك .        <sup>b</sup>الفقرا الحيدريه الروام .        <sup>a</sup>قالقوط .

---

* This place, according to the Arabic geographers, is situated on the eastern coast of China. Edrīsī says, that the tenth part of the second climate (الجزء العاشر من الاقليم الثاني) contains the eastern districts of China, the city Sūsat El Sīn...... and Sīnīat El Sīn (ينضمن البلاد الصينية) &c. And Ibn El Wardī وصينية الضين ... الشرقية مدينة سوسة الصين . اما صين الصين فهو نهاية As to Sīn El Sīn, it is the extreme eastern part العمارة في المشرق وليس وراد الا البحر المحيط which is inhabited, and beyond which there is nothing but the ocean.

† The verb حذف seems here to be used in rather an unusual sense: and were it not repeated, it might be supposed to be an error of the copyists for جدف, which is generally taken in this sense. The passage is: ويحذفون في هذه المراقب بمحانيف كالصواري الكبار يقف علي المعذاف, &c.

ginger, which they cultivate in cisterns (made for that purpose), and placed on the sides of them. In these also are houses constructed of wood, in which the higher officers reside with their wives : but these they do not hire out to the merchants. Every vessel, therefore, is like an independent city. Of such ships as these, Chinese individuals will sometimes have large numbers : and, generally, the Chinese are the richest people in the world.

Now, when the season for setting out had arrived, the Emperor of Hindustan appointed one of the junks, of the thirteen that were in the port, for our voyage. El Malik Sambul, therefore, who had been commissioned to present the gift, and Zahīr Oddīn, went on board : and to the former was the present carried. I also sent my baggage, servants, and slave-girls on board, but was told by one of them, before I could leave the shore, that the cabin which had been assigned to me was so small, that it would not take the baggage and slave girls. I went, therefore to the commander, who said, There is no remedy for this ; if you wish to have a larger, you had better get into one of the kakams (third-sized vessels) : there you will find larger cabins, and such as you want. I accordingly ordered my property to be put into the kakam. This was in the afternoon of Thursday, and I myself remained on shore for the purpose of attending divine service on the Friday. During the night, however, the sea arose, when some of the junks struck upon the shore, and the greatest part of those on board were drowned ; and the rest were saved by swimming. Some of the junks, too, sailed off, and what became of them I know not. The vessel in which the present was stowed, kept on the sea till morning, when it struck on the shore, and all on board perished, and the wealth was lost. I had, indeed, seen from the shore, the Emperor's servants, with El Malik Sambul and Zahīr Oddīn, prostrating themselves almost distracted : for the terror of the sea was such as not to be got rid of. I myself had remained on shore, having with me my prostration carpet and ten dinars, which had been given me by some holy men. These I kept as a blessing, for the kakam had sailed off with my property and followers. The missionaries of the King of China were on board another junk, which struck upon the shore also. Some of them were saved and brought to land, and afterwards clothed by the Chinese merchants.

I was told that the kakam in which my property was, must have put

into *Kawlam. I proceeded, therefore, to that place by the river. It is
situated at the distance of ten days from *Kālikūt. After five days I came
to *Kanjarkarā, which stands on the top of a hill, is inhabited by Jews,
and governed by an Emīr who pays tribute to the King of *Kawlam. All
the trees (we saw) upon the banks of this river, as well as upon the sea-
shores, were those of the cinnamon and bakam,* which constitute the fuel
of the inhabitants: and with this we cooked our food. Upon the tenth
day we arrived at Kawlam, which is the last city on the Malabar coast.
In this place is a large number of Mohammedan merchants; but the king
is an infidel. In this place I remained a considerable time, but heard
nothing of the kakam and my property. I was afraid to return to the
Emperor, who would have said, How came you to leave the present, and
stay upon the shore? for I knew what sort of a man he was, in cases of
this kind. I also advised with some of the Mohammedans, who dissuaded
me from returning, and said: He will condemn you because you left the
present: you had better, therefore, return by the river to *Kālikūt.

I then betook myself to *Jamāl Oddīn, King of *Hinaur, by sea, who,
when I came near, met me and received me honourably, and then appointed
me a house with a suitable maintenance. He was about to attend on divine
service in the mosque, and commanded me to accompany him. I then
became attached to the mosque, and read daily a khatma or two.† At
this time the King was preparing an expedition against the *island of
Sindābūr. For this purpose he had prepared two and fifty vessels, which,

<hr>

جمال الدين ‏.‎ ‏ قالقوط ‏.‎ ‏ كولم ‏.‎ ‏ كنجركرا ‏.‎ ‏ قالقوط ‏.‎ ‏ كولم ‏.‎

جزيرة سندابور ‏.‎        هنور ‏.‎

<hr>

* Mr. Apetz translates this passage, " arbores cinnamomi et Cæsalpiniæ Sappan." The original is,
اشجار القرفة والبقم ‏.‎ That the first signifies cinnamon there is perhaps little doubt: but I know
not whether Mr. Apetz is right or not in his interpretation of the second. It may not be amiss,
however, to give an extract respecting it from the medical dictionary already cited. بقم چوب
درختي است كه از طرف هند خيزد وزنكبار وصباغان استعمال كنند و طبيعت او كرم وخشكست
&c. Bakam is the wood of a tree which grows on the shores of India. It is used by dyers in
dyeing black. It is in its nature warm and dry.

† The passage is, واقرا في كل يوم ختمة او اثنتين, which means that he daily read the Koran
through once or twice.

when ready, he ordered me to attend with him for the expedition. Upon this occasion I opened the Korān, in search of an omen;* and, in the first words of the first leaf which I laid my hand upon, was frequent mention of the name of God, and (the promise) that he would certainly assist those who assisted him. I was greatly delighted with this; and, when the King came to the evening prayer, I told him of it, and requested to be allowed to accompany him. He was much surprised at the omen, and prepared to set out in person. After this he went on board one of the vessels, taking me with him, and then we sailed. When we got to the island of Sindābūr, we found the people prepared to resist us, and a hard battle was accordingly fought. We carried the place, however, by divine permission, by assault. After this the King gave me a slave girl, with clothing and other necessaries; and I resided with him some months. I then requested permission to make a journey to Kawlam, to inquire after the kakam with my goods. He gave me permission, after obtaining a promise that I would return to him. I then left him for [o]Hinaur, and then proceeded to [p]Fākanawr, and thence to [q]Manjarūr, thence to [r]Hīlī, [s]Jarafattan, Badafattan, [u]Fandarainā, and Kālikūt, mention of which has already been made. I next came to the city of [x]Shāliāt, where the shāliāts are made, and hence they derive their name. This is a fine city: I remained at it some time, and there heard that the kakam had returned to China, and that my slave girl had died in it: and I was much distressed on her account. The infidels, too, had seized upon my property, and my followers had been dispersed among the Chinese and others.

I then returned to Sindābūr to the King Jamāl Oddīn, at the time when an infidel king was besieging the town with his troops. I left the place, therefore, and made for the [y]Maldive Islands, at which, after ten days, I arrived.

---

[o] هَنَور. [p] فاكنور. [q] مَنجرور. [r] هيلي. [s] جرفتن. [t] بدفتن.
[u] فندرينا. [x] الشاليات. [y] جزائر ذبيه المهلي.

---

* فاستفتحت بالمصحف تفاؤلا. This seems to be a very favourite practice in the East. The omen is termed a *fāl* (فال), and the verses which direct how it is to be obtained, are called a *fāl nāmah* (فال نامه). A copy of this is generally found in most of the fine copies of the Korān.

## CHAPTER XIX.

*Description of the Maldive Islands—Natural productions—People—Customs—Trade—Currency—*
*Origin of Mohammedanism here—A Queen governing the principal island—They write generally on*
*palm leaves, with an iron style—Power of the Judge: his revenue—Isle of Kalnūs—Voyage to*
*the principal isle—Introduced to the husband and vizier of the Queen—Food of the islanders—*
*Takes the office of Judge—Marries three wives—Suspected by the Vizier—Divorces his wives, and*
*visits the other islands—Mulūk Island—Its fertility—Distance from the coast of Coromandel.*

THESE islands constitute one of the wonders of the world; for their
number is about two thousand, nearly a hundred of which are so close to
each other as to form a sort of ring; each of which, nevertheless, is surrounded by the sea. When vessels approach any one of them, they are
obliged to show who they have on board; if not, a passage is not permitted
between them; for such is their proximity to each other, that the people of
one are recognized by those of another.

The greatest trees on these islands are those of the cocoa-nut, the fruit
of which they eat with fish. Of this sort of trees the palm will produce
fruit twelve times in the year, each month supplying a fresh crop: so that
you will see upon the trees, the fruit of some large, of others small, of
others dry, and of others green. And this is the case always. From these
they make palm-wine, and oil olive; and from their honey, sweetmeats,
which they eat with the dried fruits. This is a strong incentive to venery.
I had some slave girls and four wives during my residence here,*......The
people are religious, chaste, and peaceable. They eat what is lawful, and
their prayers are answered. Their bodies are weak. They make no war:
and their weapons are prayers. They are by no means terrified at the
robbers and thieves of India, nor do they punish them; from the experience

---

* The passage, which will not bear translating, is this: وقد كان لي بها جواري وأربع نسوة
وكنت اطوف عليهن في الليلة الواحدة مدة مقامي بها. This tree is, no doubt, the kettule of
Knox, who says, " It groweth straight, but not so tall or big as the cocoa-nut tree. It yieldeth
a sort of liquor, which they call tellegie: it is rarely sweet and pleasing to the palate, and is
wholesome to the body, but no stronger than water: they take it down from the tree twice, and
from some good trees thrice in a day. An ordinary tree will yield some three, some four gallons
in a day—the which liquor they boil, and make a kind of brown sugar, called jaggory; but if
they use their skill, they can make it as white as the second-best sugar, and fit for any use, &c.
—Knox's Ceylon, p. 30, edit. 1817.

that every one who steals, will be exposed to some sudden and grievous calamity. When any of the war-vessels of the infidel Hindoos pass by these islands, they take whatsoever they find, without being resisted by any one. But if one of these infidels should take for himself (surreptitiously) but a single lemon, his chief* will not only severely punish him, but will impress most seriously upon his mind, the fear of some horrible consequence to follow. Excepting this one case only, they are the most gentle people possible towards those who visit them: the reason probably is, the delicacy of their persons, and their ignorance of the art of war.

In each of these islands are several mosques, which, with the rest of their buildings, are constructed of wood. They are a cleanly people, each individual washing himself twice daily, on account of the great heat of the sun. They very much use perfumes, such as the gālia,† and scented oils. Every woman must, as soon as her husband has arisen and said his prayers, bring him the box of colyrium for his eyes, with the perfumes, and with these he anoints and perfumes himself. Both the rich and poor walk barefoot. The whole country is shaded with trees, so that a person walking along, is just as if he were walking in a garden. The water of their wells is not more than two cubits from the surface of the earth.

Whenever a traveller enters these islands, he may marry for a very small dowry one of the handsomest women for any specific period, upon this condition, that he shall divorce her when he leaves the place; because the women never leave their respective districts. But, if he does not wish to marry, the woman in whose house he lodges will cook for him, and otherwise attend on him, for a very small consideration. The greatest part of their trade consists in a sort of hemp, that is, thread made of the fibres of the cocoa-nut. It is made by macerating the nut in water, then by beating

---

* The Maldive chief governor is probably here meant.

† According to Golius, " odoramenti genus: *hinc* galia *dictum*, et *vulgo* galia *moscata.*" *Gi.* The Medical Dictionary of Ibn Hosain ascribes to it the properties of reducing hard swellings, and, when mixed with oil, particularly that of the bān seed, is effectual in removing the earache : he states that its scent is delightful, and that when mixed with any drink, has the property of intoxicating ; that it is good for the epilepsy, and to cure barrenness. The words are :

غاليه شيخ الريس كويد اورام صلبــرا نرم كرداند واكر در روغن چيزي يا روغن حب البان بكذاراند

(بكذارند) ودر كوش چكاانند درد زايل كرداند و نوشيدن وي مصروعرا نافع بود ... وچون در شراب

حل كنند وبخود كسي دهند مست شود و بوئيدن وي مفرح دل بود ... وابستنيرا يارى دهد .

it with large mallets till it is quite soft; they then spin it out, and afterwards twist it into ropes.*   With this thread the ships of India and Yemen
are sewn together, of which, when they happen to strike against a rock,
the thread will yield a little, but will not soon break, contrary to what
happens when put together with iron nails.  This is the best sort of hemp.†
Each population catches the fish of its own island only, which they salt,
and send to India and China.  The currency used instead of coin, is the
ᵉWada.‡  This is sea shell-fish, which they take upon the shore, and then
bury in the earth till the flesh is entirely wasted away, the hard part
still remaining.  This is the Wada which is so abundant in India: it is
carried from these islands to the province of Bengal; and there also passes
instead of coin.

ᵉ ودع .

* Knox, speaking of the kettule tree of Ceylon, says, " it bears a leaf like to that of a betel-
nut tree, which is fastened to a skin as the betel-nut leaves were; only this skin is hard and
stubborn, like a piece of board.  The skin is full of strings as strong as wire; they use them to
make ropes withal."—Ceylon, p. 30.

† We have the following account respecting these islands in the two Mohammedan travellers
of the ninth century (Pinkerton, vol. vii. p. 182).  " Between this sea and that of Delarowi are
many islands, to the number, as they say, of nineteen hundred, which divide those two seas
from each other, and are governed by a queen."  To this last particular the editor objects in a
note ; yet it is curious enough, that a queen held the supreme power when our traveller resided
there.  It is also remarkable, that our traveller makes the islands two thousand in number ;
but he mentions nothing about the ambergris, said to be found there in the ninth century ;
while both agree in stating, that a sort of palm-tree bearing cocoa-nuts is found, and that the
fibres of these are used as hemp.  We are told, in a note by the editor, that these islands are,
by the best writers, made to amount to about twelve thousand; and it is then said, that *Male dive*
means in the Malabar tongue a thousand islands.  That द्वीप *Dweep*, means an island in the
Sanscrit there can be no doubt; but it is very doubtful whether the other etymology is true.
Ibn Batúta derives their name from the principal island, Mohl, as a proper name; and if this
be true, the meaning of their name will be the *Mohl islands*.  That the Lakadives are so
called from their number is highly probable, *Lakkha* or *Laksha* लक्ष meaning *a hundred thousand* in Sanscrit, and *Dweep* an island, as before : and the name implying an indefinitely large
number of isles generally.

‡ According to Golius, the Concha Veneris, but according to the author of the Kámoos
حرز بيضا تخرج من البحر بيضاء شقها كشق النواة تعلق لدفع العين .  A white shell which is
taken out of the sea, the fissure of which is white like that of the date-stone.  It is hung (about
the neck) to avert the evil eye.

The women of the islands of India cover their faces, and also their bodies, from the navel downwards: this they all do, even to the wives of their kings. When I held the office of judge among them, I was quite unable to get them covered entirely. In these islands the women never eat with the men, but in their own society only. I endeavoured, while I was judge, to get my wives to eat with me, but I could never prevail. Their conversation is very pleasing; and they, themselves, are exceedingly beautiful.

The cause of these islands becoming Mohammedan was, as it is generally received among them, and as some learned and respectable persons among them informed me, as follows. When they were in a state of infidelity, there appeared to them every month a spectre from among the genii. This came from the sea. Its appearance was that of a ship filled with candles. When they saw him, it was their custom to take and dress up a young woman who was a virgin, and place her in the *idol-temple which stood on the sea-shore, and had windows looking towards him. Here they left her for the night. When they came in the morning, they found her vitiated and dead. This they continued doing month after month, casting lots among themselves, and each, to whom the lot fell, giving up and dressing out his daughter for the spectre. After this there came to them a western Arab, named *Abu'l Barakāt the Berber. This was a holy man, and one who had committed the Korān to memory. He happened to lodge in the house of an old woman in the *island of Mohl.* One day, when he entered the house, he saw her with a company of her female inmates weeping and lamenting, and asked them what was the matter. A person who acted as interpreter between him and them said, that the lot had fallen upon this old woman, who was now adorning her daughter for the spectre: for this it was she was crying: this too was her only child. The Mogrebine, who was a beardless man, said to her: I will go to the spectre to-night instead of thy daughter. If he takes me, then I shall redeem her: but if I come off safe, then that will be to the praise of God. They carried him accordingly to the idol-house that night, as if he had been the daughter of the old woman, the magistrate knowing nothing whatever of the

---

‏ᵃ برخانه .    ᵇ ابو البركات البربري .    ᶜ بجزيره المهل .‏

* The principal island of the group.

matter. The Mogrebine entered, and sitting down in the window, began to read the Korān. By and bye the spectre came, with eyes flaming like fire; but when he had got near enough to hear the Korān, he plunged into the sea. In this manner the Mogrebine remained till morning, reading his Korān, when the old woman came with her household, and the great personages of the district, in order to fetch out the young woman and burn her, as it was their custom. But when they saw the old man reading the Korān, just as they had left him, they were greatly astonished. The old woman then told them what she had done, and why she had desired him to do this. They then carried the Mogrebine to their King, whose name was <sup>d</sup>Shanwān, and told him the whole of the affair; and he was much astonished at the Arab. Upon this the Mogrebine presented the doctrine of Islamism to the King, and pressed him to receive it; who replied: Stay with us another month, and then, if you will do as you now have done, and escape from the spectre with safety, I will become a Mohammedan. So God opened the heart of the King for the reception of Islamism before the completion of the month,—of himself, of his household, his children, and his nobles. When, however, the second month came, they went with the Mogrebine to the idol-house, according to former custom, the King himself being also present; and when the following morning had arrived, they found the Mogrebine sitting and reading his Koran; having had the same rencontre with the spectre that he had on the former occasion. They then broke the images, rased the idol-house to the ground, and all became Mohammedans. The sect into which they entered was that of the Mogrebine; namely, that of Ibn Mālik. Till this very day they make much of the Mogrebines, on account of this man. I was residing for some time in these islands, without having any knowledge of this circumstance; upon a certain night, however, when I saw them exulting and praising God, as they were proceeding towards the sea, with Korāns on their heads, I asked them what they were about; when they told me of the spectre. They then said: Look towards the sea, and you will see him. I looked, and behold, he resembled a ship filled with candles and torches. This, said they, is the spectre; which, when we do as you have seen us doing, goes away and does us no injury.

---

<sup>d</sup> شنوان .

When I first came to the island of Mohl, a woman was sovereign, because the King mentioned above had left no male issue; the inhabitants therefore gave to his eldest daughter, Khodīja, the supreme rule. Her husband, [e]Jamāl Oddīn, the preacher, then became her prime minister.

It is a custom with them to write out copies of the Korān and other books on paper only. Letters, orders, and legal decisions, they inscribe on palm leaves of the cocoa-nut tree, with a crooked sharp-pointed instrument some-. what like a knife. The army of this [f]Princess consists of foreigners, to the number of about one thousand men. Their laws mostly originate with the judge, who, for the authority with which his orders are obeyed, is more like a king. He enjoys, by right of his office, the revenue of three islands : a custom which originated with their king [g]Shanwāza, whose proper name was [h]Ahmed, and this still remains in force.

When I first arrived at these islands, the ship in which I was, put into port in the island [i]Kalnūs, which is a beautiful place, containing several mosques. Upon this occasion some of the learned and pious inhabitants took me to their houses, and entertained me with great hospitality. The commander of the ship in which I had been, then went with me to the island in which the Queen resided; and after which, the other islands of these parts are named. I sailed with him in order to see her; and after passing by many of the islands, came to it. Our practice was, to sail in a large boat during the morning; about the middle of the day we said our prayers, and then dined in the boat. And thus, after ten days, we came to the island [j]Zabīah El Mohl, i. e. the Maldive island. In this I landed, and a report was made to the Queen's vizier, Jamāl Oddīn, who was also her husband. Upon this he sent for me. I went to him, and was very honourably received and entertained. He also appointed a house for my residence, sent me a present of victuals, fruits, clothing, and an [k]alms-gift of the [l]Wada (or shells), which are the currency of these parts, and used instead of coin.

The food of the greater part of the inhabitants of these parts is rice, which they cook and lay up in saucers, and small potted plates, with spiced flesh, fowl, and fish. Upon this, in order to assist digestion, they

---

[e] جمال الدين .   [f] هذه السلطانه .   [g] شنوازه .   [h] احمد .   [i] كلنوس .

[j] ذبية المهل .   [k] حانبا .   [l] الودع .

drink El Kurbānī; that is, the honey of the cocoa-nut made into spiced wine; this easily digests, excites the appetite, and communicates strength to the frame.

After this the Vizier desired me to take the office of Judge, and to remain among them. He gave me a house, and a large garden, in which were built many other houses. He also sent me a carpet, vessels, a dress of honour, and made me ride upon a horse; although it is a custom with them, that none except the Vizier should thus ride. The rest of the nobles and others either ride in a ᵐpalanquin, a machine formerly described, or walk on foot. He also sent female slaves for my service; and I married three wives. The Vizier also frequently came himself and conferred his favours upon me: for which may God reward him.

When, however, I had married my wives, and my relations became, through them, numerous and powerful in the island, the Vizier began to be afraid of me, lest I should get the upper hand of him, when no such thought had entered my mind. This resulted purely from their weakness, the fewness of their troops, and their inexperience in the art of war, as already noticed. He hated me mortally in his own mind, began to inquire into my affairs, and to watch my proceedings. This was all known to me, and it became my intention to leave the place: but this was also a matter of dread with him, because I might then possibly bring an army upon him from the Maabar districts of Hindūstān, the king of those parts, ⁿGīāth Oddīn, having married a sister to one of my wives when I resided in Dehli, and with whom I was on terms of friendship.

I then divorced all my wives except one, who had a young child, and I left that island for those which stretch out before it. These form numerous ᵒgroups, each ᵖgroup containing many islands. In some of these I saw women who had only one breast, which much astonished me. Of these islands, one is named Mulūk. In this, large ships destined for the districts of Maabar put into harbour. It is an island exceedingly rich in vegetation and soil, so that when you cut a branch from any of its trees, and plant it either on the road or on a wall, it will grow, throw out leaves, and become a tree. In this island I saw a pomegranate tree, the fruit of which ceased

---

ᵖ اقليم .          ᵒ climates) اقاليم) .          ⁿ غياث الدين .          ᵐ دوله

not to shoot during the whole year. Between the Maldive islands and the Maabar districts there is a distance of three days, with a moderate wind.

---

## CHAPTER XX.

*Arrival in Ceylon—Visits the King at Battāla—Natural productions—Pearls—Obtains permission to visit Adam's Peak—Arrives at Manār Mandalī—Port of Salāwāt—Kanhar, the capital of Ceylon, described—Mosque of the Sheikh Othmān—The Emperor Kinār: his white elephant —large rubies found all over Ceylon—Description of the cave Ista Mahmūd—Būzūta— Monkies—Estuary of reeds—Old woman's house—Cave of Bābā Tāhir—Of Sībak—The fierce leech—The seven caves—Ridge of Alexander—Description of Adam's Peak—Customs of Pilgrims—Fish Port—Village of Karkūn—Of Dildīnūh—Of At Kalanja—City of Dīnaur—Great Idol-Temple, with Brahmins, Jogees, and daughters of the Nobility—Kālī—Kalambū— Battāla.*

WHEN we sailed, however, the wind changed upon us, and we were near being lost; but arrived at last at the ⁹island of Ceylon, a place well known, and in which is situated the mountain of ʳSerendīb. This appeared to us like a pillar of smoke, when we were at a distance of nine days from it.* When we got near the land, we saw a harbour, into which we endeavoured to put, but were threatened by the Reis, who was in a ship. The reason of this was, the harbour was in a district belonging to an infidel prince, who had no intercourse with the captains of Mohammedan vessels, as other infidel princes had. He was likewise a very stupid being. He had also ships with which he occasionally transported his troops against the Mohammedans. Beside all this, we were in danger of drowning, unless we could enter the port: I said to the Reis, therefore, Allow me to come on shore, and I will ensure thy safety, and that of those about thee, with the King. To this he consented, and myself, with some of my followers only, were brought on shore. The infidels then came about us and said: What are you? I answered, I am a relation of the King of the Maabar districts, and am on a voyage to visit him: whatever is in the

---

⁹ جزيرة سيلان .    ʳ سرنديب .

* Knox says, " it is sharp like a sugar-loaf."—Ceylon, p. 5.

ship, is a present for the King of the Maabar. They then went to their king, and told him this. He therefore sent for me, and I went to him. He is king of the city of ˢBattāla,* which is small, and surrounded by two wooden fences. The whole of its shore abounds with ᵗcinnamon wood, bakam, and the ᵘkalanjī aloe;† which, however, is not equal to the ˣKamārī, or the ʸKākulī, in scent. The merchants of Malabar and the Maabar districts transport it without any other price than a few articles of clothing, which are given as presents to the king. This may be attributed to the circumstance, that it is brought down by the mountain torrents, and left in great heaps upon the shore. Between this city and the Maabar districts, there is a voyage of one day and night. The king of Ceylon, ᶻAyarī Shakartī, by name, has considerable forces by sea. When I was first admitted to his presence, he rose and received me honourably, and

---

ˢ بطَّاله .  ᵗ باعوادِ القِرفه .  ᵘ العود الكلنجي .  ˣ القماري .  ʸ قاتلي .  ᶻ ايري شكرتي .

---

* Perhaps the Batticalaw of Knox, which he expressly tells us lies to the *westward* of the island, while the maps place Batticaloa (which I suppose must mean the same place) to the eastward.—Ceylon, p. 3.

† The Medical Dictionary of Ibn Hosain speaks of the Kākulī in the following terms: قاتلي نباتيست مانند اشنان ودر طعم وي شوري بود با قبض اوستخوان ان ابن عمران كويد مانند كثوث بون در فعل وطبيعيت وبكرم وخشك بود . The Kākulī is a plant like the Alkali. In taste it is salt and astringent; its stone, as Ibn Imrān says, is like the Dodder plant in operation: it is of a warm and dry nature: and Edrīsī, speaking of Fandaraina says (8th part of the 2d climate), تحط به مراكب التجار من جزاير الهند ومراكب السند ايضا وبشمال هذه المدينة وعليها جبل ساي العلو كثير الشجر عامر بالقري والمواشي وينبت في حوافيه القاقله ومهيا تحمل الي ساير اقطار الارض . ونبات القاقله تكون اشبه الاشيا بنبات الشهرانج Into this place put the merchant vessels from the islands of India and Sindia. On the north of it is a very high hill, abounding in trees, with villages and cattle: about the skirts of it grows the kākula, and hence is transported to other parts of the earth. This plant is of all things the most like to the shahrānj (شهرنج placentarum genus? Castell). The قماري Kamārī or Kimārī, is, according to Golius, so called from a place named قمار Kimār, in India. Ibn Batūta tells us, a little farther on, that both قاقله Kākula and قمارة Kamāra, the places where these plants are produced, are situated in Java (مل جاوه Mul Jāva).

Knox tells us, that the cinnamon-tree grows wild in the woods as other trees, and by them no more esteemed. It is as much in plenty as hazel in England, &c.—Ceylon, p. 31. On the aloes, &c., see Knox, pp. 36, &c.; edition by Philalethes, p. 5 and 7, &c.

said : You are to be my guest for three days. Security shall be forwarded
to the people of the ship, because your relation, the King of the Maabar,
is my friend. After thanking him, I remained with him, and was treated
with increasing respect.

One day, when I was admitted to his presence, he had with him a great
number of pearls, which had been brought from the pearl-fishery, and
these his companions were sorting. He asked me, whether I had ever seen
pearl-diving, in any country which I had visited. I said, yes, I had, in
the island of *Fīnas. He said: Do not be shy; ask for what you wish.
I answered: My only desire in coming to this island was, to visit the
blessed foot of our forefather Adam ;* whom these people call Bābā, while
they style Eve, Māmā. This, replied he, is easy enough. We will send
some one with you, who shall conduct you thither. The ship (said I)
which brought me here, shall return to the Maabar ; and when I return, you
shall send me there in one of your ships. He answered, It shall be so.
When I told this to the commander of the ship, he refused to accede to it;
and said, I will wait for you, should you be absent a whole year. This I
told to the King, who said: He may stay at my charge until you return.
He then gave me a palanquin, which his servants carried upon their
shoulders. He also sent with me four Jogees, who were in the habit of
visiting the foot-mark every year; with these went four Brahmins, and ten
of the King's companions, with fifteen men carrying provisions. As to
water, there is plenty of it to be found on the road. We then proceeded
on our journey; and on the first day crossed a river in a boat made of
reeds, and entered the city of *Manār Mandalī, which is handsome, and
situated at the extremity of the territory of the infidel king, who had
entertained and sent us out. We then proceeded to the port of *Salāwāt,

---

*c* بندر سلوات    *b* منار مندلي .    *a* فينس .

---

* This is, without doubt, the foot of some Buddh, as already noticed, p. 30. Knox says
of this hill, " On the south side of Conde Uda is a hill, supposed to be the highest on this
island, called in the Chingulay language Hamalell, but by the Portuguese and European nations
Adam's Peak. It is sharp like a sugar-loaf, and on the top a flat stone, with the print of a
foot like a man's on it, but far bigger, being about two feet long. The people of this land count
it meritorious to go and worship this impression," &c.,—Ceylon, p. 5. The Cingalese assert,
that the foot-mark is that of Buddh. Ib. p. 144; Addition, pp. 210, 215.

which is a small town.  The roads, however, over which we travelled,
were rough and abounding with water.*  In these there were many elephants: but they never touched either pilgrims or strangers, in consequence of the blessing obtained by the Sheikh [d]Abu Abd Allah Ibn
Khafīf, the first who opened this road of pilgrimage to the foot.  The infidels
would not formerly allow the Mohammedans to make this pilgrimage, but injured them; nor would they either sell, or give them any thing to eat.  But
when it happened that the elephants killed all the companions of this Sheikh,
one of them sparing and carrying him on his back from among the mountains to an inhabited district, the infidels ever after thought highly of the
Mohammedans, admitted them into their houses, and fed them.  And to
this very day they speak of the Sheikh in the most extravagant terms of
respect, and call him [e]" the greatest Sheikh."†  After this we arrived at the
city of [f]Kankār,‡ which is the seat of the Emperor of Ceylon.  It is built
in a valley between two hills, upon an estuary called the estuary of rubies,
and in which rubies are found.  Without the city is the mosque of the
[g]Sheikh Othmān of Shirāz, which both the Emperor and the people of the
city visit, and for which they have great respect.

The Emperor is an infidel, and is known by the name of [h]Kinār.§  He
has a white elephant, upon which he rides on feast days, having first
placed on his head some very large rubies.  This is the only white elephant

[d] ابو عبد الله بن خفيف .        [e] الشيخ الاكبر .        [f] كنكار .        [g] الشيخ عثمان الشيرازي .

[h] يعرف بالكنار .

---

* Knox says, " the king careth not to make his country easy to travel, but desires to keep it
intricate."—Ceylon, p. 5.

† According to Knox, a certain former king granted permission to the Mohammedans to
build a mosque at Candy, with other privileges.—Ceylon, p. 171.  See the notes, p. 42.

‡ This is, perhaps, a corruption of the Tattanour of Knox, " in which," he says, " stands
the royal and chief city Candi."—Ceylon, p. 3.  The district of *Canducarre* (which approaches
nearer in sound to our word), might, indeed, have been the seat of royalty in his times.

§ According to the list of Emperors subjoined to Knox's Ceylon, p. 340, Dālam Agali Raja
must have ruled Ceylon at this time; his reign continuing from A.D. 1327 to 1347.  The name
*Agali*, however, seems much nearer in sound to our Ayarī (ايري).  In that case, either our
traveller or the author of that list has mistaken a Governor for the Emperor.  All that can
be said, perhaps, is that the coincidence in the name is curious.  Knox tells us, however, that
this country formerly consisted of nine kingdoms.—Ceylon, p. 63.

I had ever seen.\* The ruby and [i]carbuncle are found only in this country. These are not allowed to be exported, on account of the great estimation in which they are held: nor are they elsewhere dug up. But the ruby is found all over Ceylon. It is considered as property, and is sold by the inhabitants. When they dig for the ruby, they find a white stone abounding with fissures. Within this the ruby is placed. They cut it out, and give it to the polishers, who polish it until the ruby is separated from the stone. Of this there is the red, the yellow, and the cerulean. They call it the [k]Manīkam.† It is a custom among them, that every ruby amounting in value to six of the golden dinars current in those parts, shall go the Emperor, who gives its value and takes it. What falls short of this goes to his attendants. All the women in the island of Ceylon have traces of coloured rubies, which they put upon their hands and legs as chains, in the place of bracelets and ancle-rings. I once saw upon the head of the white elephant seven rubies, each of which was larger than a hen's egg. I also saw in the possession of the king [l]Ayarī Shakartī, a saucer made of ruby, as large as the palm of the hand, in which he kept oil of aloes. I was much surprised at it, when the King said to me, We have them much larger than this.

We then proceeded from Kankār, and came to a cave known by the name of [m]Istā Mahmūd, then to the estuary of [n]Būzūta,‡ which in their language signifies monkies, animals which are in great numbers in the mountains of these parts. These monkies are black, and have long tails: the beard of the males is like that of a man. I was told by the Sheikh Othmān and his son, two pious and credible persons, that the monkies have a leader, whom they follow as if he were their king. About his head is tied a turban com-

---

[n] بوزوته .    [m] اسطا محمد .    [l] ايري شكرتي .    [k] المنيكم .    [i] البهرمان .

---

\* Knox saw an elephant in the king's possession " spotted or speckled all the body over." Ceylon, p. 41.

† This is most likely a Sanscrit or Pali word, although we do not find it in Mr. Wilson's Sanscrit Dictionary. It is to be found, however, in the Bengáli Vocabulary of Mr. Forster, as well as in the Bengáli Dictionary of Dr. Carey, the latter of whom gives it in the two following forms, viz. মানিক and মানিক৹ mániko and mánikyo, a precious stone, a ruby. Every traveller, I believe, bears testimony to the production of precious stones of this sort in this island, but I believe they are not very valuable.

‡ This appears to me to be a corruption of the Persian word بزنه buzna, a monkey. See Knox's Ceylon, pp. 49-50, who describes them as exceedingly daring and mischievous.

posed of the leaves of trees; and he reclines upon a staff. At his right and left hand are four monkies, with rods in their hands, all of which stand at his head whenever the leading monkey sits. His wives and children are daily brought in on these occasions, who sit down before him; then comes a number of monkeys, which sit and form a sort of assembly about him. One of the four monkeys then addresses them, and they disperse. After this each of them comes with a [o]nut, a lemon, or some of the mountain fruit, which he throws down before the leader. He then eats, together with his wives, children, and the four principal monkeys; they then all disperse. One of the Jogees also told me, that he once saw the four monkeys standing in the presence of the leader, and beating another monkey with rods; after this they plucked off all his hair. I was also told by respectable persons, that if one of these monkeys happens to attack, and be too strong for a young woman, he will ravish her.

We next proceeded to the [p]estuary of reeds, where rubies are also found. The next place we arrived at is known by [q]"The house of the old woman," which is the farthest inhabited part of the island of Ceylon. Our next stage was the cave of [r]Bābā Tāhir, who was one of the pious: the next, the cave of [s]Sībak, an infidel king, who retired to this place for the purposes of devotion. Here we saw the [t]fierce leech, which they call the [u]zalaw. It remains in trees, or in the grass near water. When any one comes near to it, it springs upon him, and the part of the body attacked will bleed profusely. People generally provide themselves with a lemon for this occasion, which they squeeze over him, and then he drops off. The place upon which the leech has fastened they cut out with a wooden knife made for that purpose.

It is told of a pilgrim who passed by this place, that a leech fastened upon him, so that the skin swelled; and, as he did not squeeze the lemon on him, the blood flowed out and he died.*

---

[o] موزة . [p] خور الخيزران . [q] بيت العجوز. [r] بابا طاهر. [s] السيبك .
[t] العلق الطيار. [u] الزلو.

---

* Knox describes these leeches as being rather troublesome than dangerous; his words are: "There is a sort of leeches of the nature of ours, only differing in colour and bigness; for they are of a dark reddish colour like the skin of bacon, and as big as a goose-quill; in length some two or three inches. At first, when they are young, they are no bigger than a horse-hair, so that

We next came to a place called the [x] seven caves, and after this to the [y] ridge of Alexander, in which is a cave and a well of water. At this place is the [z] entrance to the mountain. This mountain of Serendīb is one of the highest in the world : we saw it from the sea at the distance of nine days. When we ascended it, we saw the clouds passing between us and its foot. On it is a great number of trees, the leaves of which never fall. There are also flowers of various colours, with the red rose,* about the size of the palm of the hand, upon the leaves of which they think they can read the name of God and of his Prophet. There are two roads on the mountain leading to the foot (of Adam) ; the one is known by " the way of Bābā," the other, by " the way of Māmā," by which they mean Adam and Eve. The way called that of Māmā is easy : to it the travellers come upon their first visiting the place ; but every one who has travelled only upon this, is considered as if he had not made the pilgrimage at all. The way named Bābā is rough, and difficult of ascent. At the foot of the mountain where the entrance is, there is a minaret named after Alexander, and a fountain of water. The ancients have cut something like steps, upon which one may ascend, and have fixed in iron pins, to which chains are appended ;† and upon these those who ascend take hold. Of these chains there are ten in number, the last of which is termed [a] " the chain of witness," because, when one has arrived at this, and looks down, the frightful notion seizes him that he shall fall. After the tenth chain is the cave of [b] Khizr,‡ in which there is a large space ; and at the entrance a

خضر. [b]   سلسلة الشهادة. [a]   دروازة الجبل. [z]   عقبة اسكندر. [y]   بالسبع مغارات. [x]

they can scarce be seen. In dry weather none of them appear, but immediately upon the fall of rains, the grass and woods are full of them. These leaches seize upon the legs of travellers. Some will tie a piece of *lemon* and salt in a rag, and fasten it unto a stick, and ever and anon strike it upon their legs to make the leeches drop off : others will scrape them off with a *reed, cut flat and sharp in the fashion of a knife*," &c.—Ceylon, pp. 48-9. See also the addition by Phiḷalethes, p. 264.

* " There are roses red and white, and several sorts of sweet smelling flowers."—Ceylon, p. 35.

† " Pilgrims and travellers climb to the sacred summit of Adam's Peak by means of an iron chain, which is fastened to the rock, and the links of which serve as footsteps."—Knox's Ceylon, Add. p. 210.

‡ Various are the opinions of the Orientals as to this personage, whether he was a prophet, a walī, a saint, or an angel ; whether he was Moses, Jeremiah, Elias, Elisha, St. George, &c. &c. However, all agree in thinking very highly of him ; some believing him to be in heaven, others

well of water,* full of fish, which is also called after his name. Of those, however, no one takes any. Near this, and on each side of the path, is a cistern cut in the rock. In this cave of Khizr the pilgrims leave their provisions, and whatever else they have, and then ascend about two miles to the top of the mountain, to the place of (Adam's) foot. The holy foot (mark) is in a stone, so that its place is depressed. The length of the impression is eleven [c]spans. The Chinese came here at some former time, and cut out from this stone the place of the great toe, together with the stone about it, and placed it in a temple in the city of Zaitūn: and pilgrimages are made to it from the most distant parts of China. In the rock, too, in which the impression of the foot is, there are nine excavations which have been cut out: into these the infidel pilgrims put gold, rubies, and other jewels: and hence you will see the Fakeers, who have come as pilgrims to the well of Khizr, racing to get first to the excavations, in order to obtain what may be in them. We, however, found nothing but a little gold with some rubies, which we gave to our guide.

It is customary for the pilgrims to remain in the cave of Khizr for three days; and during this time to visit the foot both morning and evening. This we did; and when the three days were expired we returned by the path of Māmā, and came down to the cave of [d]Shīsham, who is [e]Sheth, the son of Adam. After this we arrived at the [f]fish port, then at the village of [g]Karkūn, then at the village of [h]Dildinūh, then at the village of [i]At Kalanja, where the tomb of [k]Abū Abd Allah Ibn Khafīf is situated. All these villages and tilled lands are upon the mountain. At its foot, and near the path, is a [l]cypress, which is [m]large and never drops the leaf. But as to its leaves, there is no getting to them by any means; and these people's heads are turned with some strange and false notions respecting

---

[h] دلدينوه .     [g] كركون .     [f] خور السمك .     [e] شيث .     [d] شيشم .     [c] شبرا .

[m] شجرة عادية .     [l] درخت روان .     [k] ابو عبد الله بن خفيف .     [i] ات قلنجه .

---

still on the earth, but invisible. Mr. Hamaker, in his notes on the " Liber de expugnatione Memphidis et Alexandriæ," has perhaps given the greatest and most authentic variety of opinions about him. See pp. 161-2, with the authorities there cited; and the Kāmoos, sub voce خضر which he has not noticed.

* This is, probably, the well mentioned by Philalethes in his Additions to Knox's Ceylon; p. 212.

them. I saw a number of Jogees about the tree, waiting for the falling of one; for they suppose that any person eating one of them, will grow young again, however old he may be.* Beneath this mountain is the great estuary at which the rubies are obtained; its water appears wonderfully blue to the eye.

From this place we proceeded, and in two days arrived at the city of [n] Dīnaur, which is large, and inhabited by merchants. In this is an idol, known by the same name, placed in a large temple; and in which there are about a thousand Brahmins and Jogees, and five hundred young women, daughters of the nobility of India, who sing and dance all night before the image. The officers of the city revenue attend upon the image. The idol is of gold, and as large as a man. In the place of eyes it has two large rubies; which, as I was told, shine in the night-time like two lighted candles.

From this place we travelled to [o] Kālī, which is a large town; then to [p] Kolambū (Colombo), which is the finest and largest city in Serendīb. After three days we arrived at the city of [q] Battāla, from which we had been sent by its king, with his servants, to visit (Adam's) foot. This we entered, and were received honourably by the king, who furnished us with provisions.

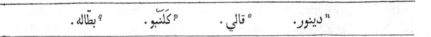

[q] بطّاله .      [p] كَلَنْبُو .      [o] قالي .      [n] دينور .

---

* This is, probably, the *Bagauhah*, or *god-tree* of Knox, which, he says, " is very great and spreading; they have a very great veneration for these trees, worshipping them upon a tradition that the Buddou, a great god among them, when he was upon the earth, did use to sit under this kind of trees." It is held meritorious to plant them, which they say he that does, *shall die within a short while after, and go to heaven.* That is, as our traveller, perhaps, understood it, shall be re-born into another and better state of being: the Buddhists holding the metempsychosis.

## CHAPTER XXI.

*Return to the coast of Coromandel—Arrival at the palace of Ghīāth Oddīn—Short account of the governors of those parts—War with the Hindūs—The Hindū king taken and slain—Fattan— Different animals kept in the same cage—Matarāh—Ghīāth Oddīn dies—Succeeded by his brother's son, Nāsir Oddīn—Fattan—Kawlam—Hinaur—Taken prisoner by the Hindūs—Kālikūt— Arrival at the Maldive islands—Bengal—Sadkāwān—Mountains of Kāmrū—The Sheikh Tebrīzī—Miracles ascribed to him—Jabnak—Blue River—Satarkāwān—Barahnakār—Produce—Character of the people—Customs.*

AFTER this, we sailed with the vessel, which had waited for us, to the Maabar districts. But when we had made half the voyage, the wind rose upon us, and we were near drowning. We then cut down our mast, and every moment expected death. Providence, however, was favourable to us; for there came boats from the infidel inhabitants of the Maabar, which brought us to land. I then told them, that I was the messenger of their King, and that he was my relation; upon which they landed us, and treated us very honourably. They wrote to the King on this, as I also did, telling him what had happened. After three days came an Emīr from the Sultan, with a number of cavalry; for me they brought a palanquin and ten horses, to carry me. We then set out for the presence of the King, ͬGhīāth Oddīn El Dāmgānī, who at this time enjoyed the supreme power in the Maabar districts. These parts formerly belonged to the Emperor of Hindūstān, the Sultan Mohammed. They were then seized by the Sherīf, ͬJalāl Oddīn Hasan Shāh, who held them for five years. After this he appointed ͨAlāi Oddīn, one of his Emīrs, as his successor; but he was killed in a warlike excursion by an accidental arrow. After this, his brother's son, Kotb Oddīn, came to the supreme rule; but he was killed, in consequence of his bad conduct. After this, one of the Emīrs of the Sherīf Jalāl Oddīn came into power, that is, this Ghīāth Oddīn, who married a daughter of Jalāl Oddīn; the mother of which daughter was sister to my wife when I was Judge in Dehli.

When I had got near his house, he sent one of his chamberlains to meet me; and, when I entered, he received me graciously, and gave me a seat. He was at this time in his camp; so he erected three tents for me opposite

ͬغياث الدين الدامغاني ·      ͬجلال الدين حسن شاه ·      ͨعلاي الدين ·

those of his Judge, "Sadar El Zamān. He also sen' me a carpet, provisions, and presents.

This was a very warlike prince; and as he happened to be in the neighbourhood of an infidel, whose army amounted to one hundred and twenty thousand men, an attempt was made to take these Maabar districts out of the hands of the Mohammedans. This infidel prince accordingly made an attack on the town of ˣKiān, which belongs to the Maabar, and in which there were six thousand soldiers, put them to the rout, and besieged it. This was reported to the Sultan, and that the town was nearly lost. He then marched out with his forces, which amounted to seven thousand, every man of whom took off his turban, and hung it upon the neck of his horse, which is, in India, an intimation that they are bent upon death. They then made a charge upon the infidel king, while his men were taking their mid-day repose and besieging ʸKiān, and put them to the rout. The greater part of them was killed; nor did one, except the cavalry, or those who concealed themselves in the woods, escape. The Sultan was taken prisoner, his wealth seized, himself afterwards killed, and I saw his body hanging against a wall in the town.

I then left the King's station, until he should return from his expedition, and came to the city of ˢFattan, which is large and beautiful, and situated upon the sea-shore. Its harbour is truly wonderful. In this city there are grapes and good ᵃpomegranates. I saw in this place the ᵇSheikh Sālih Mohammed of Nīsābūr, one of the fanatical Fakeers who suffer their hair to flow down loosely upon their shoulders. This man had seven foxes with him, all of which ate and sat with the Fakeers. There were also with him thirty other Fakeers, one of whom had a gazelle with a lion in the same place, which was unmolested by the lion. I then proceeded for the purpose of presenting myself to the Sultan at the city of ᶜMaturāh, which is large, and not unlike Dehli. In this I found a great mortality, which had destroyed the greatest part of the inhabitants. The King, Ghiāth Oddīn returned at this time to his palace sick, and soon after died. He appointed his brother's son, ᵈNāsir Oddīn, to be his successor. In this

---

" صدرالزمان .    ˣ كيان .    ᶻ كيان .    ᶻ فتن .    ᵃ الرمان الطيب .

ᵇ الشيخ الصالح محمد النسابوري .    ᶜ متراه .    ᵈ ناصر الدين .

place, too, I caught a fever which nearly destroyed me; but, as Providence restored me to health, I requested permission of the King Nāsir Oddīn to proceed on my journey, which was granted. I then returned to the city of *Fattan (Pattan), and thence by sea to ʃKawlam, one of the cities of Malabar, where I remained three months, on account of the sickness which had happened to me. From this place I set out to visit the Sultan ᵍJamāl Oddīn of Hinaur, who had received a promise from me to return. The infidel Hindoos, however, came out against us in twelve war vessels, between (the last place mentioned and) ʰFākanūn; and, giving us severe battle, at length overcame us, and took our ship. They then stripped us of all. From me they took all the jewels and rubies given me by the King of ⁱBattāla, as well as the additional presents of the pious Sheikhs, leaving me only one pair of trowsers: and thus were we landed nearly naked. I then returned to ᵏKālikūt, and entered one of the mosques. When some of the lawyers and merchants, who had known me in Dehli, heard of my situation, they clothed and received me honourably. I then thought of returning to the Emperor of Hindustan: but I was afraid of his severity, and that he might ask me, why I had separated from the present. I then went on board another ship, and this pleased me, and returned to the ˡMaldive Islands, on account of the little boy I had left there. When I had seen him, however, I left him in kindness to his mother. The Vizier then furnished me with provisions, and I sailed for ᵐBengal, which is an extensive and plentiful country. I never saw a country in which provisions were so cheap. I there saw one of the religious of the west, who told me, that he had bought provisions for himself and his family for a whole year with eight dirhems. The first town I entered here was ⁿSadkāwān,* which is large and situated on the sea-shore.

---

ⁱ بطّاله .      ʰ فاكنون .      ᵍ جمال الدين الهنوري .      ʄ كولم .      * فتن .

ⁿ سدكاوان .      ᵐ بنجاله .      ˡ لمحزاير ذبيه .      ᵏ قالقوط .

---

* The name of this place is variously written; in some cases we have سُترِكاوان Sutirkāwān, in others سدكاوان according to our MSS. In the تاريخ بدايوني we have سناركانون and ستاركانون It was, no doubt, the name of a place then in Bengal; but whether it is still in existence or not the geographers do not inform us. We are told, in the author just mentioned, that Mohammed Shāh made an expedition, in A.H. 741, A.D. 1340, to this place, and took Fakhr Oddīn, the king

The king of Bengal was at this time [o] Fakhr Oddīn: he was an eminent man, kind to strangers and persons of the Sūfī persuasion: but I did not present myself to him, nor did I see him, because he was opposed to the Emperor, and was then in open rebellion against him. From [p] Sadkāwān I travelled for the mountains of [q] Kāmrū, which are at the distance of one month from this place. These are extensive mountains, and they join the [r] mountains of Thibet, where there are musk gazelles. The inhabitants of these mountains are, like the Turks, famous for their attention to [s] magic. My object in visiting these mountains was, to meet one of the saints, namely, the Sheikh [t] Jalāl Oddīn of Tebrīz. This Sheikh was one of the greatest saints, and one of those singular individuals who had the power of working great and notable miracles. He had also lived to a remarkably great age. He told me, that he had seen [u] El Mostaasim the Calif in Bagdad: and his companions told me afterwards that he died at the age of one hundred and fifty years; that he fasted through a space of about forty years, never breaking his fast till he had fasted throughout ten successive days. He had a cow, on the milk of which he usually breakfasted; and his practice was to sit up all night. It was by his means that the people of these mountains became Mohammedans; and on this account it was, that he resided among them. One of his companions told me, that on the day before his death he invited them all to come to him; he then said to them: To-morrow I depart from you, *Deo volente,* and my vicegerent with you is God besides whom there is no other God. When the evening of the following day had arrived, and he had performed the last prostration of the evening prayer, he was taken by God. On the side of the cave in which he had resided was found a grave ready dug, and by it a winding sheet and burial spices. The people then washed and buried him in them, and said their prayers over him. When I was on my jour-

---

[o] فخر الدين . [p] سدكاوان . [q] كامرو . [r] جبال التسبت ? [s] بمعاناة السحر .
[t] جلال الدين التبريزي . [u] المستعصم .

---

mentioned by our traveller, prisoner, carried him to Laknoutī, and there put him to death. The words are: در سنه احدي واربعين وسبع مايه سلطان محمد بقصد تسخير سناركانون رفته فخر الدين را باسيري گرفته در لكهنوتي آورد و بقتل رسانيد . There must be a trifling error in one or both of these dates.

ney to see this Sheikh, four of his companions met me at the distance of
two days, and told me, that the Sheikh had said to the Fakeers who were
with them, A western religious traveller is coming to you: go out and
meet him. It was, said they, by the order of the Sheikh that we came
to you; notwithstanding the fact, that he had no knowledge whatever of
my circumstances, except what he had by divine revelation. I went with
them accordingly to his cell without the cave, near which there was no
building whatever. The people of this country are partly Mohammedans,
and partly infidels; both of whom visit the Sheikh and bring valuable
presents. On these the Fakeers, and other persons who arrive here,
subsist. As for the Sheikh himself, he confines himself to the milk of his
cow, as already mentioned. When I presented myself to him, he arose
and embraced me. He then asked me of my country and travels, of which I
informed him. He then said to the Fakeers: Treat him honourably. They
accordingly carried me to the cell, and kept me as their guest for three
days. On the day I presented myself to the Sheikh he had on a religious [x] garment, made of fine goat's hair. I was astonished at it, and said
to myself, I wish the Sheikh would give it me. When I went in to bid him
farewell, he arose and went to the side of the cave, took off the goat's
hair garment, as well as the fillet of his head and his sleeves, and put
them on me.

The Fakeers then told me, that it was not his practice to put on this
garment: and that he had put it on only on the occasion of my coming,
for he had said to them: This garment will be wished for by a Mogrebine;
but an infidel king shall take it from him, and shall give it to our brother
[y] Borhān Oddīn of Sāgirj, whose it is, and for whose use it has been made.
When I was told this by the Fakeers, I said: As I have a blessing from
the Sheikh, and as he has clothed me with his own clothes, I will never
enter with them into the presence of any king either infidel or Moslem.

After this I left the Sheikh. It happened, however, after a considerable time, that I entered the country of China, and went as far as the city
of [z] Khansā. Upon a certain occasion, when my companions had all left
me on account of the press of the multitude, and I had this garment on, and

was on the road, I met the Vizier with a large body. He happened
to cast his eyes upon me, and called me to him. He then took me by the
hand, and asked me why I had come to this country; nor did he leave me
until we came to the King's palace. I wished to go, but he would not
allow me to do so, but took me in to the King, who interrogated me about the
Mohammedan sovereigns; to all which I gave answers. He then cast his
eyes upon the garment, and began to praise it, and said to the Vizier:
Take it off him. To this I could offer no resistance, so he took it; but
ordered me ten dresses of honour, and a horse with its furniture, and
money for my necessities. This changed my mind. I then called to mind
the words of the Sheikh, that an infidel king should take it; and my wonder was increased.

After a year had elapsed, I entered the palace of the King of China at
*Khān Bālik,* my object was to visit the cell of the Sheikh Borhān Oddīn
of Sāgirj. I did so, and found him reading, and the very goat's-hair garment I have been mentioning was on him. I was surprised at this, and
was turning the garment over in my hand, when he said, Why do you turn
the garment over, do you know it? I said, I do; it is the garment which
the King of Khansā took from me. He answered: This garment was made
for me by my brother Jalāl Oddīn, for my own use, who also wrote to me
to say that the garment would come to me by such a person. He then
produced the letter, which I read, and could not help wondering at the
exactness of the Sheikh. I then told him of the origin of the story. He
answered, My brother Jalāl Oddīn was superior to all this : he had a perfect
control over human nature ;† but now he has been taken to God's mercy.
He then said, I have been told, that he performed the morning prayer every
day in Mecca; that he went on the pilgrimage annually, because he was
never to be seen on the two days of *Arafat and the feast, no one knowing
whither he had gone.

When, however, I had bid farewell to the Sheikh Jalāl Oddīn, I travelled
to the city of *Jabnak, which is very large and beautiful; it is divided by

---

<sup>c</sup> جبنق .     <sup>b</sup> يومي عرفة والعيد .     <sup>a</sup> بخان بالتى .

---

\* Cambalu, or Pekin, as will be shewn hereafter.

† هو يتصرف في الكون    See the note at page 64.

the river which descends from the mountains of Kāmrū, called the [d] Blue
River. By this one may travel to Bengal and the countries of [e] Laknoutī.
Upon it are gardens, mills, and villages, which it refreshes and gladdens
like the Nile of Egypt. The inhabitants of these parts are infidels, tribu-
tary to the Mohammedans. By this river I travelled for fifteen days, proceeding from road to road, till I came to the city of [f] Sutirkāwān.* Here I
found a junk which was proceeding to [g] Jāva (Sumatra), between which
and this place there is a distance of forty days. I proceeded, therefore,
and after a voyage of fifty days, came to the countries of the [h] Barahnakār,†
a people who have mouths like those of dogs. This is a vile race. They
have no religion, neither that of the Hindoos nor any other. They live in
houses made of reeds upon the sea-shore. Their trees are those of the [i] banana, the [k] fawfel and the [l] betel-nut. Their men are of the same form with
ourselves, except that their mouths are like those of dogs ;‡ but the women
have mouths like other folks. The men go naked, without the least covering whatever: one only among them (I saw) who had put his virilia into a
painted hollow reed, which was hung to his belly. The women cover themselves with the leaves of trees. One who had had much intercourse with them,
told me that they copulate like beasts, without the least concealment.
The men will have thirty or more wives; but adultery is not committed.
Should any one, however, be convicted of this crime, his punishment is, to
be hanged till he is dead, unless he brings either a friend or slave who is
willing to be hanged for him : he may then go free. The sentence for the
woman is, that the King shall command all his servants to trample upon

---

[h] البرهنكار .        [g] جاوه .        [f] ستركاوان .        [e] اللكنوتي .        [d] النهر الازرق .

[l] التنبول .        [k] الفوفل .        [i] الموز .

---

* See the note at p. 194.

† Nearest in sound to this, as far as I can see, appears to be the Carnacobar of our maps;
but then we must by rather a violent metathesis make the *k* and *b* change places, and otherwise vary the orthography, The description, however, seems to answer sufficiently near to
suit the inhabitants of the Nicobar islands, of which this is one : if, indeed, our *Barahnakār* is
not the *Barnagul* or *Barnagar* of Hamilton, chap. xxxiv. ; but this seems scarcely possible.

‡ Among some of the inhabitants of the Eastern Archipelago, I believe, they have a custom
of making their lips project outwards, by means of a stick so fixed in their teeth as always to
keep its place. Not long ago a family thus disfigured was exhibited in London.

her one after another, till she dies : she is then thrown into the sea. The women resist the men to a degree beyond their nature. But the men, from their baseness of character, and fear about the women, will not allow any one of the merchants to proceed on the sea in the front of their houses. They will merely consult and trade with them, carrying them fresh water on the backs of elephants. When we put into their port, their King came to us riding upon an elephant, upon which there was something like a saddle-cloth made of skin. The King himself was dressed in goat-skin, the hairy part of which he had turned outwards; upon his head was a turban of coloured silk, and in his hand a short silver spear. With him was a number of his relations riding upon elephants, and using a lauguage which no one could understand, unless he had been some time among them. We sent him the usual present: for every ship putting into any port of India is expected to send a present to the magistrate of the place. Now these people buy and receive as presents, she elephants, over which they put their saddle-cloth, but do not completely [m]clothe them. But any ship not giving them their present, they will so work upon with their magic, that the sea will rise upon it, and it will perish; or they will return upon and injure it.

---

# CHAPTER XXII.

*Arrival at Sumatra—Fruits—Currency—City of Sumatra—Introduction to the King—Royal bounty—Religion—Shāfia sect of Mohammedans—Provisions for a voyage to China—Arrival at Java—Natural productions—Camphor—Cloves—Aloes—Frankincense—Superstitious custom for the production of good Camphor—Description of Nutmeg—Mace—Arrival at Kākula—Customs in Java—Voyage in the Pacific—Arrival at the country of Tawālisī—Warlike character of its inhabitants; and of the Women in particular—Kailūka—Reigning Queen—Apparently of Turkish extraction—Regiment of Women.*

We then left this place, and in fifteen days arrived at the island of [n]Java, the place from which the [o]incense of Java receives its name.* This is a

---

[m] فيكسونها الفيلة ولا يلبسونها .        [n] جزيرة الجاوه .        [o] اللبان الجاوي .

---

* We are told in Crawfurd's History of the Islands of the Indian Archipelago, vol. i. p. 517, &c. that the frankincense or benzoin is produced only in Sumatra and Borneo, and (p. 516) that

green and blooming island. The greater part of its trees are, the cocoa, the fawfel, and the betel-nut, cloves, the Indian aloe, the ᵖshakī, the ᵩbaran-sakī (barkī?),* grapes, the sweet orange, and the camphor reed. The inhabitants traffic with pieces of tin and gold, not melted, but in the ore (as coin). They have not many rich perfumes. More of these are to be found in the countries of the infidels (Hindoos perhaps). Nor are there many in the Mohammedan countries.

When we had arrived at the shores of this place we put into the port, which is a small village, in which there are some houses, as well as magazines for the merchants; and from this the city of ʳSumatra† is at the distance of four miles. At that place resides the King. When we had got into port the magistrate of the place wrote to the King, informing him of my arrival, who sent one of his nobles, and the judge who attended the presence, to meet me. With them was sent one of the King's own saddle horses for myself, and other horses for my companions: I mounted, therefore, and set out for Sumatra. The King, at that time, was ˢEl Malik El Zāhir Jamāl Oddīn, one of the most eminent and generous of princes;‡ of the sect of Shāfia, and a lover of the professors of Mohammedan law. The learned are admitted to his society, and hold free converse with him, while he proposes questions for their discussion. He is a great hero for the faith; and so humble, that he walks to his prayers on the Friday. He is too strong for his infidel neighbours; they therefore pay tribute to him. The inhabitants of his districts are of the sect of Shāfia; and they attend

---

ᵖ الشكي .    ᵩ البرنسكي (بركي ؟) .    ʳ مدينة سمطرة .    ˢ الملك الظاهر جمال الدين .

---

the camphor is found only in the same places, if we except Japan. In another part of his work, vol. ii. p. 481, &c. we find that no Mohammedan prince reigned in Java so early as the times of our traveller; and from the mention of Sumatra in our next paragraph, it seems reasonable to conclude, that the Java here mentioned must be Sumatra. A little farther on we have some account of Mul Jāva (مل جاوه) which must be the Java of our maps. See also the Histoire des Mongols, tom. i. p. 612–13, note. Mr. Marsden tells us, Hist. Sumat., p. 148, that the camphor is produced in Sumatra only.

* These have already been described as growing in Hindūstān, see p. 105, where a passage is adduced from Mr. Crawfurd to shew that they are also produced in these islands.

† Sometimes written in our MS. شمطرة Shumutrah.

‡ See History of the Indian Archipelago, vol. ii. pp. 304–13.

him willingly on his warlike expeditions. When I came to his residence, his Viceroy met me in an obliging manner, bringing with him dresses of honour,* which he put upon me and upon my companions. They then brought us victuals, with the fawfel-nut and betel-leaf. After this, I returned to the lodgings which they had prepared for me in a garden, and had completely furnished with couches, and every necessary utensil. Morning and evening they brought us the tamarisk and other fruits from the Vizier. On the third day, which was the Friday, they told me that the King was coming to the mosque, and that my first interview with him would be there. I accordingly went thither; and at last the Sultan came. I saluted him; he then took me by the hand, and asked me of the King of India, and of my travels; and I answered him accordingly. After prayers he sat and discussed religious questions with the professors of divinity, being dressed as they were, until the evening. This is his and their usual practice; nor does he ever come to the mosque, except in the garb of a [t]professor of divinity. When the evening is past, he enters a vestry in the mosque, and there changes his robes for those of royalty, with an upper garment of richly embroidered silk. He then rides to his residence.

I remained partaking of his hospitality for fifteen days, and then requested permission to pursue my journey to China: a thing which he is not always prepared to grant. He gave me permission, however, and fitted me out with provisions, fruit, and money. May God reward him. He also put me on board a junk bound for China.

I then proceeded for one and twenty days through his dominions, after which we arrived at the city of [u]Mul Jáva,† which is the first part of the territories of the infidels. The extent of these territories is that of two months' journey. In these is found almost every sort of perfume. They produce the [x]aloe, the [y]kákulí, and the [z]kamárí, [a]Kákula and [b]Kamára being situated in these countries.‡ But in the territories of [c]El Malik El Záhir

---

[c] القماري .      [y] القاقلي .      [x] العود .      [u] مل جاوه .      [t] بلباس الفقها .

[c] الملك الظاهر .      [c] قاقله .      [b] تماره .      [a] قاقله .

---

* واحضر بقيا فيها الخلع فكساني واصحابي

† This is, no doubt, the Java of our maps.

‡ See notes to page 184. Mr. Crawfurd, in his History of the Indian Archipelago, vol. i. p. 519, says, speaking of the lignum aloes, " if it be a native of the Indian islands, the countries

in Java, there is only the frankincense of Java, camphor, some cloves, and Indian aloes. But we will now say what perfumes we ourselves witnessed, in the territories both of the Moslems and the infidels. Of this is the [d] frankincense, the tree of which is small, and about the height of a man: its branches are like those of the [e] artichoke. The leaves are small and thin; and the incense is a gum which is formed in the branches. More of this, however, is found in the territories of the Mohammedans than in those of the infidels. As to the camphor, its tree is a [f] reed, like the [g] reed of our own countries, except only that it is thicker, and the knots are longer. The camphor is formed within it: and when the reed is broken, both camphor and myrrh are found within the knot, and of the same form with it.* But the camphor will not form within the reed until some animal be sacrificed at the root. The best camphor is exceedingly cooling, and one dram of it will kill by bringing on suffocation. This is called with them the [h] Khar-

---

[h] الخردأنه .      [g] كقصب .      [f] قصب .      [e] الخرشف ؟ الخرشف .      [d] اللبان .

---

which produce it have not yet been ascertained." In Abu Zaid El Hasan's Commentary on the two Arab Travellers translated by Renaudot, this place is termed the " country of Komar," from whence, it is said, they bring the wood-aloes called *hud al komari.*—Pinkerton's Voyages, &c. vol. vii. p. 208.

* I have some doubts whether this is correctly translated. The passage stands thus: فاذا كسرت القصبة وجد في داخل الانبوبه علي شكله من الكافور والمر . It appears to me very probable that some mistaken account of the camphor reed, or tree, as it is here called, gave rise to Dr. Darwin's extravagant story of the upas tree of Java. Avicenna thus describes it (p. 189): الكافور اصناف القنصوري والرياجي ثم الازاد والاسفرك الازرق وهو المختلط بخشبه والمصاعد عن خشبه وقد قال بعضهم ان شجرته كبيرة يظل خلقا ويالفه النمورة ولا يوصل اليها الا في مدة معلومة من السنة هذا علي ما زعم بعضهم وينبت هذه الشجرة في نواحي الصين , &c. " Of the camphor there are various sorts, the Elkansurī, the Riāji, in the next place the Azād, the Aspharak, and the Azrak. It is mixed with its wood, and is extracted by being sublimed. Some say that its tree is large, and will shade many men. The leopard is found near it. People do not go near it except at a certain time of the year. This is what some think. This tree grows in parts of China." Dr. Darwin tells us that criminals are employed to get the gum, and that they can get it only when the wind is in certain quarters. Now, if there is a superstitious belief that men must be sacrificed in order to produce the camphor, it is probable that criminals are selected for that purpose: and if the tree can be frequented only at certain times of the year, on account of the wild beasts, this may have furnished the other part of the story; but, as the Arabs say on occasions like this, والله اعلم *but God knows best.*

dāna; it is that, at the roots of which a man has been sacrificed. Young elephants, however, are sometimes sacrificed instead of a man.* As to the Indian [i] aloe, its tree resembles that of the [j] oak, except only that its bark is thin. Its leaves are like those of the oak, but it has no fruit; nor does the tree grow large. Its roots are long and extended, and are scented within. The leaves and trunk, however, have no perfume within them. Among the Moslems this tree is considered property; but, among the infidels, the greatest part of it is not so considered. That which is private property is found at [k] Kākula, and is the best sort. This they sell to the inhabitants of Java for clothing. Of the Kamārī species, some is soft enough to receive an impression like wax. With regard to the [l] Atās, when one cuts off any of its roots, and buries it in the earth for some months, none of its strength will be lost: this is the most wonderful property of it. As to the clove, it is a thick and high tree. It is found in greater numbers in the countries of the infidels than of the Moslems. It is not claimed as property, on account of its great abundance. That part of it which is taken into different countries is the [m] īdān (wood)† What is called the [n] flowers of the clove in our countries, is that which drops from its blossom, and is like the blossom of the orange. The fruit of the clove is the [o] nutmeg, which is known by [p] the scented nut; the bark which forms upon it is the [q] mace.‡ All that has here been related, I saw with my own eyes.

---

[m] العيدان .    [l] عطاس .al عطاس .    [k] قاقله .    [j] البلوط .    [i] العود الهندي .

[q] البسباسه .    [p] جوز الطيب .    [o] جوز نوّا .    [n] نوار القرنفل .

---

* The MSS. differ in this place; the only one which is intelligible gives it thus: هو الذي يذبح عند اصول قصبه الادمي ويقوم مقام الادمي في ذلك الفيلة الصغار Mr. Crawfurd, however, describes the tree as being very large, just as Avicenna has done. See his History of the Indian Archipelago, vol. i. p. 515, iii. p. 418.

† It is said in a note in the margin of one of the MSS. اقول لعل ذلك الذي يسميه الاطبا قرفة القرنفل . الذي يتجه انه القرنفل الابيض لانه كزهر النارنج

‡ El Basbāsa, of which our word mace is no doubt a corruption. Mr. Crawfurd describes the nutmeg-tree as resembling that of the clove (vol. i. p. 503), and hence, perhaps, our traveller has been mistaken. " Appearing through the interstices of the mace," says Mr. Crawfurd, " is the nutmeg, which is loosely enclosed in a thin shell of a black glossy appearance, not difficultly broken."—P. 504, ib.

From this place we went on to the port of ʳKākula: it is a beautiful city surrounded with a stone wall of such a breadth, that three elephants may walk abreast upon it. The first thing I saw upon its shores was the wood of the Indian aloe, placed upon the backs of elephants; this they lay up in their houses, just as we do fire-wood, except that it is cheaper among them. The merchants will purchase a whole elephant-load of it for one cotton dress, which is, with these people, more precious than silk.* Elephants are in very great abundance here, and are used for riding and burden. Each man ties his elephant to his door  The shopkeepers tie them to their shops; and in the evening they will ride out, purchase, and bring home, any thing they may want, upon them. This is the custom of all the people of China and ˢKhotā.

The King of ᵗMul Jāva† is an infidel. I was introduced to him without his palace; he was then sitting on the bare ground, and his nobles were standing before him. His troops are presented before him on foot, no one in these parts having a horse except the King, for they ride on elephants generally. The King, on this occasion, called me to him, and I went. He then ordered a carpet to be spread for me to sit upon. I said to his interpreter, how can I sit upon a carpet, while the Sultan sits upon the ground? He answered: This is his custom, and he practises it for the sake of humility: but you are a guest; and, besides, you come from a great Prince. It is, therefore, right that you should be distinguished. I then sat, and he asked me about the King Jamāl Oddīn; to which I gave suitable replies. He then said: You are now my guest for three days; you may then return. I one day saw, in the assembly of this prince, a man with a knife in his hand, which he placed upon his own neck; he then made a long speech, not a word of which I could understand; he then firmly grasped the knife, and its sharpness and the force with which he urged it were such, that he severed his head from his body, and it fell on the ground.‡ I was wonder-

---

ᵗ مل جاوه .        ˢ والخطا .        ʳ قاقله .

---

* According to Mr. Crawfurd, China at this time affords one of the best markets for cotton in the world.—Vol. iii. p. 350, &c.

† It appears from Mr. Crawfurd's work, vol. ii. p. 481, &c. that the reigning princes of Java must have been Pagans at this time.

‡ A similar act is recorded by Mr. Crawfurd, but ascribed to a different cause, vol. i. p. 41. "About ten years ago," says he, "the son of a chief of the province of Jipang, possessed

ing much at the circumstance, when the King said to me: Does any among
you do such a thing as this? I answered, I never saw one do so. He
smiled, and said: These our servants do so, out of their love to us. He then
ordered the body to be taken up and burnt. He next went out in procession to the burning, in front of his prime minister, the rest of his nobles, his
army, and the peasantry; and on this occasion he made provision for the
family and relations of the deceased, whose memory is greatly honoured in
consequence of this act. One who had been present at the assembly, told
me that the speech he made was a declaration of his love to the Sultan,
and that on this account he had killed himself, just as his father had done
for the father of the present King, and his grandfather for the King's grandfather. I then returned; but was sent for by the King, to be his guest for
the three days. After this I proceeded by sea; and after a voyage of four
and thirty days, came into the "calm," that is, the still, " sea." It has a
red appearance, which is thought to be occasioned by the lands near it.
This sea has neither wind, wave, nor motion, notwithstanding its extent.
It is on account of the calm state of this sea, that three other vessels are
attached to each of the Chinese junks, by which these junks, together with
their own cargoes, are carried forward by oars.* Of these there are twenty
large ones, which may be compared to the masts of ships. To each oar
thirty men are appointed, and stand in two rows. By this means they
draw the junks along, being connected by strong ropes like cables.
This sea we passed in seven and thirty days, which we did with the greatest

كالطوانيس . <sup>x</sup>    البحر الكاهل . <sup>u</sup>

with a belief of his own invulnerability, put the matter to the test, and drawing his kris, killed
himself on the spot."

* The MSS. have المحانذيف here, as well as in the former description given of these vessels.

From the description here given of this sea, there can be no doubt that it received its name
from the Arabian merchants (i. e. the still sea) for the same reason that Magellan called it the
Pacific. What the island was at which our traveller touched, it is impossible to say with
certainty. I suppose, however, it might have been that of the Celebes, as the distance and
situation seems sufficiently to answer the time and description of his voyage. Of the word
Tawālisī I can make nothing, because, as this seems to have been the name of the king then
reigning, that name may have died with him. I leave it to others, however, to determine what
place this is.

ease.  We then came to the country of ʸTawālīsī, which is thus named
after its King, as is also his whole country.  It is extensive; and the King
will oppose the Emperor of China.  He possesses a great number of junks;
and with these he will fight the Chinese, until they offer conditions of
peace.  The people are all idolaters; handsome in appearance, and resembling the Turks.  They are much inclined to a copper colour.  They
have great bravery and strength.  Their women ride on horseback, they
excel in throwing the javelin, and will fight like men in battle.  We put
into one of their ports which is near ᶻKailūka, one of their largest and
most beautiful cities.  The magistrate of this place is a daughter of the
King ᵃWahī Ardūjā.

She sent for the persons who were in the ship, and entertained them;
and when she was informed of my being there, she also sent for me.  I
went to her, and saw her upon the throne of government.  Before her were
her women with papers in their hands on the affairs of state, which they
presented to her.  She saluted and welcomed me in Turkish; she then
called for ink and paper in my presence, and wrote with her own hand the
ᵇBismilla, and shewed it to me.  She then inquired about the countries
I had seen; and of these I gave her suitable information.  She said, I
wonder at the great wealth of India: but, I must conquer it for myself.
She then ordered me some dresses with money and provisions for my
journey, and treated me with great politeness.

I was told that in the army of this Queen there is a regiment of women,
who fight with her like men : that she made war upon a certain king, who
was her enemy; and that, when her army was near being put to the rout,
she made so furious an onset upon the king with her regiment, that she
overcame him, put him to death, and routed his whole force.  She then
took possession of all he had, and brought the slaughtered king's head to
her father, who accordingly gave her the government of these parts.  The
neighbouring princes have made her offers of marriage, which she has
refused to accept, except on one condition only, namely, that such person
shall overcome her in the tournament.  Of this, however, they have always
been afraid, dreading the reproach of being vanquished by her.

---

ᵇ البسمله .          ᵃ وهي اردوجا .          ᶻ كَيْلُوكَي .          ʸ بلاد طواليسي .

# CHAPTER XXIII.

*Arrival in China—Its great River: its course—Culture—Population—Plenty—Porcelain—
Idolaters—Reigning Monarch a descendant of Jengiz Khān—Mohammedan Colleges, &c.
—Luxury of the Chinese—Wealth—Paper Money—Revenue—How the Porcelain is made—
Skill of Chinese Artificers—Painters—Pictures of Travellers—Registry of Ships' Crews—Care
taken of Merchants' Property at Inns, &c.—Female Slaves cheap—Inns subject to the Magistrate
—The Port El Zaitūn—Meets an Officer of the Emperor of Dehli—Provided with a House,
&c.—Sets out to visit the King—Sīn Kīlān—Mohammedan Town—Meets with a Jogee; return
to El Zaitūn—Arrives at Fanjanfūr: Decription of it—Bairam Katlū—El Khansā—Jews and
Christians here—Jugglers—The Khān killed in battle—Funeral—Successor—Disaffection—
Return.*

WE then left the countries of ᶜTiālīsī, and arrived, after a voyage of
seven days with a favourable wind, at the first of the Chinese provinces.
This is a most extensive country, and abounds in good things (of every
description) fruits, agriculture, gold, and silver: and in these it is without
a parallel. It is divided by a river called the ᵈwater of life. It is also
called the ᵉriver of Sibar,* like the name of a river in India. It has its rise
in the mountains which are in the neighbourhood of the city ᶠKhān Bālik,†

ᶜطيالسي .    ᵈآب جياد .    ᵉنهر السبر.    ᶠخان بالق .

* This river, according to the lexicon of Baudrandius cited by Asseman, is called "Flu-
vius Caramoranus."

† This is, as Asseman has shewn (Biblioth. Oriental, tom. iii. P. II. p. 512-13) the *Cambalu*
of Marco Polo, and the *Pekin* of the Chinese. At this place, according to a citation made by
Nicolaus Trigautius, from the Commentaries of Mathæus Ricius, was the usual residence of the
Tartar Khāns, after they had obtained the supreme power in China. Our traveller, as we
shall presently see, also makes this place the residence of the Emperor in his times. The
extract is as follows: "Hoc nostrorum in hanc urbem regiam (Pekinum) adventu constare
denique certo cœpit, quod jamdiu opinati fuerant, hoc regnum illud ipsum esse, quod magnum
Chatajum apud reliquos auctores appellatur, et hanc urbem Pechinensem regiam esse illius,
quem magnum Can vocant, qui nunc est rex Sinarum, quæ urbs ab iisdem Cambalu nominatur...
Sinæ quippe scriptis libris quoties Tartaros nominabant, Lù dicunt, et septentrionis plagam Pà,
nec solum Pè. Tartaris vero Cam, à nobis magnus redditur: quam vocem ne ipsi quidem Sinæ
ignorant: et quoniam eo tempore, quo se Tartari in Sinarum regnum intruserunt, rex Tartarus
sedem Pechini fixit, ideo *Campalu* appellabit; et quoniam apud varios *p* consonans in *b* com-
mutatur, ideo *Cambalu* cœpit appellari." And, in the next page, "Apud Aytonum in lib. de
Tartaris, cap. 19. *Jons* appellari his verbis: Iste Cobila Can quadraginta duobus annis tenuit
imperium Tartarorum: Christianus fuit, et fundavit civitatem quæ vocatur Jons in regno

called the <sup>g</sup>mountain of the apes. It then proceeds through the middle of China, for a distance of six months, until it passes by Sīn El Sīn, both banks of which are covered with villages and farms, just like the Nile of Egypt, except that this is much more populous. In China grows the sugar-cane, and is much better than that of Egypt. All the fruits of our countries are found in China, but they are much more plentiful and cheap than they are with us.

As to the China earthenware, it is made only in the districts of El Zaitūn, and <sup>h</sup>Sīn Kīlān. It is made of earth of the mountains of those parts, which is burnt through like charcoal. To this they add a stone, which they keep in the fire for three days. They then pour water upon it, and it becomes like dust: it is then fermented for some days: the best of it, for five and thirty days; that which is inferior, for fifteen, ten, or fewer. Of this ware, some is transported to other countries. The Chinese hen is large, but the cock is still larger, and greater than (our) goose: its eggs are proportionately large.

The Chinese are all infidels: they worship images, and burn their dead just like the Hindoos. The King of China is a Tartar, and one of the descendants of <sup>i</sup>Jengīz Khān, who entered the Mohammedan countries, and desolated many of them. In all the Chinese provinces, there is a town for the Mohammedans, and in this they reside. They also have cells, colleges, and mosques, and are made much of by the Kings of China. The Chinese, generally, will eat the flesh of dogs and swine, both of which are sold in their markets. They are much addicted to the comforts and pleasures of life: but they do not much differ, either in their luxuries or their dress: for you will see one of their merchants, whose wealth is almost immense, clothed in the coarsest cotton. The only difference generally observable among the inhabitants of China, consists in the gold and silver plate which they severally possess. In the hand of every one of them is

---

<sup>i</sup> جنكز خان .           <sup>h</sup> صين كيلان .           <sup>g</sup> يعني كوه بواذينه جبل القرود .

---

Cathay, quæ major est Româ, ut dicitur; et in illà civitate moram traxit Cobila Can Imperator Tartarorum usque ad ultimam diem vitæ suæ." Asseman adds that Cobila renewed rather than repaired this city, and then cites Marco Polo to shew that the Kän resided here, and that the city was situated upon the great river.

a [k] staff, upon which he supports himself in walking; and this they call *the third leg*.

Silk is most plentiful among them, for the silkworm is found sticking and feeding upon the trees in all their districts; and hence they make their silk, which is the clothing of the poorest among them. Were it not for the merchants, it would bring no price whatever, and still, a cotton dress will purchase many silken ones.

It is a custom with their merchants, for one to melt down all the gold and silver he may have, into pieces, each of which will weigh a talent or more, and to lay this up over the door of his house. Any one who happens to have five such pieces will put a ring upon his finger; if he have ten, he will put on two. He who possesses fifteen such, is named [l] El Sashī; and the piece itself they call a [m] Rakāla. Their transactions are carried on with paper: they do not buy or sell either with the dirhem or the dinar; but, should any one get any of these into his possession, he would melt them down into pieces. As to the paper, every piece of it is in extent about the measure of the palm of the hand, and is stamped with the King's stamp. Five and twenty of such notes are termed a [n] shat; which means the same thing as a dinar with us. But when these papers happen to be torn, or worn out by use, they are carried to their house, which is just like the mint with us, and new ones are given in place of them by the King. This is done without interest; the profit arising from their circulation accruing to the King. When any one goes to the market with a dinar or a dirhem in his hand, no one will take it until it has been changed for these notes.

With respect to the earth which they lay up, it is mere tempered clay, like the dry clay with us. It is carried upon elephants, and then cut into pieces just like charcoal; they then harden it with fire, but in a more intense heat than that of charcoal. When it is reduced to ashes they knead it with water, dry it, and again burn it in the same manner, until the particles entirely disappear. Of this they make the china vessels, as we have formerly stated. The people of China are, in other respects, the most skilful artificers. In painting, none come near to them. Of what I

---

[u] تسمي بالشت .    [m] بركاله .    [l] السشي .    [k] عكاز .

myself witnessed was the following : I once scarcely entered one of their cities: some time after, I had occasion again to visit it; and what should I see upon its walls, and upon papers stuck up in the streets, but pictures of myself and my companions ! This is constantly done with all who pass through their towns. And should any such stranger do any thing to make flight necessary, they would then send out his picture to the other provinces; and wherever he might happen to be, he would be taken.

It is also a practice with them, that when a vessel leaves China, an account, as well of the names, as of the forms of the men in it, is taken and laid up. When the vessel returns, the servants of the magistrates board it, and compare the persons in it with the descriptions taken; and if one should happen to be missing, the commander of the vessel is taken, unless he can prove that the man has died by some sickness or other circumstance, or that he has left him, with his own consent, in some other of the Chinese provinces. After this, they require of the commander a register of all the goods in the vessel, which they obtain. The people of the vessel then leave it, and the King's servants take possession of, and clear it; and if they find any thing in it not entered in the register, the vessel, together with its freightage, is forfeited to the King. This is a species of oppression which I witnessed no where else.

When any Mohammedan merchant visits those Mohammedan towns which are among the Chinese, it is left to his choice whether he will take up his lodgings with a native merchant, or whether he will go to an °inn. If he prefers lodging with a merchant, an account of all he has is taken, and the native merchant is made surety for the amount, who spends upon his guest just as much as is proper. When the foreign merchant wishes to go, an inquiry is set on foot with respect to his property, and if any thing is found to have been made away with, the merchant who was made surety makes it good by fine. But should the stranger prefer going to an inn, his property is delivered up to the inn-keeper, who is made surety for it. He then expends what is necessary upon him, and this is put down to account. When he wishes to leave, an account of the property is taken, and should any thing be missing, the inn-keeper who is surety is forced to

---

° الفندق .

make it good. If however, he wishes to have a concubine, he may buy a female slave and reside with her in the inn. Female slaves are very cheap in China; because the inhabitants consider it no crime to sell their children, both male and female. They do not, however, force them to travel with their purchasers; nor, on the other hand, do they hinder them from doing so, should they prefer it. In like manner, if one wishes to marry, he may do so; but, in any case, he is not allowed wantonly to destroy his own property: for they say, we are unwilling that it should be reported among the Mahommedans, that our country is a place of wantonness and profligacy; or, that merchants lose their wealth among us.

The care they take of travellers among them is truly surprising; and hence their country is to travellers the best and the safest: for here a man may travel alone for nine months together, with a great quantity of wealth, without the least fear. The reason of this is, there is in every district an inn, over which the magistrate of the place has control. Every evening the magistrate comes with his secretary to the inn, and registers in a book the names of all the inmates who are strangers: he then locks them up. In the morning he comes again with his secretary, and compares the name written down, with the person of every one in the inn. The register so made out he sends by a messenger to the presiding magistrate at the next station: from whom he also brings back vouchers that such and such persons have safely arrived with their property. This is done at every station. When any person happens to be lost, or any thing is stolen, and this is discovered, the magistrate who has the control over the inn in which the loss is sustained, is taken into custody on that account. In all the inns every thing that a traveller can want is provided.

The first city I came to in China was [p] El Zaitūn; there are, however, no olives here,* nor indeed in all China or India; this is merely the name of the place. It is a large city, and in it they make the best flowered and

----

[p] الزيتون .

----

* As this word in Arabic signifies *the olive*, the writer, perhaps, thought it necessary to warn his reader against mistaking it. The longitude and latitude of this place are according to Abulfeda 114° 8′, 17° 8′. Mr. Apetz thinks it is the same with the " Saunt yo Tawn," mentioned in Lord Macartney's voyage.

coloured silks,* as well as satins, which are therefore preferred to those made in other places. Its port is one of the finest in the world. I saw in it about one hundred large junks; the small vessels were innumerable. It is a large estuary of the sea, running into the land until it meets the great river. In this, and other Chinese towns, each inhabitant has a garden and some land, in the centre of which is his house; and on this account it is that their cities are so large.†

On the day of my arrival at this place, I saw the Emīr who had been sent ambassador to the Emperor of India, and who returned with us (to Malabar) when the junk foundered and went down; he, however, escaped with his life. He told the officer of the Dīwān of me, who placed me in a very handsome house. I was afterwards visited in this by the Mohammedan judge, the Sheikh El Islām, and a number of the Mohammedan merchants, who treated me with great respect, and made a feast for me, These merchants are, on account of their residing in an infidel country, extremely glad whenever a Mohammedan comes among them: on such occasions they give him alms of their wealth, so that he returns rich like themselves.

When the magistrate of the city heard of my arrival, he wrote immediately to the Khān, who is their Emperor, to acquaint him of my having come from India. I requested of him, however, that he would send a person to bring me to ⁹Sīn Kīlān, to the Emīr of that place, until he should receive the Khān's answer. To this the magistrate agreed, and sent a person with me, who conducted me to him. I embarked, therefore, in a vessel on the river, and made a voyage of twenty-seven days, in each of which we put into some village about noon, bought what we happened to want, then said our prayers, and proceeded on in the evening. On the next this was

⁹صين كيلان .

* As the word here used, viz. الكمخا does not occur in the common dictionaries, it may not be amiss to give an explanation of it. The following is taken from the King of Oude's Persian Dictionary, entitled the Seven Seas: كمخا بكسر اول وسكون ميم وخاي ٬خذ بالف كشيده بمعني جامهٔ منقشه آمدد كه بالوان مختلف بافته باشند و بفتح اول هم كفته اند بمعني جامهٔ منقش يكرنك i. e. Kimkhā, &c. meaning a flowered garment, which they weave with various colours. When pronounced kamkhā it means a flowered garment of one colour only.

† Such seems to have been ancient Babylon, with its hanging gardens and grazing lands. See Rennell's Geography of Herodotus.

repeated, and so on till we got to Sīn Kīlān. At this place, as well as El Zaitūn, the earthenware is made : at the latter of which, the river called the <sup>r</sup>water of life enters the sea; and which they, therefore, call the <sup>s</sup>conjunction of two seas.

This Sīn Kīlān is one of their greatest and best formed cities. In the middle of it is a great temple, which was built by one of their kings. This he endowed with the revenue of the city and of the surrounding villages. In this are apartments for the sick, the aged, the blind, and the great Fakeer Sheikhs, and the endowment affords them provisions in great plenty. A picture of this king is painted in the temple, and worshipped by the inmates. In a certain part of this province is a town in which the Mohammedans reside. It has a market, a mosque, and a cell for the poor. Here is also a Judge and a Sheikh El Islām : nor is there any doubt that there must be, in all the towns of China, Mohammedan merchants who have a Judge and a Sheikh El Islām, to whom their matters are referred. In this place I resided with one of the merchants, and remained among them for fourteen days ; during which time, not a day passed without my receiving presents from them. Beyond this city, neither the Mohammedans nor infidels of China have another. Between it and the obstruction of Gog and Magog* there is, as I was told, a distance of sixty days The people who inhabit that place eat all the men they can overcome : and hence it is that no one goes to those parts. I did not see any one, however, in these parts, who had either seen the obstruction himself, or who had seen one who had seen it.

I was also told in ʿSīn Kīlān, that a considerable personage was in that neighbourhood, who was upwards of two hundred years old ; that he never ate, drank, spoke, or took any delight whatever in the world, his powers were so great and so perfect ; and that he lived in a cave without the city, in which also his devotions were carried on. I went to the cave, and saw him at the door; he was exceedingly thin, and of copper colour. He had marks of a devotional character about him; but had no beard. When I I saluted him, he seized my hand and smelled it. He then said to the

---

آب حياه <sup>r</sup>.    مجمع البحرين <sup>s</sup>.    صين كيلان <sup>t</sup>.

---

* Some have thought that by this expression is meant the great wall. See Asseman, Bib. Orient. tom. iii. P. 2, p. dxiv.

interpreter : This man is just as much attached to this world, as we are to the next. He said to me : You have seen a wonder. Do you remember when you came to an island in which there was a temple, and a man sitting among the images, who gave you ten dinars of gold? I answered, I do. He rejoined : I am the man. I then kissed his hand. He then considered for a little time, and went into the cave, seeming to repent of what he had said. And as he did not come out again, we forced ourselves, and went in after him. Him, however, we did not find; but there was one of his companions, who had before him a number of the paper notes. These, said he, are your feast; so go back. I said, We wait for the old man. He replied: If you stay here for ten years, you will not see him ; for it is his practice, that when he has exhibited one of his mysteries to any one, that man sees him no more. Nor suppose that he is absent; the fact is, he is now present. I much wondered at this, and returned. I have, on a former occasion, related the affair of the Jogee, who gave us the dinars, when among the images in the temple of a certain island.*

After this, I told the story of the old man to the Judge of the town, and the Sheikh El Islām, who said: Such is his general practice with those strangers who go to see him ; but no one knows what religion he is of. The person, continued he, that you supposed to be one of his companions, was the old man himself. I have been told, too, that he had disappeared for about fifty years, but returned to this place within the last year ; that the Sultan and others beneath him, visit the old man, and that he gives each of them presents suitable to his station. He gives presents, in like manner, to the poor who visit him. In the cave in which he lives there is nothing to attract the attention; and his discourse is of times that are past. He will occasionally speak of the Prophet, and say : Had I been with him, I would have assisted him. He also speaks of "Omar Ibn Khatāb, and with peculiar respect of ˣAli son of Abu Tālib. I was told by ʸAuhad Oddīn of Sanjar, the head of the merchants, that he one day entered the cave, when the old man took him by the hand. I had, said he, imme- diately the idea that I was in a large palace, that the Sheikh was sitting in it upon a throne, with a crown on his head, and his servants standing

---

ʸ اوحد الدين السنجاري .          ˣ علي بن ابي طالب .          " عمر بن خطاب .

* See page 164.

before him. I thought I saw the fruits falling into streams there; and taking one to eat, I found myself in the cave standing before him, and him laughing at me. I had, however, a severe fit of sickness in consequence of this, which did not leave me for some months. After this I visited him no more. The people of this country think he is a Mohammedan, but no one has seen him pray, though he is constantly fasting.

I now returned to the city of El Zaitūn by the river; and, soon after my arrival, came the answer of the Khān to his Lieutenant there, in which it was ordered, that I should be honourably provided for, and sent to the presence, either by land or by the river, as I might choose. They accordingly provided me with vessels and servants, and I proceeded at the charge of the Sultan by the river, leaving one village in the morning, and arriving at another in the evening. This we did for ten days, and then arrived at the city of ᵃFanjanfūr, which is a large and handsome place situated in a plain, and surrounded with gardens, something like the plain of Damascus. Here I was met by the Judge, the ᵃPresbyters of Islamism, and the merchants, with the Emīr of the city and the officers of his forces, by whom the Emperor is entertained in the most honourable manner. I accordingly entered the city. It has four walls. Between the first and second of these are the Emperor's servants, who watch the city; between the second and the third, are the troops of cavalry, and the city magistrate; between the third and fourth are the Mohammedans; where also I took up my residence with their Sheikh, ᵇZahīr Oddīn. Within the fourth wall are the Chinese; and this is the largest part of the city. It was strange enough that, one day, when I was at a feast which they had made for me, in came one of the great Mohammedan Fakeers, whom they welcomed by the title of the ᶜSheikh Kawām Oddīn. After the salutation, and his joining our society, I was wondering at his appearance, and had looked on him for some time, when he said: Why do you continue looking at me, unless you know me? I then asked him of his native place. He said, it was ᵈSubta (Ceuta). I said: Well, I am from ᵉTanjiers. He then renewed his salute and wept; and at this I wept too.* I then asked, whether he had been in India. He

ᵃ فنجنفور . ᵃ مشايخ الاسلام . ᵇ ظهير الدين . ᶜ بالشيخ قوام الدين . ᵈ سبته . ᵉ طانجه .

* We here recognize something like the simple and affecting scene between Jacob and Rachel

said : Yes ; at the palace in Dehli.  When he said this, he came to my
recollection; and I said, are you*El Bashīrī ?*  He said : Yes.  He had
come to Dehli with my uncle, *Abul Kāsim El Mursī, when he was young
and before a beard had appeared on his cheek.  He was then one of the most
clever at retaining the Korān by memory, and of those termed *benchers.
I had mentioned him to the Emperor of India, who accordingly wished to
retain him in office.  But this he did not accept of.  His wish was to go to
China.  The Emperor had given him three thousand dinars, and he had
then set out for China.  In China he was put in office among the Mohammedans, and became possessed of great wealth.  After this, he sent me
several presents.  His brother I met, some time after, in Sūdān; what a
distance between these two brothers !  In *Kanjūrā I resided fifteen days :
I then proceeded by the river, and after four days arrived at the city of
*Bairam Katlū, which is a small place, the inhabitants of which are very
hospitable.  In this place there were not more than four Mohammedans,
with one of whom I resided for three days, and then proceeded by the
river a voyage of ten days, and arrived at the city of *El Khansā.  The name
of this place is similar to that of the poetess *El Khansā,† but I do not
know whether the word is Arabic or not, or whether the Arabic has any
agreement or not with their language.

This is the largest city I had ever seen on the face of the earth : its length
is a journey of three days, in which a traveller may proceed on and find
lodgings.  It is, as we have already said of the manner of building among
the Chinese, so constructed, that each inhabitant has his house in the middle
of his land and garden-ground.  This city is divided into six cities : all of
which are surrounded by a wall, and of which we shall presently say more.

---

ك بيرم قطلو .      ؟ بقنجورا .      ᵏ الموطا .      ᵍ ابو القاسم المرسي .      ʳ انت البشيري .

ᵐ الخنسا .      ˡ الخنسا .

---

at the well.  Gen. 29, 10—12 : " And it came to pass, when Jacob saw Rachel the daughter
of Laban, his mother's brother, &c. he lifted up his voice and wept."

* According to Ferishta and others, this should seem to be the name of an office in the court
of Dehli.

† For some account of this poetess, see M. de Sacy's Chrestomathie Arabe, tom. ii. p. 413,
edit. 2.  The place is probably the Chensi of the maps.  See also Assemani, Biblioth. Orient.
tom. iii. P. ii. p. 512.

When we approached this city we were met by its judge, the presbyters of Islamism, and the great merchants. The Mohammedans are exceedingly numerous here. This whole city is surrounded by a wall: each of the six cities is also surrounded by a wall. In the first reside the guards, with their commander. I was told that, in the muster-rolls, these amount to twelve thousand. I lodged one night in the house of the commander. In the second division are the Jews,* Christians,† and the Turks who worship the sun: these are numerous, their number is not known: and theirs is the most beautiful city. Their streets are well disposed, and their great men are exceeding wealthy. There are in the city a great number of Mohammedans, with some of whom I resided for fifteen days; and was treated most honourably. The third division is the seat of the government. In this resides the chief "commander of all China, with the forces. When I entered its gate, my companions were separated from me, on account of the press, and I remained alone. I was here met by the prime minister, who carried me to

---

" امير امرآ الصين .

---

* It does not seem possible, without positive history on the subject, to ascertain at what period the Jews entered China. Some fix upon the year 224 before Christ: others on other periods less ancient: but, as far as I can see, not much reliance is to be placed on any one of them. The reader may, however, consult the tract by Christoph. Theoph. de Murr, containing the Notitiæ S.S. Bibliorum Judæorum in Imperio Sinensi, with the Diatribe de Sinicis S.S. Bibliorum Versionibus, Halæ ad Salam, 1805, and the works there mentioned.

† These were, probably, some of the Nestorian Syrian Christians, who seem to have been first sent into China for the purpose of propagating the Christian faith, from the churches in Malabar, commonly styled the Christians of St. Thomas, &c. See the Bibliotheca Orientalis of Asseman, tom. iii. P. II. pp. 512-552, where every particular relating to the history of these Christians is discussed in a very able and interesting manner. We are told, in p. 519, that the Chinese call the Christians *Terzai* or *Tersai*, which, according to a conjecture of Trigautius, must be either Arabic or Persic, not Armenian. The truth is, it is the Persic تَرْسَا tarsä, a general name given to Christians by the Persians, as may be seen in the Dabistän, the Gulistän of Sadī, &c.; and if it be true that the Chinese so term them, one would be led to suppose, that Christianity must first have gone from Persia to China. Asseman concludes upon the words of Trigautius: " Christianos in Sinarum regno Nestorianos fuisse, non Armenios, neque ex Armenia, sed partim ex Assyria et Mesopotamia, partim ex Sogdiana, Bactriana et India illuc convolasse, eo maxime tempore, quo Tartari in illud regnum invaserunt, ipse Marcus Paulus Venetus, qui a Trigautio citatur, pluribus in locis affirmat, ubi quoties Christianorum in Sinis meminit, eos Nestorianos vocat." Asseman argues, however, that Christianity was not originally Nestorianism in China. But his interesting article should be read throughout.

the house of the commander of the forces, the Emīr ° Kartī. This was the person of whom I have already given some account, who cast his eyes upon the goat's-hair garment which had been given me by the friend of God, the ᵖSheikh Jalāl Oddīn of Shīrāz. This fourth city is the most beautiful of all the six. It is intersected by three rivers. I was entertained by the Emīr Kartī, in his own house, in a most splendid manner: he had brought together to this feast the great men of both the Mohammedans and Chinese. We had also musicians and singers. I stayed with him one night. At the banquet were present the Khān's jugglers, the chief of whom was ordered to shew some of his wonders. He then took a wooden sphere, in which there were holes, and in these long straps, and threw it up into the air till it went out of sight, as I myself witnessed, while the strap remained in his hand. He then commanded one of his disciples to take hold of, and to ascend by, this strap, which he did until he also went out of sight. His master then called him three times, but no answer came : he then took a knife in his hand, apparently in anger, which he applied to the strap. This also as-cended till it went quite out of sight : he then threw the hand of the boy upon the ground, then his foot ; then his other hand, then his other foot ; then his body, then his head. He then came down, panting for breath, and his clothes stained with blood. The man then kissed the ground before the General, who addressed him in Chinese, and gave him some other order. The juggler then took the limbs of the boy and applied them one to another : he then stamped upon them, and it stood up complete and erect. I was astonished, and was seized in consequence by a palpitation at the heart : but they gave me some drink, and I recovered. The judge of the Mohamme-dans was sitting by my side, who swore, that there was neither ascent, des-cent, nor cutting away of limbs, but the whole was mere juggling.

On this very night I entered the fifth city, which is the largest of them. It is inhabited by the common Chinese people, among whom are the most ingenious artificers. In this place are made the ᵠKhansāwīa garments. The most wonderful things they make, are dishes composed of reeds glued together, and painted over with colours, such that when hot meat is put into them they do not change their colour. Ten of these may be put into one another ;

---

ᵠ الثياب الخنساوية .       ᵖ جلال الدين الشيرازي .       ° قرطي .

and the person seeing them would suppose them to be only one. For these they have a cover, which contains them all; and their softness is such, that should they fall from a height they would not break. They are wonderful productions.

After this, I entered the sixth city, which is inhabited by sailors, fishermen, ship-caulkers, and carpenters. I was told after this by the wealthy Mohammedans, that some of the relations of the great [r]Khān had revolted, and that they had collected an army, and gone out to give him battle; they had collected an hundred companies of cavalry, each company of which amounted to ten thousand. The Sultan had on this occasion, of his own particular friends and stipendiaries, fifty thousand cavalry; and of foot soldiers, five hundred thousand. He was also opposed by the greater part of the nobles, who agreed that he ought to abdicate the throne, because he disregarded the regulations of the Yasāk,* laid down by his ancestor Jengiz Khān. They accordingly went over to the side of his uncle's son, who had set up a claim against him. They also wrote to the Khān, advising him to abdicate the throne; and promising that the province of [s]El Khansā should be apportioned to him. This he refused to accede to, and gave them battle; but after a few days he was put to the rout and killed, before I had arrived at his palace.† The news of this soon came to the city, and drums

---

[r]القان الاعظم .    [s]الخنسا .

---

* لانه كان غير احكام اليساق. See p. 91, note.

† I can find no account whatever in De Guignes or others of the death of this Emperor; but, as no change seems to have happened in the dynasty, and, according to our traveller, the uncle's son succeeded to the throne, no notice might generally have been taken of the circumstance. The dynasty of Yuen seems to have reigned from the latter end of the thirteenth century of our era to 1369, during which period nine Emperors of the descendants of Jengiz Khān are said to have held the supreme power in China. Now, it is very remarkable, that, of the first eight of these the longest reign is only thirteen years, while the ninth is made to continue through a period of thirty-six, i. e. from 1333 to 1369. It strikes me, therefore, that this reign is too long, and that the reign of another Emperor ought to be inserted between the eighth and ninth of them, in order to make the account probable; and if the relation of our traveller be true, such reign actually took place: and with the close of this the Yuen dynasty ceased. See Asseman, Biblioth. Orient. tom. iii. P. II. p. 535. De Guignes, tom. i. P. I. p. 279. In the last of which we are informed of several rebellions having taken place

and trumpets were sounded accordingly during the space of two months, for joy at the accession of the new Khān. The Khān who had been killed, with about a hundred of his relatives, was then brought, and a large sepulchre was dug for him under the earth, in which a most beautiful couch was spread, and the Khān was with his weapons laid upon it. With him they placed all the gold and silver vessels he had in his house,* together with four female slaves, and six of his favourite Mamlūks, with a few vessels of drink. They were then all closed up, and the earth heaped upon them to the height of a large hill. They then brought four horses, which they pierced through at the hill, until all motion in them ceased; they then forced a piece of wood into the hinder part of the animal till it came out at his neck, and this they fixed in the earth, leaving the horses thus impaled upon the hill.

The relatives of the Khān they buried in the same manner, putting all their vessels of gold and silver in the grave with them. At the door of the sepulchres of ten of these, they impaled three horses in the manner just mentioned. At the graves of each of the rest, only one horse was impaled. This was a notable day; all the people of the city, Chinese, Mohammedans, and others, were present on the occasion, and had on their mourning, which consists of a sort of white hood. I know of no other people who do so on such occasions.

When, however, the former Emperor was killed, and Fīrūn, the son of his uncle who had made war against him, had been put in power, he chose to fix his residence at ʿKora Karūm,† on account of its nearness to the

---

ٔ قراقروم .

---

during the reign of the last prince of the Yuen dynasty: and one of these is, perhaps, that related by our traveller.

* See a very curious note on this subject in Mr. Marsden's Translation of Marco Polo, n. 878, p. 451, whence it appears that the Russians found great quantities of plate, arms, &c. in the graves of the Tartar chiefs; and Bell's Travels in Asia, Pinkerton, vol. vii. pp. 335-6.

† According to D'Herbelot, Caracoram, ville qui Octai Kaan fils de Genghizkhan bâtit dans le pays de Cathai après qu'il l'eut subjugué: elle fut aussi nommée Ordu Balik, et c'est peut-être la même que Marc Paul appelle Cambalu. Mungaca ou Mangu Caan, fils de Tuh Kan, et petit fils de Genghizkhan, quatrième Empereur des Mogols, faisoit son séjour ordinaire dans cette ville. Voyez le titre de Cara Khotān. See also Histoire des Monguls, Liv. II. chap. i. p. 347.

territories of his uncle the "King of Turkistān and ˣMāwarā El Nahr. But those nobles, who had not been present at the death of the former Khān, revolted. Upon this occasion they stopped up the roads, and the disaffection spread itself like a flame. The leading men among the Mohammedans advised me to return to the city of El Zaitūn, before the confusion should become general: and accordingly, they petitioned the minister of King Fīrūn to give me permission, which he did, with an order for my maintenance, according to custom.

---

## CHAPTER XXIV.

*Returns by the river to El Zaitūn—Sails for Sumatra : driven by adverse winds : at length gets to Sumatra—Marriage ceremony—Sails for Hindustan : arrives at Kawlam.—Kālikūt—Zafār in Arabia—Maskit El Torayāt—Port of Shiah : Kelba—Telhān—Hormuz—Kūzistān—Lār—Janja Būl— Kaldūn — Hakān—Saman—Sabā—Shīrāz — Isphāhān—Basra—Kūfa—Ambār—Damascus — Aleppo — El Khalīl—Damietta—Cairo—Aidhab—Judda—Mecca—Jerusalem—Cairo—Alexandria—Jarba—Fez—Tanjiers—Gibraltar—Andalūsia.*

I THEN returned by the river, descending from El Khansā to ʸ Kanjanfūr, and thence to the city of El Zaitūn. When I got there I found some junks bound for India, and got into one belonging to El Malik El Zāhir King of Sumatra, whose servants are Mohammedans. In this we sailed with a good wind for ten days. The sky then became obscure and dark, and a storm arose, in consequence of which the vessel got into a sea unknown to the sailors. The people in the junk were all terribly afraid, and wished to put back : but it was impossible. After this we saw, one morning at day-break, a mountain in the sea, at the distance of about twenty miles, and towards this the wind was carrying us. The sailors wondered at this, because we were far from land ; and because no mountain had been observed in that part of the sea. It was certain that, if the wind should force us to it, we should be lost. We then betook ourselves to repentance and prayer to Almighty God, with all our hearts ; and, in addition to this, the merchants made many vows. The wind then

---

became calmed in some degree: when, after sun-rise, we perceived that
the mountain we had seen was in the air, and that we could see light
between it and the sea.   I was much astonished at this : but, seeing the
sailors in the utmost perturbation, and bidding farewell to one another, I
said, Pray what is the matter?   They said, What we supposed to be a
mountain, is really a Rokh,* and if he sees us, we shall assuredly perish,
there being now between us and him a distance of ten miles only.   But
God, in his goodness, gave us a good wind, and we steered our course in a
direction from him, so that we saw no more of him ; nor had we any knowledge of the particulars of his shape.

After two months from this day, we got to ᶻJava, and shortly after
landed at ᵃSumatra.   Here we met with the King of the place El Malik
El Zāhir, just returning from a victory, and bringing many captives with
him.   He received us very honourably, and supplied us with every thing
necessary.   He was then about to marry his son and heir.   I was present
at the wedding, and witnessed the ᵇcloseting.   It was a strange ceremony;

---

ᵇ يوم الخلوه .            ᵃ سمطره .          ᶻ الجاوه .

---

* The name of a bird so large that he is able to take up and fly away with a whole
rhinoceros at once.   The King of Oude's Persian Dictionary (sub voce رخ) gives the following
account of it : نام جانوريست كه او نيزمانند عنقا در خارج وجود ندارد وآن كه معروف است
كه . فيل وكركدن را طعمهٔ بچههاي خود ميكند غلط ودروغ معلوم ميشود   It is the name of an
animal, which like the Ankā (or Sīmurg, the fabulous bird said to be on the mountain Kāf)
has no external existence.   The one, commonly believed to feed its young with the elephant and
rhinoceros, is known to exist only in error and falsehood.

In Mr. Marsden's interesting edition of the Travels of Marco Polo, we have a similar, but
more particular, account of this bird.   " Persons," says the traveller, " who have seen this bird
assert, that when the wings are spread they measure sixteen paces in extent from point to point ;
and that the feathers are eight paces in length, and thick in proportion."   We are told, a little
lower down, that the Grand Khān having heard of this extraordinary bird, sent messengers to
the island of Magastar, or San Lorenzo, to inquire about it, and that they brought back a
feather of it, which highly gratified his majesty.   This, however, the traveller states on the report
of others (p. 707).   Mr. Marsden's opinion on the subject is stated in note 1440, where he says,
he believes it to be the albatross magnified into a monster.   The bird, he thinks, might occasionally migrate from more southern latitudes to the island of Madagascar.   What Ibn Batūta
saw was, probably, a real mountain ; the light he saw under it, might perhaps have been occasioned
by what is termed the *mirage*.

I never saw any thing like it elsewhere. It was this : They set up a large sort of pulpit in the court-yard of the palace, and covered it with silk. The bride then came from the inner apartments on foot; with her were about forty ladies, carrying her train; these were the ladies of the Sultan, his nobles, and ministers. They were all unveiled and exposed to the gaze of high and low. This, however, is not customary among them, except on the occasion of some noble marriage. The bride now ascended the pulpit, preceded by musicians and singers, male and female, who danced and sang. After this came the bridegroom, who was the King's son, mounted on an elephant, and sitting on a throne placed on the back of the animal. Over his head was an awning. He had a crown on ; and on his right and left were about a hundred young men, sons of Governors, Ministers, and Generals. These were all clothed in white, and riding on horses caparisoned. On their heads were caps set with gold and jewels; and every one of them was beardless. When the prince came in, dirhems and dinars were scattered among the people. The Sultan himself sat and witnessed the whole. The prince then alighted and walked to his father ; and taking hold of his foot kissed it. He then ascended the pulpit to the bride, who rose to him and kissed his hand. He then sat by her side ; the ladies standing before them richly dressed out. The fawfel-nut and betel-leaf were then brought in, and the bridegroom taking some in his hand put it into her mouth. The bride next took some, and put it into his mouth. The bridegroom then took a betel-leaf, and put it into his mouth, then into her's. The bride did the same to him. The covering of the pulpit was then let down upon them, and the whole was carried into the interior of the palace.* When the people had feasted themselves, they all dispersed.

I remained in this island for two months as the King's guest. I then was put on board one of the junks, the Sultan having presented me with some lignum aloes, camphor, cloves, sandal-wood,† and provisions. I then set sail for Kawlam, where I arrived after a voyage of forty days. After

---

* See Marsden's History of Sumatra, p. 266, &c. ; Crawfurd's description of marriage ceremonies in Java, vol. i. pp. 88-93.

† On this wood as found in the islands of the Indian Archipelago see Mr. Crawfurd's work, vol. i. pp. 519-20.

this I went to Kālikūt in Malabar. I then went aboard a vessel, and after
a voyage of eight and twenty days came to [e]Zafār. This was in the month
of Moharram, in the year forty-eight (i. e. A. H. 748; April, A.D. 1347.)
At this time I found its King, [d]El Malik El Nāsir, son of El Malik El
Moghīth, the same person who reigned when I formerly visited this place.*
From this place I sailed to [e]Maskit El Torayāt, then to the port of [f]Shiah,
then to the port of [g]Kelba, the name of which is the feminine form of Kelb
(a dog); then to [h]Telhān; all which places are subject to the government of
[i]Hormuz, but are considered as belonging to [k]Ammān. I then proceeded
to [l]Hormuz, and stayed there three days. From this place I went to
[m]Kuristan (Kūzistān), and from thence to [n]Lār, then to [o]Janja Bāl, from this
place to [p]Kaldūn, where I remained three days. I then proceeded to [q]Hakān;
then to [r]Saman, then to the city of [s]Sabā, and thence to [t]Shīrāz, when I
found [u]Abu Is-hāk, the reigning king;† but who was then absent from Shīrāz.
I then went on to [x]Māin, then to [y]Bazdkhāsh (Yezdkhās), then to [z]Kalīl,
then to [a]Kansak, then to [b]Isphahān, then to [c]Tostar, then to [d]El Hawāir, (Hawaiza?) then to [e]Basra, then to [f]Meshhed Ali Ibn Abi Tālib, then to [g]Kūfa,
then to [h]Sarsar, then to [i]Bagdad, where I arrived in the month of Shawāl
in the year 48 (i. e. 748), the King of which was at that time the [k]Sheikh
Hasan, son of the aunt of the Sultan Abu Saīd. After this I proceeded
to the city of [l]Ambār, then to [m]Hīt, then to [n]Hadītha, then to [o]Ana, then
to [p]El Rahba,‡ then to [q]El Sakhna, then to [r]Tadmor, then to [s]Damascus of

[c] ظفار .    [d] الملك الناصر ابن الملك المغيث .    [e] مسقط التريات .    [f] مرسي شيه .

[g] مرسي كلبه .    [h] تلهان .    [i] هرمز .    [k] عمان .    [l] هرمز .    [m] كورستان .    [n] اللار .

[o] جنج بال .    [p] كالدون .    [q] حكان .    [r] سمن .    [s] سبا .    [t] شيراز .    [u] ابو اسحق .

[x] ماين .    [y] بزدخاش (يزدخاس ؟) .    [z] كليل .    [a] كنسك .    [b] اصفهان .    [c] تستر .

[d] الحواير (العويزه ؟) .    [e] البصرة .    [f] مشهد علي .    [g] الكوفة .    [h] صرصر .    [i] بغداد .    [k] الشيخ

حسن ابن عمة السلطان ابي سعيد .    [l] الانبار .    [m] هيت .    [n] الحديثه .    [o] عانه .

[p] الرحبه .    [q] السخنه .    [r] تدمر .    [s] دمشق الشام .

---

* See p. 54.

† Abu Is-hāk was, according to Mirkhond, the reigning King in Persia at this time; and, in
this very year he undertook an expedition against Karmān, see p. 40.

‡ El Harawi, after stating that this was one of the districts belonging to Emessa, proceeds
to say, that there is in the Meshhed of this place, عظم فخذ لبعض الجبابرة طوله مقدار ثلثه اذرع

Syria; the whole time of my absence from which had been twenty full years. The chief judge of the sect of Shāfia was now [t]Takī Oddīn El Sabkī. From this place I went to [u]Aleppo, and then returned to Damascus, then to Jerusalem, and to the city of [x]El Khalīl (Hebron), then to [y]Gaza, then to [z]Damiettá, then to [a]Fāriskūr, then to [b]El Mahalla El Kobra (or the great station), then to [c]Damanhūr, then to [d]Alexandria, then to [e]Caïro. At this time there was a general plague throughout Egypt. I was told that the number of those who died daily in Caïro amounted to one and twenty thousand. The reigning prince at the time I entered Egypt was [j]El Malik El Nāsir Hasan Ibn El Malik El Nāsir Mohammed Ibn Kalāwūn. I then proceeded from Caïro on the way to Upper Egypt, for [g]Aidhāb. There I took shipping, and got to [h]Judda, then to [i]Mecca, may God ennoble it! I arrived at this place in the month of [k]Shaabān, in the nine and fortieth year (i. e. A. H. 749); and in this year I performed the pilgrimage. I then returned with a Syrian caravan to [l]Taiba, the city of the prophet. I visited his grave, and returned with them to Jerusalem. I then hired a passage back to Caïro; but, as a desire of seeing my native country now came upon me, I prepared to take my journey to the west. I travelled, accordingly, to Alexandria: and, in the month Safar, A. H. 750, I set sail and arrived at the island of [m]Jarba. From this place I sailed in another vessel to [n]Fez, then to [o]Safākus, then to [p]Milyāna, then to the city of [q]Tūnis, then to

| | | | | | |
|---|---|---|---|---|---|
| [a]فاريسكور. | [z]دمياط. | [y]غزه. | [x]الخليل. | [u]حلب. | [t]تقي الدين السبكي. |
| [f]الملك الناصر حسن ابن | [e]مصر. | [d]الاسكندريه. | [c]دمنهور. | | [b]المحلة الكبري. |
| [k]شعبان. | [i]مكه. | [h]جده. | [g]عيذاب. | [j]الملك الناصر محمد بن قلاوون. | |
| [q]تونس. | [p]مليانه. | [o]سفاقس. | [n]فاس. | [m]جربه. | (Medina) طيبه. [l] |

وعرضه مقدار شبرين وقيل وزنه خمسة وثلثون رطلا بالرجي (بالرحبيّ) وذكر بعض العلماء ان الرحبة
لم يكن بها اثر واتما احدثها ملك بن طوق وليس بصحيح وانما بناها النمرود بن كوش وهي مدينة
مذكورة في التوراة   A thigh bone of one of the giants, the length of which is three cubits: its width is that of two spans. It is said that its weight is five-and thirty ratls (of Rahba). Some of the learned, however, say that there is no monument of antiquity in Rahba, and that it was first built by Malik Ibn Tauk; which is not true: for it was built by Nimrod, son of Kūsh; and it is a city mentioned in the Bible.—It is, probably, the city Rehoboth, which we are told, Gen. x. 11, was built by Ashur. This is, no doubt, the truth: and, if so, the historians mentioned here, as well as by Mr. Ewald in his Mesopotamia of El Wākedī (p. xiii) are to be treated as fabulous.

[r]Tilimsān : then to the [s]palace of Fez, where I arrived in the latter part of the month Shaabān, in the year 750. The reigning king at this time was the Commander of the Faithful, [t]Abu Anān. I presented myself to him, and was honoured by a sight of him. The awe that surrounded him, made me forget that of the King of [u]Irāk; his elegance, that of the Emperor of India; his politeness, that of the King of [x]Yemen; his bravery, that of the King of the Turks; his mildness, that of the Emperor of Constantinople; his religious carriage, that of the Emperor of [y]Turkistān; his knowledge, that of the King of [z]Sumatra; for he so overwhelmed me with his favours, that I found myself quite unequal to express my gratitude. In Fez, too, I terminated my [a]travels, after I had assured myself, that it is the most beautiful of countries. The poet has truly said of it:

> † Ask me my proof: Why in the west
> Countries you find the sweetest, best?
> 'Tis this: Hence rides the full orbed moon,
> And hither hastes the sun at noon.

It was now my wish to visit the tomb of my father; and accordingly I left Fez for Tanjiers. From that place I went to [b]Subta. It then occurred to me, that I should have pleasure in the warfare for the faith; I therefore set sail from Subta to Spain; and the first place I saw was the [c]Hill of Victory. This is one of the greatest refuges of Islamism, and one which forced sorrow down the necks of the idolaters. From this place commenced Islamism, in the *great victory*; for here landed [d]Tārik Ibn Ziād, the slave of Mūsa Ibn Nasīr, at the time of his passing over to Spain. From this circumstance it was named after him, and called [e]Jabal Tārik

---

[r] تلمسان .   [s] حضرة فاس .   [t] ابو عنان .   [u] العراق .   [x] اليمن .   [y] تركستان .

[z] جاوه .   [a] والقيت عصي التسيار بفاس .   [b] سبته .   [c] جبل الفتح .   [d] طارق بن زياد

مولي موسي ابن نصير .   [e] جبل طارق .

---

الغرب احسن الارض     ولي دليل عليه

البدر يرقب منه     والشمس تسعي اليه

---

* See the Histoire génerale des Huns by De Guignes, tom. i. p. 347. See also " Histoire de la Domination des Arabes et des Maures en Espagne et en Portugal, depuis l'invasion de ces peuples jusqu'à leur expulsion definitive ; redigée sur l'histoire traduite de l'Arabe en Espagnol de M. Joseph Conde," Paris, 1825, tom. i. pp. 68-105; and the Annales Muslemici, tom. i. pp. 262-3, and 426-7, tom. iii. p. 583.

(corruptedly *Gibraltar*). It is also called the *Hill of Victory*, because his beginnings had their commencement here. But, a despicable foe had had possession of this place for about twenty years, until our Lord the Sultan [f]Abu El Hasan reduced him, and sent his son with an army, which he strengthened with many reinforcements, and obtained a complete victory. He then rebuilt and strengthened its fortifications and walls, and stored it with cavalry, treasure, and warlike machines. This was one of his good deeds, the effects of which still remain.*

I proceeded from the hill of victory (Gibraltar), which is one of the most extensive and handsome strongholds of Islamism, where I had met its celebrated and learned men, of whom one was my maternal uncle's son, [g]Abu El Kāsim Ibn Batūta, after I had remained there some days, and then went to the city of [h]Marbella, which is a strong and handsome place. From this place I went to the city of [i]Malaga, one of the chief cities of Andalūsia. Its charming districts lie together, and enjoy the advantages both of sea and land. It abounds with excellent productions, so that eight ratls of grapes are sold for a small dinar. Its figs and pomegranates are unequalled.

From this place I travelled to the city of [k]Tabsh, from that to [l]Hama, which is a small town, and in which there are warm springs. I then went to Granada, the chief city of [m]Andalūsia, which, for its structures and

---

[i] مالقه .    [h] مربله .    [g] ابو القسم بن بطوطه .    [f] مولانا السلطان ابو الحسن .

[m] الاندلس .    [l] حمه .    [k] تبش .

---

* Abu'l Hasan, according to Mr. Conde, mounted the throne of Fez in 1330, and held Gibraltar during the greater part of his reign. At what time he gained possession of it, we are not told; but that he was in the habit of supplying his friends and allies in Spain with troops and ammunition, there can be no doubt. The French translator and editor of Mr. Conde's work is most likely correct when he says, " Cet Abul Hasan ne fut point roi de Maroc, comme on l'a dit, mais roi de Fez." Tom. iii. p. 187. But, whether he is so, when he further says, *ib.* " Il n'est pas non plus exact de dire, avec quelques historiens Espagnols, qu' Abul Hasan envoya en Espagne son fils Abdelmélek avec une armée ; Abdelmélek n' était point fils, mais général du roi de Fez—" Ibn Batūta has not informed us ; for he has said nothing about the name of this son of the King of Fez : he has only told us, that he sent his son : and so far it is probable the Spanish historians are correct. In a note a little lower down (p. 213), we are told that, " Plusieurs historiens Espagnols disent qu'à cette occasions Abul Hasan envoya une armée sous la conduite d'Aly, un de ses fils...Les Arabes affirment positivement un fait bien different, puis qu'ils disent qu' Abul Hasan n'envoya point de secours." I merely remark, that Ibn Batūta here agrees with the Spanish historians in the fact of a *son* of Abul Hasan's having been sent : and by them he is here named Ali, not Abdelmélek.

suburbs is unequalled in the whole world. It is divided by the well-known river [n]Shenīl; besides this, however, there are many other rivers, as well as cisterns, gardens, orchards, and palaces, surrounding it on all sides. The King of Granada was at this time [o]Abu El Walīd Yūsuf Ibn Nasir. I never met him, on account of a disease under which he then laboured.* His noble and excellent mother, however, sent me some dinars for my support. I here met some of the learned men of the place, of whom the most surprising was a young man named [p]Abu Jaafar Ahmed Ibn Rizwān El Jadhānī. His astonishing peculiarity was this, that although he was brought up in a desert, and had never either studied or given himself any trouble about learning, yet he produced poetry so good as scarcely to be equalled by the most accomplished writers. The following is a specimen.†

Friend, from whom 'tis pain to part,
Take thy station in my heart.
Through my eye, its lucid door,
View the structure o'er and o'er;
There enthroned thou'lt always see
Every chamber filled with thee.
But when from thee, with pain distrest
I feel the void within my breast,
My vacant eyes too well declare
Their favourite inmate is not there:
But, when thy charms my spirits fill,
I close my lids to keep thee still.

---

[n] شنيل . [o] ابو الوليد يوسف بن نصر. [p] ابو جعفر احمد بن رضوان الجذاني .

---

* This prince, who is styled by Mr. Conde (tom. iii. p. 229) "le vertueux Jusef Abul Kégag, was assassinated at Granada in 1354, and was succeeded in the throne by his son Mohammed the Fifth.

†يا من اختار فوادي منزلا    بابه العين التي ترمقه
فتح الباب (a)فوادي بعدكم    ارسلوا طيفكم يغلقه

(a) One of the MSS. reads سهادي, and for ارسلوا, فابعثوا. The species is that termed البسيط, and consists of six feet, of the measure مستفعلن فاعلن مستفعلن repeated, with its variations. See Clarke's Prosody, p. 55, &c.

## CHAPTER XXV.

*Gibraltar— Subta—Asīlā—Salā — Morocco—Miknāsa—Fez—Sigilmāsa—Thagārī—Tās-hāla—*
*The great Desert—Abu-Lātin — Mālī—Zāgharī—Kārsanjū—Hippopotami—Customs at court*
*—Tambactū—Kawkaw—Nakda or Tukadda—Hakār—Sigilmāsa—Fez.*

FROM Granada I went to the *Hill of Victory,* and from that place took
shipping and sailed to ⁹Subta; then to ⁷Asīlā, then to ⁸Salā.* I then
travelled from that place by land to ᵗMarrākish (Morocco), which is a most
beautiful city, of extensive trade and territory. One of its poets has thus
described it.

> † Morocco blest, in site, in health,
> Brave in nobles, great in wealth:
> Here will the homeless wand'rer find,
> Welcome to cheer his drooping mind:
> One only doubt can now remain,
> Such as to give a moment's pain:
> Whether the eye or ear can boast,
> The privilege of blessing most.

ᵗ مرّاكش .     ⁸ سلا .     ⁷ اصيلا .     ⁹ سُبْتَه .

* This is, according to Abulfeda, an ancient and thickly inhabited city, having on its west the
ocean, and on its south a river, with gardens and vineyards. It is said that Abd El Mūmin, its
high priest, built a large palace on the bank of the river on its south and adjoining the sea: and,
that his followers choosing the parts adjoining, built the city which was called El Mehdīya. Salā,
it is added, is a moderate-sized district of the extreme western division, and the nearest part of
it to Spain. Its soil consists mostly of red sand: the river is large, and is subject to the reflux of
the tide. The city abounds with provisions. The districts subject to its rule are on its south, and
are called Tāmasnā, abounding with cultivation and pasturage. وسلا مدينة قديمة ضخمة في غربها

البحر المحيط وفي جنوبها النهر والبساتين والكروم وبني عبد المومن امامها من الشط الجنوبي علي النهر
والبحر المحيط قصرا عظيما واختط خاصته حوله المنازل فصارت مدينة سماها بالمهديه وسلا متوسطة بين
بلاد المغرب الاقصي وقريبه من الاندلس وتربتها رمل احمر ونهرها كبير يصير فيه المد وهي مدينة كثيرة
الرخا والرخص وسلا معاملة كثيرة في جنوبي سلا يقال لها تامسنا كثيرة الزرع والمرعي .&c. See also
D'Herbelot, sub voce " Sala."

| | |
|---|---|
| وحبذا اهلها السادات من سكن | †الله مرّاكش الغرآ من بلد |
| اسلوه بالانس عن اهل وعن وطن | ان حلّها نازح الاوطان مغترب |
| ينشاء التحاسد بين العين والاذن | بين المحديث بها او بالعيان لها |

This verse is of the sort termed البسيط, and is of the measure فعلن مستفعلن فاعلن مستفعلن
repeated. See Clarke's Prosody, p. 53, &c.

From this place I went to "Miknāsa,* then to the palace of "Fez,† and
presented myself to the Commander of the Faithful, the Sultan ʸAbu Anān,
may God give him happiness.‡   After this I bade him farewell, with an

---

ʸابو عنان .          فاس ˣ .          مكْناسه "

---

* This place is near Fez, and situated on its north.  It is remarkable for the great number of
its olives.  Ibn Saïd has said that Miknāsa consists of two white cities, separated from each
other the distance of a horse's course.  It is one stage from Fez.  Its river is called the Fulfal.

وممّا بقرب من فاس مدينة مكْناسه وهي عن فاس في الشمال وهي مشهورا بكثرة الزيتون ومن
المشترك مكناسه بكسر الميم وسكون الكاف ونون والف وسين مهمله وها قال ابن سعيد ومكناسه
مدينتان بيضان بينهما شوط فرس وهي عن فاس علي مرحلة ولمكناسه نهر يسمي فلفل .&c.

See
also Ulenbroek's Iracæ Descriptio Proleg., p. 13.

† Fez is, according to Abulfeda, placed in the different longitudes and latitudes of 8° 8′,
34° 8′, 8° ′8, 35° 35′, 20° 50′, 38° 8′.   He then describes it :

وفاس مدينتين يشتق بينهما نهر وفي
فاس عدة عيون يجري وللمدينتين ثلثة عشر بابا والمياه تجري باسواقها وديارها وحمامات وليس
بالغرب ولا بالمشرق مثلها في هذا الشان وهي مدينة محدثة اسلامية و نقل ابن سعيد عن الحجازي
انهم لما شرعوا في حفر هذه المدينة وجدوا فاسا في موضع الحفر فسميت بذلك قال وعلي انهارها
داخل المدينة نحو ستمایة جحر ارحي تدور بالماء دايما واهل فاس مخصوصون برفاهية العيش والفاس
قلعة باعلي مكان بها و يشتق القلعة نهر وفي فاس ثلث جوامع يخطب فيها ومنها الي سبتة عشرة
ايام ومخرج نهرها علي نصف يوم من فاس يجري في مرج وازاهر حتي يدخلها قال في كتاب
الاطوال وفاس قصبة طنجه ,&c.

Fez consists of two cities, between which runs a river, and con-
tains several springs which supply streams.  Both cities have in all thirteen gates.  The water
thus supplied runs into the streets, houses, and baths, a thing witnessed neither in the east nor
the west.  The place was founded since the times of Islamism.  Ibn Saïd has related after
El Hijāzī, that when they began to dig for the foundations they found an axe (فاس fäs) in the
excavations, and hence it took its name.  It is said, that there are within the city and upon its
river about three hundred water-mills constantly worked by the stream.  The people are remarkable
for the comforts of life which they enjoy.  El Fäs is its citadel, which is situated on the highest
spot in it, and through which the river runs.  There are here three mosques, in which there is
preaching ; and from it to Subta is a distance of ten days.  The source of its river is half a
day's journey from the city; it then runs through meadows and among flowers until it enters
the place.  Fez is said, in the Atwāl, to be a village of Tanjiers.  See also D'Herbelot, under
Fas.

‡ There is so much confusion and error in Mr. Conde's history of these times, that it seems
quite impossible to determine from him who this Abu Anān was, or when his reign commenced.
The French translator and editor of this work says (p. 339), il est vraisemblable que cet Abu
Salem est le même que Fariz; que son frère Omar, élu dans un premier moment de trouble, ne

intention to visit ᵉSūdān (Nigritia), and came to ᵃSigilmāsa, which is a very handsome city. It produces many very good dates (fruit), and in the abundance of these it may be compared with Basra, except only that those of this place are the best. I lodged at this place with the theologian, ᵇMohammed El Bashīrī, the brother of him I had seen in the city of ᶜKanjanfūr, in China. I proceeded from this place in the beginning of the month Moharram, and of the year 753 (February 1352), with a large company of merchants and others; and, after a journey of five and twenty days, arrived at ᵈThaghārī,* a village in which there is nothing good, for its houses and mosque are built with stones of salt, and covered with the hides of camels. There is no tree in the place; it has nothing but sand for its soil; and in this are mines of salt.† For this they dig in the earth, and find thick tables of it, so laid together as if they had been cut and placed under ground.‡ No one, however, resides in these (houses) except

---

ᵈ ثغازي .    ᶜ تنجنفور .    ᵇمحمد البشيري .    ᵃ سجلماسه .    ᵉ السودان .

---

conserva point la couronne, et qu'elle passa à Abu Zeyan. Ce qui augmente l'embarras, c'est que d'autres font succeder à Abul Hasan un autre de ces enfans nommé Abu Hanan ou Aluan. M. Conde cite même ce dernier comme regnant a Ceuta," &c. From the work of Ibn Khaldūn, however, the history of the Berbers, which now lies before me, it appears that Abu Anän was a son of the Sultan Abul Hasan, and that he left the lieutenancy of Tilimsān and succeeded to the supreme power in Fez, A.H. 749, A.D. 1348. As it is my intention to edit and translate this work, I shall forbear giving any extracts from it at present, merely stating, that it is full and particular on the circumstances of these times in Africa.

* One of the MSS. has تغازي Tagāza constantly, Mr. Kosegarten تغازا Tagāzā.

† Edrīsī, however, tells us that the only salt mines known in Sūdān are situated in the island of Awlīl, which is in the sea; and that from this place ships bring the salt, which is thence carried to the different parts of Sūdān; that these ships enter the Nile, and pass on to Salī, Takrūr, Barīsī, Ghāna, Nakāra, Kūgha, &c. فاما جزيره اوليل فهي في البحر وعلي مقرابة من الساحل وبها الملاحة المشهوره ولا يعلم في بلاد السودان ملاحة غيرها ومنها يحمل الملح الي جميع بلاد السودان وذلك ان المراكب تاتي الي هذه الجزيرة فتوسق بها الملح وتسير منها الي موضع النيل و بينهما مقدار مجري فتجري في النيل الي سلي وتكرور وبريسي وغانه وساير البلاد ونقاره وكوغه وجميع بلاد السودان How this can all be true I know not; I merely give it to shew the opinions of the Arabs in the times of Edrīsī.—Sect. i. clim. i.

‡ Mr. Kosegarten's copy adds..." quarum binæ (i. e. tabulæ) cameli onus efficiunt" (p. 46). See his notes, p. 50. In Major Denham's Narrative, p. 24, we have an account of some very extensive salt-pits.

the servants of the merchants, who dig for the salt, and live upon the dates
and other things which are brought from *Sigilmāsa,* as well as upon the
flesh of camels.  To them come the people of ᶠSūdān from their different
districts, and load themselves with the salt, which among them passes for
money, just as gold and silver does among other nations; and for this
purpose they cut it into pieces of a certain weight, and then make their
purchases with it.† The water of ᵍTaghārī‡ is poisonous; we found it
injurious.  Of this they take, however, to carry them over the desert,
which is twenty stages in extent, and is without water.§  After passing
this we arrived at ʰTās-hālā‖ a stage at which the caravans stop and rest

---

ᵉ سجلماسه .        ᶠ السودان .        ᵍ تغاري .        ʰ تاسهالا .

---

* Abulfeda gives the longitude and latitude of this place from the Kānūn, 20° 8′, 31° 30′;
from Ibn Saīd 18° 34′, 36° 34′; and describes it thus : سجلماسه قاعدة درعه شرقي سجلماسه و
ولاية مشهورة ولها نهر يأتي من الجنوب والشرق وينقسم فيمرّ علي سرقي سجلماسه وغربيها وعليها البساتين
الكثيرة ولسجلماسه ثمانيه ابواب ومن ايها خرجت تري النهر والنخيل وغير ذلك من الشجر وعلي
جميع بساتينها ونخلها حايط يمنع غارة العرب مساحته اربعون ميلا وهي مدينة تلي الصحرا الفاصله
بين بلاد المغرب وبلاد السودان وليس في جنوبها ولا غربيها عمارة قال ابن سعيد واهلها يسمون
الكلاب ويأكلونها وارضها سخه سهله .  Sigilmāsa is eastward of Darha, and is the capital of the district so called.  It has a river which comes from the south-east, divides, and passes by the east
and western parts of the city.  It abounds in gardens, and has eight gates; at which gate soever
of these you go out, you will see the river, the palms, and other trees.  Around all the gardens and
palms there is a wall intended to keep off the predatory Arabs, and this encloses a space of forty
miles.  The city adjoins the desert which divides between the western districts and Sūdān.  No
building is to be seen either to the south or west of it.  Ibn Saīd has said that its inhabitants
poison dogs and eat them, and that its soil is soft and easy of culture.  See also D'Herbelot,
under Segelmessah.

† " A handful of salt (purchased) four or five good-sized fish."—Denham's Narrative, p. 46.

‡ تغازي  Taghāza, as before.

§ Mr. Kosegarten's MSS. adds here والكماة بهذه الصحرا كثيرة ويكثر القمل بها جدا فيجعل الناس
في اعناقهم خوطا فيها الزيبق ليقتلها , &c. which he translates thus : " Tuberibus vero abundat;
magna etiam in eo ricinorum copia, quamobrem homines cervici imponunt virgam argento vivo
munitam, qua illos occidant."

‖ One of the MSS. reads تاسهلا  Tāsahlā : Mr. Kosegarten's copy تأسهل .

three days,* and then prepare to enter the great [i]desert, in which there is
neither water, bird, nor tree; but only sand and hills of sand, which are
so blown about by the wind, that no vestige of a road remains among
them.† People can travel, therefore, only by the guides from among the
merchants, of which there are many. The desert is, moreover, exposed
to the light, and is dazzling.‡ We passed it in ten days.§ We then came
to the city of [k]Abu Lātin,‖ in the beginning of the month Rebīa El

---

[k] ابو لاتن .        [i] صحرا .

* Mr. Kosegarten adds ومنها يكتب التجار لاهالي اي ولاتن ليكتروا لهم دورا ويستاجرون رجلا
من اهل مسوفة ليتوجه امامهم بالمكاتيب, &c. "Inde etiam litteras dant mercatores ad incolas
urbis Eiwelàten, quibus domus sibi conducere jubeant, et aliquem Messôfitarum mercede con-
ducunt, qui litteras ferens ipsos præcedat," &c. I have no doubt, however, that for مسوفة
in this extract we should read مسوّقة (in one MS. مسـّـقة), a word often used for *merchants* in our
MS. and in some cases where Mr. Kosegarten's has التجار. Instead of "Messofitarum," then
we should have *Mercatorum* in the translation, and in the several places in which this word occurs.
See his notes, p. 50. زغاو is with us زعاف, which is, no doubt, correct.

† So in Denham's Narrative, p. 13.

‡ So Major Denham in his journey to Mourzuk, Narrative and pp. xix, lii., 28.

§ Mr. Kosegarten's copy has *two months*, شهرين, which is probably the true reading. Mr.
Kosegarten has a very extraordinary passage here, which I cannot forbear noticing, it is this:
والشياطين كثيرة بها وربما استهوت المسافر بالمكاتيب فهلك وبسببه يهلك اكثر القافلة لانه اذا وصل
تلقا القافلة من اهل ايولاتن بالما من مسيرة اربع ايام فاذا هلك لم يتلقاهم احد فيهلك اكثرهم عطشا
Which he translates (Desertum, &c.): "dæmoniis frequentatum, quæ sæpe virum litteras ferentem
ita fascinant, ut mortem obeat; quo facto major etiam agminis pars interire solet. Nam si
vir salvus ad Eiwelàten pervenit, Eiwelàtenis incolarum multi, aquam ferentes, ad quatuor
dierum iter agmini obviam eunt, si vero perierit, obviam iis fit nemo, et plerique eorum absu-
muntur siti." Having met with nothing like this, either in Ibn Batūta or any other Oriental
traveller, I very much suspect there is some error in the text. Now if we read الشياطَة
instead of الشَياطِين we shall have all clear and consistent. The translation will then be, Et
æstas est in eo maxima, ita ut qui iter cum litteris fecerit sæpe errare inducatur atque intereat:
idcirco pars maxima agminis peribit quoque, quippe qui, &c. The want of water being
evidently assigned as the cause why numbers of the caravan perish. I have no doubt, therefore,
that there is an error in Mr. Kosegarten's MS.

‖ One of the MSS. constantly reads ايولاتن *Ayūlātin*, not declining the word, as the others do
as if compounded of Abu and Lātin. Mr. Kosegarten has occasionally this word. See Mr.
Kosegarten's notes, p. 50.

Awwal.  This is the first district of [l]Sūdān; which, as they say, belongs
to a lieutenant of the Sultan of the countries of [m]Farbā (which means a
lieutenant).  When we had got to this place, the merchants stowed their
goods in an open area, and charged some blacks with the custody of them.*
At this place I lodged with a man from [n]Salā.  But it was my wish to
return from [o]Abu Lātin as soon as I had witnessed the vile dispositions of
the blacks, and the contempt in which they held the white people.  It then
occurred to me, however, that I would complete my knowledge of these
countries; and accordingly we remained at [p]Abu Lātin fifty days.  It is
an exceedingly hot place, with a few small palm trees in it, under the
shade of which they sow the melon.  The water of the place is found in
pits, having been absorbed by the sand.†  Mutton is in great plenty.‡
Their clothing is all brought from Egypt.  The greater part of the inhabitants are merchants.  Their women are exceedingly beautiful, and more
respectable than the men.  The character of these merchants is strange
enough, for they are quite impervious to jealousy.  No one is named after
his father, but after his maternal uncle; and the sister's son always succeeds to property in preference to the son : a custom I witnessed no
where else, except among the infidel Hindoos of Malabar.  But these are
Mohammedans, who retain their prayers by memory, study theology, and
learn the Korān by rote.  As to their women, they are not shy with
regard to the men, nor do they veil themselves from them, although they
constantly accompany them at prayers.§  Any one who wishes to marry
one of them may do so; but he must not take her with him out of the
country; and, even if the woman should wish to go, her family will not
allow her.  It is a custom among them, that a man may have a mistress,
of women strangers to him, who may come and associate with him, even
in the presence of her own husband and of his wife.  In like manner, a

---

[p] ابو لاتن .       [o] ابو لاتن .       [n] سلا .       [m] فربا .       [l] اول عماله سودان .

* See Mr. Kosegarten's Notes, p. 50, and Major Denham's Narrative, p. 20.

† ومآوها احسآ .

‡ Major Denham frequently speaks of the sheep he saw and partook of in Sūdān.  Narr.
p. 107, &c.

§ A similar account is given of the Tuarick women in Major Denham's Narrative, p. 65, as
well as of others generally throughout this narrative.

man will enter his own house, and see the friend of his wife with her alone, and talking with her, without the least emotion or attempt to disturb them; he will only come in and sit down on one side, till the man goes.* Upon a certain day I went in to the Judge of *Abu Lātin, who was an eminent man, at that time my host, and with whom I had formed a friendship. I saw with him a handsome young woman, and wished to leave him: for I knew his wife, and that this was a different person. The woman smiled at me, but did not blush. He said: This is my female friend; she is no stranger. I remonstrated with him, and said: This is a strange woman; you are an eminent Kāzī, and Judge of the Mohammedans: how, then, can you be alone with her? He said: This is our custom; nor is there any suspicion from our being in society together. He did not, however, benefit (by my advice), nor did I visit him after this.†

I then proceeded from "Abu Lātin ‡ to 'Māli,§ the distance of which is a journey of four and twenty days, made with 'effort. The roads are safe, so I hired a guide and proceeded with three of my companions. These roads abound with trees, which are high, and so large that a caravan may shade itself under one of them.‖ As I passed by one of these trees, I saw a weaver weaving cloth within a cleft of its trunk. Some of these will grow so corrupt,¶ that the trunk will become like a well and be filled with

---

<sup>ع</sup> للمجد .    <sup>ء</sup> مالي .    <sup>r</sup> أبو لاتن .    <sup>٩</sup> أبو لاتن .

---

* Two of our MSS. differ here from Mr. Kosegarten's; our passage is, ومن عادتهم ان الرجل &c. , يكون له من النسا الاجانب صاحبة تاتي اليه وتصاحبه بمراي من زوجها وزوجته ايضا. &c. This is noticed to warn the reader not to conclude, that either Mr. Kosegarten or myself is wrong, because our translations do not happen to agree. I shall not think it necessary to notice all the varieties, but only those which seem to be of moment.

† See Mr. Kosegarten's notes, p. 50.

‡ Mr. Kosegarten's ايو لاتن is sometimes with us ابو لاتن or ابي لاتن as the case may require. In one place Mr. Kosegarten gives اي ولاتن (p. 42, line 9), which I have no doubt is intended for ابي لاتن. It is impossible to say which reading is the true one.

§ Ibid, p. 51. This is the Melli of Leo Africanus, and Major Denham's Narrative, p. 179.

‖ Major Denham speaks of immensely large tamarind and other trees in Sūdān, p. 159, &c.

¶ The original, with Mr. Kosegarten, is قد استآس داخله , which he translates, " interiora ita sunt excavata," &c. With me it is وبها اشجار استآشت . The last word here is the only

the rain-water, and from this the people will drink.  Sometimes the bees
will be in these in such numbers that they will be filled with honey,
which travellers take for their use.  It is affirmed by Ibn Jazzī El Kelbī,
the Epitomator (of this work), that there are in Andalūsia two chesnut trees
such, that a weaver may sit and weave cloth in them.  Ibn Batūta proceeds: The gourd grows so large in "Sūdān, that they will cut one into
halves, and out of these make two large dishes*.  The greatest part of
their vessels, moreover, are made of the gourd.  After ten days from our
leaving Abu Lātin we came to the village ˣZāgharī which is large, and
inhabited by black merchants.  Among these lives a number of white people, of the ʸIbāzīa sect of hereticst.

We then left this place and came to the great river, which is the Nile.
Upon it is the town of ᶻKārsanjū,‡  from which the Nile descends to

ᶻ كَارَسَنْجُو.        ʸ اباضيه المذهب الخوارج .        ˣ زاغري .        " السودان.

one about which there can be any difficulty; and, if our MSS. may be relied on, our word must
signify *became corrupt*, taking the root to be اِسَ, which Golius gives as equivalent to افسـد
*corrupit*, and prefixing the syllable اسـت to the tenth conjugation, we shall have اسْتآسَ, fem.
استآسَتْ, which must mean *it became corrupt, rotten, &c.;* as in استولى *he became* ولي or
*governor*, استوزر *he became vizier*, and the like.  But Mr. Kosegarten has اسن for the root,
and then the verb must also mean *it became corrupt*, and not *excavated*: the general meaning,
however, is tolerably near.  But what are we to say to Mr. Burckhardt, who has taken this for
the name of the tree, and has called it the Istaset?  See Appendix iii. to his Travels in Nubia,
p. 536.

* Gourds are in abundance in Sūdān. Denham's Narrative, p. 14, &c.

Mr. Kosegarten has a passage here, which I deem worthy of transcription; it is this:
والمسافر بهذه الصحرا لا يحمل ما ولا زادا وانما يحمل قطع الملح والسلع العطرية واكثر ما يعجبهم منها
القرنفل والمصطكا فاذا وصل قرية جا نسا السودان باللبن والدجاج والارز والدقيق وباعوه منه بالملح
والعطر الا ان ارزهم يضر اكله بالبيضان ,&c.  His translation is: " qui per hoc desertum iter fa-
ciunt, neque aquam neque comeatum secum vehunt, nisi frusta salis, et mercimonia aromatica,
quorum gratissima incolis sunt caryophylla et mastiche.  Quum ad urbem accesserint, Nigrorum
mulieres afferunt lae, gallinas, oryzam et farinam, (he should have added, atque istis salem
et aroma emunt) " oryza eorum vero alborum valetudini infesta."  On the gourd see his note,
p. 51, and Major Denham's Narrative, p. 25.

† Mr. Kosegarten adds وجماعة من السنين المالكية " et aliquot Sunnitæ Malikitæ."

‡ Mr. Kosegarten has كَارَسَخُوا.  See his note on this place, p. 51, who seems to have no doubt
that Ibn Batūta's account of the course of the Niger must be the true one.  See also Leo
Africanus, who doubts this; edit. 1632, p. 7.

<sup>a</sup>Kābāra, then to <sup>b</sup>Zāga,* the inhabitants of which were the first (in these parts) to embrace Islamism.† They are religious, and fond of learning. From this place the Nile descends to <sup>c</sup>Tambactū,‡ then to <sup>d</sup>Kawkaw,§ of

كُوكُو.<sup>d</sup>  تَنِبُكْتُوا.<sup>c</sup>  زَاغَه.<sup>b</sup>  كَابَرَه.<sup>a</sup>

---

* This is probably the Zagāwa (زغاوه) of Abulfeda, who thus describes it after Ibn Saïd :

قال ابن سعيد وقاعدة الزغاويين حيث الطول نه (يه؟) والعرض ند (يد؟) وقد اسلم اهلها ودخلوا في طاعة الكانمي وفي جنوبها مدينة زغاوه ومحلّات الزغاويين والتاجوين ممتدة في المسافة التي علي اعوجاج النيل وهم جنس واحد غيران التاجوين احسن صورة وخلقا من الزغاويين قال في العزيزي ومن دنقله الي بلاد زغاوه في سمت الغرب عشرون مرحلة.

The principal city of the people of Zagāwa is where the longitude is 55° (15 ?) and the latitude 54° (14 ?). They have embraced Islamism, and are subject to those of El Kānam. In the south of this district is the city of Zagāwa. The villages of the people of Zagāwa and Tājū are extended through the space situated upon the windings of the Nile. They are people of the same stock, except that those of Tājū are the handsomest and best behaved. It is said in the Azīzī, that from Dongola to the country of Zagāwa westward is a distance of twenty stages.

† Our MSS. have here واهل زاغه قدماً في الاسلام, &c. Mr. Kosegarten divides one of the words thus : واهل زاغه قد ما في اسلام, &c, which he thus translates. " Sagha, cujus incolæ sacra islamitica non nimis curant," &c., which, as far as I can see, is erroneous.

‡ Mr. Kosegarten writes this word *Tumbuktu*, but without any authority mentioned for doing so. Mr. Burckhardt always writes it *Timbuctoo*, just, I suppose, as he heard it pronounced by the Arabs. Our MSS., however, when they have the vowel points write تَنِبُكْتُوا, *i. e.* Tambactū, or تُنِبُكْتُوا, Tumbaktū, but never Timbuctū. Mr. Kosegarten's MS. probably had تَنِبُكْتُوا. Leo Africanus writes the first syllable with ọ, and in Bello's Map we have *Tonbacktoo*. Denham, p. 109.

§ Abulfeda says of this place (كوكو, *i. e.* وهو صاحب تلك البلاد مقر وكوكو سعيد ابن قال)

كافر يقابل من غربيه مسلمي غانه ومن شرقيه مسلمي الكانم ولكوكو نهر منسوب اليا وهي في شرقي نهرها قال في القانون وكوكو واقعة بين خط الاستوا وبين اول الاقليم الاول قال في العزيزي وعرض كوكو عشر قال وهم مسلمون.

It is said by Ibn Saïd that Kawkaw is the residence of the Sultan of these parts, and that he is an infidel : opposite to him on the west are the Moslems of Ghāna, and on the east, those of El Kānam. This place has a river named after itself : but the place itself is to the eastward of this its river. It is said in the Kānūn that Kawkaw is situated between the equinoctial line, and the beginning of the first climate. It is said in the Azīzī, that the latitude of Kawkaw is 10 degrees ; and that the inhabitants are Moslems. Of the Ghāna just mentioned he says :

وبمدينة غانه محل سلطان بلاد غانه ويدعي انه من نسل الحسن بن علي عليهما السلام والي غانه تسير التجار المغا به من سجلماسه في بر مقفر ومفاوز عظيمة نحو خمسين يوما ولا يحضرون منها غير

both which we shall give some account. It then proceeds to the town of
*Mūlī, which is the extreme district of /Mālī. It then goes on to ⁸Yuwī,*
the greatest district of Sūdān, and the king of which is the most potent. No
white person can enter here; for, if he attempt to do so, they will kill him
before he reaches it. The Nile then descends from this place to the countries of *Nubia, the inhabitants of which are Christians; then to 'Dongola,
which is the largest district they possess; the king of which is named *Ibn
Kanz Oddīn, who became a Mohammedan in the times of 'El Malik El
Nāsir. The Nile then descends to the cataracts, which terminate the regions
of Sūdān, dividing them from Upper Egypt.†

From ᵐKārsanjū, I went to the river ⁿSansara,‡ which is about ten miles
from °Mālī. I then went to the city of ᵖMālī, the residence of the King.

---

ᵏ ابن كنز الدين .      ' دنقله .      ʰ النوبه .      ⁸ یُوِي .      /مَالي .      * بلدة مُولي .

ᵖ مالي .      ° مالي .      ⁿ صَنْصَرَ .      ᵐ كَارسَنْجُو .      ' الملك الناصر .

---

الذهب الاحمر وقد حكي ابن سعيد ان لغانه نيلا هو شقيق نيل مصر قال ومصبه في البحر المحيط
عند طول عشرة ونصف وعرض اربع عشرة فيكون بين مصبه وبين غانه نحو اربع درج وغانه علي
ضفتي نيلها قال وغانه مدينتان احداهما يسكنها المسلمون والاخري الكفار .      In the city of Ghāna is
the residence of the King of the districts of Ghāna, who lays claim to being a descendant of
Hasan son of Ali. To this place travel the western merchants from Sigilmāsa through an
immense desert of fifty days, and from it they bring nothing but red gold. Ibn Saīd has said
that it has a Nile, which is a branch of the Nile of Egypt, and that it flows into the ocean in the
longitude of 10½ and in the latitude of 14°, so that between this place and Ghāna is a
distance of about 4 degrees. Ghāna stands on both sides of its river. It is also said that Ghāna
contains two cities, one of which is inhabited by Moslems, and the other by infidels. Our MSS.
give the former of these places كوكو kaukau, not kūkū. Abulfeda is silent on the subject. Mr. K.
has كوك which he writes kôk.

* One of our MSS. give بُوِي Buwī. Mr. Kosegarten has يوي, but no vowels; he writes
however, Joi. This is, most probably, the " Yeou " of Major Denham, which he places on the
bank of a river, Narr. p. 147.

† Mr. Kosegarten has a remarkable addition here, which is this: " hoc loco in littore fluminis
crocodilum vidi, scaphæ minori similem." ورايت التمساح بهذا الموضع علي الساحل كانه قارب صغير .
Major Denham also saw crocodiles in Sūdān, pp. 156, 228, and perhaps on the very same river.

‡ See Mr. Kosegarten's note on this river, p. 51.

I there inquired for the residence of the white people, and lodged with them;* they treated me very honourably. The Mohammedan Judge of the blacks, who was a celebrated Hāji, made me his guest, and sent me a present and a cow.† I was sick two months in ⁹Māli. But God restored me.

It happened that ʳMansī Soleimān,‡ the Sultan of ˢMāli, a most avaricious and worthless man, made a feast by way of kindness. I was present at the entertainment with some of our theologians. When the assembly broke up, I saluted him, having been brought to his knowledge by the theologians. When I had left the place he sent me a ᵗmeal, which he forwarded to the house of the Judge. Upon this occasion the Judge came walking hastily to me, and said: Up, for the Sultan has sent you a present. I hastened, expecting that a dress of honour, some horses, and other valuables, had been sent; but, behold! they were only three crusts of bread, with a piece of fried fish, and a dish of sour milk. I smiled at their simplicity, and the great value they set on such trifles as these. I stayed here, after this meal, two months; but saw nothing from him, although I had often met him in their friendly meetings. I one day, however, rose up in his presence, and said: I have travelled the world over, and have seen its kings; and now, I have been four months in thy territories, but no present, or even provision from thee, has yet reached me. Now, what shall I say of thee, when I shall be interrogated on the subject hereafter? Upon this, he gave me a house for my accommodation, with suitable provisions. After this, the theologians visited me in the month of ᵘRamadān, and, out of their whole number, they gave me three and thirty ˣmethkāls of gold. Of all people, the blacks debase themselves most in presence of their king: for when any one of them is called upon to appear before him, he

---

ˣ مثقالا .        ᵘ رمضان .        ᵗ الضيافة .        ˢ مالي .        ʳ مَنْسِي سليمان .        ⁹ مالي .

---

will immediately put off his usual clothing, and put on a worn-out dress, with a dirty cap; he will then enter the presence like a beggar, with his clothes lifted up to the middle of his legs; he will then beat the ground with both his elbows, and remain in the attitude of a person performing a prostration. When the Sultan addresses one of them, he will take up the garment off his back, and throw dust upon his head; and, as long as the Sultan speaks, every one present will remain with his turban taken off.* One of the best things in these parts is, the regard they pay to justice; for, in this respect, the Sultan regards neither little nor much. The safety, too, is very great; so that a traveller may proceed alone among them, without the least fear of a thief or robber.† Another of their good properties is, that when a merchant happens to die among them, they will make no effort to get possession of his property: but will allow the lawful successors to it to take it. Another is, their constant custom of attending prayers with the congregation; for, unless one makes haste, he will find no place left to say his prayers in. Another is, their insisting on the Koran's being committed to memory: for if a man finds his son defective in this, he will confine him till he is quite perfect, nor will he allow him his liberty until he is so. As to their bad practices, they will exhibit their little daughters, as well as their male and female slaves, quite naked.‡ In the same manner will the women enter into the presence of the King, which his own daughters will also do. Nor do the free women ever clothe themselves till after marriage. The greatest part of them will eat stinking dead bodies, dogs and asses.§

I travelled, in the next place, from <sup>y</sup>Mālī, the Sultan having given me a hundred <sup>z</sup>methkāls of gold, which place I left in the month Moharram, in

---

<sup>z</sup> مثقال .      <sup>y</sup> مالي .

---

* These customs were witnessed by Major Denham and his companions. See his Narrative, pp. 118, 168, 237, &c.

† See Mr. Kosegarten's note, p. 51. Leo Africanus says, speaking of the parts about the Niger: " Longa est admodum via, secura tamen atque tuta." (P. 11, edit. 1632.)

‡ So Major Denham attests, Narr. pp. 145, 147, 169, &c.

§ See also Denham's Narrative, p. 145.

the year fifty-four (A. D. February, 1353), and came to a "gulf which branches out of the Nile, and upon the banks of which there were very large beasts. I wondered at them, and thought they were elephants from the great numbers there are in those parts:* but when I saw them enter the water I enquired about them, and was told, that they were [b]sea-horses,+ which go out to graze, and then return to the water. They are larger than the land horses, and have manes and tails: their heads are like those of horses, and their legs like those of elephants. I was told by some credible black [c]Hājis, that the infidels of some parts of Sūdān will eat men; but that they will eat none but blacks, because, say they, the white are injurious on account of their not being properly matured; and, that when their Sultan happens to send his ambassadors to one of the Kings of the black Mohammedans, and intends to honour them with a feast, he also sends to them a black slave, whom they kill and eat, and then return their thanks for the honour and favour done them.‡

After some days I arrived at the city of [d]Tambactū,§ the greater part of the inhabitants of which are merchants from [e]Lathām, which is a district of [f]Mālī. Here is also a black magistrate, on the part of the Sultan of [f]Mālī. I next arrived at the city of [g]Kawkaw, which is large, and one of the most beautiful in Sūdān. They here transact business with the [h]cowrie‖ (see p. 178), like the inhabitants of Mālī. After this, I arrived at the city of [i]Bardāma,¶ the inhabitants of which protect the caravans. Their

---

<sup>a</sup> خَلِيج .   <sup>b</sup> خيل البَحر .   <sup>c</sup> الحجيين .   <sup>d</sup> تُنبكتُوا and تَنبكتُوا al. تنبكتو .   <sup>e</sup> اهل الشام .

<sup>f</sup> مالى .   <sup>g</sup> كوكو .   <sup>h</sup> ودع .   <sup>i</sup> بَرْدَامَةً .

---

* Major Denham witnessed large numbers of these animals, p. 187, &c.

† See Mr. Kosegarten's note, p. 51, and Major Denham's Narrative, pp. 154, 162, 177, 231, &c.

‡ There must be some error in the text here.

§ Mr. Kosegarten's work adds وبينها وبين النيل اربعة اميال ومن تنبكتو ركبنا النيل في قارب منحوت من خشبة واحدة كنا ننزل كل يوم بالقري ونشتري الزاد بالملح والعطر الي ان وصلنا الي مدينة كوكوا, &c. which he translates, " a Nilo quatuor milliaribus distat. E Tumbuctu in scapha, quæ e unius arboris trunco confecta erat, per Nilum invecti, singulis diebus in oppida divertimus, commeatumque sale et aromatibus coëmimus, donec ad urbem Kuku appulimus." See his note also, p. 51.

‖ So in the Journal of an excursion from Murmur to Kano, Denham's Narrative, p. 51, &c.

¶ Mr. Kosegarten has بُرْدَامَة Burdāma.

women are chaste and handsome.   I next arrived at the city of ¹Nakdā,*
which is handsome, and built with red stone.   Its water runs over copper
mines, which changes its colour and taste.   The inhabitants are neither
artizans nor merchants.   The copper mine is without Nakdā, and in this
their slaves are employed, who melt the ore and make it into bars.   The
merchants then take it into infidel and other parts of Sūdān.   The Sultan
of Nakdā is a Berber.†   I met him, and was treated as his guest, and was
also provided by him with necessaries for my journey.   I was afterwards
visited by the commander of the faithful in Nakdā, who ordered me to
wait on him, which I did, and then prepared for my journey.   I then left
this place‡ in the month ¹Shaabān, in the year fifty-four (A.D. 1353),
and travelled till I came to the territories of ᵐHakār, the inhabitants of

---

ᵐ هكار.          ¹ شعبان.          ᵏ نكدا.

---

* One MS. reads تكذا tukdhā and تكدا.   Mr. Kosegarten has تكدا takaddā. with a considerable addition to the text, the translation of which is : " Tekedda scorpiis abundat.   Segetes
ibi raræ.   Scorpii morsu repentinum infantibus adferunt mortem, cui remedio occurritur nullo ;
viros tamen raro perimunt.   Urbis incolæ in sola mercatura versantur ; Ægyptum adeunt, indeque
vestes pretiosas afferunt ; de servorum et mancipiorum multitudine inter se gloriantur."

   † See on these people the note at p. 17, that these are a part of the same people is highly
probable with me : and the reason of their being found so far in the interior might have originally
been necessity, arising from their inability to cope with the powerful Arab dynasties of the
north.   Mr. Seetzen supposed the Berbers of Libya and Nubia to be of the same race.   Mr.
Burckhardt doubts this.   See Travels in Nubia, Appendix iii. p. 535, note.

   ‡ Mr. Kosegarten has : " Dein reditu ad Sedschelmâsse parato, cum viatorum agmine Tekeddam
reliqui, et Tewât petii.   Septuaginta ab illa stationibus distat, quibus in trajiciendis viatores
commeatum secum vehunt, cum in via nihil ejusmodi reperiatur, nisi lac et butyrum, quæ
vestibus emuntur.   Accessimus Kahor ( كاهر ) quæ e terris Sultani Kerkerici ( كركري ), est, pabu-
loque abundat.   Inde profecti, per dies tres iter fecimus per desertum habitaculis vacuum,
aqua carens ; dein per dies quindecim iter fecimus per desertum aqua non carens, sed habitaculis
vacuum.   Inde in locum bivii pervenimus, ubi via quæ in Ægyptum tendit, descedit a via, quæ ad
Tewât ducit.   Ibidem putei, quorum aquæ super ferrum decurrit ; si quis vestem iis lavat nigra
fit.   Inde, post iter per dies decem institutum, pervenimus ad Dehkar," ( دهكار i. e. our هكار
above)......" Per eorum terras in quibus herbæ raræ mensem unam iter prosecuti, accessimus Būdā
( بودا ) — ex urbibus Tewâti majoribus est.   Qua relicta, in urbem Sedschelmâsse venimus, frigi-
dam, nivibus abundantem," &c.

which are a tribe of the Berbers, but a worthless people. I next came to
"Sigilmāsa, and from thence to °Fez, the residence of the commander of
the faithful, to whom I presented myself and kissed hands. I now finished
my travels, and took up my residence in this country. May God be
praised.

---

"سجلماسة .   °فاس .

THE END.

**COSIMO** is a specialty publisher of books and publications that inspire, inform, and engage readers. Our mission is to offer unique books to niche audiences around the world.

**COSIMO BOOKS** publishes books and publications for innovative authors, nonprofit organizations, and businesses. **COSIMO BOOKS** specializes in bringing books back into print, publishing new books quickly and effectively, and making these publications available to readers around the world.

**COSIMO CLASSICS** offers a collection of distinctive titles by the great authors and thinkers throughout the ages. At **COSIMO CLASSICS** timeless works find new life as affordable books, covering a variety of subjects including: Business, Economics, History, Personal Development, Philosophy, Religion & Spirituality, and much more!

**COSIMO REPORTS** publishes public reports that affect your world, from global trends to the economy, and from health to geopolitics.

FOR MORE INFORMATION CONTACT US AT
**INFO@COSIMOBOOKS.COM**

✳ if you are a book lover interested in our current catalog of books

✳ if you represent a bookstore, book club, or anyone else interested in special discounts for bulk purchases

✳ if you are an author who wants to get published

✳ if you represent an organization or business seeking to publish books and other publications for your members, donors, or customers.

**COSIMO BOOKS ARE ALWAYS AVAILABLE AT ONLINE BOOKSTORES**

VISIT **COSIMOBOOKS.COM**
BE INSPIRED, BE INFORMED